AF538453

"John Harrington's *Photographs from the Edge of Reality* is a real how-to book that gives aspiring shooters insight into the real world of assignment photography. Harrington has done it again when it comes to describing his innovative approach to his profession and his ability to share it with the world."

—David Hume Kennerly, Pulitzer Prize–winning photographer

"When John Harrington goes on assignment, you go with him. It's more than just loading your memory cards and batteries. It's figuring out where you need to be and how to get there. John is a pro at business, and with his new book, he shares some of his hard-won secrets for how to make your clients as happy with your pictures as you are."

—David Burnett, award-winning photojournalist
and co-founder of Contact Press Images

"Great stories from a great guy. Read this book."

—Bill Frakes, award-winning photographer

"John shows you the world of Washington, DC photography behind the pomp and power posturing. If you want to learn how to do it right, then this is the book for you."

—Cameron Davidson, award-winning photographer

"With this book, John does not attempt to glorify or sugar-coat what it is REALLY like to be a news photographer. This leads to a much more introspective and interesting look into the behind-the-scenes world that most will never get to experience. I can see this book appealing to both photographers as well as everyday people who are interested in the details of what happens BEHIND the camera—not just in front of it."

—Vincent Laforet, Pulitzer Prize winner and former
New York Times photographer

Photographs from the Edge of Reality:

True Stories About Shooting on Location, Surviving, and Learning Along the Way

John Harrington

Course Technology PTR
A part of Cengage Learning

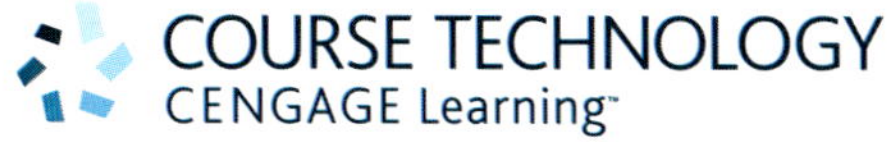

Australia, Brazil, Japan, Korea, Mexico, Singapore, Spain, United Kingdom, United States

COURSE TECHNOLOGY
CENGAGE Learning™

Photographs from the Edge of Reality: True Stories About Shooting on Location, Surviving, and Learning Along the Way
John Harrington

Publisher and General Manager, Course Technology PTR: Stacy L. Hiquet

Associate Director of Marketing: Sarah Panella

Manager of Editorial Services: Heather Talbot

Marketing Manager: Jordan Castellani

Acquisitions Editor: Megan Belanger

Project and Copy Editor: Cathleen D. Small

Interior Layout: Shawn Morningstar

Cover Designer: Mike Tanamachi

Indexer: Kelly Talbot Editing Services

Proofreader: Kim V. Benbow

Printed in the United States of America
1 2 3 4 5 6 7 12 11 10

Library of Congress Control Number: 2010936614

ISBN-13: 978-1-4354-5782-9

ISBN-10: 1-4354-5782-X

Course Technology, a part of Cengage Learning
20 Channel Center Street
Boston, MA 02210
USA

Cengage Learning is a leading provider of customized learning solutions with office locations around the globe, including Singapore, the United Kingdom, Australia, Mexico, Brazil, and Japan. Locate your local office at: **international.cengage.com/region.**

Cengage Learning products are represented in Canada by Nelson Education, Ltd.

For your lifelong learning solutions, visit **courseptr.com.**
Visit our corporate Web site at **cengage.com.**

To Charlotte—

*My best friend, my champion,
my partner, my muse.*

For my girls—

*These are some of the stories I'll
recount to your children.*

Acknowledgments

It is with heartfelt thanks that I express my appreciation and gratitude to the professionals, friends, and family who have had an influence on my life and development over the years. To my siblings—Laura Rettinger, Robert Harrington, and Suzanne Seymour, and my extended Harrington/Seymour/Taylor siblings—thank you for allowing me to grow up with and through you.

To Charlotte Richardson: Thank you for your efforts in helping me to clarify these stories and for your recollections of projects we worked on together that helped remind me of just how difficult many of these assignments were. Thank you for *always* being there for me during the many years we've been friends.

To my editors: Project editor Cathleen Small, and acquisitions editor Megan Belanger, thank you for shaping and helping to make sense of the stories and getting them organized in a logical way, and to Shawn Morningstar, for her gentle guidance on how to best present the text and visuals.

To my office staff on hand for this book—Talley Lach, Suzanne Behsudi, and Lindsay King—thank you for your hard work and efforts amidst the many personal and professional distractions during the production of this book.

To Ken Weber, who published my first photo essay, which led to my working for my first editor, David Hill, at *The World & I* magazine. Thank you both.

To photographer Nick Crettier, who is a mentor and friend, both professionally and personally. To photographers Michael Spilotro and Ken Cedeno, both of whom have challenged everything I know about photography, sometimes just trying to prove me wrong, but always trying to be helpful. And to Mark Finkenstaedt, Bill Auth, Paul Morse, David Hobby, David Burnett, Cameron Davidson, Jessica D'Amico, Jamie Rose, Jeff Snyder, Karen Ballard, David Hume Kennerly, Bob McNeely, Vincent Laforet, Ralph Alswang, Cliff Owen, Bill Frakes, and Bill Foster for your friendship and professional guidance over the years.

About the Author

John Harrington arrived in the nation's capital in 1985 as a student and began his formal freelance career in 1989, before graduating from college. He built a successful photography business and has spoken at numerous courses, seminars, and meetings on the subjects of business practices for photographers and his creative vision. Among the organizations he's made presentations before are the American Society of Media Photographers, Advertising Photographers of America, National Press Photographers Association, the White House News Photographers Association, PhotoPlus Expo, the Smithsonian Institution, Corcoran School of Art and Design, and the University of Maryland. In 2007 John was awarded the International Photographic Council's Leadership Award at the United Nations. He has worked for more than 20 years as an active photographer in Washington, DC and around the world, with both editorial and commercial clients. Editorially, his credits include the Associated Press, *The New York Times, The Washington Post, Time, Newsweek, U.S. News & World Report,* the National Geographic Society, *USA Today, People,* MTV, and *Life,* among hundreds of others. Commercially, John has worked with more than half of the top Fortune 50 companies and even more of the top Fortune 500. John has worked on ad campaigns for Siemens, Coca-Cola, General Motors, Bank of America, and XM Satellite Radio, to name a few, which have been seen worldwide.

In addition to this book, John has authored *Best Business Practices for Photographers,* now in its second edition, and his photography has illustrated four books, three specially commissioned by the Smithsonian Institution's National Museum of the American Indian: *Meet Naiche* (2002), *Meet Mindy* (2003), *Meet Lydia* (2004), and *Patriotism, Perseverance, Posterity: The Story of the National Japanese American Memorial* (2001).

John is currently serving his second term as the president of the White House News Photographers Association and has served on the boards of the local chapters of the Art Directors of Metropolitan Washington, the American Society of Media Photographers, and the American Society of Picture Professionals.

Table of Contents

Introduction

As I traveled around the world as a photographer, it quickly became apparent that stories such as, "I was stuck on an overnight train, sleep deprived, en route to Warsaw, Poland, as border guards were demanding my travel documents at 4 a.m. in a language I didn't understand...," or, "I found myself celebrating the Fourth of July with the Mexican ambassador, being serenaded by Ben Vereen...," or, "The president looked right at me as he was walking down Pennsylvania Avenue..." all seemed surreal to friends, family, and even colleagues. They seemed, in fact, made up or unreal. Fortunately, my reason for being there is to document (with a camera) these circumstances seemingly from the edge of reality—hence the title of this book.

Very early in my career, I began writing dispatches and sending them off to family, usually by email, well before the age of the Internet as it is today. It saved me time, as I didn't have to recount the stories repeatedly and chance leaving something out.

Yet, over time, my life got a bit crowded, and I lost the time to do these dispatches as I used to. However, as most photographers will tell you, their photographs are not just images to them, but an instant reminder of not just what was seen through the viewfinder, but also the environment outside of the frame—from weather, to assignment challenges, to the shot that got away.

I also remember lighting setups, and on film assignments I can remember f-stops, shutter speeds, and usually focal lengths, too. It's a form of instant recollection that I am putting down on paper here—not just to weave a tale from assignments past, but to bring these stories back to life and share with you, dear reader, what went into the assignment. The challenges overcome, the missed shots, the lighting setups, and even, in some instances, the full take, so you can see how a moment in time gets captured and selected...

Previously, I wrote the book *Best Business Practices for Photographers*, and you'll find some of that information in this book too; but if you're looking for a business guide, that would be the book to buy. However, if you want to read about actual assignments and how they were achieved—from photographing presidents, to working on assignment in Eastern Europe, to capturing the biggest names in rock-and-roll and Hollywood, often making something out of nothing—then this is the book for you.

In more than 20 years as a photographer—and, God willing, at least another 20 or so more—I have had the good fortune to travel the world on someone else's dime to make great images. Here are the stories behind some of them.

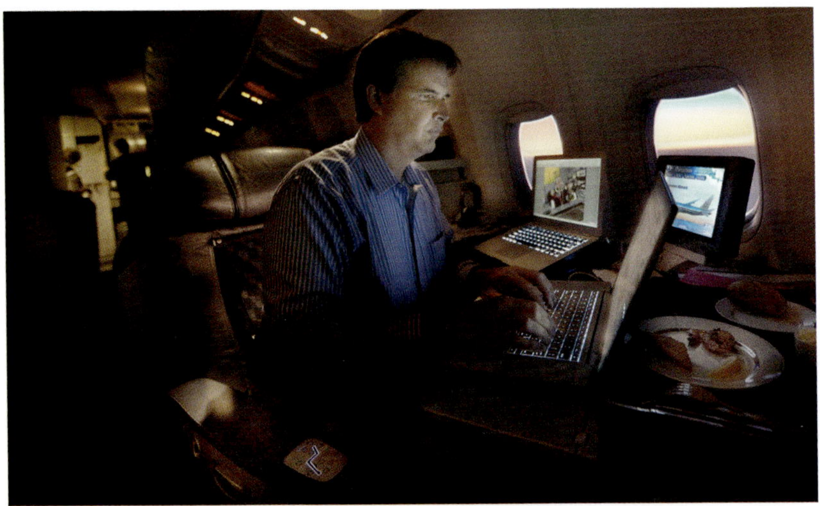

En route to Europe on assignment, somewhere over the Atlantic, working on a dispatch as the sun sets.

Ascending to an Historic Summit: Bush and Gorbachev

Everybody has a story about "how it all began." This is my story. It was late spring of 1990, and the Cold War was thawing rapidly. I was just a few weeks away from graduating college when I learned that the credentialing process was to begin for the summit between President George H.W. Bush and Soviet leader Mikhail Gorbachev. By this point I'd had a bit of success in working with one client—*The World & I* magazine—on a freelance basis. So, I approached them about covering the summit.

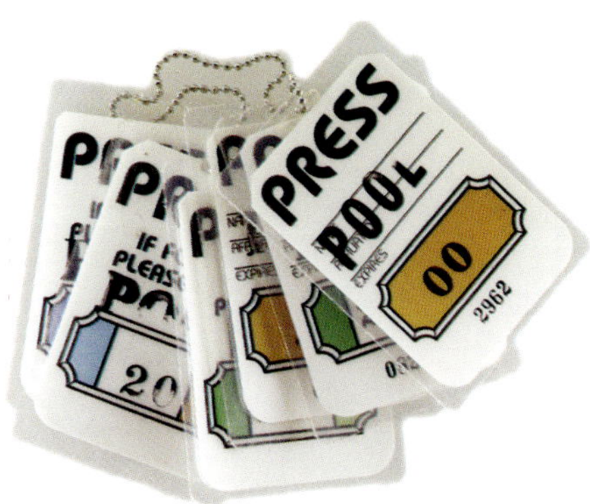

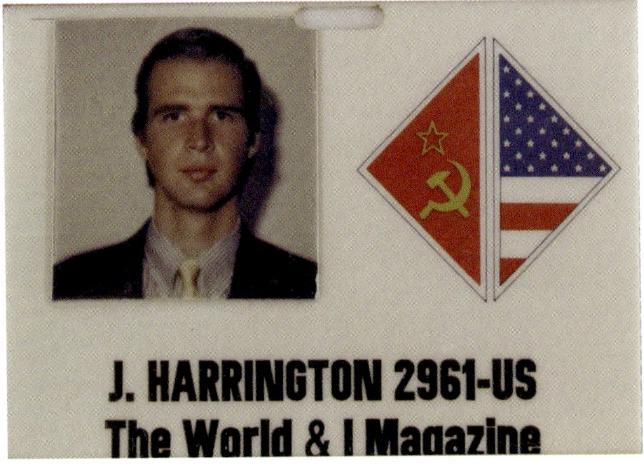

My very first press credential.

Because I had a track record with them, they were amenable to giving me an assignment, and they wrote a letter requesting a credential. I was 23 years old at the time and far less schooled in the ways of the world or even how the press corps worked. Yet, I wanted to make it work, somehow.

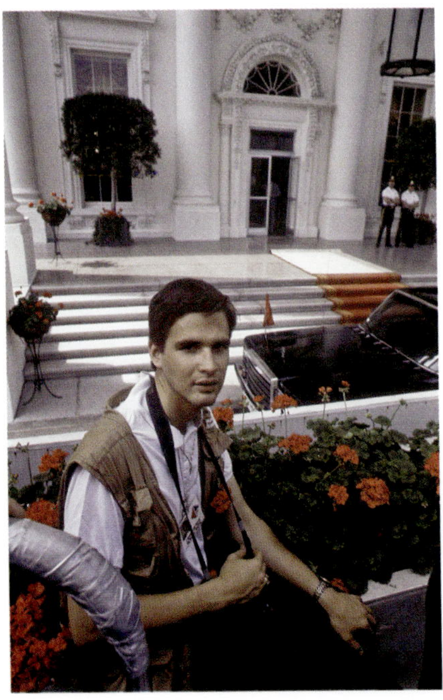

Sitting on the edge of the flower boxes at the North Portico of the White House before President Gorbachev arrives for the state dinner in his honor.

I sent in the letter and the requisite headshot for my credential, and I waited. A few weeks later, I was told I had a credential and just one press pass—to the arrival ceremony on the South Lawn of the White House. Although I thought this was really cool, I was disappointed because I wanted to be everywhere doing everything—how little I knew!

The visit began in May, and each event was controlled by a pool pass. I won't go into detail on what a pool is, because I'll do that in the next chapter. Suffice it to say that being in the pool this time meant I was a part of a small cadre of photographers given access, and, in this case, I did not have to share my images with other photographers, as "poolers" nowadays do.

The first event was the arrival ceremony, and I had a pass for that. For each event, the press was screened at the press-filing center at George Washington University, then taken by motorcade to the event, and then returned to the GWU center. As I was waiting for the bus to depart for the arrival ceremony, I learned we were waiting for several people who had not claimed their pool passes by checking in and who would not be allowed into the event. This got me to thinking during the downtime before the ceremony....

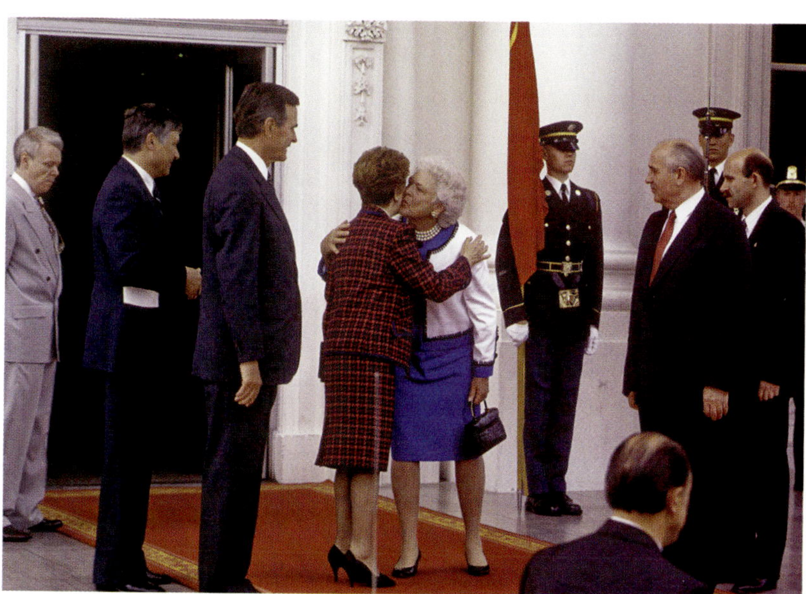

On the ride back, I (politely) cornered the press handler and made a proposition. I suggested that it seemed a waste for photo positions to go unused, and that the more photographers the more coverage, so why not distribute any unclaimed passes by way of a waiting list that could be made up in the time leading up to the next event? The press handler thought about it for a minute and agreed with me that it was a good idea.

The next event was to be a luncheon at the Russian Embassy, and I said, "Can I be on the waiting list for the embassy luncheon?" I was told yes, so I rushed off the bus, re-cleared security, and waited at the front of the line. When the call time came for the embassy, I made it in because I was on the waiting list, and someone didn't show.

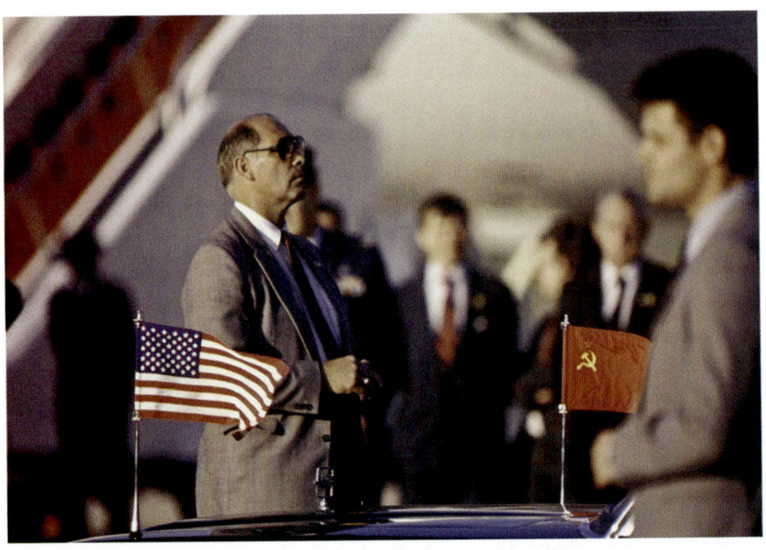

Secret Service on duty around President Gorbachev's limousine.

Coming back from the embassy, I positioned myself to be off the bus first so I could repeat this again. I ended up going to Camp David, getting into the Oval Office, and covering the signing ceremony in the East Room of the White House. In the end, I had more than a dozen passes through this system I had invented and somehow gotten approval for. I was, of course, missing all manner of classes near the end of the semester, but I didn't care.

Ascending to an Historic Summit: Bush and Gorbachev

President Bush and President Gorbachev disembark Marine One at Camp David.

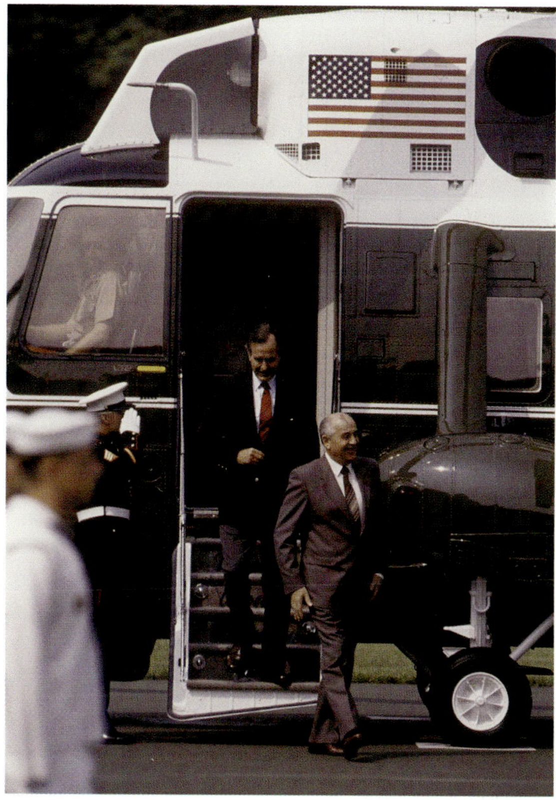

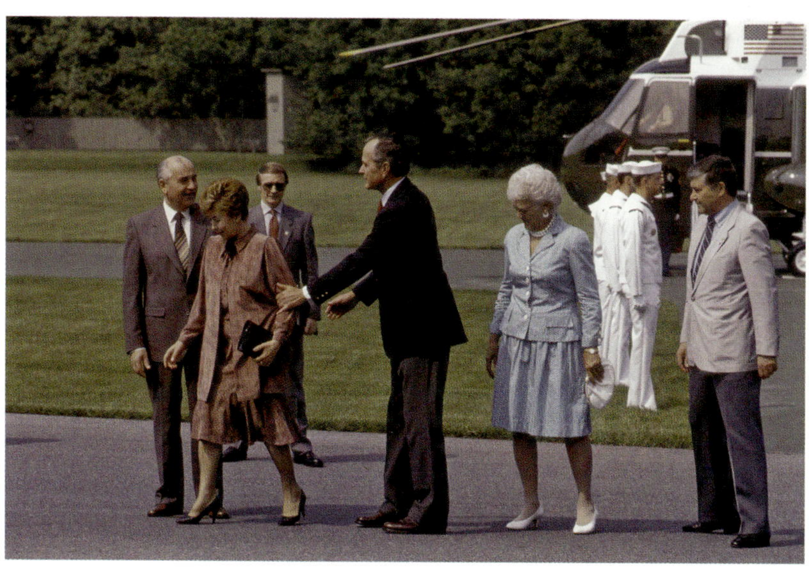

The Gorbachevs and the Bushes get arranged properly for a press photo op at Camp David.

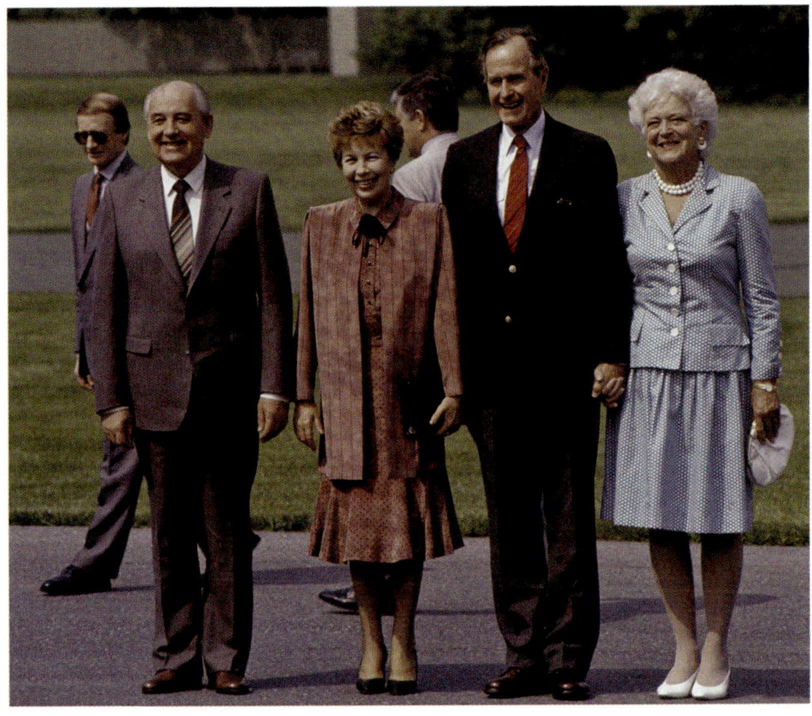

The Gorbachevs and the Bushes pose for a press photo op at Camp David.

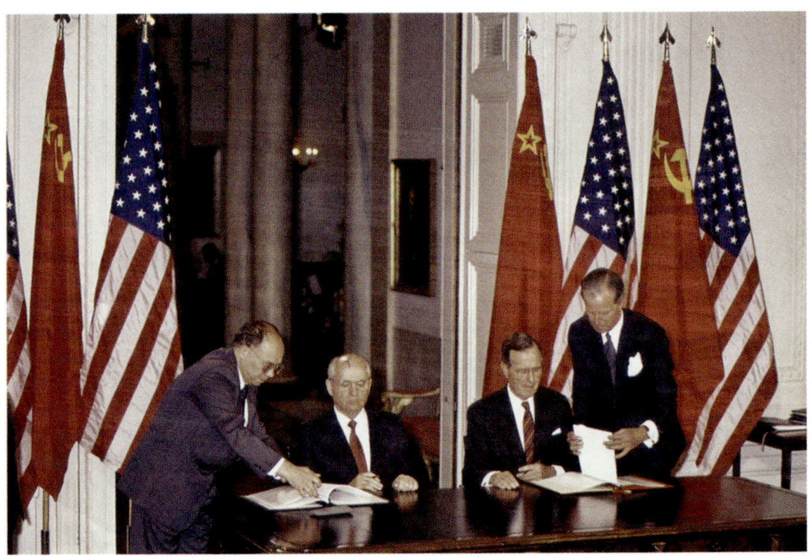

After the summit was over, I turned up at the magazine with all my credentials proudly displayed around my neck. I wanted to impress the photo editor, and it must have worked. I handed him all my film to process, and he asked how I had gotten into so many events, so I explained my little system. He processed my film, and within about a week he told me I had so many images that they didn't need to get them from the news agencies. Instead, they could get them solely from me, and the entire two-page spread about the summit would be just my images.

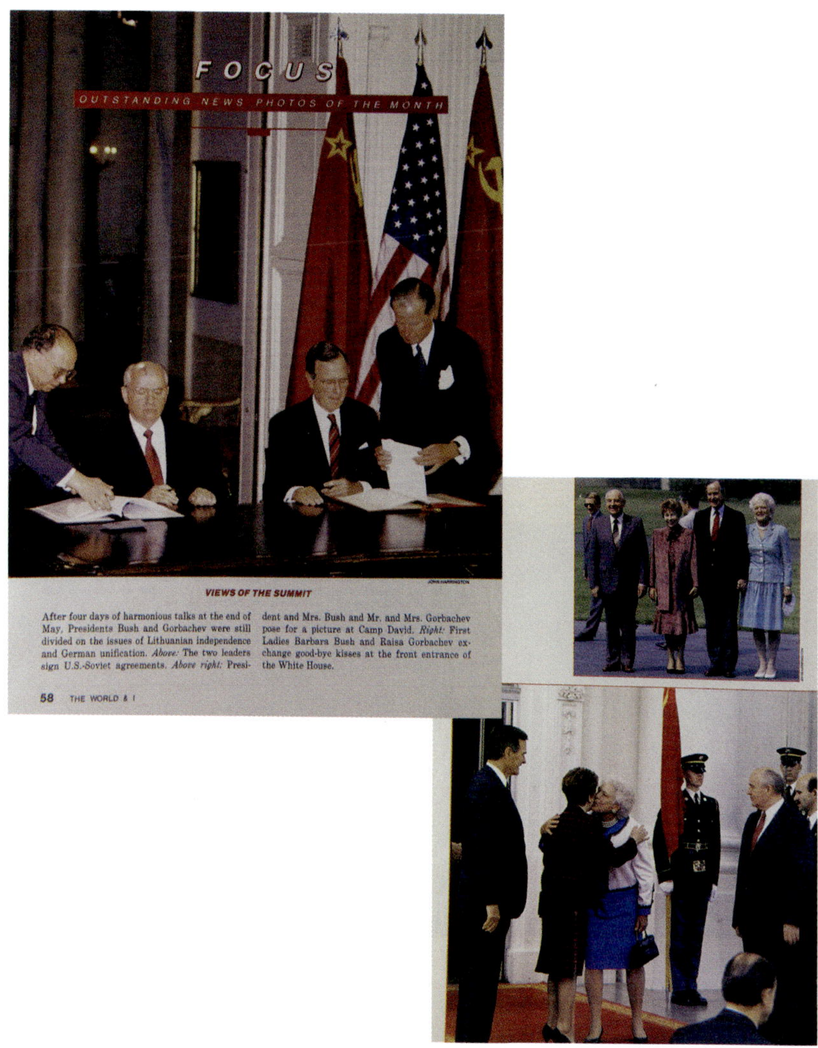

FOCUS

OUTSTANDING NEWS PHOTOS OF THE MONTH

JOHN HARRINGTON

VIEWS OF THE SUMMIT

After four days of harmonious talks at the end of May, Presidents Bush and Gorbachev were still divided on the issues of Lithuanian independence and German unification. *Above:* The two leaders sign U.S.-Soviet agreements. *Above right:* President and Mrs. Bush and Mr. and Mrs. Gorbachev pose for a picture at Camp David. *Right:* First Ladies Barbara Bush and Raisa Gorbachev exchange good-bye kisses at the front entrance of the White House.

58 THE WORLD & I

After I graduated in September of that year, the staff photographer for the magazine told me that he was going to move to another job, and if I wanted the staff photography job at the magazine, he would recommend me for it. I was honored and humbled. His boss, the photo editor, agreed with the recommendation, since I had proven my abilities already. Yet, when I met with the publisher of the magazine, my portfolio consisted only of images his magazine had published.

"Don't you have anything else to show me?" came the inquiry.

"No sir, just images that your magazine has published. And I have enjoyed all the assignments to date and would love to work here full time." And with that and no formal training in photography, my first job out of college was as staff photographer for *The World & I* magazine. I immediately applied for credentials to cover Capitol Hill, and I was told when I got "card access" credentials to the White House that I was the youngest photographer to be covering the White House on a regular basis. Whether or not this was true, it surely was an eye-opening experience from day one, and I learned that where there's a will, there's a way—and sometimes you have to make your own way.

Pool Spray in the Oval

When you're a member of the press corps, taking photographs in the Oval Office of the White House is usually a brief experience. Over the years, the time allotment has gotten shorter and shorter. Nowadays, it's usually about 20 seconds. I've had the privilege of being in there as a guest of the president, sans camera, as well as accompanying delegations during a private meeting with a president. Although when I've not been under such time constraints I've had far more of an opportunity to, as the saying goes, "make art," choosing my angles and moments to capture, my normal experience lasts well under a minute.

When you're standing outside "the Oval" on the colonnade looking over the Rose Garden, a number of things are going through your mind—who's in front of you, how many people are in front of you, where you'll position yourself during the precious few seconds you'll have, what lens you'll want to utilize, and so on. It used to be that you needed to consider whether you were using a strobe, but with digital at high ISOs being the norm, jettisoning the strobe means you don't have to wait for flash recycles, and you can squeeze off a few more frames.

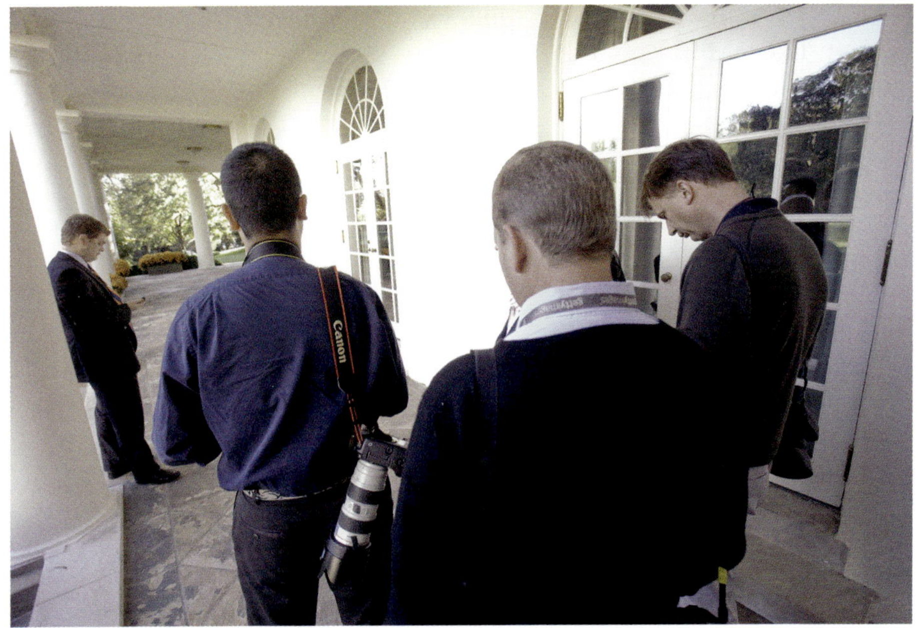

Waiting in the colonnade to go into the Oval.

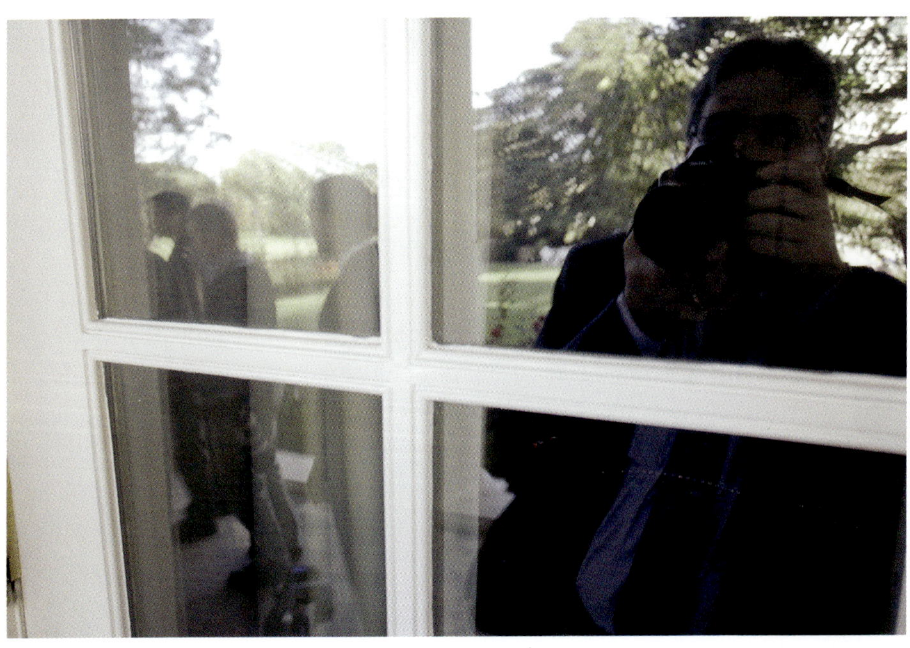

A quick snap of me in the window, waiting to get into the Oval, with the Rose Garden in the background.

There are many strategies to going in: If you're last in the line, you likely won't get a head-on shot, so perhaps you go for the side shot and then a frame showing the many members of the press there, with an ultra-wide lens. You can also linger for a couple seconds as the rest of the photographers are getting up and make a few frames that might look less scripted than those your colleagues made a few minutes ago. Most times, the wire-service photographers (the Associated Press, Reuters, and Agence France Presse) are at the front of the line, so they're going for the head-on, low-angle shot. Although that is a staple of newspapers around the country, knowing what they are getting allows you to get into a different position and make a slightly different image.

There are essentially two settings in the Oval for photography. The first is of two world leaders seated side by side in front of the fireplace. The second—and less common—setting is of the president at his desk, usually signing a bill with congressional leaders looking on.

Earlier this day, we had traveled by motorcade to a nearby hotel as the president gave remarks to the Grocery Manufacturers Association and also named the new Secretary of Agriculture—Ed Schafer—to a cabinet post. Now, late in the afternoon on a busy news day, the president was signing a bill in the Oval, and the press was called in to document the event. In this case, President George W. Bush was signing the Internet Tax Freedom Act Amendments Act of 2007—a bill to amend the Internet Tax Freedom Act, which extends the moratorium on taxes for purchases made on the Internet. This seems like a mouthful—what it does is save you from paying taxes on purchases you make on the Internet when the sale is taking place outside of your state.

The president was joined by several members of Congress, among them Rep. Goodlatte of Virginia, Sen. Sununu of New Hampshire, and Sen. Alexander of Tennessee. I made a few of the obligatory front-on images within the first few seconds and then quickly shifted to my left to do a side shot of the press pool in action.

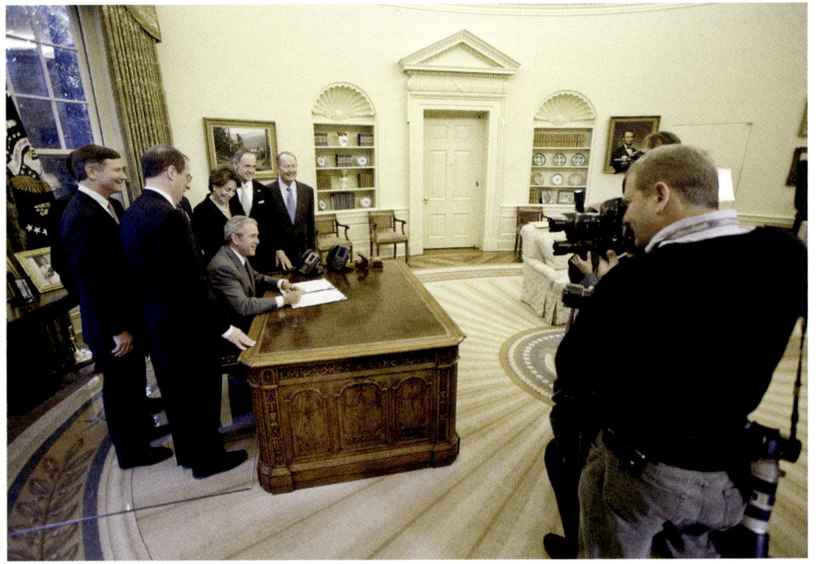

A side shot of the signing ceremony to show the press documenting the event.

Now would be a good time to explain what a "press pool" is. In press circles in Washington, a pool is essentially an abridging of the First Amendment rights of the press. Consider, for example, that you have 50 news outlets that want to cover a news event. Clearly, you could not fit all of them into the Oval. So, the White House (and other news-centric bodies around the city) essentially says, "Well, guys, we can't fit 50 of you into the space we have, so either no one can come in or five of you come in and each of you five agree to share your images among 10 others." Thus, in concept, each group of 10 has to "pool" its needs and resources into the hands of one (hopefully) able-bodied photographer.

At the White House, the wires (AP, Reuters, AFP) have steadfastly refused to pool images (much to their credit), and the news magazines (*Time, Newsweek*, and *US News*) all have agreed to a "mag pooler." Sometimes the newspapers (*Washington Post, The New York Times*, and so on) have agreed to a "newspaper pooler."

And then there is a collection of other independent stills poolers (ISP poolers) made up of folks such as Bloomberg News, Getty Images, Corbis, Black Star, United Press International, Consolidated News Pictures, European Press Agency, Polaris, Sipa Press, and Abaca USA.

That day, I was the "pooler" for the ISP, and my images not only were distributed by my agent (Black Star), but also were distributed by the other eight ISP members under their own banner. While I retain the copyright to the images and the revenue from the licensing of my images through Black Star, I do not through the other eight. Fair? No. Yet until someone with the financing and legal backing to make an impact fights this, it is the status quo.

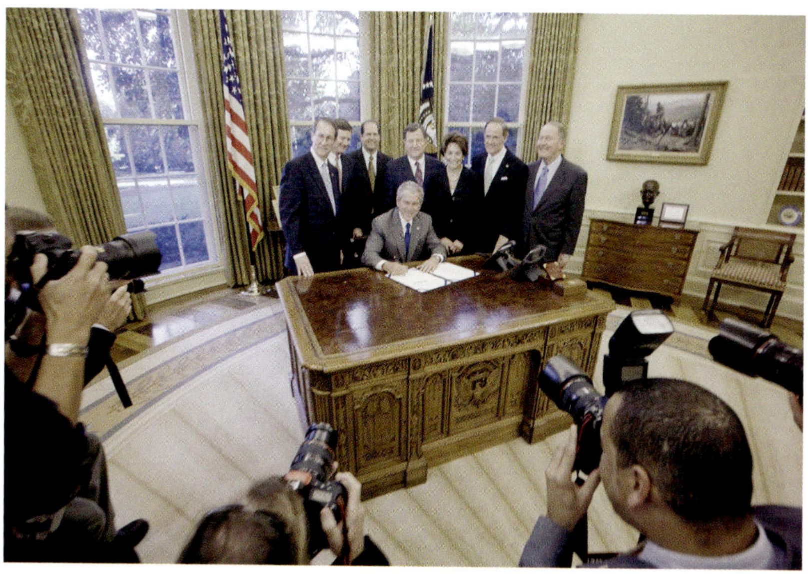

The signing ceremony with a wider angle of view to show the press documenting the event.

After about 20 seconds, the "op" (short for "photo op" or "photo opportunity") was called, and we were escorted out. At this point, it's a rush to see who can get their images emailed out the fastest to the waiting news outlets. I had prewritten my caption and was already online. As I was hustling the 50 or so yards through the maze past Secret Service agents and narrow corridors from the Oval to my desk in the press room, I was tagging the images I wanted so that when I opened the card folder in Photo Mechanic, I could immediately view the ones I thought were best, process them out as JPEGs from the Camera Raw file, and then apply the caption, upload, and distribute. So, within about three or four minutes of the end of the event, my first image of about a half-dozen was outbound to the waiting pool members and on to news outlets worldwide.

Lean Green Entertaining Machine

Kermit the Frog. In fact, you need only say "Kermit," and everyone knows exactly who you're talking about. Perhaps even more than the single-namers Madonna, Cher, or even Elton, Kermit is known—and loved—worldwide. I'd had the privilege of working with Cookie Monster, Elmo, and a few other Muppets in the past, but working with Kermit, as I had once before, was exciting—no doubt for some boyhood reason I couldn't pinpoint.

The first time I worked with Kermit, I was on the set of the *Today Show* with Katie Couric, and Kermit was promoting the U.S. Mint's 50 State Quarters program. I really didn't have an opportunity to give Kermit any direction, as that was happening without my input thanks to those in charge of the *Today Show*. I was just along for the ride.

During breaks, I was able to get a few images of Katie and Kermit. She seemed almost as excited as I was to be in the presence of green greatness, and it showed on her face.

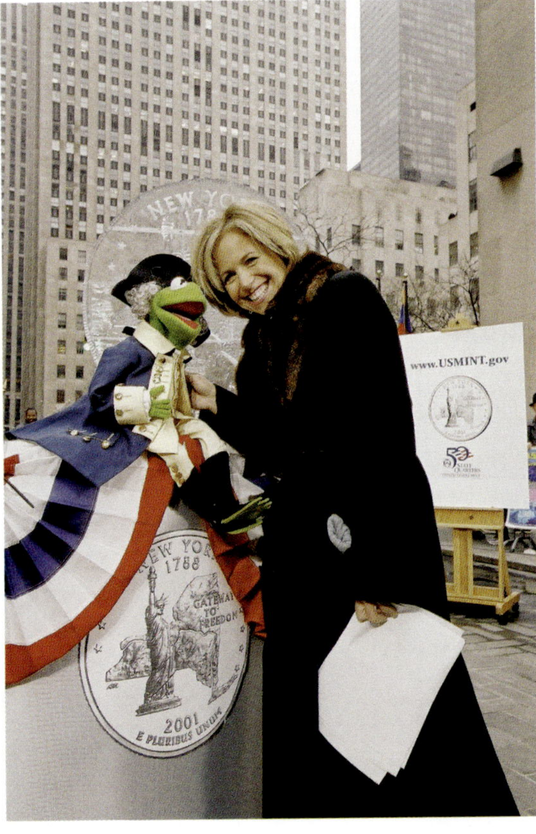

Katie Couric and Kermit the Frog on the set of the *Today Show* to promote the New York State quarter launch.

My next opportunity, however, called for me to work directly with Kermit, not just for posed photographs with Congressional staff, but also during a panel discussion with people involved in promoting and protecting zoos in the United States. The conversation was scripted, and I was able to observe how Kermit got set up and comfortable and how Kermit was able to focus directly on the speakers. I was also able to observe exactly how he was animated for the event.

During a break, it was suggested that we do a portrait of Kermit with the Capitol in the background, which meant it was just me, Kermit, and...well, you know, his "handler." Working with Kermit's "friend" to get just the right look was a lot of fun, and I couldn't believe that I was actually working with Kermit.

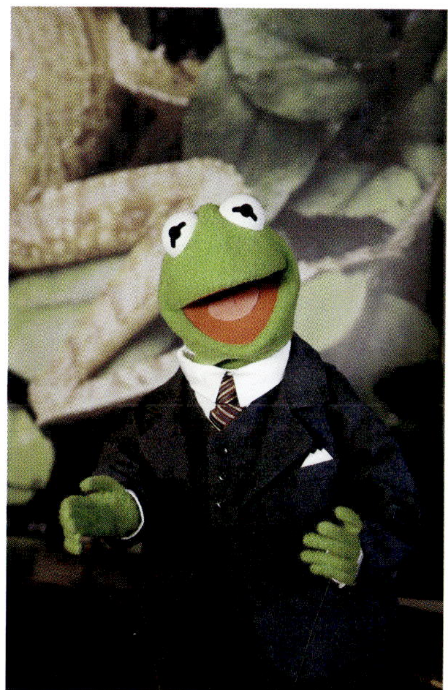

Portrait of Kermit the Frog, who visited Capitol Hill to call attention to the plight of amphibians on Wednesday, March 12, 2008.

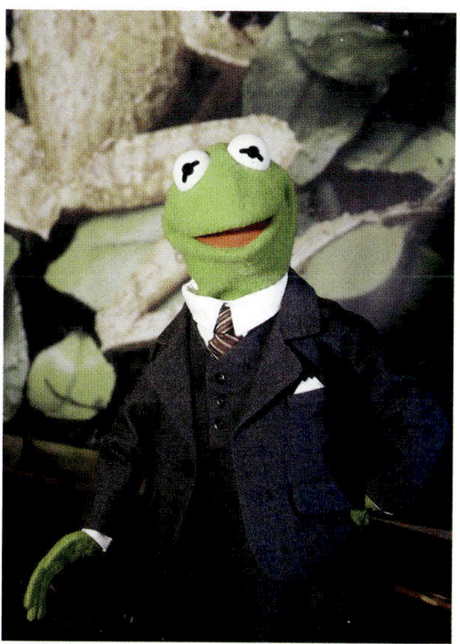

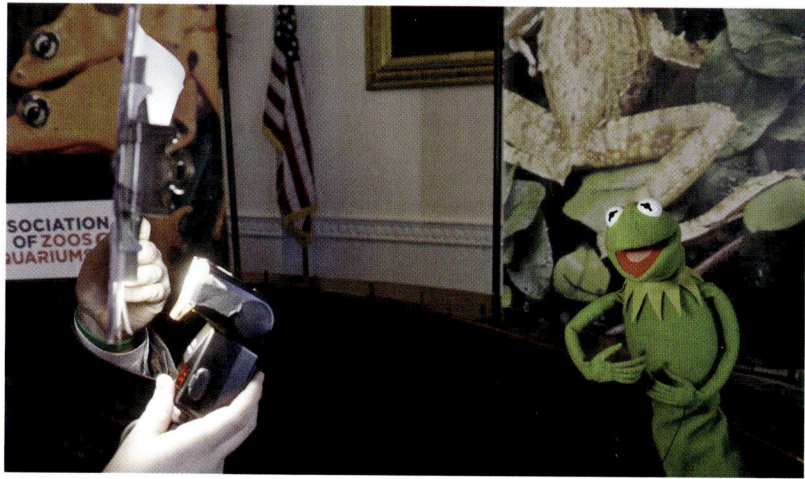

The simple lighting setup of off-camera flash for portraits of Kermit the Frog.

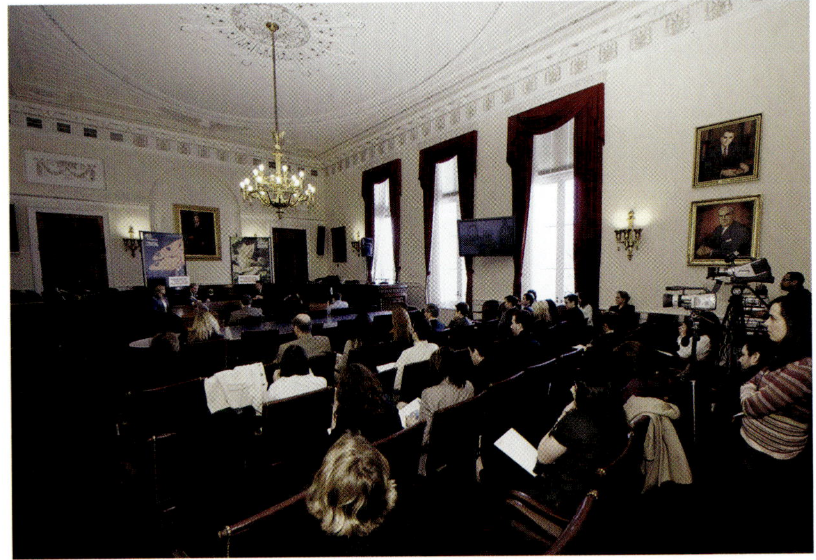

Kermit the Frog visits Capitol Hill.

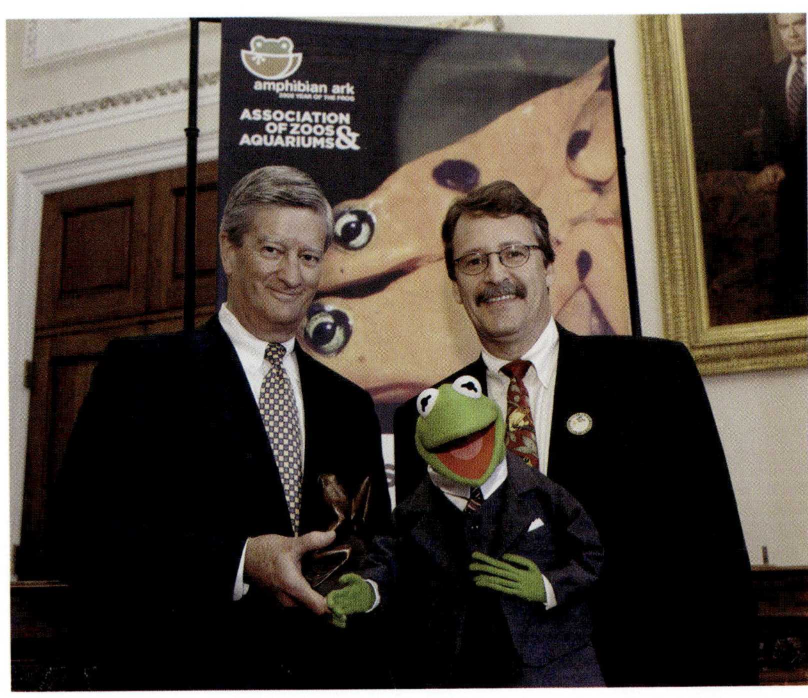

Opposite page: Kermit the Frog poses in front of the U.S. Capitol.

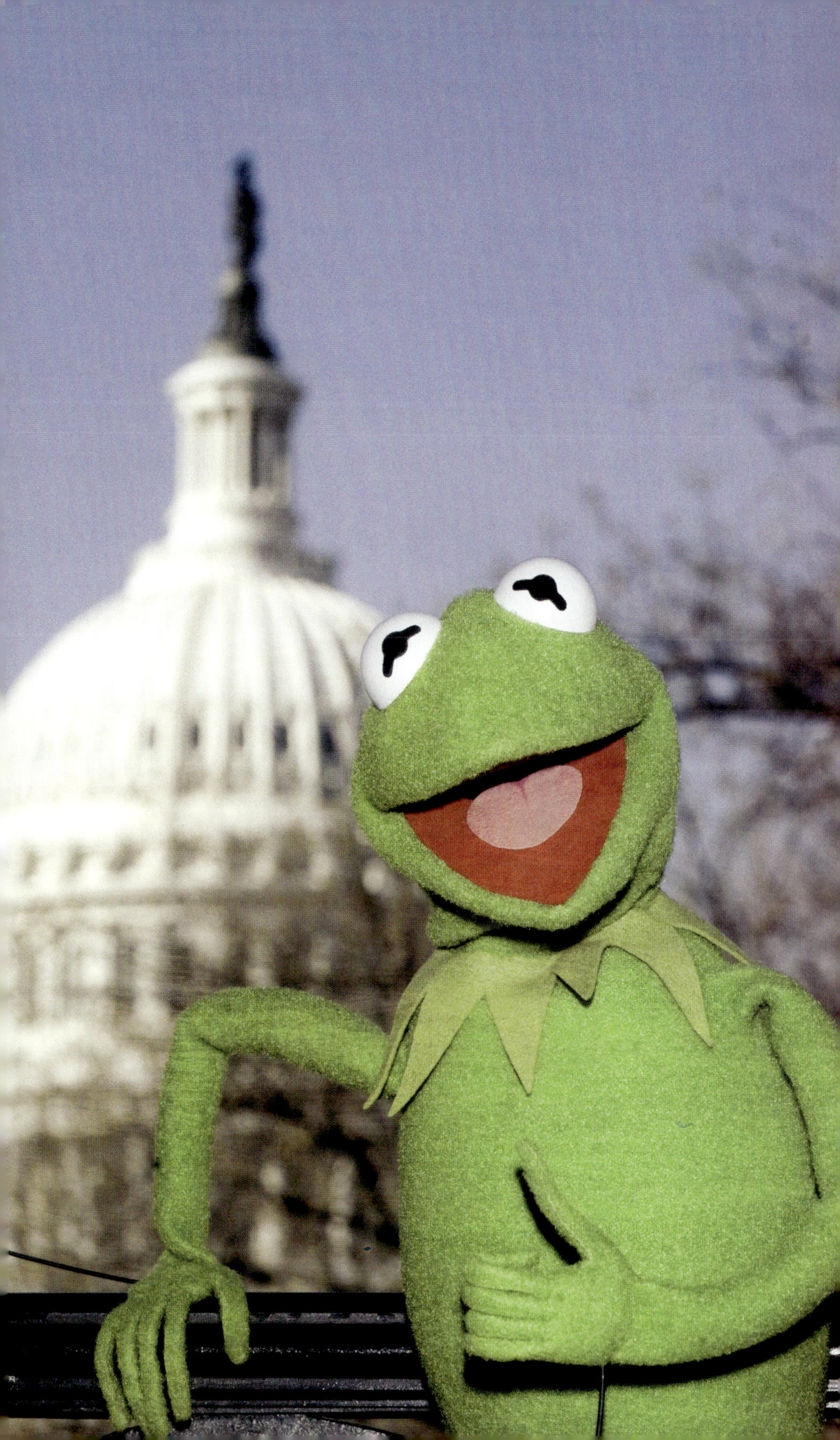

When I called my mom afterward and told her, she just said, "Wow, that's cool," but when I called my sister—who is just three years younger than me—she said, "No way! I don't believe you." Yup. Cool indeed. Working with Kermit. Long live the Muppets! Honored to have been in his presence.

Harrier Jet Liftoff: No Time for Indecision

At the end of the Gulf War, it was decided that there would be a huge celebration of the success of the military in the war. America needed a win, as the last big war had been Vietnam, and the government had sorely mishandled the homecoming for those soldiers, so a proper celebration was in order.

As plans evolved, it was decided to bring in representative aircraft to the Mall, in downtown Washington, DC. If you've never been to the Mall, it's a two-mile stretch of grass between the U.S. Capitol and the Lincoln Memorial, with the Washington Monument in the center. Flanking the Mall are almost all of the Smithsonian Institution museums, and it is often called America's backyard. Marches, protests, and rallies all are held here, with the setting of the U.S. Capitol as a powerful backdrop for any event.

Such was the case here, and it was decided that all the aircraft that could would be flown in. It wasn't possible to build a runway, so fixed-wing aircraft were brought in on flatbed tractor-trailers. However, the helicopters and the Harrier Jump Jet, with its vertical takeoff and landing capability, were all flown in. Accredited media received a binder of information on the arrival and location for each of the aircraft that were coming in. They all were due to be in at first light, and I planned to be there. The maneuvers would take about an hour or two to accomplish, but it seemed to me to be an amazing photo opportunity that I just couldn't miss. Well, I did—at least part of it.

I awoke in my Capitol Hill row house to the sounds of the thump-thump-thump of helicopter rotors overhead, and I cursed as I realized that I had overslept. Not a good sign. I quickly grabbed my gear and made a beeline for the location I thought would make a good vantage point—a slight berm rising above street level just to the east of the Washington Monument. I got there, and the Harrier jet had arrived first. I was kicking myself; I was so angry for having overslept. Yet I focused on the remaining helicopters, which looked amazing backlit by the rising sun and against a silhouetted Capitol dome. I shot and shot and shot until I ran out of film, yet I was frustrated by having missed the shot I wanted.

When I reviewed the film, I learned that although I had great images, I was a bit under-lensed. Even though I had a 300mm lens, I could have used a 600mm for some of the shots.

The parade and pomp and circumstance surrounding the multi-day celebration went off well, and I made a really great image of the president greeting General Norman Schwarzkopf, who led the parade down Constitution Avenue.

At the conclusion of the festivities, all of the aircraft had to leave, again with the precision that only the military can bring to bear. With the experience of the arrival under my belt, I decided to lens-up and rent a 600mm lens for the shot I had in mind. With the liftoff scheduled to begin a few hours before sunset, with the Harrier followed by the rest of the helicopters, I got in position well ahead of time, not wanting to be late again. I aligned myself exactly with the center of the jet and the Capitol dome, and a 600mm lens was perfect—the compression that the telephoto created made it look like the jet was literally parked on the grass right in front of the Capitol. Further, I was so tight that there was a small margin of error on the wing tips within the frame, left to right.

About 30 minutes before the Harrier was scheduled to lift off, one of my mentors—and someone whom I held in the highest regard—photographer Fred Maroon, came to right where I was standing to check out the view. I had assisted Fred in college when he came back to his alma mater (and now mine) to do a coffee-table book on the school, and Fred was held in such high regard that Leica called on him to do many of their catalogs and brochures for their cameras. I said hello to Fred, and he walked about 20 or so feet to my left and set up. I was so thankful that I had been there first, because there was no way I would have been comfortable enough to set up my own camera near his, feeling I might be encroaching on his position—and how dare I do that?

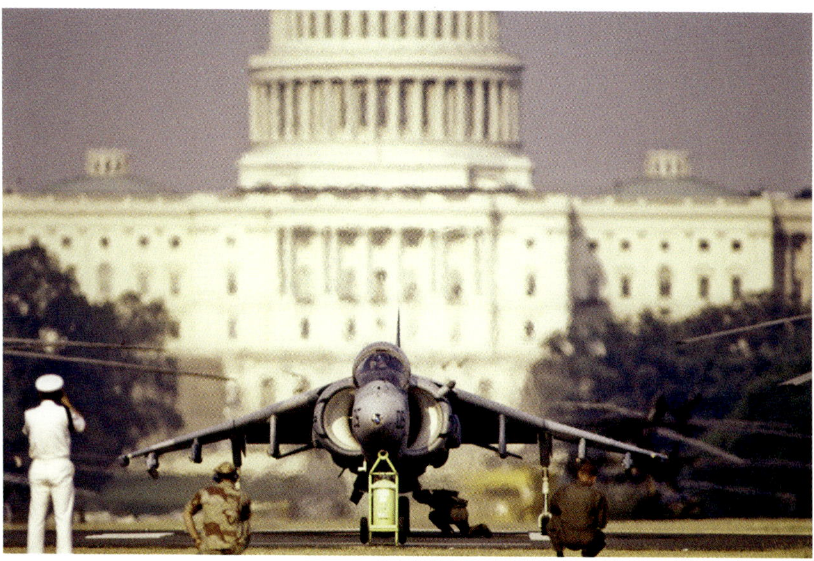

The Harrier Jump Jet just before it fires up its engines and departs from the National Mall.

Fred had selected a 300mm lens for his Leicas, and I was there with my 600mm lens, wondering whether I had made a wrong choice, second-guessing myself in the minutes before launch. I did have my 300mm lens, but should I switch?

The launch sequence began, and the jet's engines fired up. I had a frame or two on my roll of 36 that I had shot of the plane on the ground, and so I waited until the wheels lifted off the ground and slowly began firing. I knew I wouldn't have time to change the roll of film, so I had to be judicious with my film consumption.

As the plane crested the top of the building, I knew the images were getting good, and by the time the plane reached the top of the frame—and thus also the top of the Capitol dome—I ran through the last frame on the roll, the 37th frame on a roll of 36.

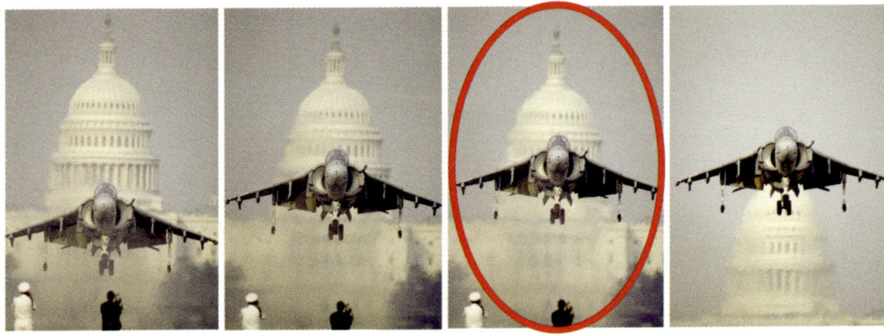

In the end, my gut told me to stick with the 600mm, but I would be lying if I said I didn't look to my left to see what Fred was doing. However, the knowledge I had gained from the landing sequences as they were arriving earlier told me that I was best staying with my 600mm lens, and I was pleased with the result. Although I shot the rest of the aircraft departing as well, the image of the Harrier remains to this day one of my iconic images in my archive. It was commissioned by the Smithsonian's National Air and Space Museum as a poster, and it was one of the top-selling inspirational posters sold by a poster company.

Opposite page: The Harrier Jump Jet departs from the National Mall following the June 8, 1991 celebration of the end of the Gulf War, in which Kuwait was liberated following the invasion by Iraq. This image in the series was, in my estimation, the best one.

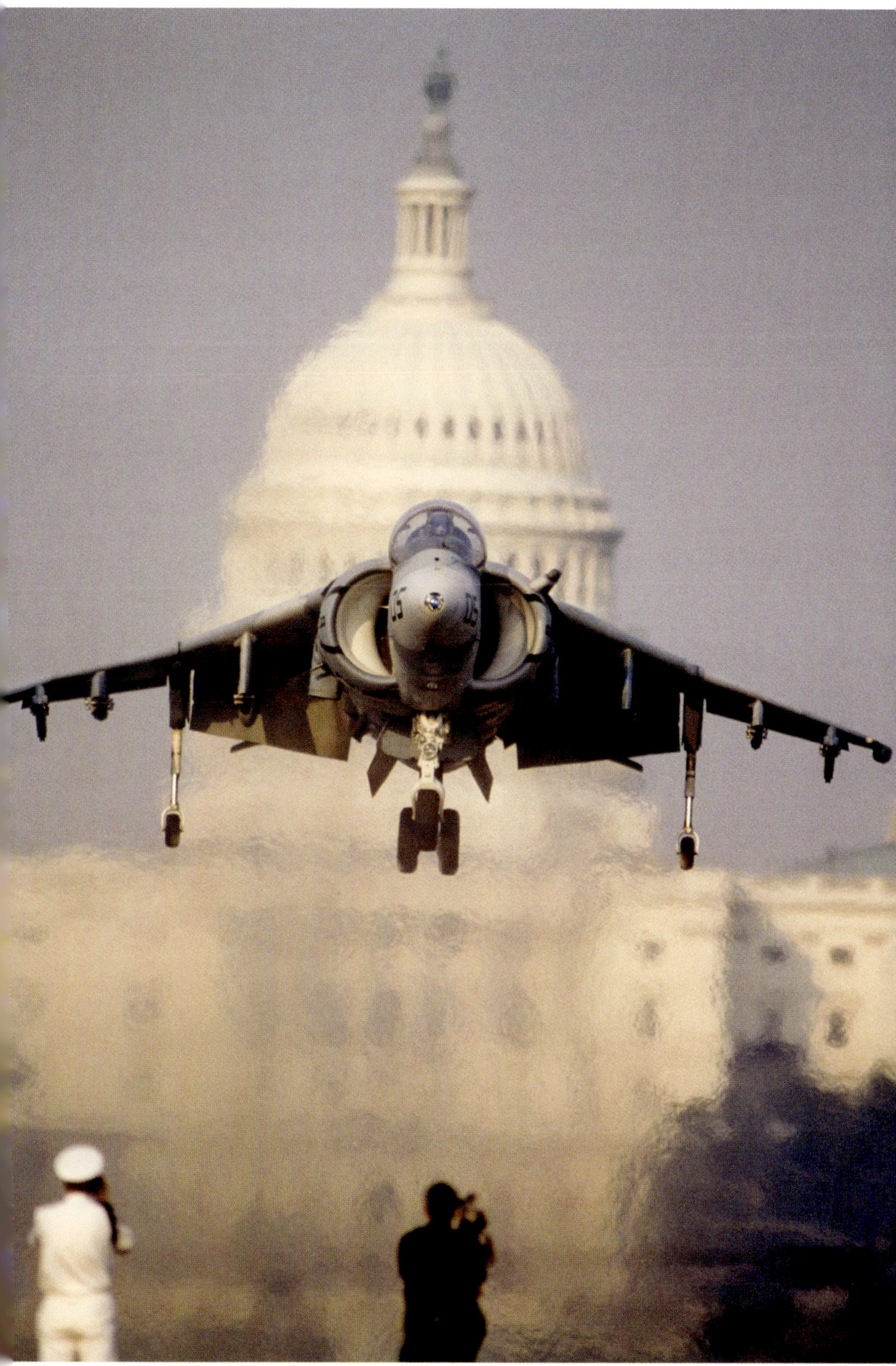

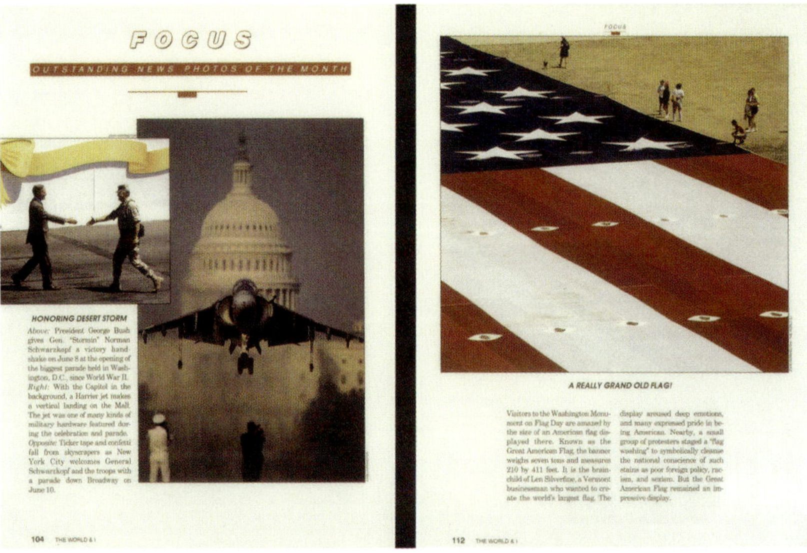

FOCUS

OUTSTANDING NEWS PHOTOS OF THE MONTH

HONORING DESERT STORM

Above: President George Bush gives Gen. "Stormin" Norman Schwarzkopf a victory handshake on June 8 at the opening of the biggest parade held in Washington, D.C., since World War II. *Right:* With the Capitol in the background, a Harrier jet makes a vertical landing on the Mall. The jet was one of many kinds of military hardware featured during the celebration and parade. *Opposite:* Ticker tape and confetti fall from skyscrapers as New York City welcomes General Schwarzkopf and the troops with a parade down Broadway on June 10.

104 THE WORLD & I

FOCUS

A REALLY GRAND OLD FLAG!

Visitors to the Washington Monument on Flag Day are amazed by the size of an American flag displayed there. Known as the Great American Flag, the banner weighs seven tons and measures 210 by 411 feet. It is the brainchild of Len Silverfine, a Vermont businessman who wanted to create the world's largest flag. The display aroused deep emotions, and many expressed pride in being American. Nearby, a small group of protesters staged a "flag washing" to symbolically cleanse the national conscience of such stains as poor foreign policy, racism, and sexism. But the Great American Flag remained an impressive display.

112 THE WORLD & I

The spread in the magazine where several of my images documented the patriotic celebration marking the end of the Gulf War.

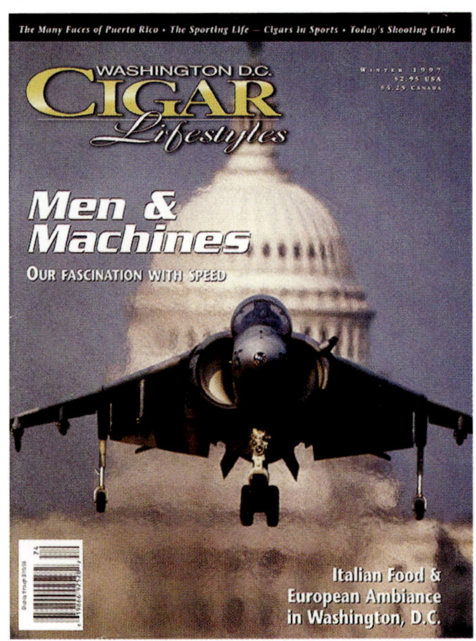

The cover of *Cigar Lifestyles* magazine was one of many of the reuses of the Harrier image.

Don't Let the Fear of Striking Out Get in Your Way

The title of this chapter is a quote from the legendary Babe Ruth, and it is quite appropriate for me. Let's get something clear from the beginning: I am not a sports photographer. However, that did not preclude me from dreaming of one day photographing the World Series. I figured I'd have to be working for one of the "majors" to get one of the coveted few press credentials that would let me make pictures during the ultimate sports event. So when the call came from my client (XM Radio) to accompany their on-air talent as well as the PR effort surrounding their right to broadcast Major League Baseball, I didn't quite know what to do—I was so excited.

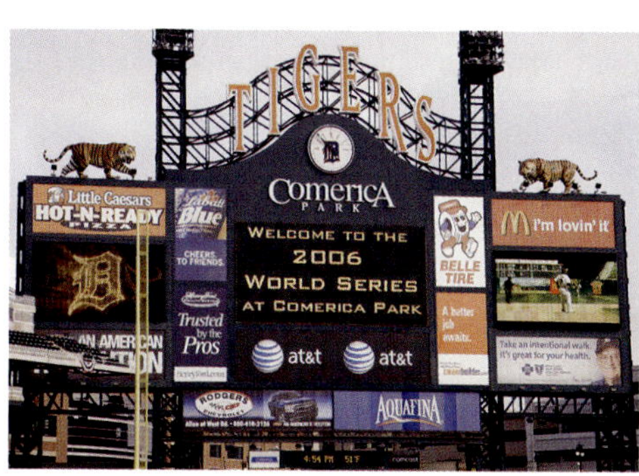

The Detroit Tigers scoreboard during Game 1 of the 2006 World Series.

Of course I said I could do it, and I prepared my estimate for what would be several days' worth of work in Detroit, as well as travel to and from the city. Fortunately, I didn't have to manage the logistics of hotel rooms that were convenient to the stadium or transportation to and from a security and logistical nightmare; I only had to worry about my flights.

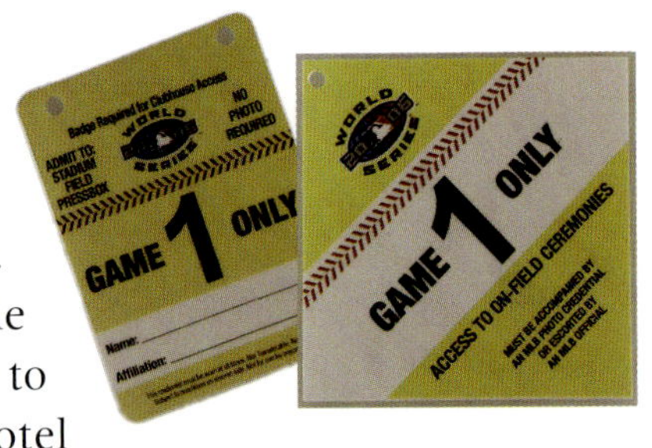

After my cost proposal was approved, I booked my flights and had to provide headshots and other security information so it could be confirmed that I was not any kind of security threat. I knew that getting my credentials would be the key to the access I needed to do my job, whether it was covering the on-air talent calling the game in the press box or accompanying them onto the field before and after the game for player and VIP one-on-one interviews.

I flew in the day before the Series and met my contact, who gave me the best credentials he could get me. Unfortunately, I knew it wasn't the full access that XM Radio had a right to and that I needed to completely do my job. I decided I would make the best of the credentials I had, and I began working on the simpler parts of my shot list.

In pre-game meetings with my client, we discussed the need for me to document all of the accommodations that they had for VIP guests, such as sky boxes, hospitality suites, and meet-and-greets with hall-of-famers, as well as the in-stadium advertising that was posted throughout the stadium. Also on the list were the approximate times when there would be in-stadium giveaways, as well as ads that would appear briefly on the Jumbotrons. Although this may not be overly exciting stuff at first blush, it was important to my client, and it was what got me into the game.

As fans began entering the stadium, I was able to knock out a large number of the easy shots so that I could focus on the on-air talent doing their job before the game. As players and VIPs with coveted "on-field" access filtered onto the field before the game, I was in a good position to accompany them onto the field. My earlier concerns about not having the correct access because the credential I had was limited turned out to be true, and I found myself in a quandary as I scrambled to get the correct credential that would get me onto the field.

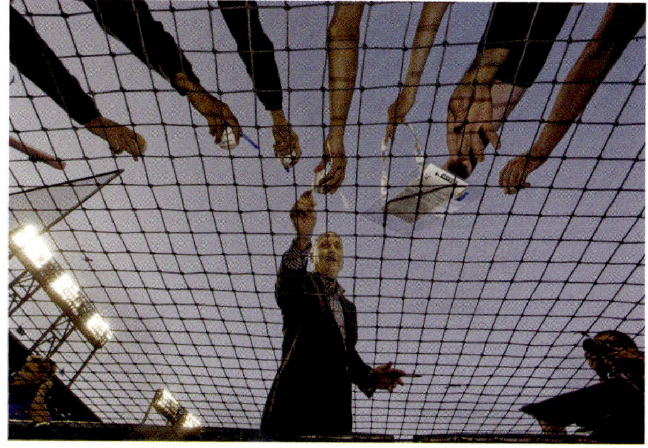

Cal Ripkin reaches out to fans to sign autographs at the edge of the stadium.

A few phone calls later, my client handed me the proper credential, which allowed me to effectively do my job up close and personal with the on-air talent and VIPs who were there. Unfortunately, someone else needed that credential during the game, so I had to return it when I left the field. Although I knew that I wouldn't be on the field during the game (no one but the players would), I also knew I was facing a bit of a dilemma regarding post-game interview coverage access.

As the game began, I located the person to whom I needed to return the credential and reluctantly, albeit with a smile on my face and a word of thanks and appreciation, handed it over. As I made my way up to the press box, the sun had long ago set. Being in the open-air catwalks of the stadium, I started to shiver.

It was cold, and I hadn't brought a jacket because it was so hot earlier in the day that I thought I didn't need one. Before I made it to the press box, a vendor who was servicing the sky suites with top-of-the-line apparel and World Series trinkets was moving her cart from one suite to another. The only jacket she had was an MLB World Series jacket that cost $175. I was cold and had hours more work ahead of me, and shivering my way through this assignment was *not* an option, so I plunked down my credit card and settled into my savior.

I made it into the press box and shot some great images of the commentators hard at work, juxtaposed against the playing field, and then I headed to where my client's guests were seated to photograph the VIPs. As the game went on, I made wide shots of the opening ceremonies and all of the pageantry that was taking place, as well as the client-specific needs. I knew that wide shots as well as shots of players my client would be interviewing or had relationships with could be useful if I caught them depicted positively while playing the game, so I filled the active game time focused on the game and the players with that in mind, since I had no on-field access, nor the long lenses that I would normally have if I were there specifically to cover the game itself.

As the game neared the ninth inning, my only need was the post-game on-field photography showing the on-air talent doing their jobs. Calls to my previous contact reminded me of what I already knew—the credentials that got me onto the field before the game would not do so afterward, and there wasn't a credential that would do what I needed available to me. With great determination, I headed to the ramp where the press that was headed onto the field had assembled, waiting for the final out to end the game. From years of experience, I knew that often acting like you belong can replace the credential that says you really *do* belong, and no one will question your presence. I hung back, hoping to find myself in the middle of a throng of photographers, out of the reach of credential checkers who might miss me in the crush of movement and the flurry of activity as the photographers rushed the field.

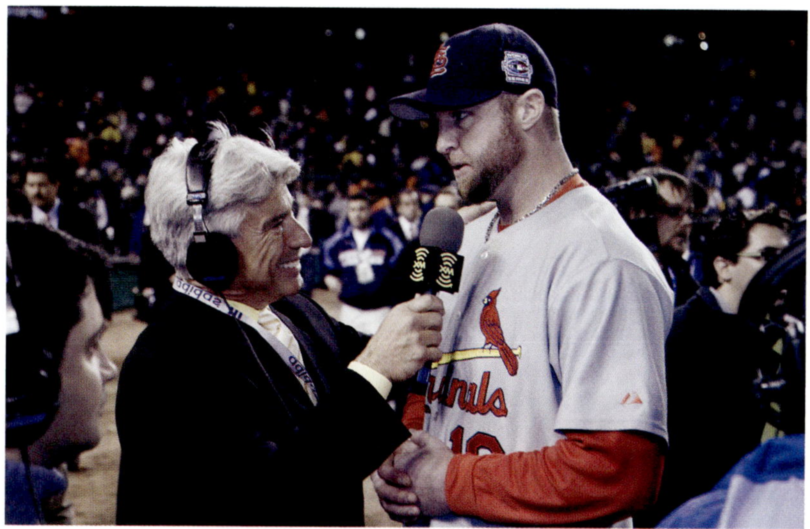

An XM Radio announcer interviews one of the Cardinals players following the game. Note the jacket in the background.

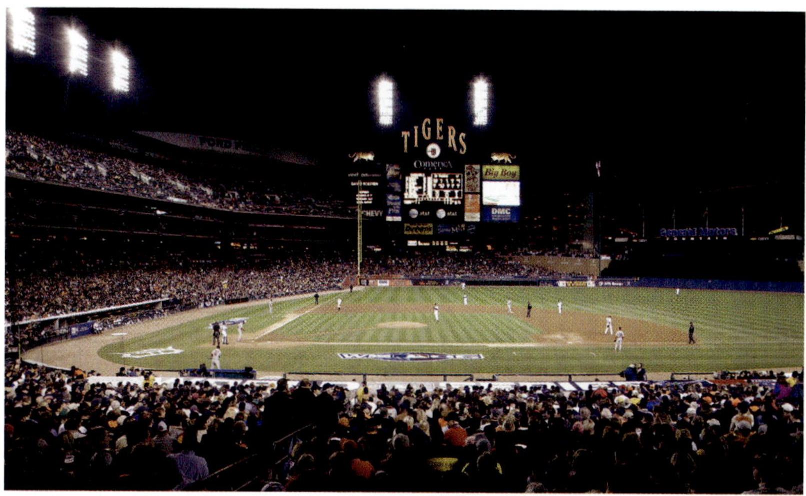

On-field action during Game 1 of the 2006 World Series.

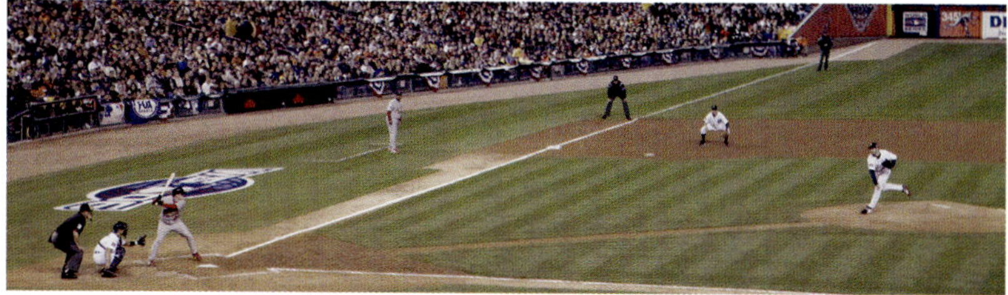

The most important photographers to go onto the field were those working for Major League Baseball, and they slipped right up to the front of the line so that they could be the first onto the field. As they slipped passed me and 15 or 20 more of my colleagues, I instantly knew I would have no problem getting onto the field and going wherever I wanted.

Fortunately for me, the photographers working for the MLB were keeping warm in the same jacket I was—the only difference was some small text that said "MLB Photos" embroidered on the sleeve. I tucked my less-than-powerful credentials inside my jacket with just the lanyard visible near my neck, zipped up the coat halfway, and held my camera in front of me as cadre of photographers began their rapid movement. No one asked to see my credentials because the jacket said it all!

I got onto the field and did my job in the veritable mosh pit of photographers. I could have gone anywhere I wanted, but I didn't want to abuse the opportunity that had serendipitously presented itself, which might have cut short my time on the field. I did get a couple of quizzical looks and raised eyebrows from the other similarly jacketed photographers because I clearly wasn't with them, nor did they know me.

As I wrapped up the last of my on-field pictures, I headed toward the tunnel I had come out of and unzipped my jacket. No one ever checks people departing a credentialed area, so I vanished into a sea of people and headed back to my shuttle bus for the seemingly long ride to my hotel room. I was exhausted but still on an adrenaline high from my incredible adventure at the first game of the World Series. I still have the jacket hanging in my office as a reminder of what's possible with a mix of luck, determination, and a bit of desperation.

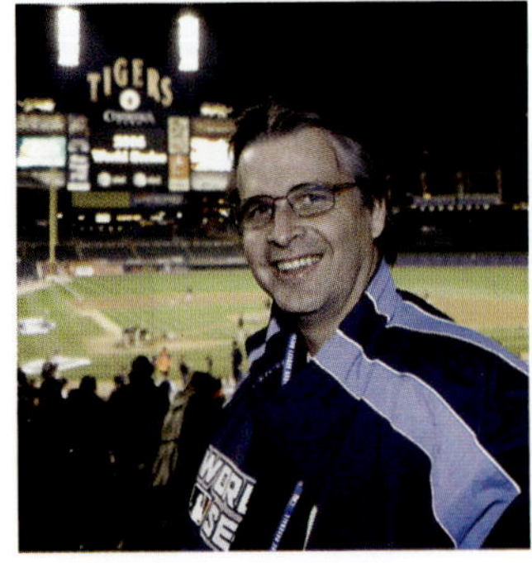

Wearing the remarkable 2006 World Series jacket after my success on the field.

Ice Cream Social with Obama

It was June 20, 2009, and it was my day to cover the White House. It was a very hot Saturday, the day before Father's Day, and nothing was on the president's schedule, which looked like this:

THE WHITE HOUSE
Office of the Press Secretary

FOR IMMEDIATE RELEASE June 19, 2009

WEEKEND GUIDANCE AND PRESS SCHEDULE FOR SATURDAY, JUNE 20 AND SUNDAY, JUNE 21, 2009

The President will spend the weekend in Washington, DC. He has no scheduled public events.

Saturday's In-Town Travel Pool
Wires: AP, Reuters, Bloomberg
Wire Photos: AP, Reuters, AFP
TV Corr & Crew: ABC
Print: New York Daily News
Radio: AP
Magazine Photo: TIME
Sunday's In-Town Travel Pool
Wires: AP, Reuters, Bloomberg
Wire Photos: AP, Reuters, AFP
TV Corr & Crew: CBS
Print: New York Post
Radio: AURN
Magazine Photo: TIME

Press Schedule for Saturday, June 20, 2009
EDT
10:00AM Pool Call Time
Press Schedule for Sunday, June 21, 2009
EDT
11:30AM Pool Call Time
##

Yet, even with no official public events on the president's schedule, for protective purposes (meaning an unexpected movement off the White House grounds or some national emergency that would make news), we had to be there. The denotation of a 10:00 a.m. "Pool Call Time" meant that the White House would promise to have no announcements or activities before 10:00 a.m. without first letting members of the press know with enough advance warning (usually) to get to the White House to cover said events. However, on this day, things didn't go quite as planned.

I arrived at the White House just before 10:00 and set up for what would likely be a quiet day. There were hints that the president might go golfing...or might not. We all hoped that maybe we'd get some ice-cream outing, but we didn't have high hopes. Something, anything, to break up the boredom.... Yet it's not a fully relaxed boredom, because you still have to be ready to move with a moment's notice to the motorcade in the event that something happens, and more than one of my colleagues has missed the motorcade because he or she wasn't fast enough. I didn't ever want to fall into this category.

At 3:00, we were given what's known as a "travel lid," meaning that the White House would keep a lid on any news until we were notified with enough time to return. There's something called a "lunch lid," where we have about an hour to safely leave the White House to get a sandwich, without the fear that when we're gone something will happen. A "travel lid" means that even if there were news out of the White House, the press office promises that it won't involve travel off the grounds. A "full lid" means that there will be no more news out of the White House for the day, unless, of course, they notify us with enough time to get back—or so they say.

So, with a travel lid in place, it would have been safe for me to depart, and in fact the wire-service photographers and *Time* magazine's photographer did just that. I, however, opted to stay on until we had a full lid, just in case. At about 3:20, a full lid was called, and I began to pack up. I got to my car about 10 minutes later and got a panicked phone call from a colleague of mine who was a member of the pool, telling me that they had called the travel pool back in, as the president was doing an "off the record movement."

An "OTR," as it is known, is where the president has decided to go somewhere at the last minute, and because of the nature of that unexpected movement, with the destination being known only to a select few people, it is generally considered safe for the president to turn up unannounced somewhere, because no one would have had the time to plan some unpleasantness directed at him.

Despite that, an advance team was sent out the moment the president decided to go to this as-yet-unknown-to-us destination, to secure it—discreetly—to the extent possible within that limited timeframe.

I immediately turned and ran back to the Northwest Gate of the White House and got cleared through security, and then I ran to the Press Room, catching my colleagues just as we were passing through to the Rose Garden and the waiting motorcade. We all were speculating about where we were headed, and Ben, our press liaison, wouldn't let on. When we saw President Obama's daughters get into the SUV, we thought for sure he was headed on an ice-cream excursion, but exactly where?

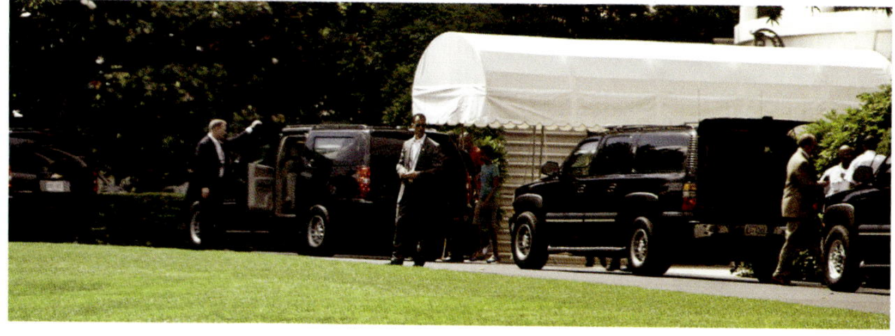

President Barack Obama and his two daughters, Sasha and Malia, get into an SUV for an off-the-record movement (accompanied by a phalanx of Secret Service agents and press members), which ended up being a trip to get ice cream at the Dairy Godmother in Alexandria, Virginia.

The motorcade departed the White House at 3:40 p.m., and we headed south. We traversed the Potomac River, no doubt much easier than George Washington did a few hundred years ago (and in the opposite direction, I believe), headed into Virginia. At this point, I was lost as to where we were going, if for ice cream, because all of my ice-cream destinations where in the city proper.

We continued through the streets of suburban Virginia, and the motorcade came to an abrupt halt. At 3:56, we were told, "Get out; this is it," and we all jumped from the vans and ran toward the front. We were ushered through the ad hoc security perimeter that had been quickly set up by plain-clothed Secret Service agents. We found ourselves outside of the Dairy Godmother ice-cream parlor in the Del Ray section of Alexandria, Virginia. The president and his daughters were already inside, and we were not allowed in. "Grrrrr," was all I could muster. This is not unusual when you're trying to make something out of nothing. You're really trying to show what the president is doing, but you're not able to get to where the president is actually doing it.

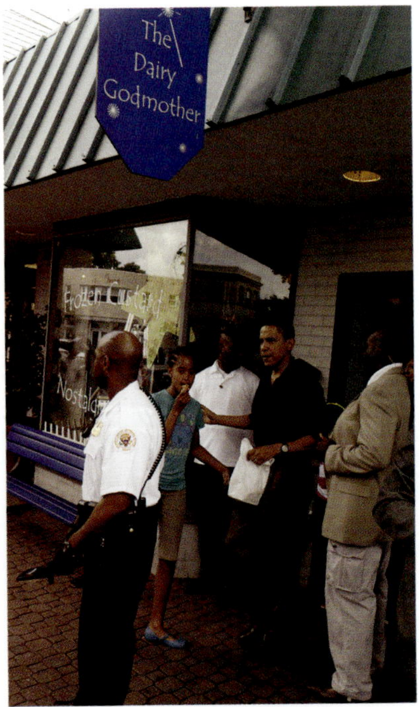

We waited outside for about 15 minutes, while the president and first daughters enjoyed their ice cream inside, socializing with the other patrons who were lucky enough to find themselves inside already. Then President Obama came out, gave a wave, and got back into the SUV to head home in the motorcade.

President Barack Obama departs the Dairy Godmother in Alexandria, Virginia.

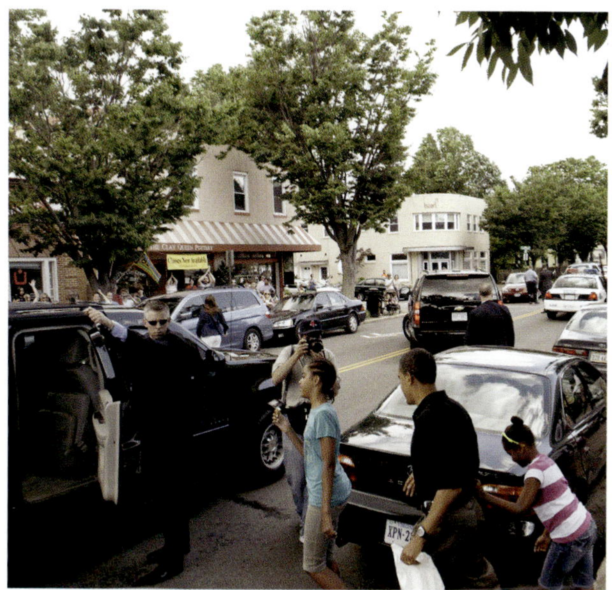

President Barack Obama, holding doggie treats as he and his two daughters head back into their SUV following an off-the-record stop at the Dairy Godmother.

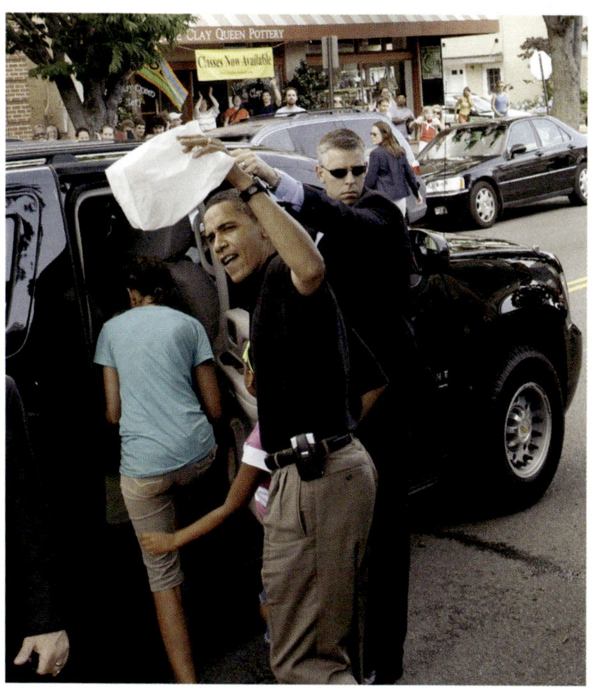

President Barack Obama shows off the doggie treats.

The pool report from my colleague at the *New York Daily News* reported the day's events as such:

Pool Report #1 June 20, 2009

Ice cream run with the girls

POTUS, riding in his motorcade SUV, departed at 3:40 p.m. from the White House with daughters Malia and Sasha in tow.

POTUS took the girls on a sugar-coated Father's Day Eve jaunt to the Dairy Godmother, a boutique ice-cream parlor in the Del Ray section of Alexandria, VA.

Malia had a waffle cone of vanilla custard, and Sasha had a cup of vanilla custard. POTUS had a cup of vanilla custard with hot fudge and toasted almonds, the shopkeeper disclosed. The trio were in the shop for about 15 mins and sat at a table and enjoyed their frozen treats.

POTUS and the girls received applause from the staff and patrons inside and a small crowd outside as they exited the ice cream shop. POTUS, carrying a bag of frozen "puppy pops" for Bo the First Dog, waved to the crowd before he hopped in the SUV.

The motorcade returned to the White House at 4:32 p.m.

For the record, your pool was unexpectedly called for this trek 25 minutes after a travel lid and 10 minutes after a full lid were issued. Hey, things change.

We now have what we are told is the real full lid for the day.

Upon arrival back at the White House, it was a rush to transmit photos out. Several of the wire photographers were transmitting from the motorcade as it drove through the city streets. I, too, was busy editing my images and would transmit as soon as I got back to my hardwired connection at the White House. I transmitted several images out and was on my way home by 5:30. So goes another day traveling with the President, even if only for ice cream.

Donny Osmond, Snoop Dogg, Weird Al, and Coolio...Oh My!

Every year a who's who of people and companies associated with consumer electronics gather in Las Vegas for an event called the Consumer Electronics Show, held by the Consumer Electronics Association. If you're a Las Vegas–based photographer, this event is no doubt a boon to your bottom line, as there are many events, press conferences, and activities that need to be photographed. For many a non-Vegas photographer, it means an all-expenses-paid trip to Las Vegas. Such was the case for me when XM Satellite Radio asked me to travel to Las Vegas to photograph their press conferences and other activities related to the show.

To create a buzz and draw attendance to their booth, XM had decided to bring to the show a number of artists and celebrities who would speak, give interviews, perform, and otherwise be in attendance. There's a saying that "politics makes strange bedfellows," but that pales in comparison to a backstage green room at the Las Vegas Consumer Electronics Show. At that show, I found myself in the green room with artists and celebrities such as Snoop Dogg, Donnie Osmond, Cal Ripken, and "Weird Al" Yankovic, among many others.

Snoop Dogg had become a part of the XM team as a result of a humorous commercial in which, while in the XM studios, his "Snoop" bling went missing, and he wandered around the studio to the various radio booths, querying a variety of well-known artists as to whether they had his bling. We were able to capitalize on this because we had this necklace with us, and I asked a number of notables whether they would mind donning it as well.

While Snoop was in the green room, the epitome of the "cool" rapper with all the appropriate accessories, in walked squeaky-clean Donny Osmond. Donny is ever the consummate professional, and if he had an adverse opinion about Snoop, you couldn't have seen it. I had worked with Donny a few years earlier for a

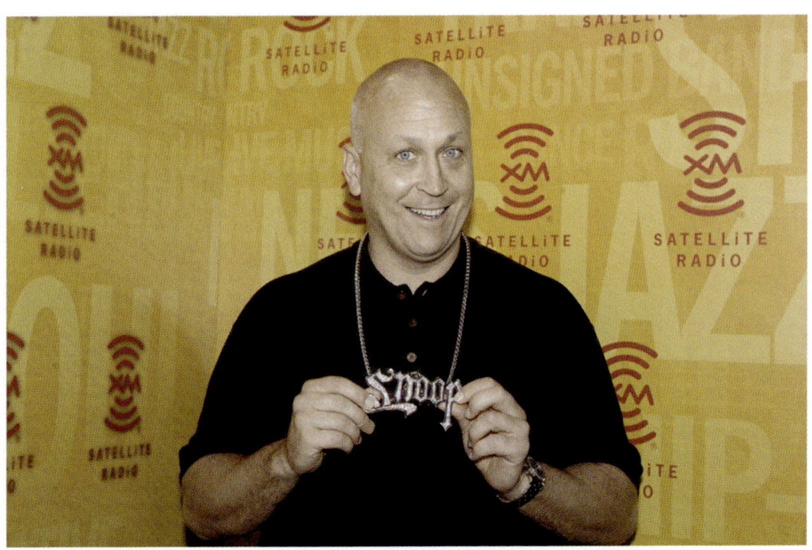

Baseball great Cal Ripken participates in a prank being played on Snoop Dogg, who, in a widely publicized XM commercial, had his bling go missing in the XM studios—several artists and celebrities agreed to wear it for the prank.

portrait session for another client, and he and I chatted briefly about that project after Snoop had passed through the green room and had given Donny a warm embrace. Donny expressed a similar warm sentiment toward Snoop, and it was smiles all around. I was busy in the small space with a very wide-angle lens and strobe fill, making images of the exchange and embrace. I can think of few moments as surreal as Donny Osmond and Snoop Dogg embracing as if they were two pals at a PTA meeting.

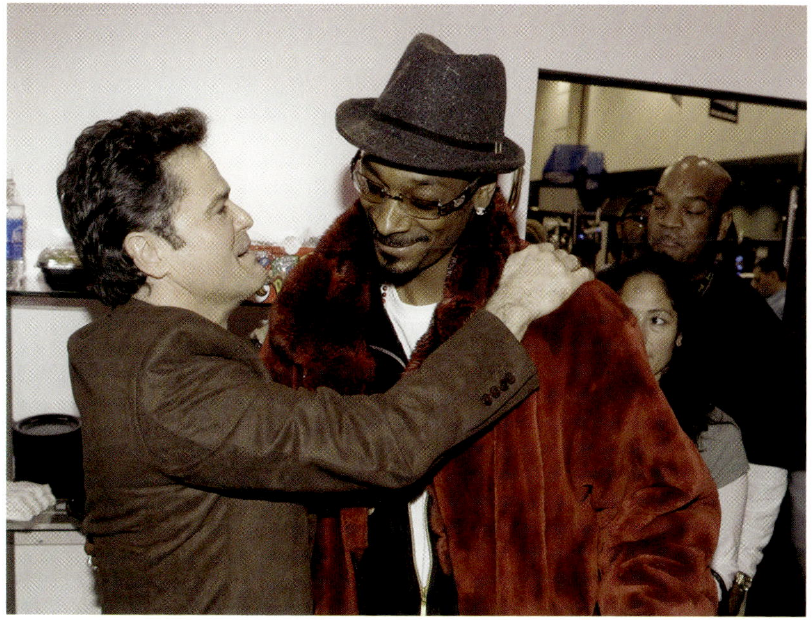

Donnie Osmond (left) and Snoop Dogg (right) in the green room backstage in the XM booth.

That, however, paled in comparison to what happened next. "Weird Al" had been on stage earlier promoting his unique brand of comedy. Following his turn on stage, he had been moved to a corner of the booth where fans could queue up and he would sign autographs and have his picture taken with them. Because I had already photographed him on stage and with a number of fans, I had migrated elsewhere in the booth to see what other photo opportunities there might be.

Vegas being Vegas, you can never predict who might come into the booth unannounced with or without an entourage. I stumbled upon an extremely well-known rapper on the opposite side of the booth, all by himself, just checking out the new XM product offerings. I immediately thought that it would be a great photo if I were able to pair up this artist with "Weird Al" Yankovic, but I knew there was a bit of an unknown factor that could come into play, because this artist was—at one point anyway—quite angry with "Weird Al." Knowing it would be a great photo opportunity, I forged ahead anyway.

I approached the artist, introduced myself, and asked whether he would mind coming over to be photographed, saying, "There's someone who I'd like to photograph you with, if you don't mind." He was amenable and followed me toward the signing area. Because of my sizable frame, he didn't see whom I was introducing him to until they were within two or three feet of each other and before I stepped out of his line of sight. I preset my focus, f-stop, shutter speed, and strobe and zoomed all the way out, knowing I would potentially have seconds to get a great photograph (if it went badly)—and, more importantly, believing that the rapper and "Weird Al" were both consummate professionals. I turned to "Weird Al" and said, "'Weird Al,' this is Coolio. Coolio, meet 'Weird Al.'"

Now, this scenario presented a bit of a risk because every time "Weird Al" did a parody song, he would seek and get permission from the record company holding the rights to the songs—even though he likely did not need it, as evidenced by the Supreme Court case regarding a Roy Orbison song parodied by 2 Live Crew. Yankovic felt that the appropriate thing to do was to get permission to do his parodies. In that vein, he had obtained permission from the record label to parody Coolio's "Gansta's Paradise," about the rough-and-tumble life of a gangster, when he did his parody called "Amish Paradise."

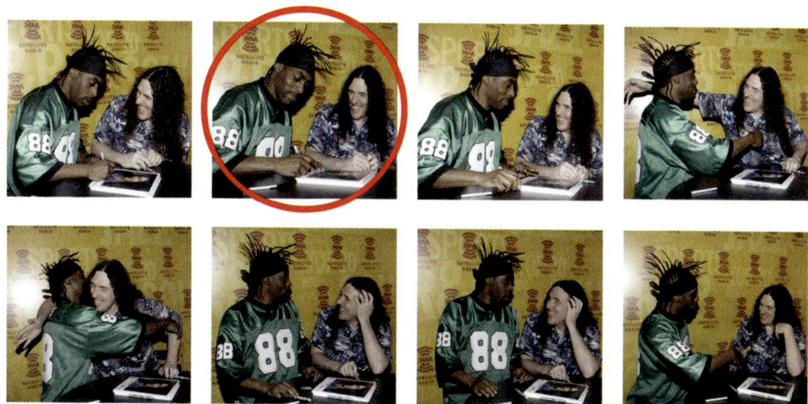

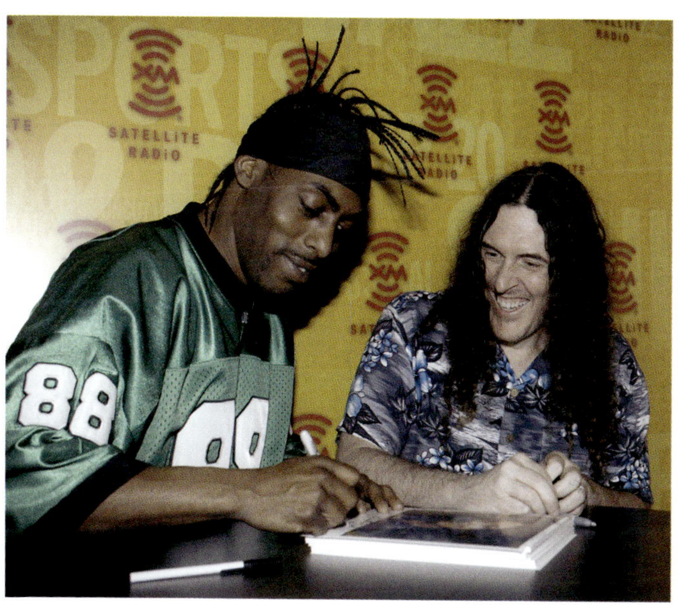

Coolio (left) breaks the ice with "Weird Al" Yankovic (right) at the XM Satellite Radio booth at the 2006 Consumer Electronics Show in Las Vegas, Nevada, on January 7, 2006.

Unfortunately, according to Coolio, his record label hadn't checked with him, and he was none too happy. Although I don't know the extent of the public statements and/or the threats that were made, suffice it to say that Coolio was definitely not happy. I had worked once before with Yankovic and knew that he was frustrated by what was clearly a miscommunication and saddened that the artist who he had parodied was upset.

When Yankovic noticed that Coolio was standing right in front of him, he looked up in shock and, as he later recounted, didn't know quite what to think. Coolio extended his right hand and said, "Hey, man. How're you doing? Let me sign some of these," and began signing his name to some of Yankovic's head shots. What ensued was a few brief moments of lighthearted and congenial back and forth between the two artists as I hurriedly made a number of frames of the two of them breaching a *détente* that had existed for a number of years.

Because of the newsworthiness of the original disagreement between Coolio and "Weird Al," it was easy to find news outlets who were interested in taking the sequence of images from that interaction. And XM, my client, was able to get some substantial publicity because it took place not only in their booth, but also in front of an XM step and repeat background.

I breathed a sigh of relief as they embraced one last time and Coolio headed off to other booths at the show. "Weird Al" later commented in an interview that he was very happy that the age-old ice had been broken and that they were now on speaking terms. And I was happy that what happens in Vegas doesn't always have to stay in Vegas, and everyone benefited from the situation.

When working with big-name celebrities, artists, singers, or actors, they can be quite flighty in certain situations, because the control they have over their image and how they are perceived in the public eye is everything. So being prepared, knowing your equipment, being able to think and work quickly, and knowing the history of the talent you are working with can often help you capitalize on what would otherwise be a non-event.

Three Locations, 45 Minutes... No Problem!

One thing I revel in being able to do is making the seemingly impossible, possible. In one such case, a high-tech Internet company needed new visuals to get people excited about their service, which was essentially a new way to allow citizens to get things done with the government. Paying parking tickets online was but one of the things that this Internet company wanted to do, and they had the backing of some big names—General Colin Powell among them.

This particular client contacted me and a few of my friends/colleagues. I came in for the briefing on the project, and they asked me about a few of my ideas and whether I thought we could get the shots they wanted done in 45 minutes. My first answer is always yes, and then I figure out how to make it happen. One setup was formal portraits, which were to take place in their downtown office, and the next setup was nearby on the steps of the General Grant Memorial, with the Capitol in the background.

I shared with them one of my ideas—one of the founders of the company wrapped in red tape, and the other founder with a pair of scissors, cutting his partner out of the red tape, symbolizing what the company could do for the average citizen.

Telling the potential client this idea was a bit risky, because I wanted to get them excited about the idea, but not to the point that they would book someone else and then give the idea to that unknowing photographer to execute. Yes, I know, ideas are not copyrightable/protected—only the tangible expression thereof is—but still, I didn't want them using my idea.

The meeting ended, and I felt good about the project. I asked who the other photographers were that the client was talking to, and I knew them both.

A few days later, after I had submitted my proposal, I got the call that I had been awarded the project. I asked the client in a casual manner why they had selected me, and they said that it was not about the money (as I had come in as the most expensive), but they selected me because they thought I was the only one who could do the assignment based upon the plan I had laid out to accomplish all the photos in 45 minutes—which is exactly what we did.

To accomplish the shots in that timeframe, we had three different setups, lights, softboxes, a generator, assistants, makeup people, a location manager, and catering. We started at the client's office, setting up lights there for the portraits. The other two locations were being set up at the same time. I kept in close contact with the assistants at the other two locations to ensure that we had both of the other setups prepared. After finishing up at the client's office in less than 10 minutes, we had them travel to the Capitol in 15 minutes, leaving 25 minutes for the remaining shot.

The second shot was of the two founders with the red tape. We had gone out and purchased a hundred or so yards of red velvet holiday ribbon, and we started wrapping up one of the founders.

I wanted to have enough left over to stream toward the camera and down the steps, to draw the eye from the camera to the subjects. The idea was that the guy wrapped in red tape should look a bit like a damsel in distress lying across the railroad tracks. We carefully laid him down entirely wrapped up, and we had his partner come in with the scissors. I wanted oversized scissors, but we couldn't find any that were reasonable and not cartoonish, so we used the biggest pair we could find. We knocked out several images and had great results. Using a huge Plume HexOval softbox and shading them with a large scrim, the light on them was extremely flattering.

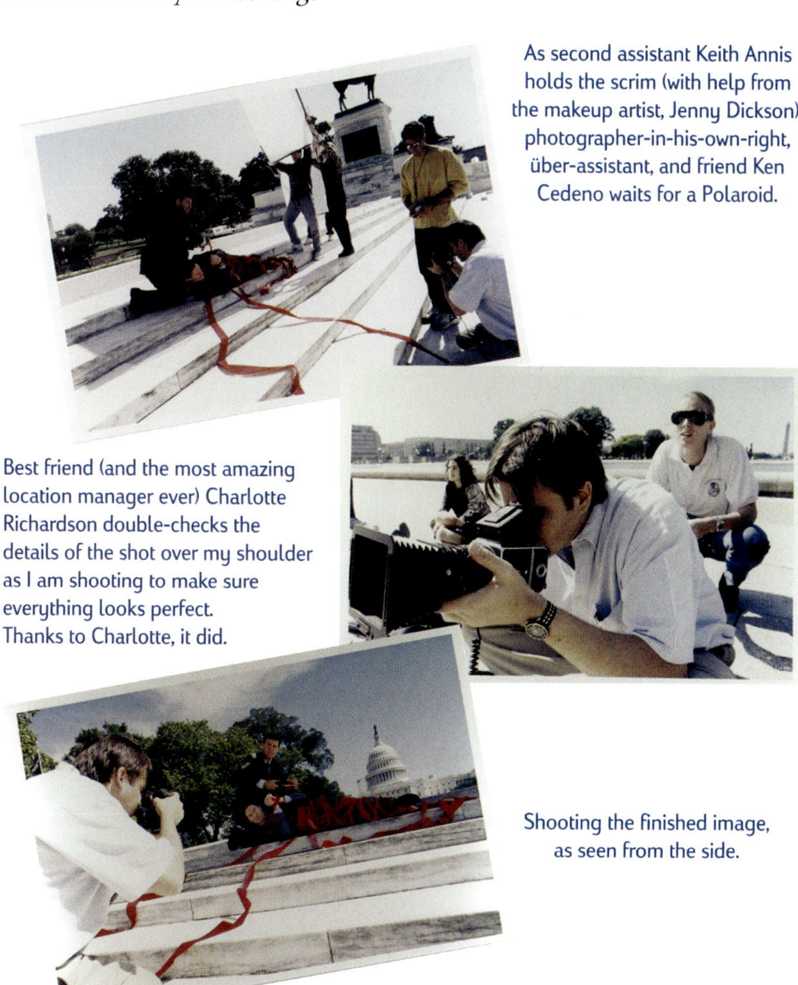

As second assistant Keith Annis holds the scrim (with help from the makeup artist, Jenny Dickson), photographer-in-his-own-right, über-assistant, and friend Ken Cedeno waits for a Polaroid.

Best friend (and the most amazing location manager ever) Charlotte Richardson double-checks the details of the shot over my shoulder as I am shooting to make sure everything looks perfect. Thanks to Charlotte, it did.

Shooting the finished image, as seen from the side.

Because we had done this one so quickly, I decided that I wanted the founders to be standing in the reflecting pool, and they seemed to go for it. The client and I had discussed this idea in a brainstorming session, but they didn't think their client would go for it; I thought different.

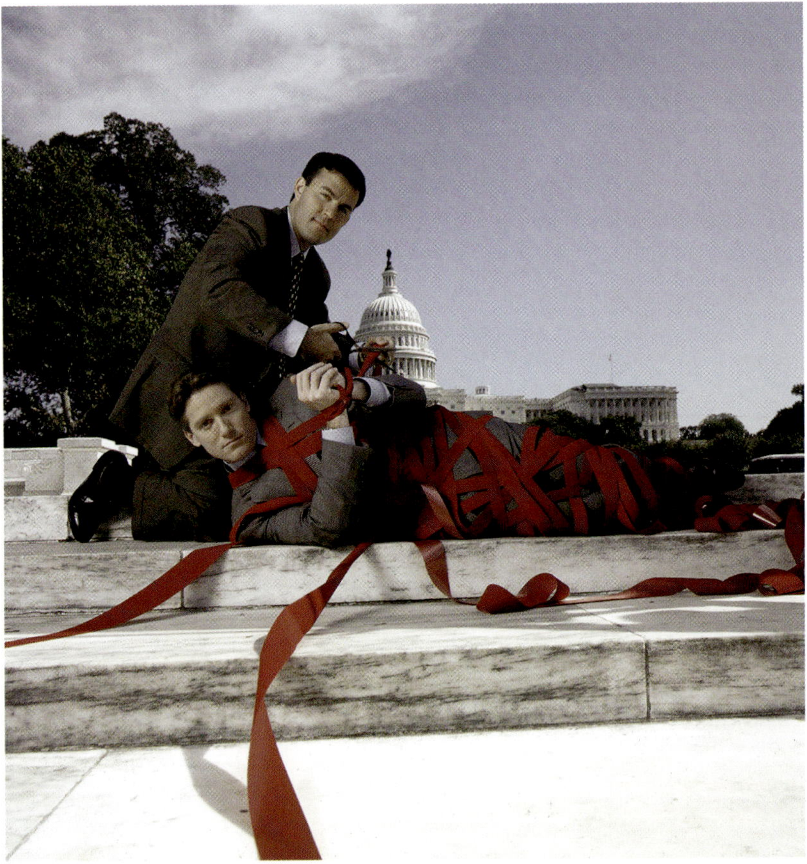

The finished image.

I suggested to the founders that I thought it would be really cool to do a shot of them standing in the reflecting pool, with their pants rolled up, reading a paper and smoking cigars. They were totally up for it. We had them step into the reflecting pool, which we thought might be a no-no, but we didn't have a definitive kibosh on it. As we started the first few frames, which included an assistant in the calf-high water holding the light and softbox that surely would have electrocuted all of them if it had fallen in the water, my location manager—the genius we all know as Charlotte—warned me that a Capitol police officer was coming over to check what we—our entire team of 10 people—were doing. I told her to intercept the officer, show him the permit, and buy me some time, which she did.

After a back-and-forth dialogue, my second assistant whispered to me that Charlotte and the officer were coming over toward me. Knowing that I had the shot and the entire shoot was a wrap with this third image in the can, I called to the two subjects that we had it, and they started walking toward the edge of the water with the shot done—and all with five minutes left on the clock!

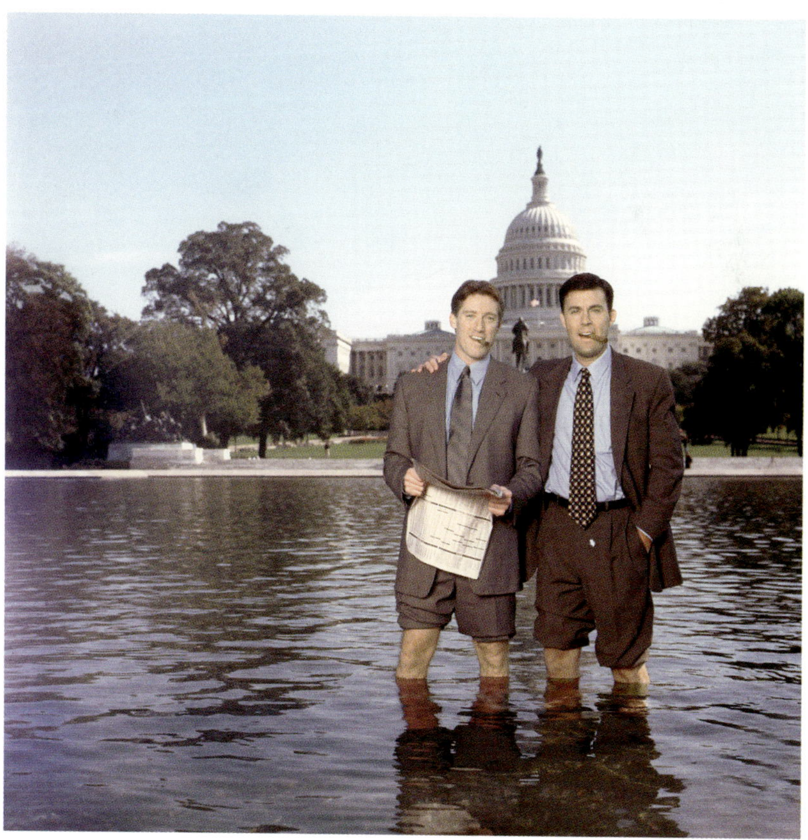

The subjects in the Capitol reflecting pool.

Rolling Stones: Shooting the *Voodoo Lounge* Kickoff

Just prior to the Rolling Stones announcing their worldwide *Voodoo Lounge* tour, I got a call from a colleague of mine asking whether I would mind shooting during the DC show at RFK Stadium. The tour was to kick off in DC in August of 1994, and this show was important. Although I've never been a huge Rolling Stones fan per se, I recognized the historical importance of the band, and since it had been widely suspected that the previous *Steel Wheels* tour might have been their last, I jumped at the opportunity to have full access to cover the entire show.

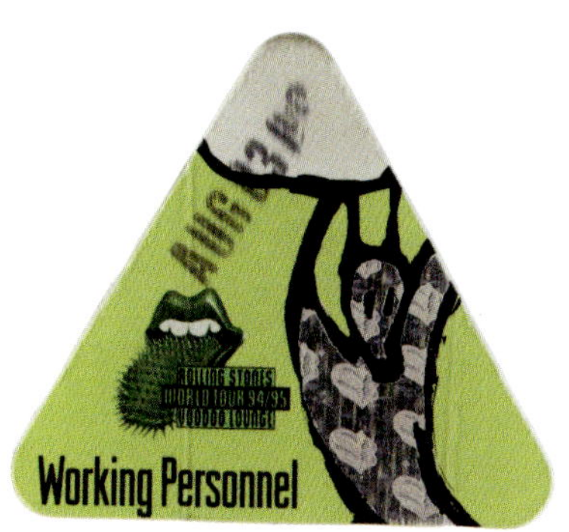

When shooting concerts, we often are limited to the first three songs, so the opportunity to shoot the entire show arises only on occasion. The beauty of being able to shoot the entire show is that you have the opportunity to make images of multiple wardrobe changes and light and effects changes, and you're able to really move around the venue and work the entire scene. In situations like this, I've always preferred to use fixed focal length lenses because of the purity of the glass, and my lenses of choice have always been 35mm f/1.4 and 85mm f/1.4, along with a 135mm and/or a 180mm f/2. I've found that these lenses—often referred to as *fast glass*—are the most optically pure and provide a clarity that far surpasses any zoom lens. Perhaps I'm being a stickler, but when I'm also shooting on Kodachrome film, I am trying to arrive as close to technical visual perfection as possible, in the hope that it will carry me if I don't quite make a "creatively perfect" image.

I arrived at the stadium by way of the crew entrance tunnel in the back—for sound check, not necessarily to make great images. I have covered many an all-day festival, and I have often found that the images made during the daylight hours lacked the mood and feel that I wanted to convey in my images. It was always the act that performed during the evening portion of these all-day festivals that benefitted from an amazing mix of shadow and light that really made the images come to life. Because of this I opted not to shoot much during the sound check; instead, I wanted the various members of the road crew to become familiar with me and comfortable with my presence.

During the actual show, with crazy fans and deafeningly loud music, any questions posed by a crew member or an overzealous security guard unfamiliar with me could not be rapidly addressed by those who had blessed me as an authorized photographer for the entire show. Thus, as I encountered crew I would make eye contact with them and nod or say "Hey" so that they would be aware that I was authorized and approved (since no one else would be in the venue during a sound check).

In addition, when the lead security for the event held their muster meeting for all the yellow-shirted "Event Staff" guards who seemed to be posted every 20 or so feet, I made a point of being nearby, organizing my gear and otherwise silently demonstrating my authorization to be there. Even though I wore a "Working Crew" credential that was lime green and visible to all, doing these preliminary demonstrations wherever possible serves me well and helps me avoid headaches, questions, and a loss of shooting time when peak action is occurring. I cannot stress enough the importance of knowing everyone you can before the high stress and adrenaline kicks in as the concert starts, causing many of the crew to make split decisions that don't go your way.

As the last rays of sun slipped past the top of the stadium rim and dusk settled, I knew that the lights would be coming on soon, and I relished the opportunity to cover the show. I could feel my creative juices begin to flow as I started to see some of the stage lights coming on.

The Counting Crows did the honors as the opening act for the tour. They were rotating with Tori Amos for various dates, but for the first show, they were the openers. The two-and-a-half-hour show was to be a *tour de force* aurally, and I wanted to capture that essence in camera.

After a brief changeover, the Rolling Stones took the stage with a light show and oversized screen as a backdrop to their performance. The light was amazing, and I was literally standing at the feet of the master, Keith Richards, as he worked his magic with guitar licks that roared out of the sound system. Much of what I did from the photo pit, I did with my 35mm f/1.4, and the clarity shows. The photo pit is the steel fencing that is the buffer between the front-row fans and the stage. This is the area where the Event Staff security works, as well as any TV cameras recording the show for future use or as IMAG—image magnification—so that the fans in the "cheap seats" can see a larger-than-life version of the performers on the big screens.

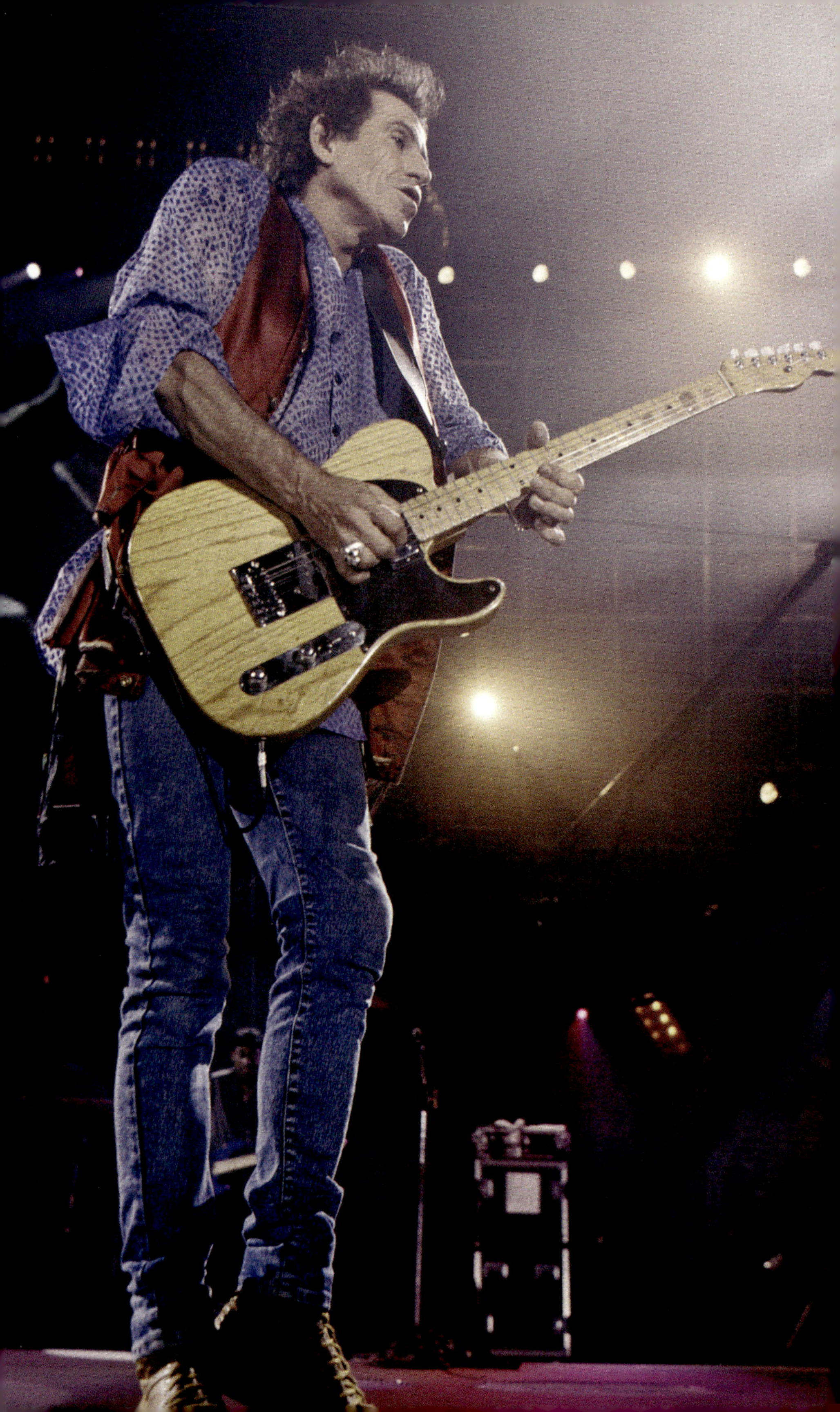

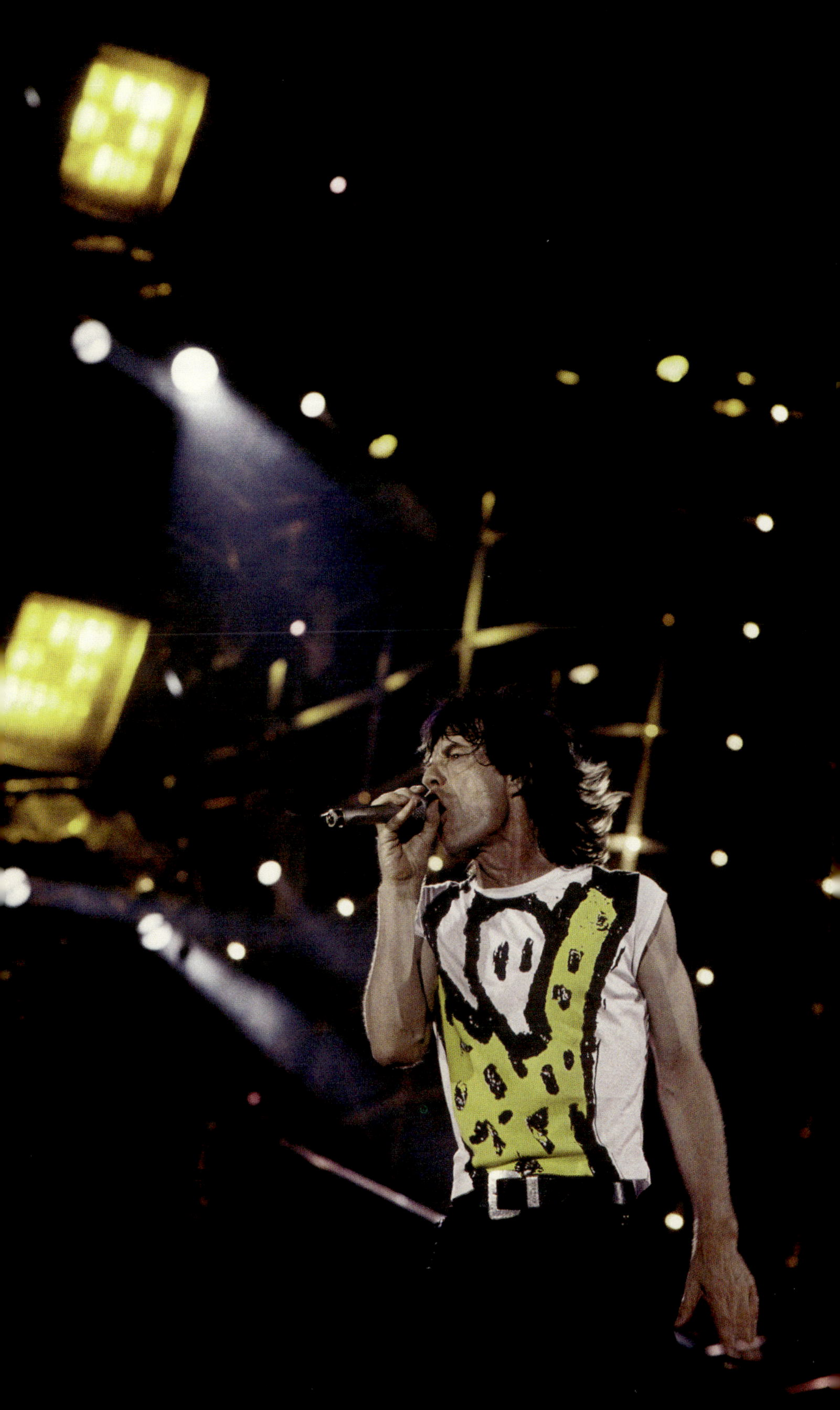

For the first three songs, I was amidst my colleagues, who were furiously working to make their images before getting the boot. As the Stones neared the end of their third song, I left the pit and decided to roam in the audience. This allowed me to avoid being swept up by the publicists corralling all my colleagues and shepherding them out the door.

My earlier efforts paid off, as all of the crew and security I encountered as I walked the path that was about 20 rows back recognized me and let me do my work uninterrupted. I switched to a longer lens and one that wouldn't be so "up the nose" so I could get some other really interesting angles.

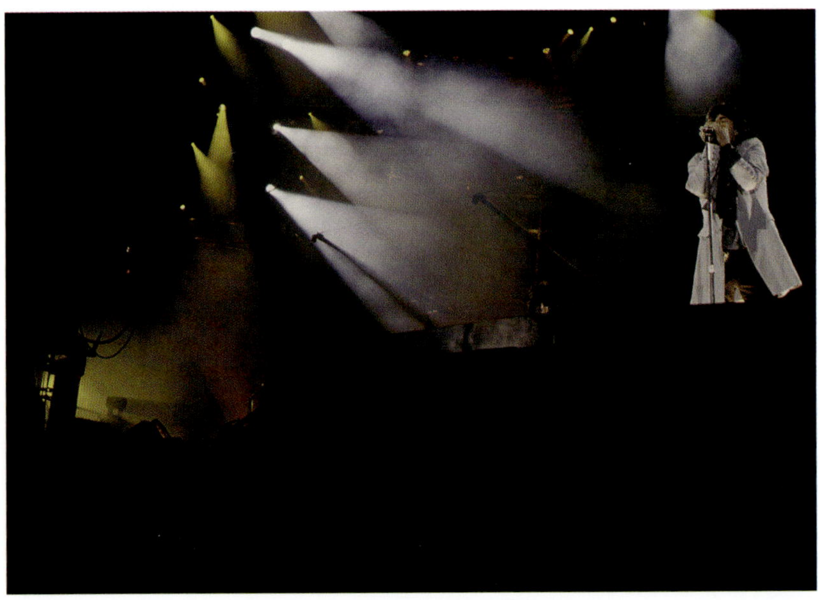

Mick Jagger on stage during the show.

The show wound down close to 11:00 as the band came out to the front of the stage and took a bow. Although reviews were less than favorable for this particular show in the days following the event, I, for one, remember the show as one I've had the most fun at—being free to make great images, unencumbered by the typical restraints of an increasingly constrictive PR machine.

An Excursion to Cuba

Unfortunately for most U.S. citizens, at least as of the writing of this book, the U.S. government doesn't allow tourists to visit Cuba because of the embargo imposed many years ago. This is a great misfortune, because stepping off of a plane and onto Cuban soil is like stepping back in time. From the cars to the architecture, little has changed since the embargo took place—and even then, ornate architecture gave hints of a glorious era long since past. The Cuban government welcomes tourism revenue in any form, and visitors from elsewhere in the world do indeed travel to the Cuban resorts. In fact, U.S. dollars are a welcome currency, provided you can actually *get there* to spend them. Cuba also welcomes U.S. citizens, and although they will look at your passport, when I visited on assignment they did not stamp my passport because they knew the U.S. government would take a dim view of my having been to Cuba.

Once I had my magazine assignment to travel to Cuba, I began the process of determining the legality and possibility of actually getting there. My calls to the U.S. State Department about travel restrictions and the U. S. Treasury about my ability to pay my bills in Cuba revealed that as a member of the press, the U.S. government would not preclude my travel there, but I might have to get a press visa from the Cuban government. My efforts in obtaining that visa were met with a refusal; however, at the same time that I was looking into the working visa, my Canadian travel agent suggested I might travel easiest through him on a tourist visa. With that in mind, and knowing that none of my American-based bank credit cards would work in Cuba, I paid as many bills as I could to my Canadian travel agent, who routed me through Canada on my way to Cuba, and I took a fair amount of U.S. currency with me.

Prior to departure, my editors and I discussed a shot list. However, I'm often leery about any shot list that's created in the real-life vacuum of an air-conditioned conference room, because it never stands up to street testing. Much like the military saying, "No battle plan survives first contact with the enemy," so, too, was this the case when I arrived in Cuba.

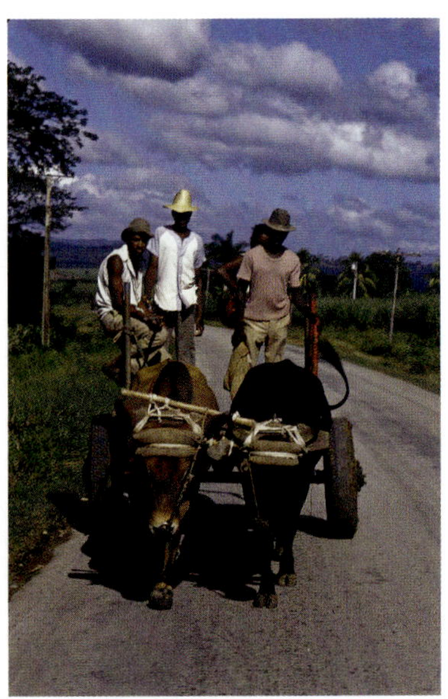
Farmers travel down the road in a cart drawn by two oxen. El Maya, Cuba.

Making it through Customs as a tourist was no problem, and I traveled with a limited amount of equipment because I didn't want to attract the attention of any Cuban officials. In truth, as I will tell you in short order, this was not to be. I arrived at a resort common in many third-world countries, with a tourist trade behind a tall wall where no locals were allowed, save for those actually working at the resort. I checked in and immediately started to determine how I would best connect my laptop to the Internet.

I'm not sure how other resorts were wired for communications, but this one required me to use dial-up and connect through an obscure service provider, and I had to use banana clips to connect my telephone port inside the wall jack. Despite my attempt to hide my wiring job from the hotel staff, this may well have been the beginning of my demise if suspicions were raised about just what a guest was doing with wires dangling out of the wall. With communication established with my editors, I set about planning my days. About half of my shot list could be accomplished on several scenic tours, but a number of the images required a private tour and guide.

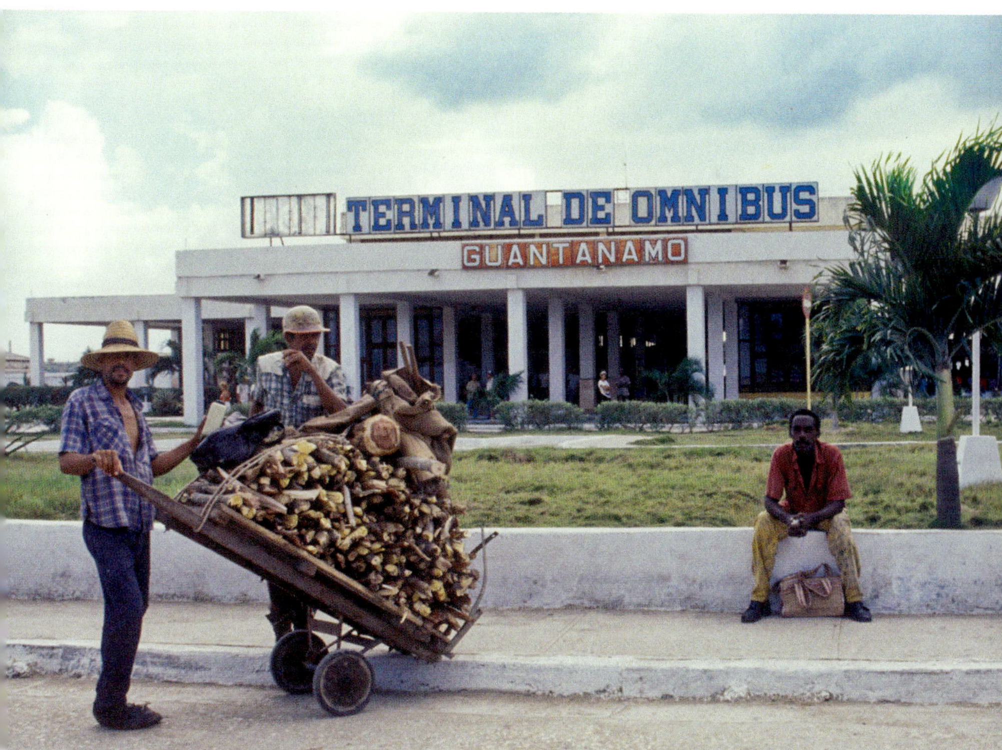

A man with a cart full of wood stands waiting for a ride in front of a bus terminal. Guantanamo, Cuba.

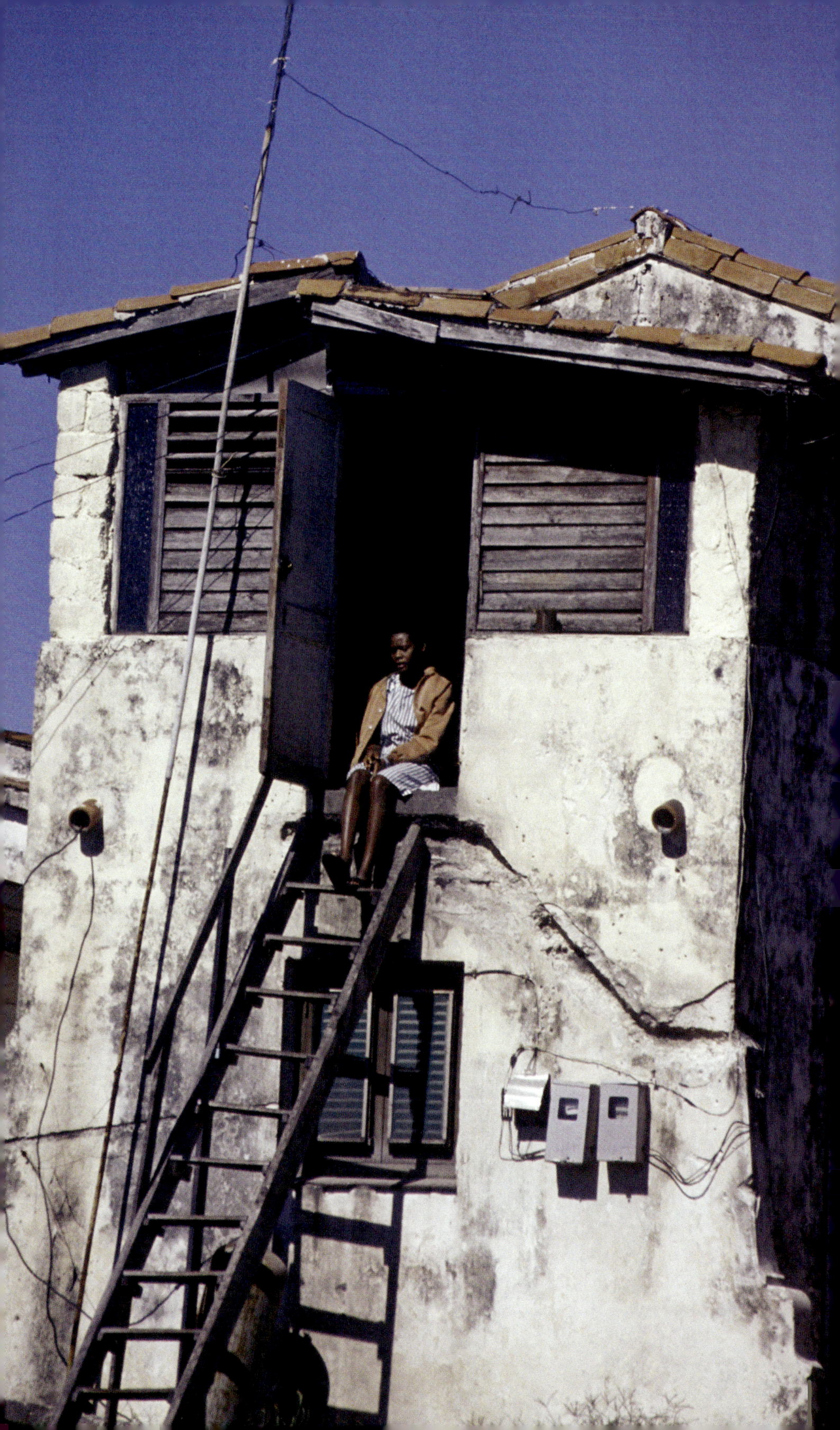

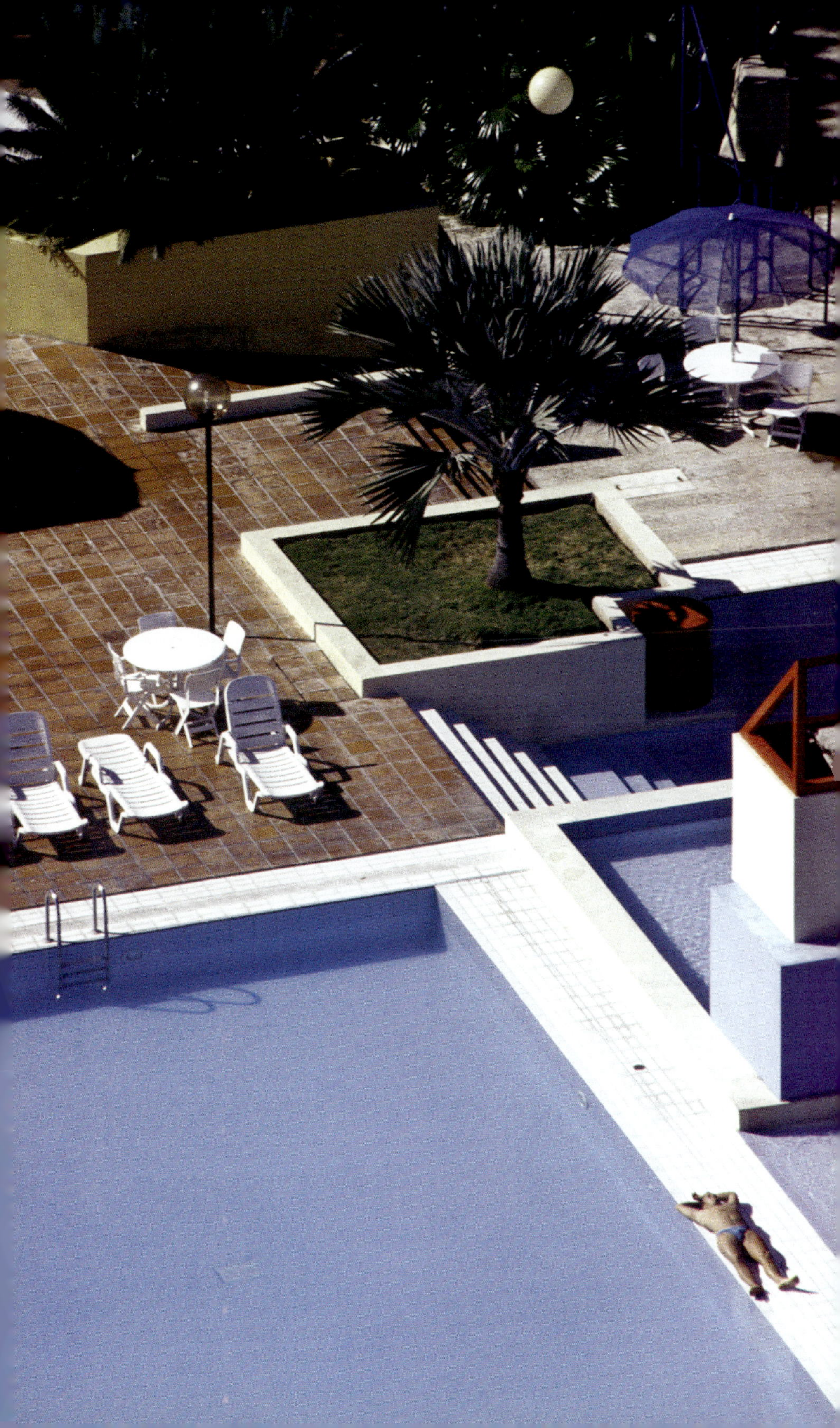

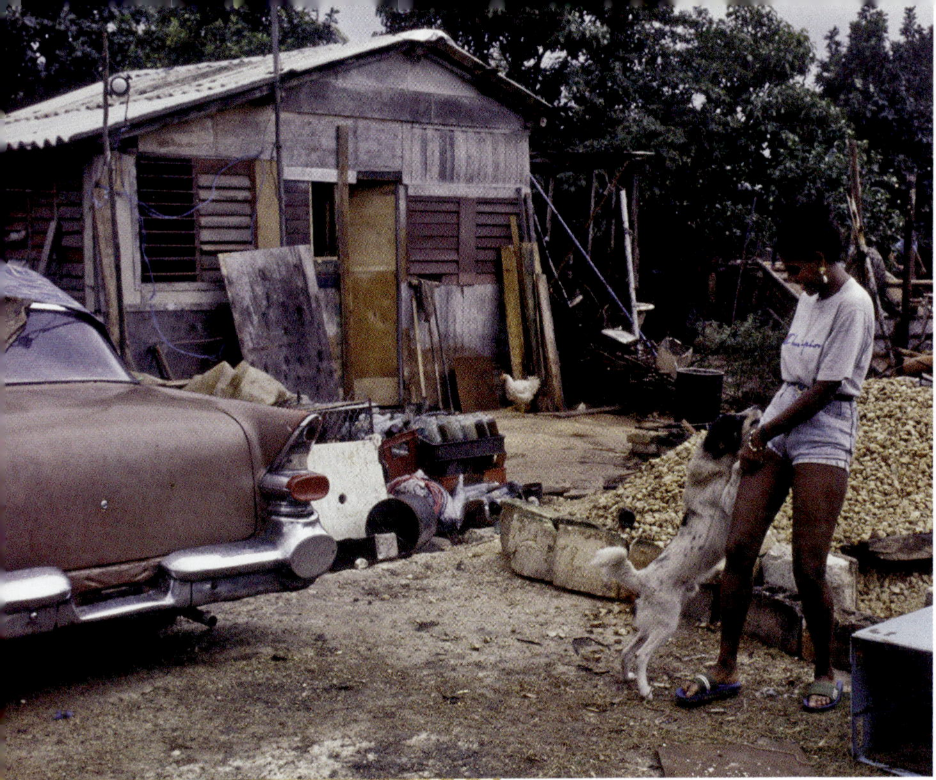

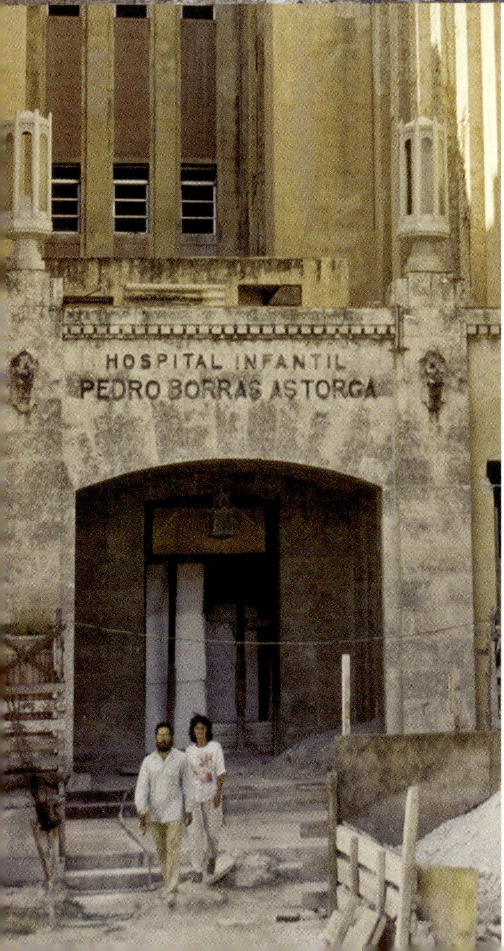

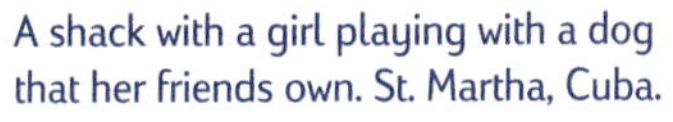

A shack with a girl playing with a dog that her friends own. St. Martha, Cuba.

Previous two pages: A Cuban woman sits on the porch of her dilapidated home in Varadero, Cuba.

A European tourist in the pool area of the Santiago de Cuba Hotel, Santiago, Cuba.

Children's Hospital in Havana, Cuba. (this page)

Bicyclist catches a ride on a truck full of homeward-bound commuters in Santiago, Cuba. (next page)

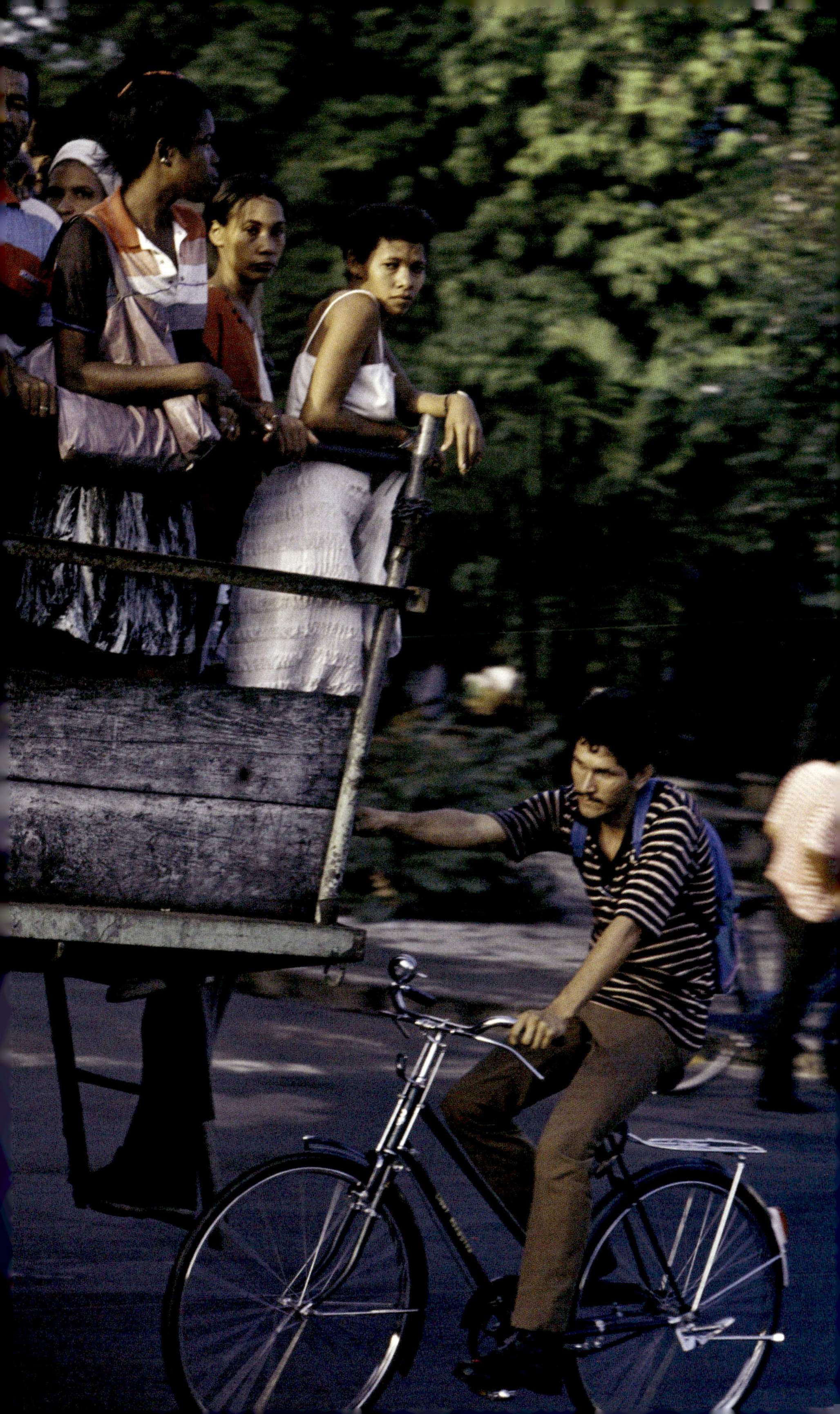

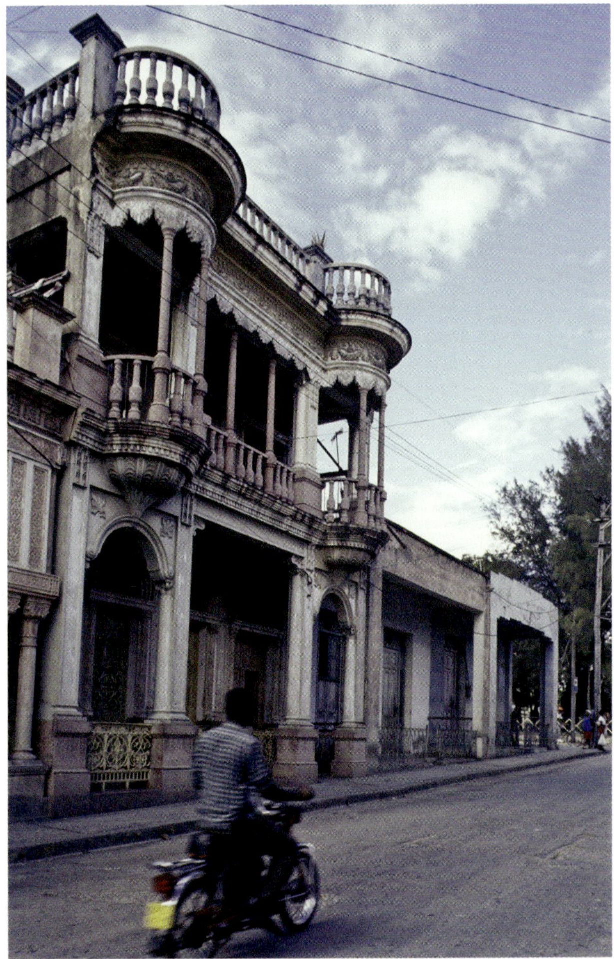

The beauty of the Victorian homes is still evident through the peeling paint. Guantanamo, Cuba.

During my group tours, I was able to secure a competent English-speaking guide whom I could hire for cash and could take out with my rental car. We made several forays into Havana and to the outskirts of the city, where a more genuine experience was to be had. On one trek, we found ourselves at La Bodeguita del Medio, where Ernest Hemingway would lounge around drinking mojitos. On another trek, we ended up outside the Capitol, at sunset, as families in their apartment buildings were sharing the last rays of sun with their line-drying clothes.

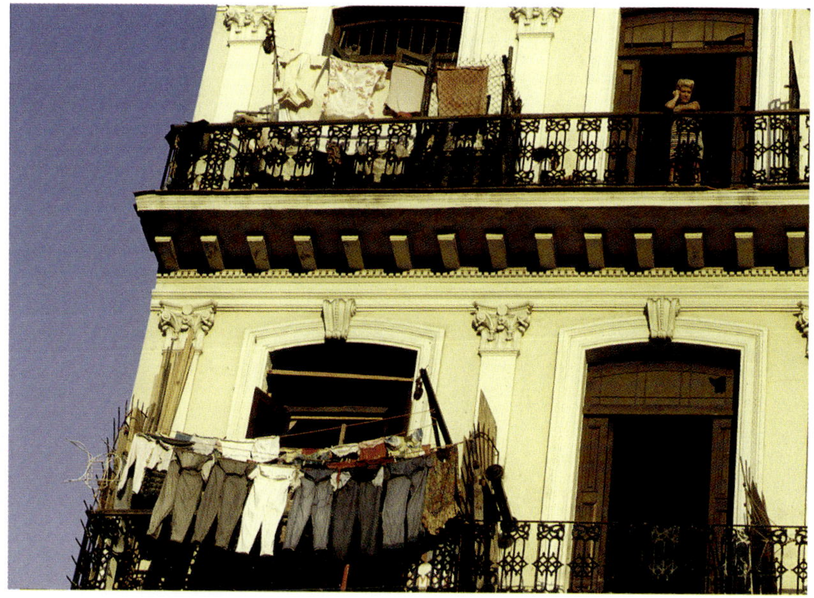

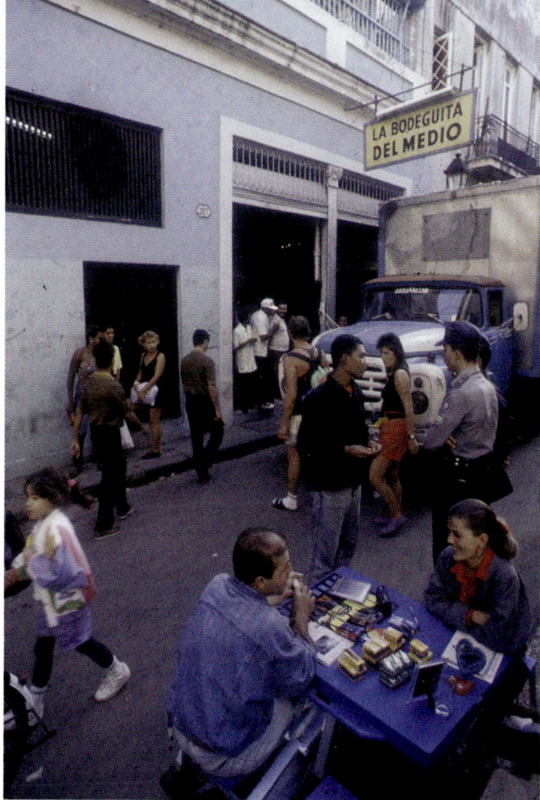

Across from the Capitol, a woman waits as her line-drying clothing catches the last rays of sun. Havana, Cuba

Outside of the bar La Bodeguita del Medio, made famous by Ernest Hemingway. Havana, Cuba.

Although my resort was on the beach a short distance outside of Havana at Varadero, I did need to take an in-country flight from Havana to Santiago to photograph the other end of the island. Each night I would store my film in a very methodical manner, in my safety deposit box, to which I was told I was the only one who had a key. It wasn't until I returned to the States that I learned this was not the case. In addition, I spent hours on end each night reviewing where I had been and whom I had photographed, as well as typing copious captions, which I then emailed back to my editors. I did this partly to preserve the information and partly to let them know that I was making progress and what my plans for the next day were.

Flying to Santiago on a Russian-made Yak-40 aboard a Cubana Airlines flight reaffirmed my appreciation for U.S. airline standards for safety. My seat was broken in a permanently reclined position, and no one seemed to care about where the exits were or how we might survive a water landing. Yet the flight was short, and I survived.

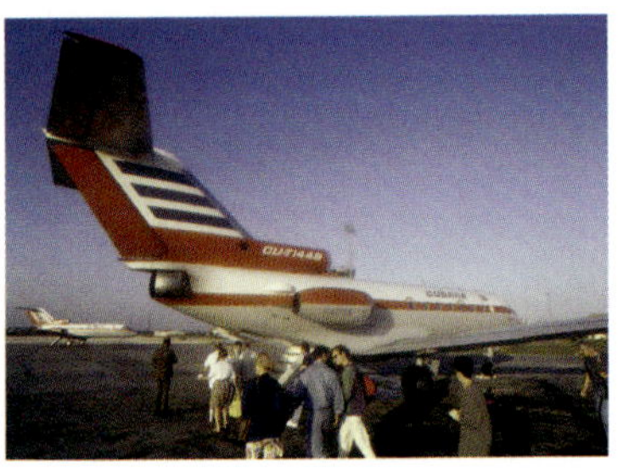

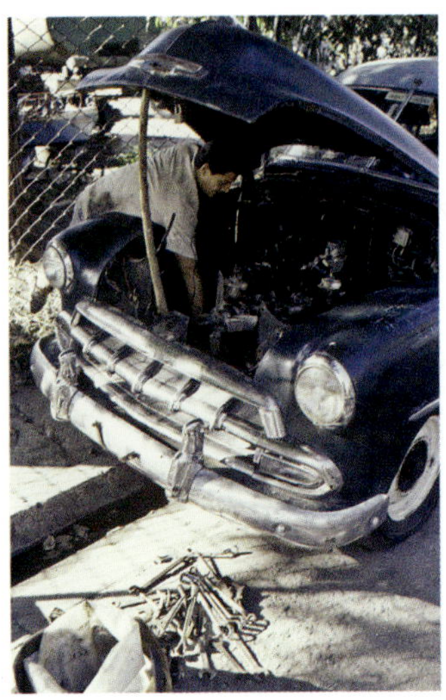

Once in Santiago, I opted to go it alone and try my hand at navigation and map reading. I accidentally found myself in a sugarcane field, which is where I made the image that would ultimately make it onto the cover of the magazine. People everywhere seemed to have no problems with having their photographs made, whether it was young adults on a motorcycle, a man working on his '60s-era car, or Cuban workers smoking cigars.

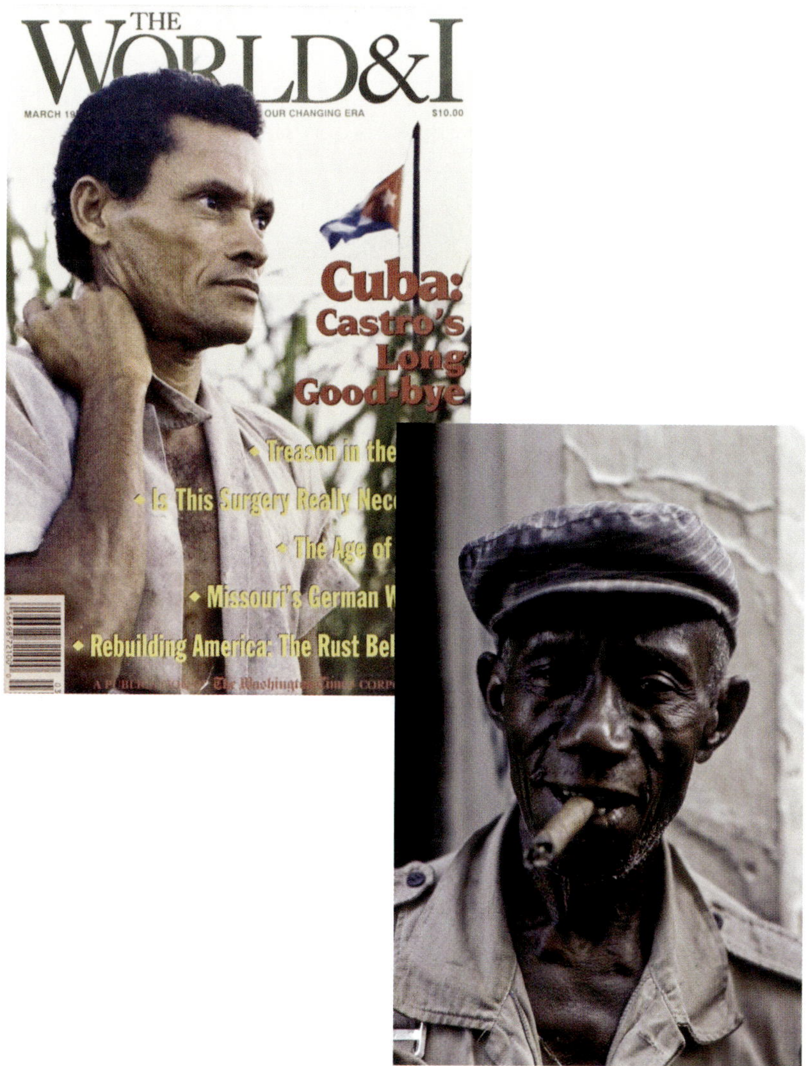

Several of my must-have shots were about the cigar industry. I needed to get into the fields and capture the making of the famed Cuban cigars. Outside Santiago, I located a field of tobacco being grown and found that there was an instructional effort underway by a very charming older man teaching young students about the growing of tobacco. He showed me the drying room and how the leaves are treated carefully during the entire process, and I was able to make a number of great images.

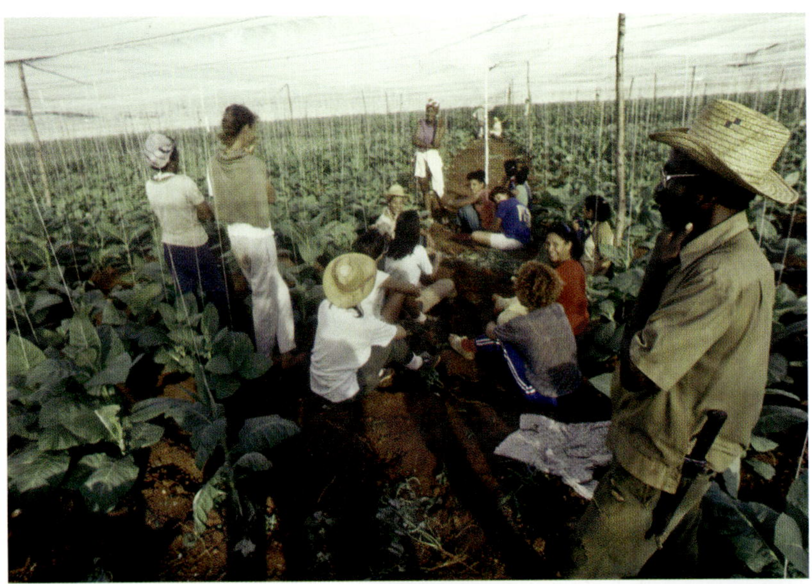

Cuban youths on a month-long visit to tobacco fields 23 km outside of Havana. Tobacco leaves are dried in dark, poorly constructed buildings near the growing fields, protecting them from animals and allowing them to dry properly. Taken near Havana, Cuba.

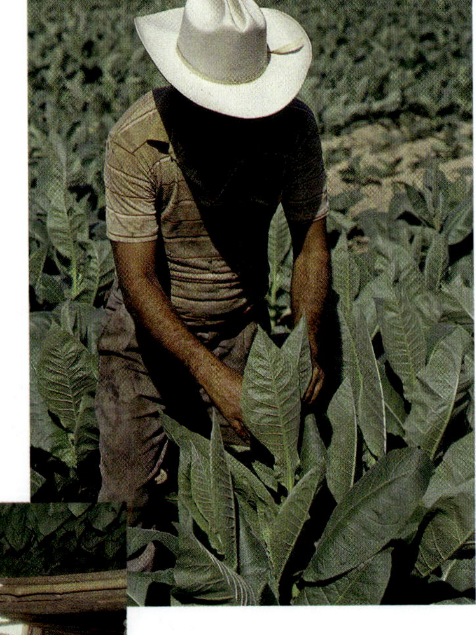

With that phase of the cigar industry covered, I made my way next to a factory. I found that many stores had factories connected to them, so once I found a store, I found a hand-rolling shop as well. It was interesting to see how carefully each cigar is made, and I could appreciate just how much they cost.

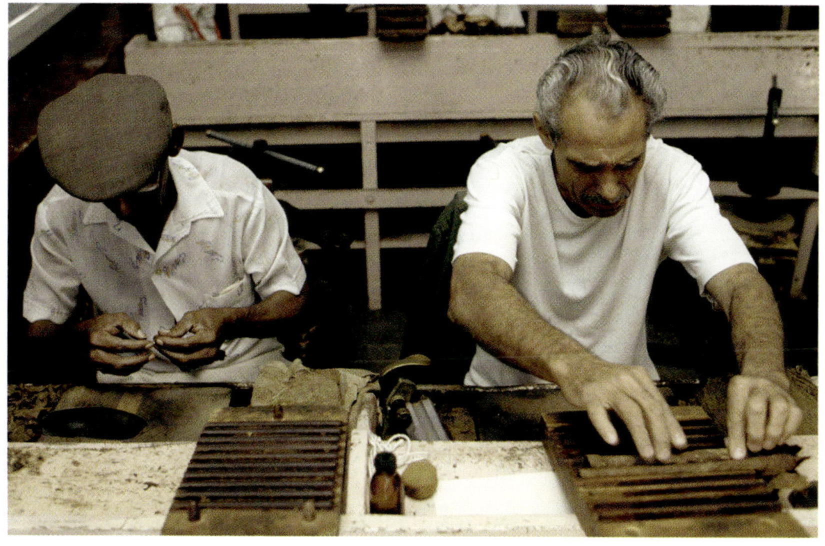

Workers prepare Cuban cigars in a cigar factory, taken in Pinar Del Rio, Cuba.

Sitting on the cold linoleum of the Santiago airport for my return flight was not my idea of fun. I had been incommunicado with my editors for several days, and although they knew this was to be the case, it was unnerving for all of us, as I genuinely felt I could get arrested and then would be stuck.

When I returned home, I felt confident that I had captured a number of images and remarkable scenes throughout Cuba, and I had certainly accomplished far more than I expected from my shot list. The only thing missing, I thought, were the hours of sleep that I had left in Cuba, which resulted in a fairly significant sleep-deprived state. I safely delivered all of my film, neatly organized in Ziploc bags, for later processing before what I vaguely recall as a few comatose days following the assignment.

When I got into the office, it was my job to hand-process all of my film. As I began to methodically retrieve the film from inside the canisters, I learned that someone had been inside my canisters before me and had pulled out the film, exposed it, and rerolled the film back into the canisters. I was able to discern this because in several instances the culprit had pulled the film out so hard that he had torn the paper where the film attached to the spindle. Apparently, someone else had a key to my safety deposit box and quite possibly was monitoring my whereabouts —although he must have been good at his trade, because even in remote areas I never noticed anyone following me or anything out of the ordinary.

Fortunately, when I encountered opportunities to shoot again something that I had already checked off my shot list, I did not pass up the opportunity. Instead, I took advantage of it, meaning that the lost subjects from my shot list could have been in excess of 30 percent of my accomplishments, but in the end were closer to 10 percent.

Looking back, as a young, idealistic photographer in my 20s, it was the good nature of the Cuban people and their hospitality that lulled me into a false sense of security in what was, and still is, a Communist country. The adage "Big Brother is watching you" definitely applied, and I had gotten off a lot lighter than most. That, in and of itself, was enough to make my stomach queasy at the thought of what could have been, and it makes me respect even more the challenges faced by my brethren telling stories in press-oppressed countries such as Iran, China, and North Korea, where, even in the era of digital, getting the news out is still a life-threatening effort.

National Geographic and the White House

When I started out as a photographer, I made my way fairly effectively into the profession. However, after a few years, someone told me I had to have goals in life. I was pretty satisfied with my life and the headway I was making in a profession, especially given that I had no formal training as a photographer. But, at the ripe old age of 25, I decided I would set two goals for myself. The first was to do an assignment for *Rolling Stone* and the second was to do an assignment for the National Geographic Society. I figured I would get to at least one of them by the time I was 40.

In the fall of 1994, National Geographic was to film a television special—*Inside the White House*—with a behind-the-scenes look at the goings-on of the White House. One of the focal points was to be a state dinner—in this case, the state dinner honoring Russian President Boris Yeltsin on September 27, 1994. I had done several state dinners before, and one Spring evening I was in attendance when the American Society of Picture Professionals (ASPP) had a tour of the White House Photo Office. I stood in the back as one of the White House editors regaled the audience with a story about how great one of my fellow photographers was. I said, to no one in particular, "I do that, too, all the time," referring to a point about covering the White House.

Unbeknownst to me, standing next to me was an editor from the NGS. The ASPP, if you don't already know this, is an organization made up mostly of picture editors and picture buyers, not photographers. So when I said that (quietly, more to myself than anyone else in particular), the editor, Margaret Sidlosky, turned to me and said, "Oh, we're working on a project on the White House. Do you have a card?" And I did. And I gave it to her. And she gave hers to me. And I gasped (silently).

A few days later, Margaret called me and asked me to come in. I agreed, hung up the phone, and began to panic. What did I have that could prove my statement from days earlier and that could, more importantly, meet the test of the NGS? I turned up early, with my best stuff to show. Margaret showed me to her office, and I showed her my stuff.

One image caught her eye—I had taken a monopod and raised it up to look down on the press making an image of then President George H. W. Bush. That did it for her, and that was what got me the assignment. She began talking to me about the project and about the stills she needed to accompany the film to promote it. We discussed details, and she handed me a contract for the assignment. And with that I walked out of the NGS offices, at the age of 26—about a year after I had set the goal, I had my first NGS assignment.

I was told I could visit the NGS equipment room for whatever gear I needed. It was mid-September, and I knew I was going to pre-light a few rooms of the White House and control them by a wireless remote that had channels, so that as I changed rooms, I could turn on and off various light packs. Walking into the workshop, I felt like a kid in a candy store. I'd heard stories about cameras made to look like various animals, remote triggering devices, and all manner of custom-made equipment cases.

One such story of legend was the motorcycle that was fitted with custom camera cases on each side that, were they priced on man hours, likely would have cost more than the motorcycle they graced. For my purposes, I just needed a *lot* of flash power, but I marveled at some of the equipment on display and the cabinets and cabinets of gear at my disposal.

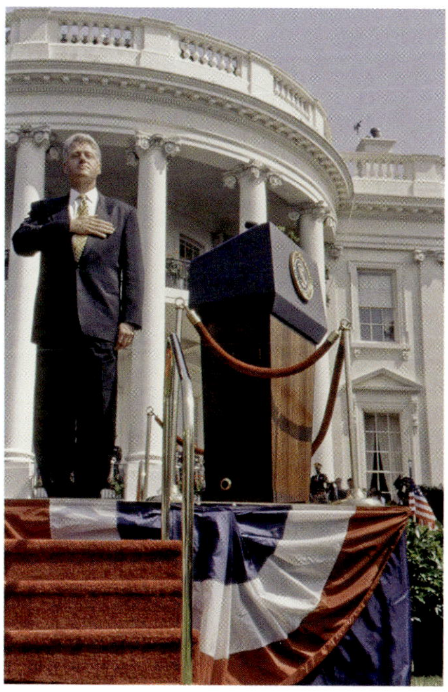

President Bill Clinton on the South Lawn during the playing of the national anthem at the state arrival ceremony for Boris Yeltsin.

I rolled into the White House early on the morning of September 27, with a close friend as my assistant to help. It took nearly an hour to get all the equipment through security and stowed in the pressroom before being deployed to the various locations in the White House. From strobes to remote cameras, I felt this was my one shot to hit one out of the park. Colleagues later would recount to me that when I rolled in with all that equipment, they—not knowing I was there for the NGS—thought all the equipment was mine personally and that, somehow, I was independently wealthy. I wish!

The first event of the day was the arrival ceremony. During the "pre-set," we were able to set up equipment and test it out before the arrival took place. I set up remotes for the arrival ceremony and then took my place on the press stand. As I was capturing my "normal" images from the press stand of President Yeltsin being received, I was simultaneously triggering remotes at the appropriate times to capture other angles.

As the arrival ceremony wound down, I collected my remotes and headed off to get exclusive access to the dining room as they were setting up for the dinner. I very much wanted an iconic image from the setup that I had visualized in my mind ahead of time—the place card that read "The President" on his place setting at the table. The White House penman and his staff hand-stroked each place card, and I thought that would be an interesting shot.

Opposite page: The president's placard is placed by the White House penman as the finishing touch on the place setting.

The president's place setting.

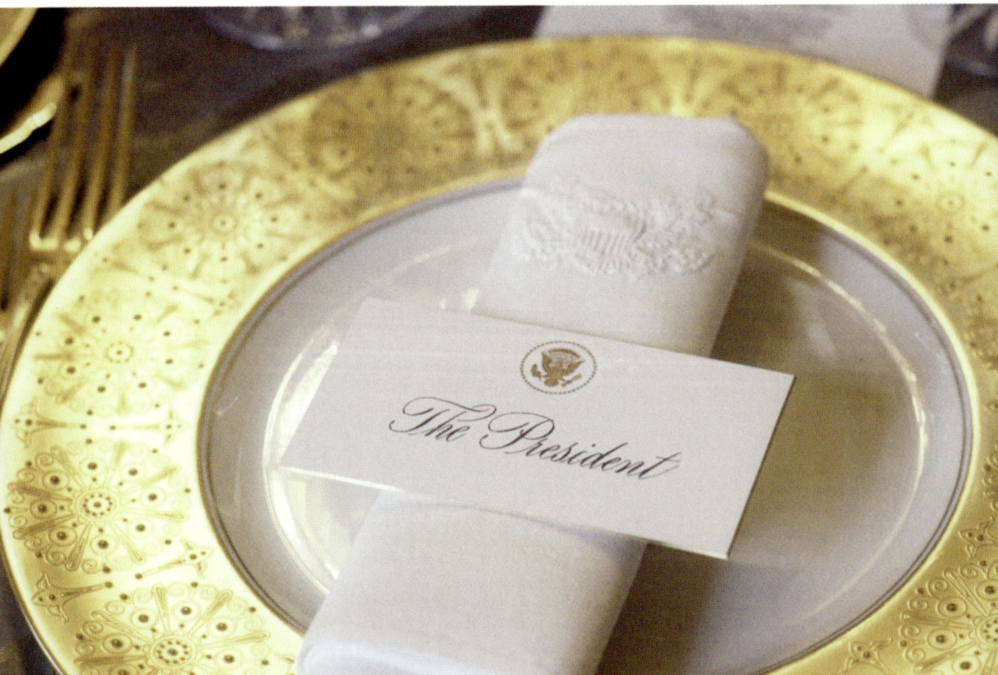

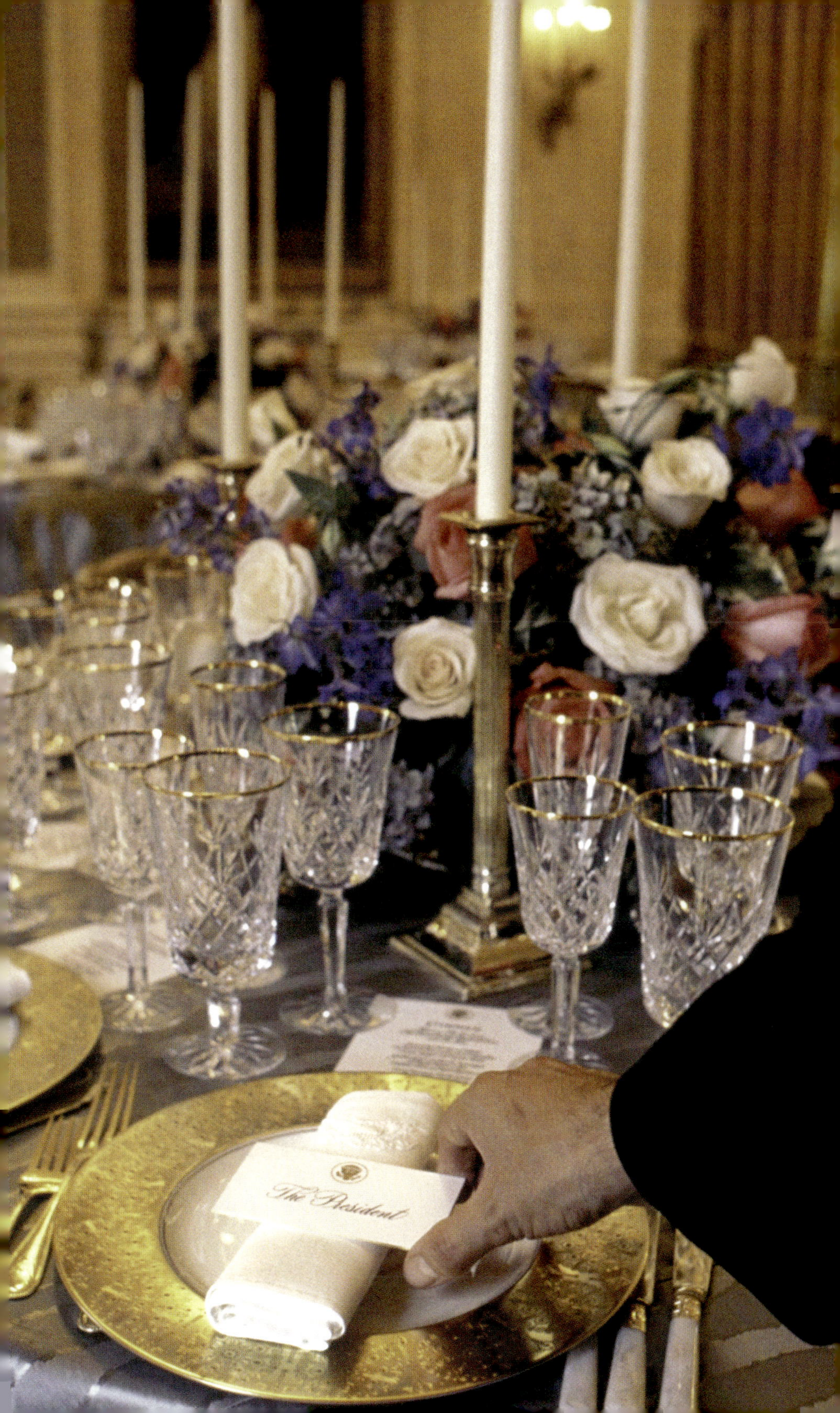
The President

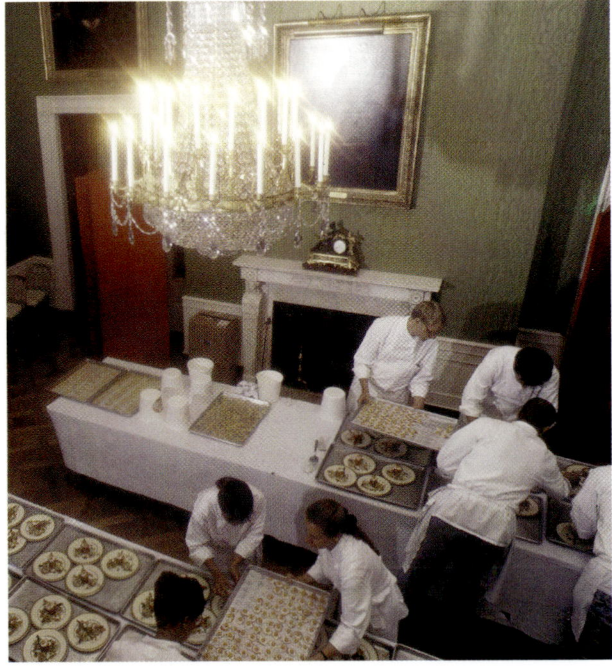

Chefs put the final touches on the first course of a state dinner for Boris Yeltsin. (Image captured by a remote camera mounted on the ceiling in the Green Room.)

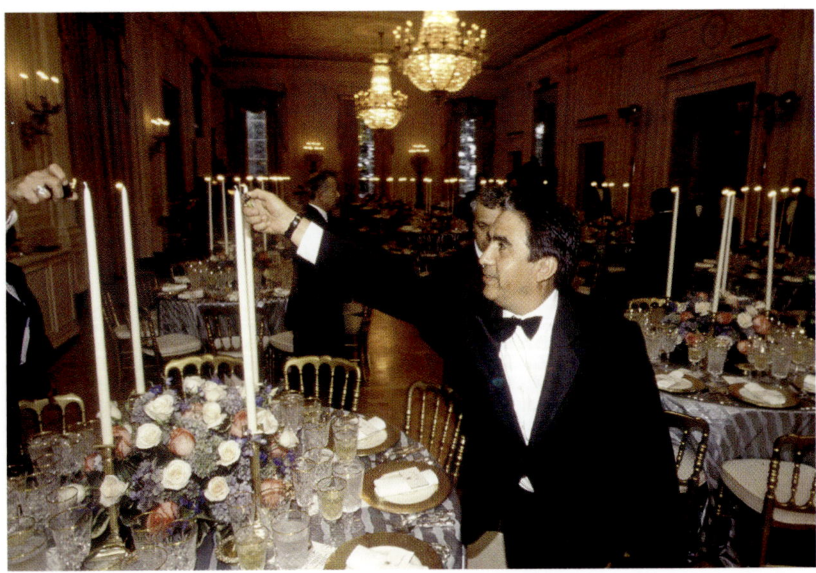

As guests are greeted by the president, butlers in the East Room light the candles on each table for the state dinner.

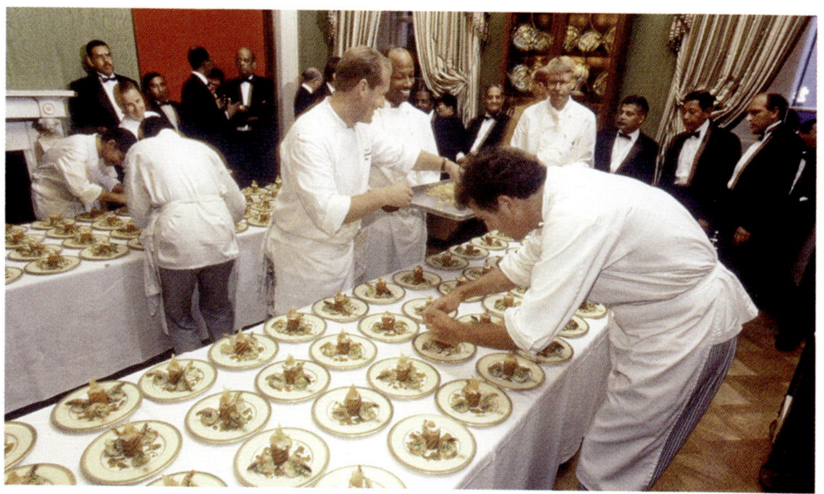

In the Green Room, chefs put the final touches on the first course of the state dinner, as the butlers await the signal to serve the dish to waiting guests.

Other images, such as the staff vacuuming, staff meetings, the musicians getting ready, and the lighting of the candles just before guests arrived were also on my list. During the evening's state dinner arrival ceremony, I was given the option to capture the event from outside the North Portico or to be inside. I opted for the inside-looking-out shot because it's an angle you never see. My only constraint was that I needed to be far enough in the background that I wouldn't show up in the video or the still images my colleagues were making outside.

I was able to make a few images in the "booksellers" area, which is where the guests are each announced to the assembled press. It is the entry point to the lower floor of the White House, where the White House Library is. (One person suggested the area got its name in the early 1900s because the Booksellers Association, seeing the shelves of the White House Library severely lacking, brought books for President Roosevelt and his family to choose from to fill the library.) After that, I made my way upstairs to the Green Room, where I had lights set close to the ceiling, along with a remote camera. The Green Room was the staging area for the White House chef Walter Scheib and his team, just off the East Room, where the guests were sitting down for dinner.

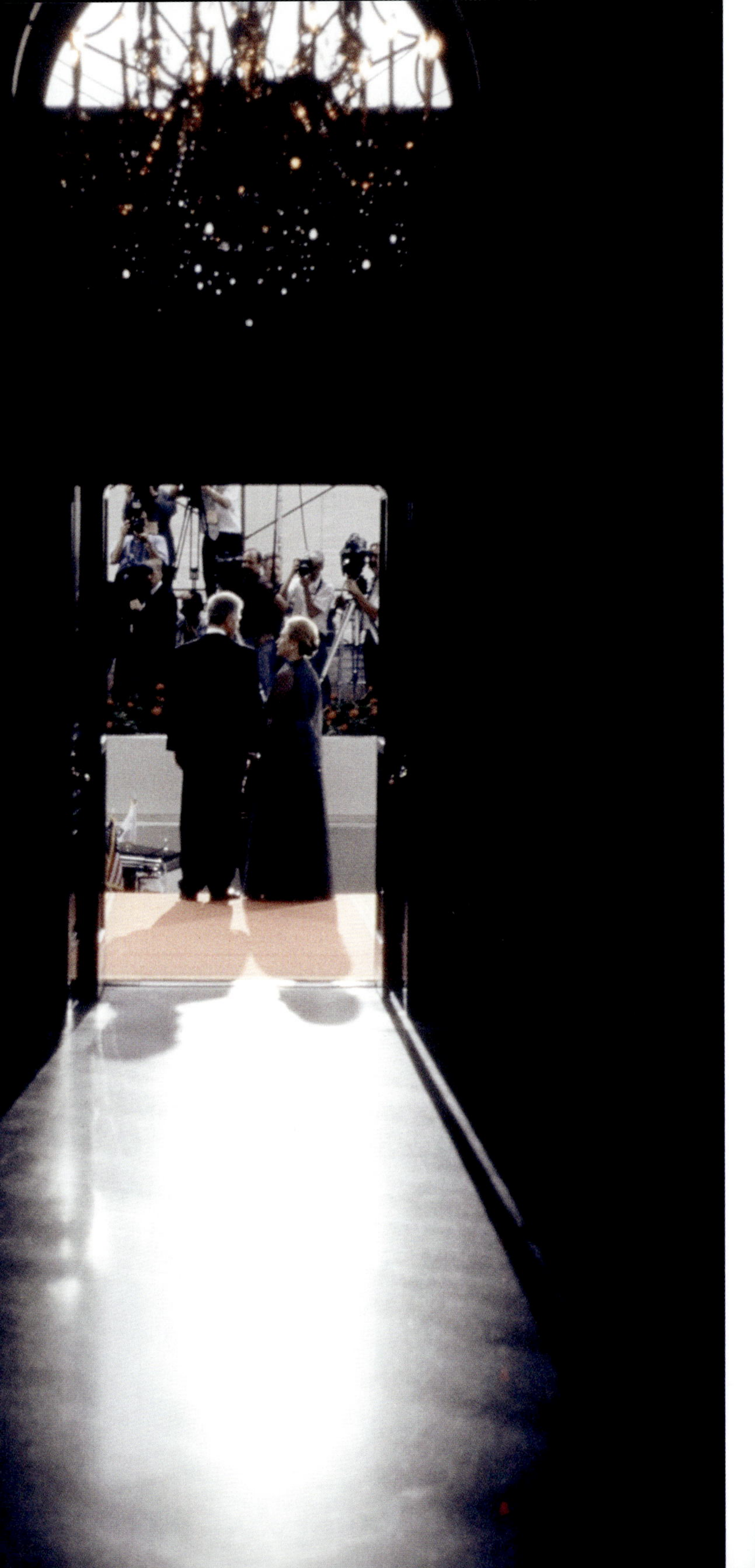

Previous page: President Bill Clinton and First Lady Hillary Rodham Clinton stand on the steps of the North Portico awaiting their official guests—the Yeltsins—at the beginning of the state dinner.

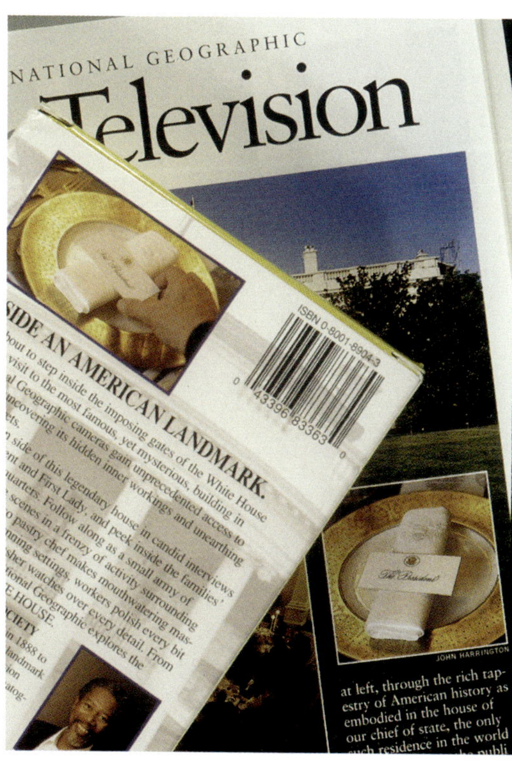

Two of the many uses of the images to promote the broadcast—on the back of the retail sale of the show and in the *National Geographic* magazine.

Then began the waiting process. We had to wait until the end of the dinner to take down all the lighting and remote cameras. It was a long and exhausting day, but I was pleased with the potential for my results. The next day, I returned to the NGS offices to drop off all my film for processing, and I spent some time writing captions for the images. When the lab indicated the images were ready, I jumped at the chance to review them. The proof was in the pudding—my images were used in a wide variety of media, from the back of the VHS sleeve to the "On Television" section of the *National Geographic* magazine. The client was very happy with the results, and within a year of setting my goals for the NGS and *Rolling Stone*, I had achieved both. So much for forty!

The Blizzard of 2010

Over the years, I have watched as my press corps colleagues have found themselves in risky situations, where just the right tool or equipment was what defined the difference between success and failure, and safety and life-threatening risk. From floods that called for a flat-bottomed boat or Jet Ski, to blizzards that paralyzed a city, the news must be gathered. Even more than the slogan "Neither snow nor rain nor heat nor gloom of night stays these couriers from the swift completion of their appointed rounds" applies to the postal carrier, it applies to the press. The news must be gathered without fail.

Following a blizzard that paralyzed DC in 2003, I decided I needed a snowmobile, just in case. I found one on eBay from a guy in upstate New York, and he offered delivery to the buyer. I had lived in Alaska for a few years of my young life, in a small village where the only forms of transportation were either a sled dog team or a "sno-go." (I know elsewhere people call them "snow machines" or snowmobiles, but where I learned to ride, we called them sno-gos.)

I knew I likely would need to get the sno-go street legal. Yes, the likelihood that a DC police officer would actually pull me over during a blizzard was slim, and I could likely show my press credentials and make my case, but I wanted to be street legal just to cover my bases.

I did my research, reading up on the rules and regulations for vehicles in DC. It seemed unlikely that I could get a license plate for it; but upon a closer reading, there also seemed to be the possibility of a loophole I could slip through, so I wouldn't need a license plate, but I would still be legal on the streets of DC. With my paperwork and the relevant regulations in hand, I paid a visit to the office of the Administrator of the Department of Motor Vehicles.

"Do you have an appointment?" questioned her secretary.

"No," I replied. "This should just take a second." The administrator was there, and after a few minutes she asked whether there was something she could help me with.

"Yes, actually, it should be brief. I just want clarification from the DMV. I'm a member of the news media, and I'm trying to properly register my snowmobile so that in the event of the next blizzard, I can do my job safely and get around to gather the news."

"Uhh, I don't think you can do that," she replied.

I countered, "Well, I would be more than willing to submit to the licensing of vehicles here in DC, but from the regulations I am reading, my snowmobile would be exempt."

"No, we don't license recreational vehicles in DC; they aren't allowed on the streets."

"Well, according to my read of the regulations, a snowmobile would be exempt from licensing requirements, and I just need a letter affirming this—unless of course you would like a license plate on it, which I'm happy to pay for."

"I'm not clear on how you believe a snowmobile would be exempt," she responded.

"Well, according to the regulations, any vehicle that travels on a track is exempt and neither is required to be tagged with a license plate, nor must go through emissions inspections. And since a snowmobile travels on a track, it would meet this test."

The administrator looked at me as if I had just told her I had three eyes. "Well, let me check with legal counsel on this. Would you excuse me a minute, please?"

I excused myself to the reception area as she got their lawyers on the phone. After a brief conversation, she invited me back in to be on the call with the lawyers.

"The law wasn't really written to include snowmobiles," came the lawyer's response. "It was meant for trolley cars on rails around the city."

I responded, "Well, Counselor, I understand your interpretation. However, I have right here a parts catalog where I can order a replacement "track" for my snowmobile, so my interpretation is equally valid. I would be happy to submit to licensing, which would solve this problem, if you would like."

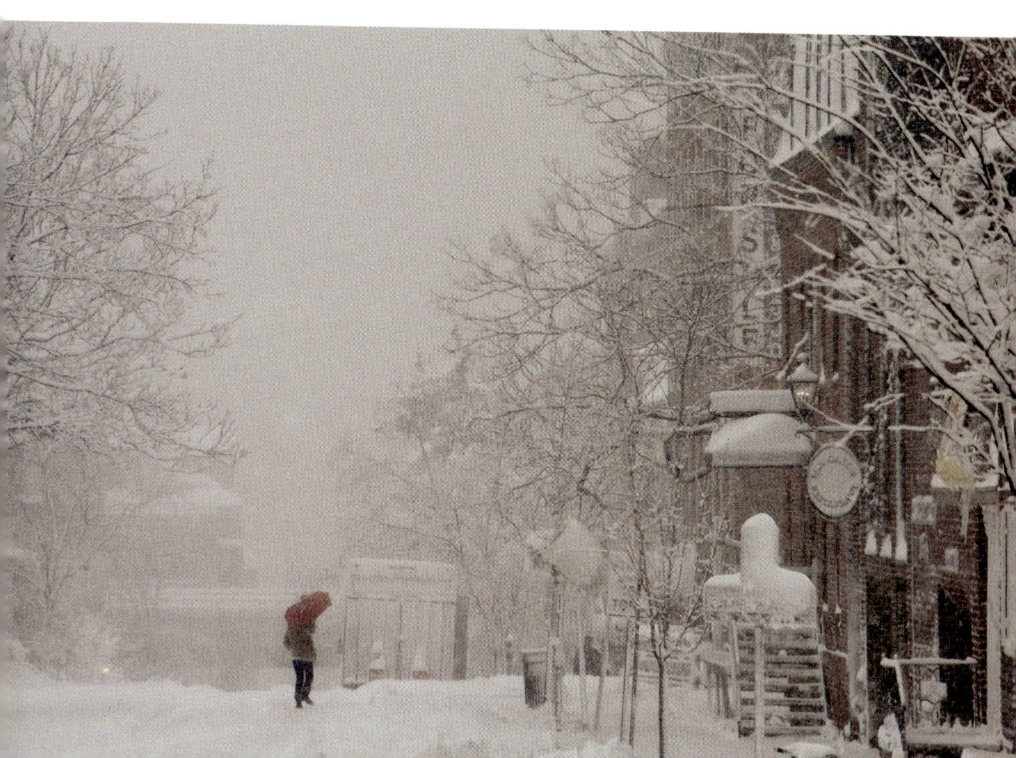

"Would you excuse us again for a minute?" asked the administrator, and again I found myself in the waiting room. After a few more minutes, the administrator came out and told me that the DMV would be issuing the first-ever license plate for a snowmobile, and my vehicle would be street legal in DC. They asked me whether I wanted a motorcycle plate or a full car-sized plate, and they issued me the tags.

I promptly built a storage box for the snowmobile, and I waited. A few snowstorms hit, and I could get it out briefly, but the stars were aligned when the Blizzard of 2010 hit the DC area. A blizzard anywhere else in the country (apart from perhaps Florida) would be a non-event. However, in DC, even an inch of snow causes complete and utter paralysis. No public transportation, usually no power, all federal government buildings closed.... Translation: It's a ghost town. People strip the supermarkets clean and set about trying to dig their cars out of the snow and then lay claim to their parking spots, sometimes using near violence as they doggedly patrol their clear spot—until the snowplow comes through and re-blocks their vehicle.

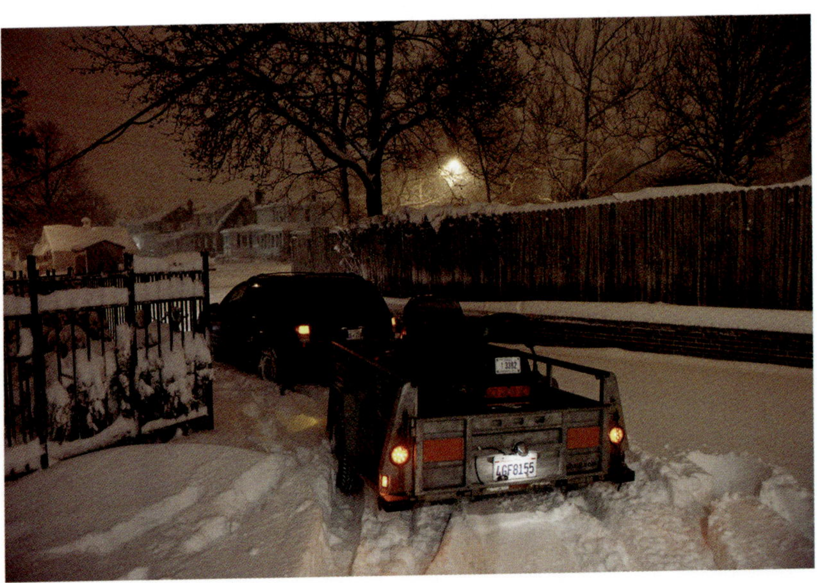

My SUV and trailer loaded with my sno-go in the alley behind my house before dawn as I leave for my assignment.

The Blizzard of 2010

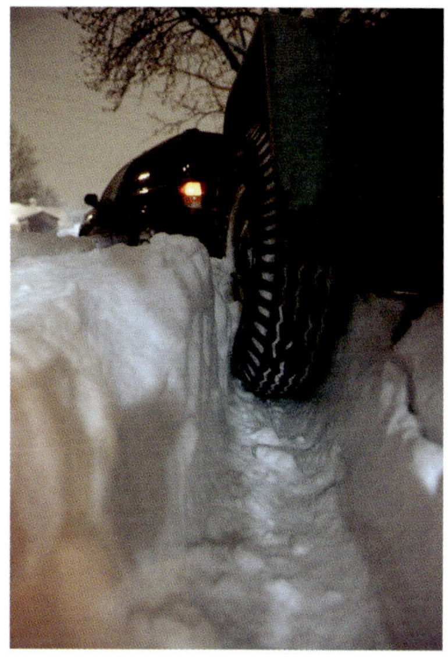

The snow was deeper than the tires on my trailer as I departed, turning it in many ways into a sled my 4×4 was towing.

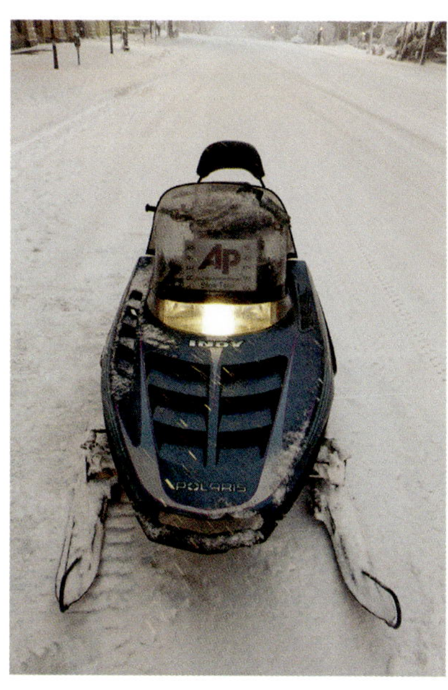

My street-legal sno-go in the middle of 13th Street NW, outside the AP offices, ready to go.

The SUV, trailer, and sno-go motorpool on hand and ready outside the AP offices in DC.

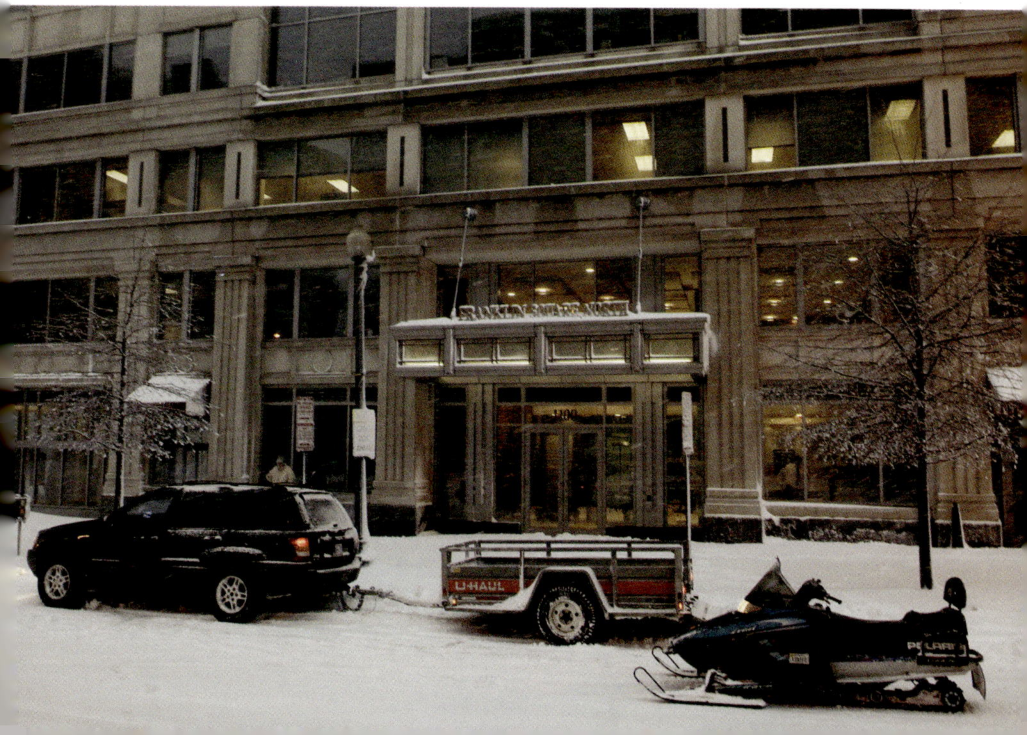

Setting aside the complete "wahoo" fun factor of having the only street-legal snowmobile in DC, I called my colleagues at the Associated Press and noted to them a day or so before the storm was coming, "I have the only street-legal snowmobile in DC and a 4×4 truck, if you have any photographers who need to get around the city." Later that day, I got a call back wanting to hire me for the storm. I had a U-Haul trailer that I was able to tow behind the 4×4 with the snowmobile secured in it. I had planned to go out and gather my own news, but why not book out my equipment as well?

The next morning I turned up at the AP offices and offloaded the snowmobile. I had been assigned to transport longtime friend and colleague (and legend in his own right) J. Scott Applewhite around the city. I didn't know whether Scott would want to be in the warmth of the vehicle or the back of the snowmobile, nor did I know what we would find in the unplowed streets, so as I waited for him to come downstairs, I buzzed around their office in northwest DC. Scott came down and said, "Oh my God, I can't believe you have that!" And off we went, in the warmth of the SUV. We trekked around the city as the snow continued to fall, and Scott made—as anyone familiar with Scott knows—great images late into the afternoon. We returned to the AP office, where he filed his images and called it a day. Tired but happy, I returned home. I had one full day of billing against the snowmobile, which almost cost-justified it.

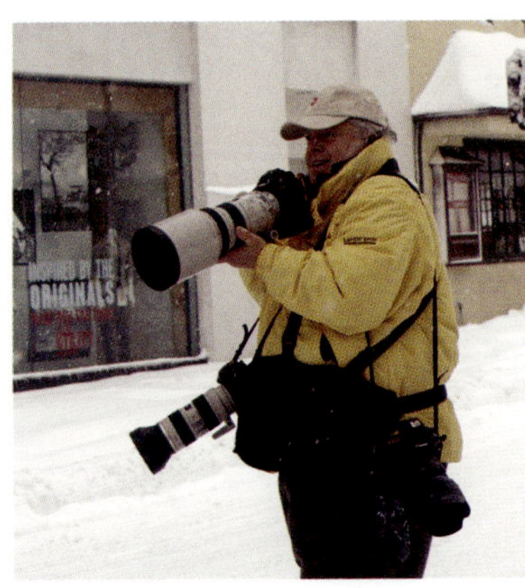

Legendary photographer and good friend J. Scott Applewhite of the Associated Press was my passenger for two days during the Blizzard of 2010. Here, Scott is looking for just the right moment to capture while standing in the middle of Wisconsin Avenue in Georgetown.

The next day, the famed Dupont Circle Snowball Fight was to take place. If you can imagine about a thousand stir-crazy, snowbound people looking to let off some steam, coupled with the instant communication abilities of Facebook and Twitter—that was where Scott and I were headed. I parked a block or so away, and I had two options: stand around and wait or offload the sno-go to buzz around Dupont Circle, in case Scott needed a quick pickup if violence occurred. This wasn't unheard of—a few months prior, a DC police officer who was hit by a snowball drew his service revolver, and all pandemonium ensued. So, I circled the round that defined Dupont Circle. I then parked the sno-go as if it was any other vehicle and got off to make a few photos of the snowball fight myself.

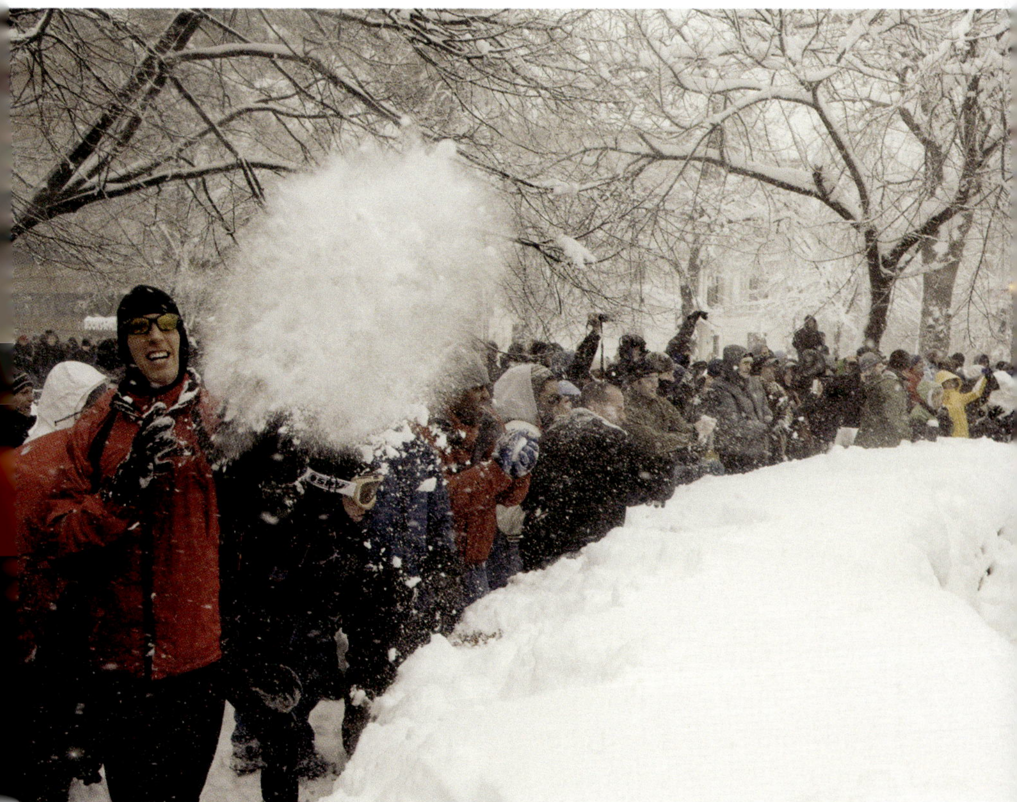

More than once I was pelted by snowballs during my coverage of the Dupont Circle snowball fight. Here, I make a frame just before a direct hit is scored on my camera and my head.

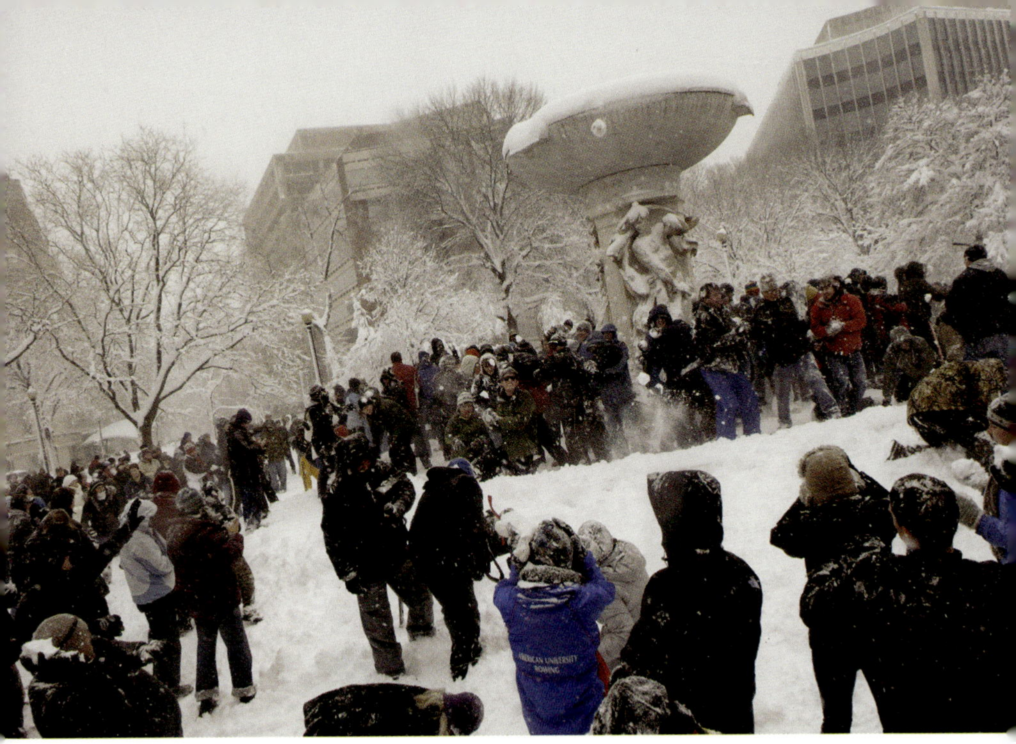

The snowball fight in full swing in the center of Dupont Circle in Washington, DC.

The day ended unceremoniously and without violence. By now the streets were clearer, and people were tired of seeing snow photos, so I wasn't needed on the third day, which was fine by me. So, on day three, I zipped all over the city making my own news photos and crossing bridges. At one point, I even found myself behind one police car as a second one pulled up behind me. No sirens, no "Pull over, sir"—no nothing. I was permitted to go along my merry way and do my job.

On reflection, though many skeptics at the DMV and across the city may have laughed when I purchased this snowmobile, I knew in my heart that with the changing climate conditions, it would be worth its weight in gold and would assist me in doing what I love to do—take photographs.

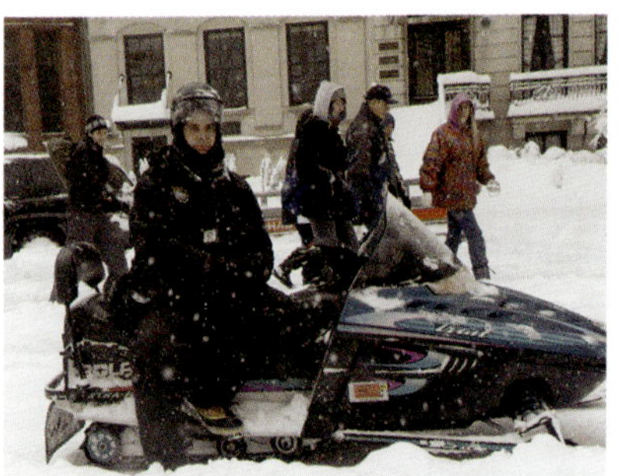

On the sno-go in downtown DC.

It's All About the Drinks

There are numerous types of advertising photography, from products, to services, to images that advocate for a particular stance on an issue. These latter types of ads are usually referred to as *advocacy ads*, because they are advocating a particular perspective. Consider, for example, what happened when Exxon and BP had their issues with oil spills. In the aftermath, both companies needed to illustrate what efforts they had made to mitigate the damage to the environment, and paid advertising with images of their efforts would illustrate the point.

During Hurricane Katrina, one of my clients called because their aircraft were being used in search and rescue. They wanted images they could use at a later date to illustrate this—images shot in a manner that would be usable by them and that would put their aircraft in a positive light. It is that type of photography we found ourselves called upon to produce for this particular project.

In this case, the issue at hand was an additional tax on a particular type of beverage. The challenge was not only to illustrate all of the beverages subject to the tax, but also to ensure that people knew this tax would be costly over the long haul.

In our preproduction meetings, we worked closely with the team that was tasked with simultaneously producing a TV commercial for the same cause. Because they had arranged the actors/talent, I conveyed to them that we needed to ensure we had print-rights to use the talent in print ads.

Fortunately for me, TV was handling many of the logistical challenges for this shoot, from makeup to lighting, and from permits to location fees. The challenge was to integrate seamlessly with equipment and a digital workstation and not get in the way of the TV side of the effort.

We arrived on set at about 4:00 a.m. on Friday, so we could be ready to shoot "dawn for dusk" with the subjects. The image was to depict a husband and wife enjoying non-alcoholic beverages around a campfire at the end of a long day. However, we were shooting this "dusk" image at first light. So, we had about 90 minutes to get set up and in position to make the image happen, knowing that the TV producer had first rights to the setup and shot, and we would be left with whatever time he deemed he didn't need at the end. In essence, the 90 minutes could divide up as 88 minutes for TV and 2 for me.

We had a bit of added pressure as well. We were in the woods, in the middle of nowhere in Maryland. The end client was sleeping restfully in another time zone, and we needed still-image approval, as there was a full-page ad appearing in the *Washington Post*. And the deadline to get the finished ad to them was 10:00 a.m. Friday. So we had to be able to edit and transmit directly from our location as soon as we had obtained approval from our client and other stakeholders, states away, within our allotted time provided by the TV producer.

As the sun eased into just the right position, our actors were in place, along with our gas-powered "campfire" and the tent in the background, placed just so. I waited patiently, hovering two feet behind the director as he took take after take as the light slowly rose. I tried not to look antsy about getting my shot as I was counting the seconds and the angle of the sun was incrementing degree-by-degree higher. When we were given the go-ahead by the director, I had just a few seconds to capture the image and get the shot. We had several images captured that would work, and the art director and ad agency owner reviewed the images and were satisfied, so we struck the set for both TV and stills and moved on to the next location.

About an hour later, the end client called, concerned that the beverages might look a bit too much like alcohol, and they didn't want that possible confusion. They then asked whether we could add a cooler and a two-liter soda bottle to the shot.

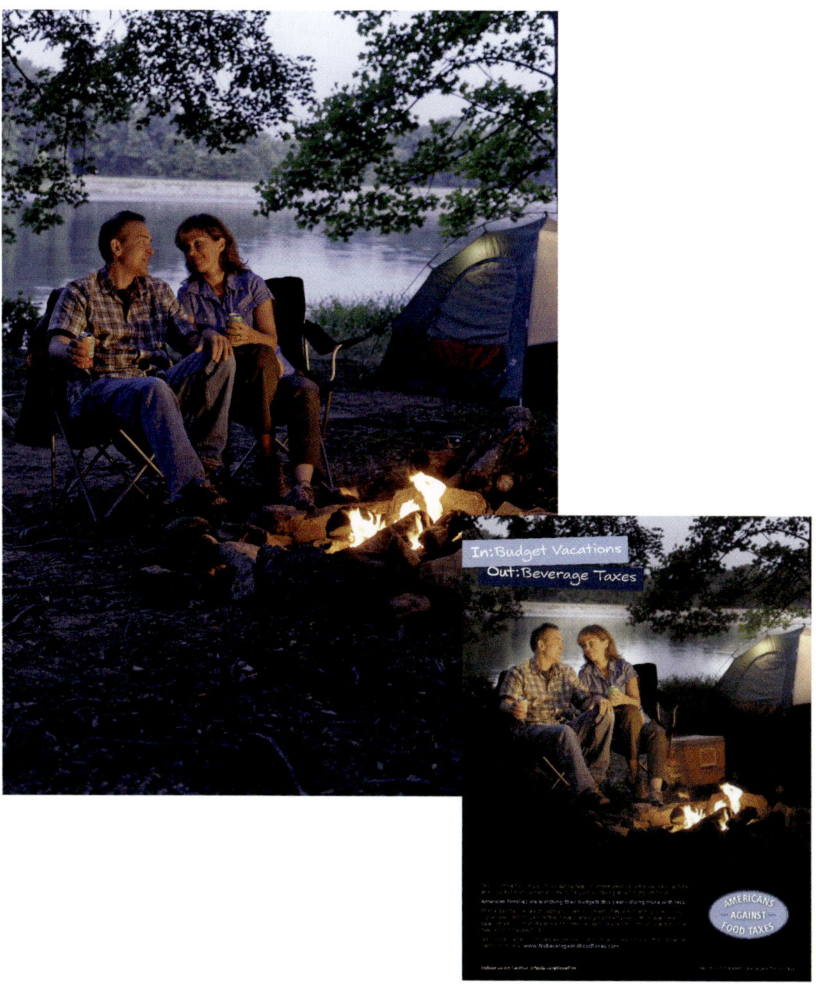

The problem was, we were an hour past sunrise, the light was different, the set had been struck, and the actors had moved on. Running to find the stylist who was managing the props, we begged, borrowed, and sweet-talked a cooler out of her, and we (temporarily) stole the generic two-liter bottle from the staging of the next shot that TV was doing, with the promise that we'd get it back to them unscathed. (All these props were made especially for these shots, and the "hero bottle" didn't have a replacement.) So, we shot the cooler and the bottle alone, dropped in approximately the same place the actors and chair were positioned before. Then at lightning speed (thank God for Photoshop), we inserted the bottle and cooler into the existing shot of the couple, immediately sent the photo for approval, and waited, yet again, for final approval, knowing we had only minutes to transmit the ad so it would make deadline for the *Washington Post*.

After what seemed like an eternity, we were given a thumbs up, and the image made it by deadline into a full-page ad in the *Post*. We had no time to rest on our laurels, however, as we had to get to the next setup; TV was already shooting the next scene, and we needed to capture that one, too. When working in tandem with TV crews, the still photographer takes a back seat to the priorities and time constraints of the TV team. However, the humble photographer still must produce creative images that are consistent with the quality of the TV side—but with a lot less time to do so. A still photographer cannot hold up a TV production when working—especially with child actors, who have a maximum number of hours they can work in a day. Although this particular shot didn't involve children, others we were doing that same day did, and there were children on set and on the clock. Knowing this and other gems of information will make the difference between you having a fruitful relationship with TV and you having a poor relationship with the medium. When you can deliver under extreme time constraints and in this environment, you will have longevity and a good working relationship into the distant future with clients like these.

From New Orleans to Crawford for a Pool Date with the President

On November 8, 2007, I went to New Orleans to give a presentation to the local chapter of the American Society of Media Photographers. They had asked me to come down and try to give them a boost after the devastation that was wrought not only on their personal lives, but also on their businesses following Hurricane Katrina. So, I presented to a small group of photographers and was invited by a long-time friend to stay with him in his home after the event. The problem was, I had just been informed that I was the pool photographer who needed to cover President Bush the next morning in Crawford, Texas, more than 500 miles away. I jumped in my rental car at about 10:00 p.m. and headed toward Crawford. It was about a 10-hour drive there, and I wanted to be on site at 8:00 a.m., because you never know what the president will be doing. And I needed to check in, as it was my day to be on call—a pool day—in the event that something happened.

A "pool" is where a group of photographers, all representing competing organizations, each acknowledge that it would be hard for all 10 or so of them to be wherever the president is, and the White House would also not allow that large of a cadre of people to be a part of the traveling "presidential bubble" of security. So where there is a limit on space, all the competing organizations agree to "pool" their needs and resources, and just one photographer is assigned to represent (and thus share his or her images with) those who could not be there. Today was my day, so I could not be late.

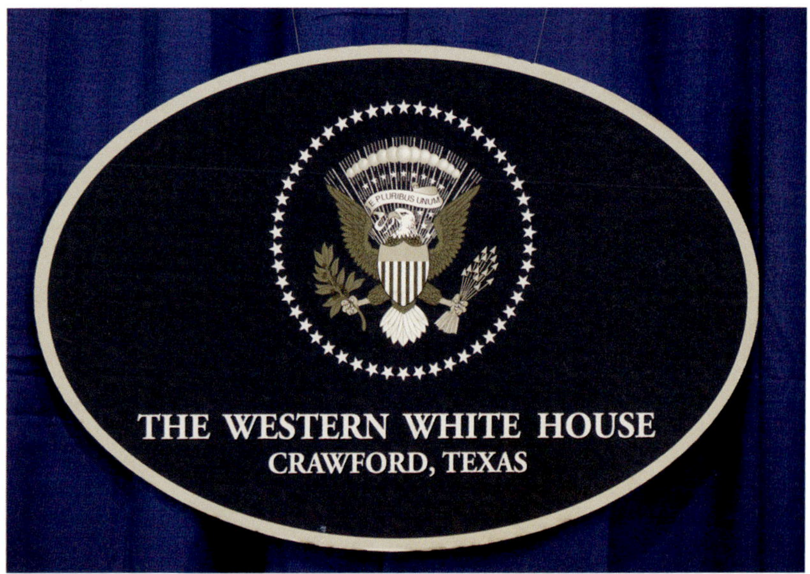

The seal on the wall of the press filing center serving the Western White House in Crawford, Texas.

I was traveling far above the speed limit, but I hadn't seen any signs, and I was relying on someone who had advised me that in some places in Texas there are no speed limits. First mistake. Then the colorful lights of a supercharged Dodge Charger in full pursuit came into my rearview mirror. I knew he wasn't headed to some shootout at the OK Corral or to the local donut shop for a refill—he was coming for me, even though it was about 3:00 a.m., and I was the only one on Interstate 10, just outside of Houston.

He pulled me over and asked for my license and registration. I showed them to him, and the "Press Photographer" police-issued badge that I carry in my wallet was visible to him. He asked about the badge, and I told him I was a photographer. He then asked where I was headed so quickly, and I told him I was due to be in Crawford for an 8:00 a.m. call time for the White House. He handed me back my license and rental car agreement and told me to drive safely. Thank goodness I was in Texas, with a Texan as president! I continued on my way, thankful that I hadn't received a ticket—just a Texas-friendly warning.

Right at about 8:00, I pulled into the school that housed the Western White House Press Filing Center and checked in. Apparently, one other photographer from our pool was there as well, thinking he had the exclusive. We talked, and I told him it was my pool day, I had come all the way to Crawford to do that, and I was not going to let this one go down without a fight. He went and talked with the press staff, and it was decided that we would both have unilateral positions—meaning that neither of us had to share images, since no one else was on hand, and we could both cover the day's activities at the ranch.

The day was uneventful until we learned that the president was hosting an informal down-home meeting with German Chancellor Angela Merkel, and she would be arriving around 6:00 p.m. So, at about 5:00, we gathered outside of the school for the security sweep. The Navy's Explosive Ordinance Disposal (EOD) technicians came in to inspect our gear, and the Secret Service checked us all with metal detectors, as is standard for every sweep. After we were cleared, we loaded into the motorcade and headed out to the helipad at the ranch. When the motorcade came to a halt about 50 yards from the rope line demarking where we could go no farther, we all hustled up to it. Because I wasn't in the first van, I found myself in the second row, which isn't such a bad thing since I am taller than most of my colleagues. For those of you who've never been to the ranch, there's a lot of brush—very Texas and without a lot of interesting scenery.

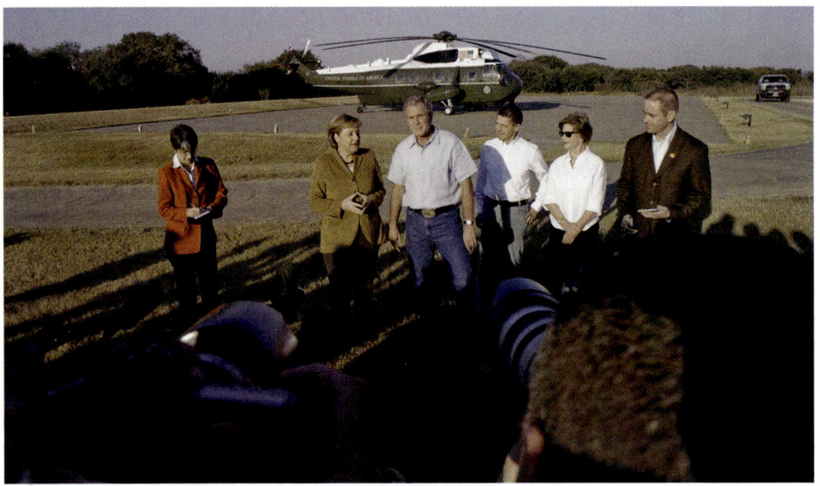

President Bush and German Chancellor Merkel (center), accompanied by translators and their spouses, talk to the press at the Western White House in Crawford, Texas, on November 9, 2007.

The helicopter touched down, and out came the German chancellor. Both she and the president came to the press line and made a few remarks. I was interested in capturing an image that told the story of the informal visit. Right near the end of the remarks, the president extended his hand and the chancellor shook it, and as genuine a moment as can be had in front of the press took place, where the president really *did* look glad to have her to the ranch as a guest.

As the press conference concluded, the president and the chancellor climbed into the president's pickup truck and drove off to the residence for their visit. That in itself was a sight to see—the president loading the chancellor of Germany into his pickup truck and heading off into the sunset! We piled into the motorcade and sped back to the filing center. There, I edited and transmitted my images, trying to get them out as quickly as possible to the waiting news outlets—and trying to keep my eyes open, as I had not slept in 36 hours.

Opposite page: President Bush welcomes German Chancellor Angela Merkel, who arrived via the helicopter in the background, to the Western White House in Crawford, Texas.

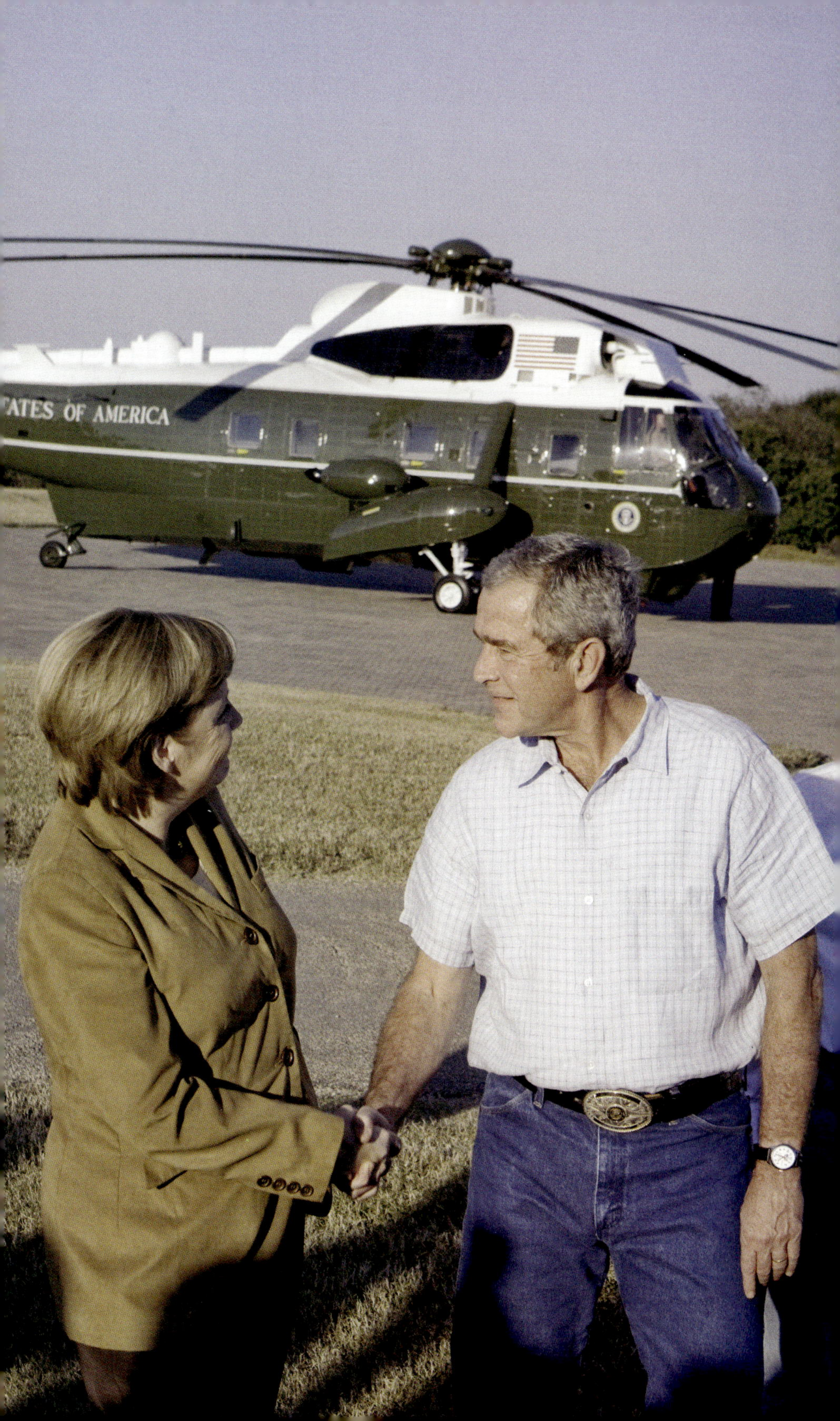
TATES OF AMERICA

I had two commitments in two different states on two different days, 500+ miles apart, and I wouldn't have traded one for another. Sometimes you have to suck it up and sacrifice sleep to make it all happen.

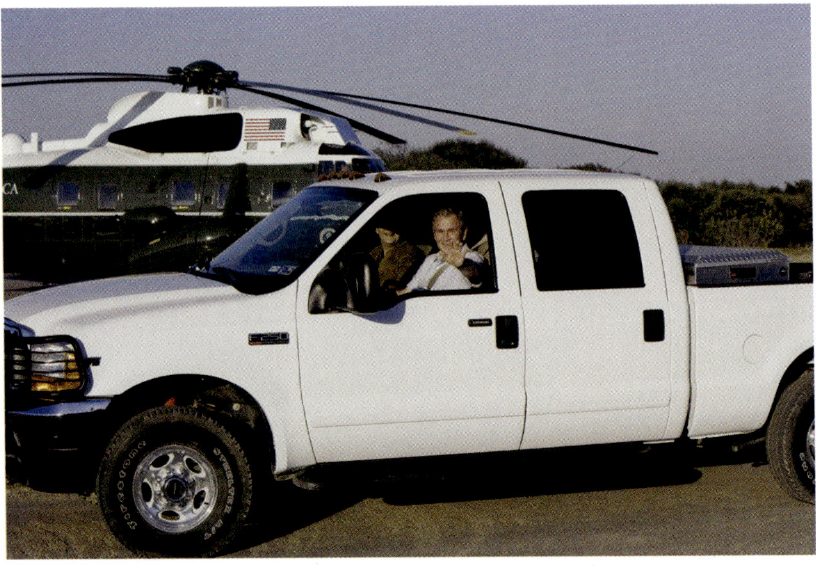

President Bush waves to the press as he and the chancellor of Germany drive toward the Western White House.

January 20th: A Truly Washington Moment

Since 1992, I've had the great privilege of being within naked eyesight of the words being spoken as each president has taken the oath of office. I know that I wouldn't have been afforded that proximity if it wasn't for my membership in what is humorously referred to as the fourth branch of government, or the Fourth Estate—the press corps.

During my first inauguration, I saw the back of President Clinton's head and the face of Chief Justice Rehnquist, but I had a decent side view during his inaugural address. During my second inauguration, also with President Clinton, I had a view from exactly the opposite side, so I was able to see President Clinton's face during that opportunity. I had a slightly more angled view when President George W. Bush was sworn in on a rainy January 20, 2001, and I had a much better angle of view when President Bush was sworn in a second time. During each successive experience, I did a thorough review of what went right, what could have gone better, and what went wrong, so that I could improve upon it in the next go-round.

One of the after-action thoughts I had following President Bush's second inauguration was the idea of having multiple cameras and multiple focal lengths all pre-positioned, pointed, and focused on the same spot; because when the president's hand is raised, you not only want a nice, tight shot, but you also want a wide, a mid-range, and a decent vertical in the event that your picture is a candidate for a cover. The challenge in doing this is that the president's hand is only raised for approximately 30 seconds during his recitation of the oath of office. As a result, you have little time to change lenses, refocus, and recompose, so a multi-camera solution all triggered by one camera solves this problem.

In the days leading up to inauguration week, we were able to preview our angle and the square footage of our space. The space was approximately 30 inches wide and 4 feet deep; however, this 4 feet had to accommodate me and my equipment, as well as leaving a 2-foot pathway behind me so that my neighbors on either side could have egress around me. So I really only had 30 inches by 24 inches to set up any equipment. On the floor of my office, I taped off a 30-inch-by-4-foot area and then added a second line at the halfway mark, where I knew I couldn't store any equipment beyond or have a tripod leg intruding on. I set up my tripod in the area and used a variety of extension rails and magic arms to attach several cameras and lenses to the single tripod, with focal ranges from 20mm through 600mm. I interconnected them using PocketWizards, although I did have some concerns about being on a similar frequency to another nearby photographer with the same basic idea.

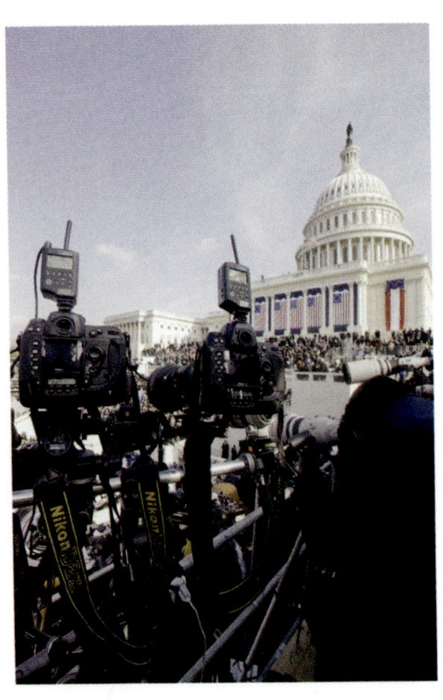

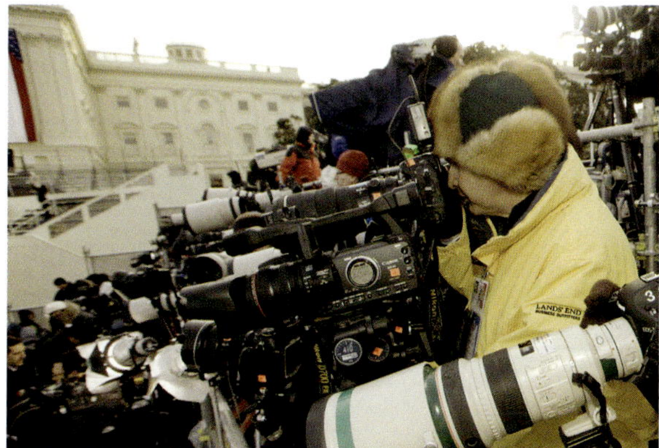

Working with one camera, with the remaining cameras all pre-focused and pre-composed, all triggered via PocketWizards during the few seconds I had to document the swearing in of President Barack Obama.

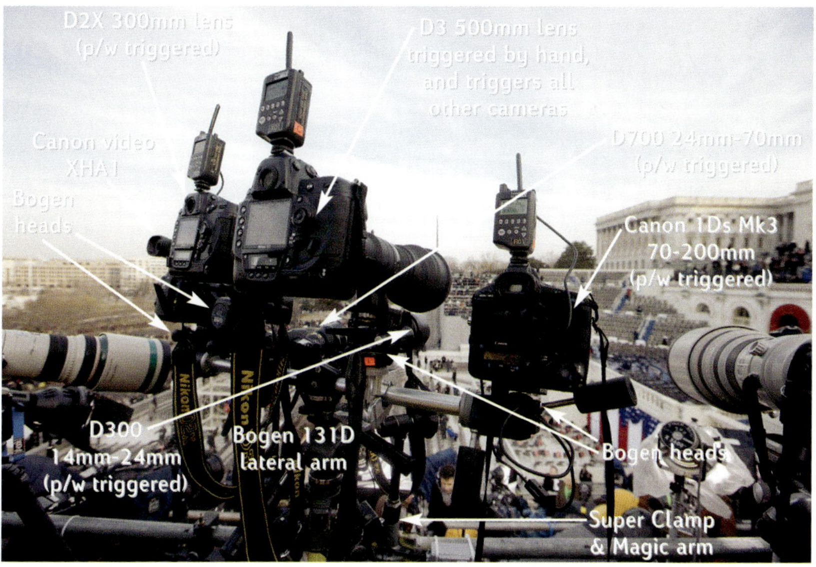

A single tripod and expansion bar holds all the cameras and varying focal-length lenses, all triggered via PocketWizards.

After I tested their connectivity and they were all firing in unison, I approached the next aspect of the picture that I wanted to capture. It is not enough for me that the president have his right hand raised; I also wanted him to be actually speaking a word with his mouth open. In thinking through the 30 seconds that the president's hand is raised, one quickly realizes that if the chief justice is reciting the words the president must repeat, then there is an approximately equal amount of time that each is speaking.

Thus, during half of the 30 seconds that the president's right hand is raised, he will be speaking.

With this in mind, I located an audio recording of President Bush's swearing in, and I played the recording repeatedly to test exactly how long I would have relative to how long he was speaking. This revealed a slight technical challenge that arose because of my camera's buffer. Although a camera can in fact shoot eight or so frames a second, any photographer will tell you that, when shooting RAW, this is sustainable for about five seconds before the buffer is full. I had 30 seconds during which I needed to capture images, but only 15 seconds where I wanted to actually be making those same images during the 30-second portion of the ceremony where the president's arm is raised.

I approached this technical challenge next. I tried a variety of cards and card speeds to determine the best configuration. In this case, using the second slot of the cameras to back up with JPEGs what the first slot was capturing in RAW cost me several extra frames, so I opted not to do that, believing that the multiple other cameras, also shooting RAW, afforded me the security that I needed, albeit in a slightly different way.

I settled on the card speeds that worked best for each camera and tested each camera based upon the cadence of the remarks as they were played back from the recording. The state-and-repeat interaction between the president and the chief justice essentially not only gave me 15 seconds where the president was speaking, but also interspersed throughout the 30 seconds' worth of buffer-2-card write time (the time that the camera needs to save the images just shot to the memory card) while the chief justice was speaking, if I was judicious in my use of the camera's release. During the testing, I found that I could capture between 34 and 37 frames during the swearing-in where the president's mouth was open. For those of you who watch the inauguration from the warmth and comfort of your own home (which is most of America, although it didn't seem that way when President Obama was inaugurated), the inauguration is always on January 20th, and it is always freezing cold. Further, we have to be up by 3:00 a.m. to be out the door by 4:00 a.m. and at the Capitol by 4:30, pushing all the cameras, tripods, cases, lenses, and other gear on carts and standing in long lines with the rest of our media brethren. We have to clear security by about 6:00 a.m. and then stand around and wait until the ceremonies begin, just before noon, which means hours and hours of standing around waiting in the freezing cold.

As most people know, batteries don't like cold weather, which means that I have to wear them inside my coat, against my body, to keep them from failing. Complicated electronic cameras don't like cold either, and the weather is prone to causing them to fail, too. These are just a few tidbits of information you learn from trial, misery, and doing things the hard way—unless you're reading this book!

Because the vice president is sworn in first, I was able to get a test of my system before the president himself was sworn in. While I certainly didn't consider the vice president a true testing opportunity (he could one day actually become the president, which would then lend additional value to this image), I knew that it would afford me an opportunity to refine my approach one last time, just before the president was sworn in.

Fortunately, not only was I able to capture some great images of the vice president's swearing-in, but one of these images was also selected to be a part of the Smithsonian Institution's permanent collection of images for their archives, following its inclusion in their exhibit "I Do Solemnly Swear," which was a companion project to the Official Inaugural Book Project.

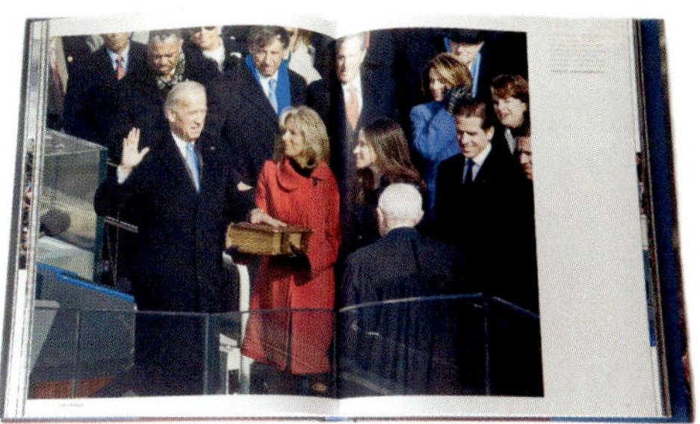

With the vice president's images made, I did a brief preview of the images captured by the other cameras and concluded that no additional adjustments needed to be made as the president rose from his seat to be sworn in. All the cameras had cleared their buffers from the vice president's images, and no one else's PocketWizard had taken over triggering my cameras, thank goodness.

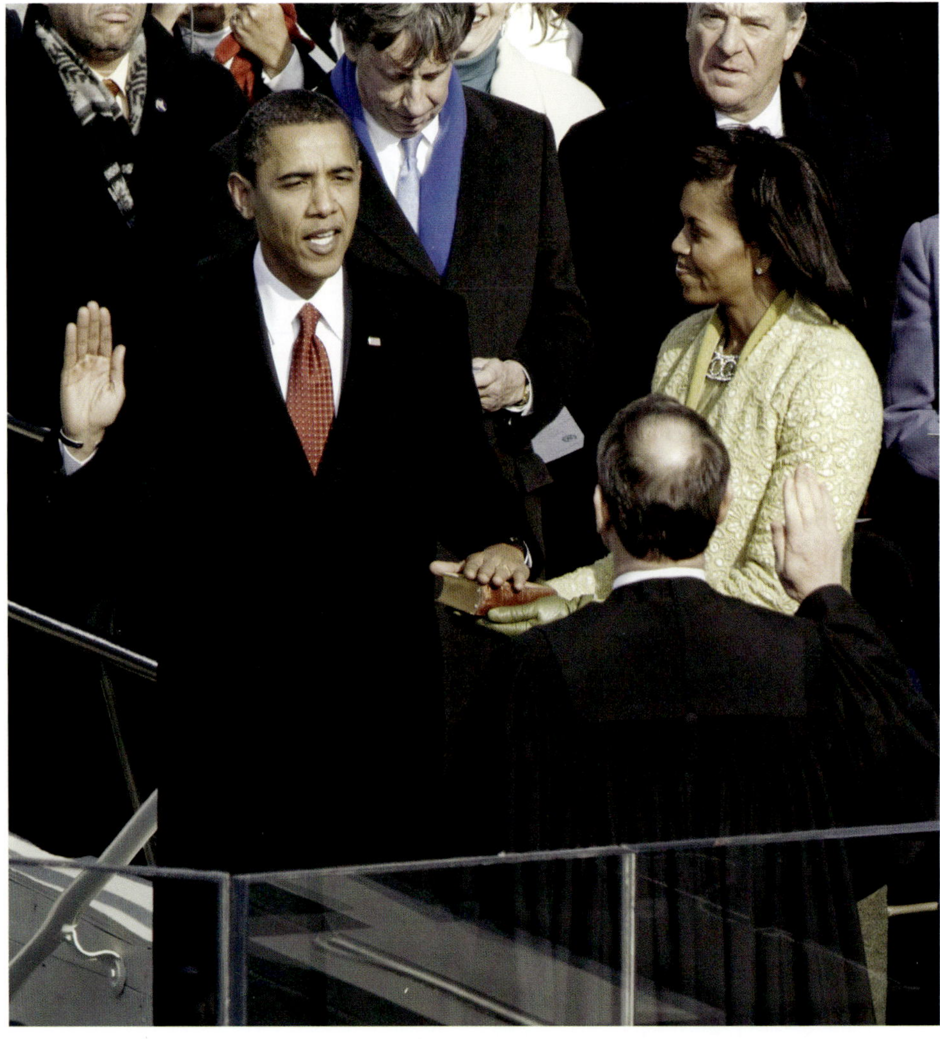

President Barack Obama repeating the oath of office recited by Chief Justice John Roberts as Michelle Obama holds the Lincoln Bible and looks on.

As the president's arm was raised, I made a single frame test with his arm up to ensure that all cameras were still in sync, and the joyous cacophony of all the cameras firing simultaneously meant that all systems were go and that all of the testing, studying, and reconfiguring had positioned me to bring my best abilities to bear at this historic moment. This day, which had started eight hours earlier with a cartload of cameras, lens cases, and all manner of other apparatuses and electronics, served me well for 15 seconds just after noon on January 20, 2009, when everything worked exactly as planned.

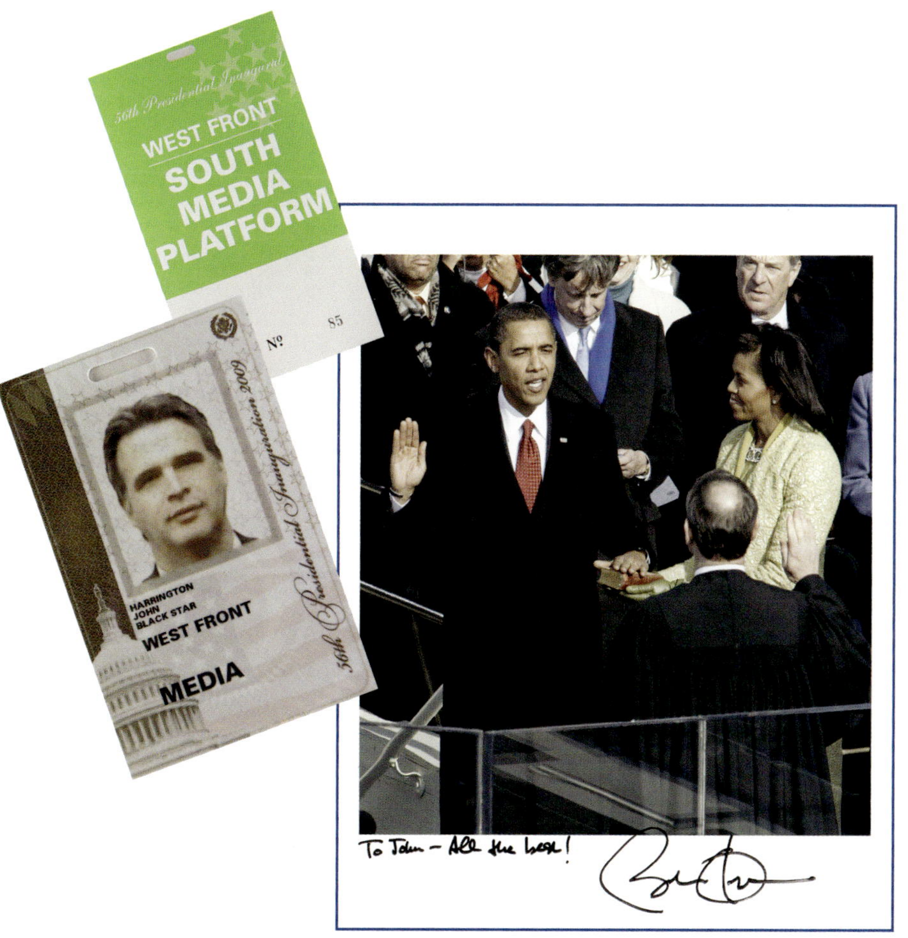

A personal note and signature from the President on my image of him repeating the oath of office.

Obama's Inaugural Walk

I've had the good fortune to photograph presidential inaugurations since 1992, beginning with the inauguration of Bill Clinton, and I brought that knowledge to bear when I was privileged to be a part of the team producing the official inaugural book during the inauguration of Barack Obama. I wore many hats during the inaugural week, which included my role in this official capacity, my coverage of the actual swearing-in ceremony as a member of the press corps, and my role as the personal photographer to a CEO of one of the major benefactors of the unofficial inauguration festivities, which required attendance at evening receptions and galas. This was most certainly a week where the phrase "no rest for the weary" applied, and the most respite that I could find was a few minutes on a freezing press riser or a cramped front seat in a black sedan between events.

One of the photographs I had always wanted to make was of a newly minted president taking what is best described as a victory walk along Pennsylvania Avenue to the White House. In my earlier inaugural experiences, the photograph that always best told the story was one that included the president, rather than just the gala of the parade.

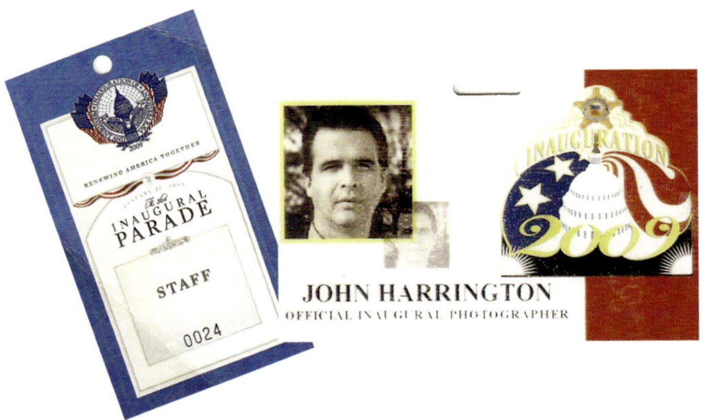

Of course, supporting photographs of the pomp and circumstance of the parade were necessary. But the ultimate picture really is one that includes the president. Previous positions I was in afforded me a long-lens view of the president motoring by in the presidential limousine with thick, green bulletproof glass, and if I was lucky, when he was in my view he would be waving in my direction. Although I understand the intense security precautions that preclude all but the foolhardy from walking the entire route—which they could do, as the parade moves at a glacial pace—there really is only one sure bet to capture an image where the president and first lady are on foot and the excitement is plain as day on their faces. That is during the last block or two that the parade travels up to the presidential reviewing stand on the north side of the White House.

I'd had the opportunity to photograph President George W. Bush's second inauguration from alongside the presidential reviewing stand, so I knew what to expect during President Obama's inauguration. I studied my images from my previous experience and did a scouting visit of the stretch that I wanted to work for my previsualized picture of President Obama. I knew that if I stayed in one of my chosen positions for too long, even wearing a "parade staff" credential, I might run into a challenge or two, so I waited in an out-of-the-way place for maximum potential access to the multiple vantage points I had contemplated, depending upon at what point the president exited the vehicle and began his walk.

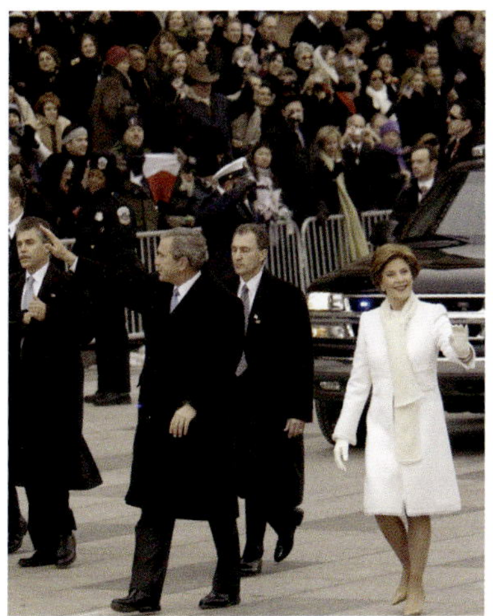

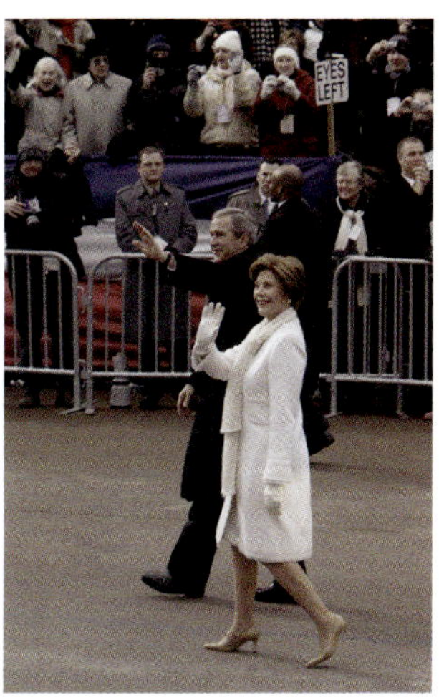

President George W. Bush and Laura Bush walk down Pennsylvania Avenue in the last few feet of their procession of the official inaugural parade before entering the reviewing stand to watch the parade go by.

I had also considered that if I made a few images from my first vantage point and then I hustled to my second vantage point and then to my third and fourth vantage points farther along the parade route (all within about a half a block along Lafayette Park on the north side), I could quadruple my opportunity to get a really great image. I could get the image that I had waited for a long time (and for which the opportunity only came along every four years).

As the president arrived, I could see his vehicle stop in the distance, and my adrenaline instantly began pumping, even though it was exceptionally cold on January 20, 2009, and I had been in that cold since well before sunrise. I could feel my body generating so much energy right then that my shivering stopped, and I no longer felt cold.

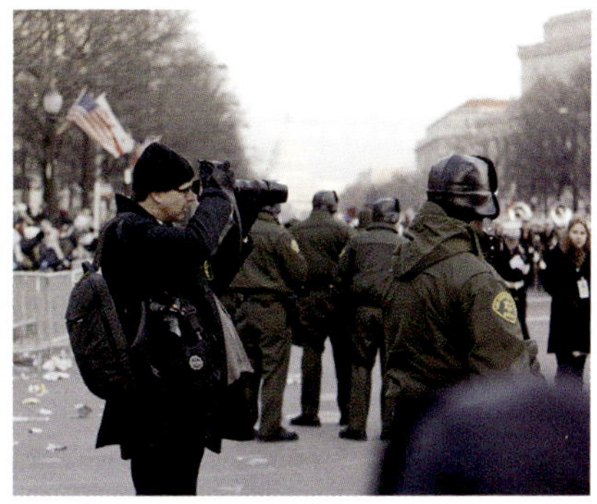

Traveling light with my laptop, backup camera, and small camera bag made it easy to work between the security barricades and the police lining the parade route.

Knowing that the picture I wanted was vertical, I tested full-length framing on other parading participants who preceded the president. I knew that the best lens would be a 70-200mm zoom, and I had also tested the focus tracking and knew that continuous focus tracking would work well for someone walking down the street.

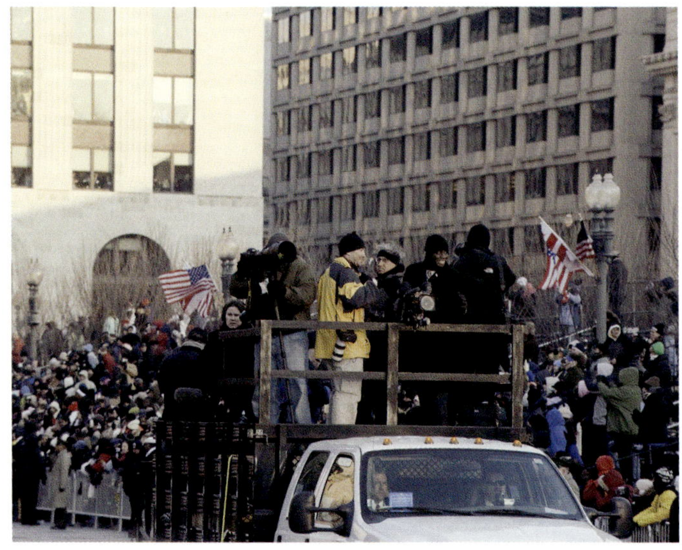

The president's vehicle is preceded by a flatbed truck full of a few dozen photographers and videographers documenting the President's procession up Pennsylvania Avenue to the White House from the Capitol.

I made a few images from my first position, and although they were suitable, they were not as good as I wanted them to be. I gave up the opportunity to make another five or ten frames so that I could reposition myself in my second position and also allow for my camera to clear some free space in the buffer, as I was shooting RAW in Slot 1 and backing up with JPEGs in Slot 2, and even with the fastest cards, I knew I needed those extra few seconds. While in position two, I made several more good frames, but I was also partially obstructed, temporarily, by the vehicles preceding the president and the president's intermittent looking and waving to the south side of the street.

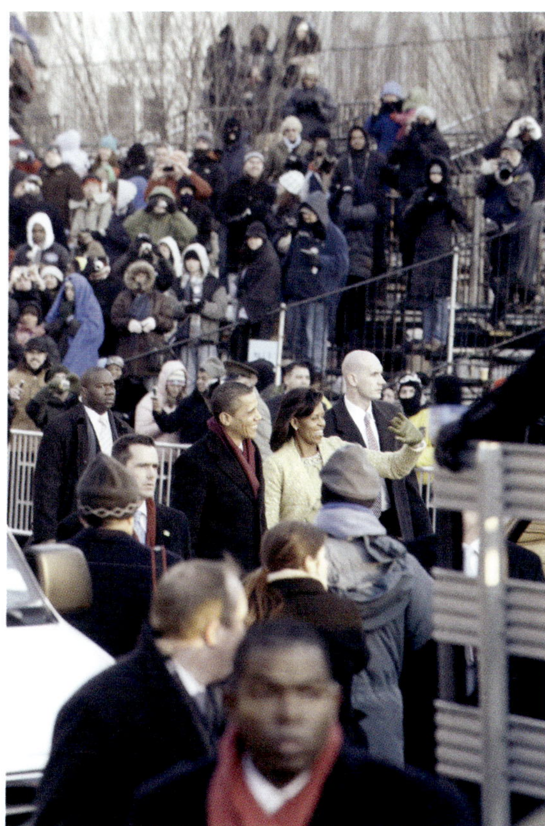

The press trucks as well as the security surrounding the president made the opportunities to get a clear photograph of the president quite difficult.

Moving again to position three—which, if I recall correctly, was right next to where Al Roker was broadcasting for NBC—I reset and reframed a third time for another go at it. This time the president was waving to the north in my direction, and I felt confident that I had "the shot." Because I could, I moved myself one last time to position four and filled my buffer with extra images simply because I didn't want to waste the opportunity.

Just after the president passed by me, I began a quick review of my images to see whether I had captured what I thought I had seen. Sure enough, I had an image where the president not only had good foot position, but also was looking directly into my camera. I couldn't imagine my good fortune, because even if the president wasn't looking at me, this image was a winner. With him looking at me, I was beside myself!

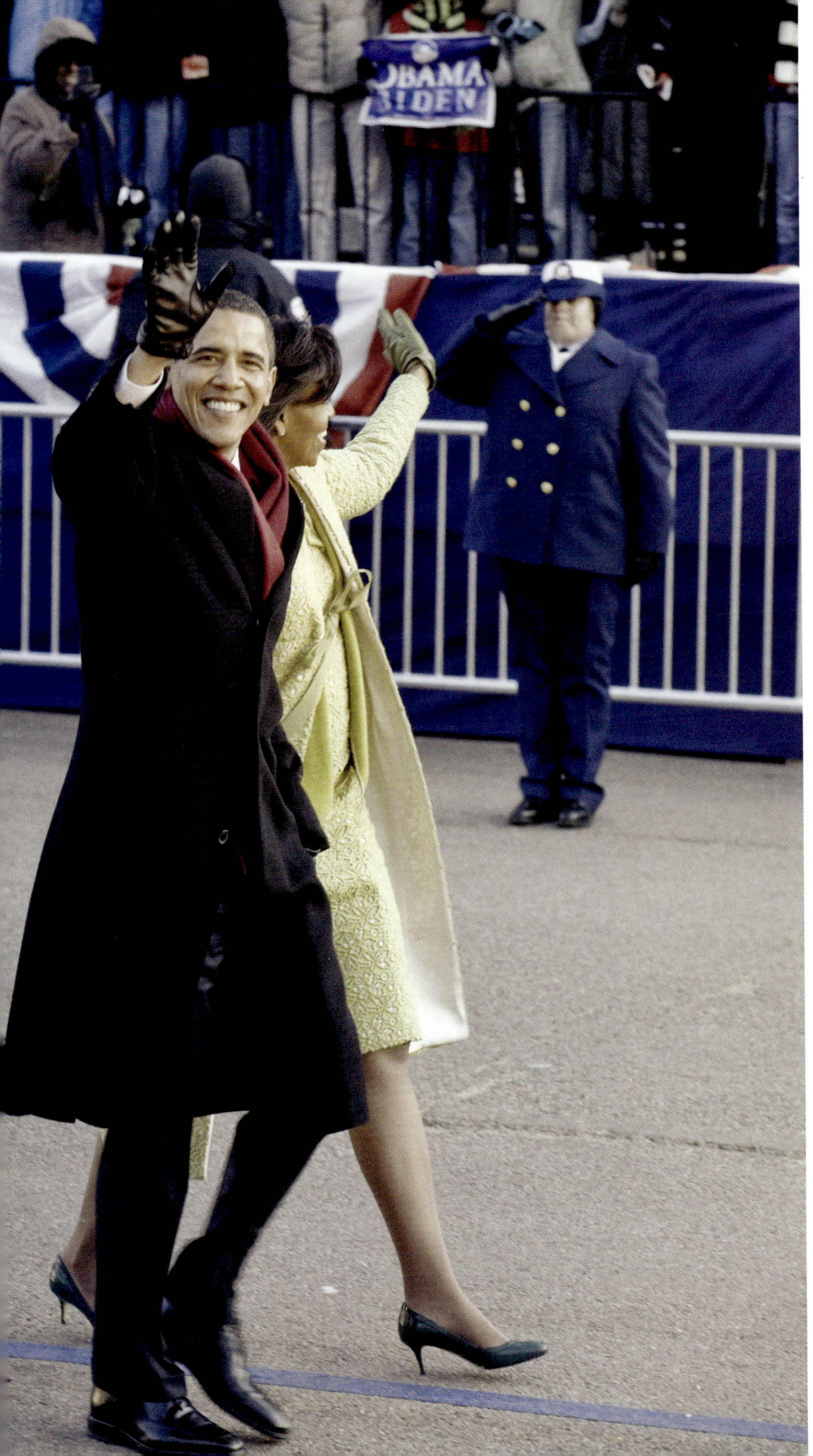

The framing of the image with the saluting female member of the military in the background and an Obama/Biden sign in the stands in the background just added to my pleasure with a job well done. I couldn't check critical focus on the image until I was back to my computer, but I felt confident that my focus was spot-on and that I would not be disappointed. When I made it back to my computer, as exhausted as I was, I wanted to forego even a brief nap before heading to cover inaugural galas and a 4 a.m. call time to be at Washington National Cathedral to cover the prayer service the next day. I had to check that this image was sharp. I loaded the card into the computer, and all of the planning had paid off. Not only did I have an image that I am proud of, but I also didn't have to wait another four years to achieve the image I had envisioned in my mind's eye.

As an interesting side note, when I had the opportunity to present the winners of the White House News Photographers Association Eyes of History Contest winners to the president in the Oval Office, all guests that day were allowed to bring their winning entry or a select image to be signed by the president. I presented two copies of two images—one of him looking at me while walking and one of him being sworn in earlier in the day. With great appreciation, I received back the one of him being sworn in, signed by him with a personal note. And with great honor, I noted that the two images of him looking at me were missing. I can only surmise that he liked them enough to keep both, and if this is the case, I'll take that as a true sign of a job well done.

Opposite page: President Barack Obama, looking right into my lens, and Michelle Obama walk down Pennsylvania Avenue near the White House in the official inaugural parade just prior to entering the reviewing stand to watch the parade go by.

Smithsonian Books

One thing I don't like doing is expecting something because of my heritage. Although I'm Native American, I don't think it's reasonable for me to expect that the Smithsonian's book division should owe me anything—such as an opportunity to be published. That said, once The National Museum of the American Indian opened, I did have a few story ideas, but I certainly didn't think that I should be afforded special consideration because I was Native.

One day, I received a phone call from a prospective client. Her name was Amy, and she started out the conversation with a series of questions about whether I was a full-time photographer and whether I was based in Washington. Then she asked whether I was Native American. Taken aback, I said that I was, and I then queried, "Why do you ask?" She responded that she had been at an event where someone we knew mutually suggested she contact me because I was Native, and she responded to our mutual acquaintance that this wasn't possible, that the Smithsonian's book division knew all the Native photographers in DC, let alone around the U.S.

She then asked why I hadn't come to the museum to introduce myself before. I replied that I don't go around wearing my heritage on my sleeve expecting something and that eventually, once the museum opened, I would've stopped in to see whether there was something I could do to contribute to its mission of educating people about what native peoples have experienced over the years. She then asked me whether I had a portfolio and if I wouldn't mind coming in to visit.

Thus, a meeting was scheduled with me, Amy, the head of the Smithsonian's book division, and the head of purchasing. The meeting began easily enough, and I showed them some of my images that I had taken when I was attending my own tribe's powwows over the years, as well as the very first story I'd ever had published, done on my father, who is a hereditary chief of the tribe. It seemed, as they looked at the photos and at me again, that there remained a question about my heritage. So, rather than beat around the bush, I addressed it: "It seems you're still wondering about my being Native, so let me show you my tribal card." This was met with a "No, no, that's not necessary," but I still pulled it from my wallet and slid it across the conference table. Sure enough, everyone wanted to look at it *closely*.

Noting that, I mentioned to them a story I'd been told by my biological father, who held a job in the legal profession, advocating for other native people. He told a story about how whenever he would go into a meeting, all people would look at were his braids, and they wouldn't pay as much attention to what he was saying. Once he cut them off and started wearing suits, he began to get more done; yet this troubled him, as he felt it was disrespectful to his heritage. An elder told him not to worry, that in order to hunt it was often necessary to don the hides and fur of the prey in order to get close enough to be effective in the hunt, and this was similar to what he was doing. In order to be taken seriously and have the attention be focused on the matters at hand, he needed to dress in a manner that wasn't a distraction, and through this he could be more effective. Thus, because I was in Washington and at the White House and Capitol and the other corridors of power throughout the city, in order for me to be most effective, dressing as I do is simply a variation on the story my father was told.

During the meeting, the discussion of copyright came up. "The Smithsonian typically wants to own the copyright to the photos. Do you have a problem with that?" I thought for a minute—not about whether I had a problem with it, but rather, about what the best way to answer the question was. I wanted to give back to my people through my photography and skills, but I also didn't want to not own the work that I created. How to answer this question?

"Well, there's a bit of a problem with that," I began. "The government, many years ago, took advantage of Native Americans by taking their property, and if you were to take my copyright, I would think that would be a modern form of what happened centuries ago." With a pregnant pause in the conversation, I made them an offer: "Why don't we share copyright? I'll not need to seek permission from you to use them as I see fit, and you'll not need to pay me again in the event that you want to reprint, reuse, or repurpose the work for your own needs." The head of the book division, after a moment's contemplation, agreed that this was a fair and reasonable way to work out both of our needs, and we had an agreement.

A short while later, a call came in for a possible book project. It was to be the first in a series titled *Our World*, about the differences that young children face being Native and living also in a modern American world. The visuals were to depict the children engaged in Native ceremonies, as well as living a more typical Western lifestyle.

The portion of the series I worked on was the first three books—*Meet Naiche*, *Meet Mindy*, and *Meet Lydia*. For those unfamiliar with Native American customs and traditions, this was no small undertaking. First, if you've ever heard of "Southern time" or have visited the Caribbean and heard of "island time," "Native time" makes both of those look like they are running a fine Swiss timepiece to keep things on schedule. Further, there are often tribal restrictions as to what anyone (whether Native or non-Native) can photograph or videotape.

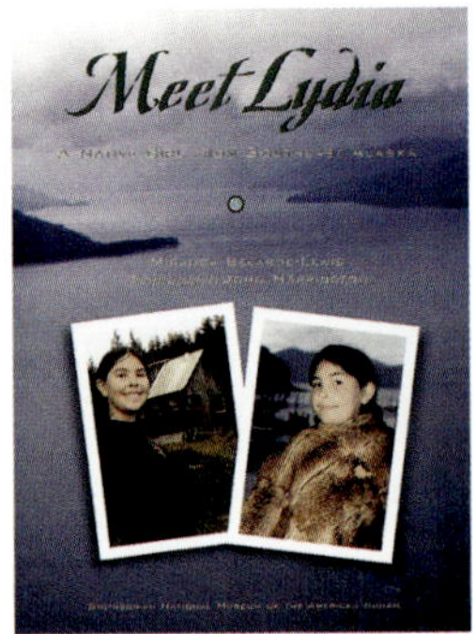

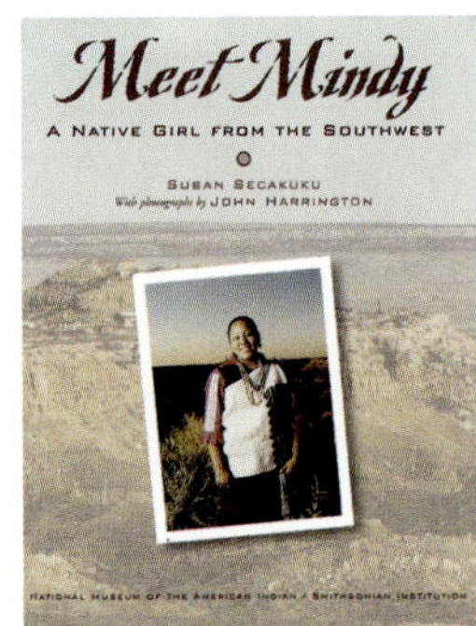

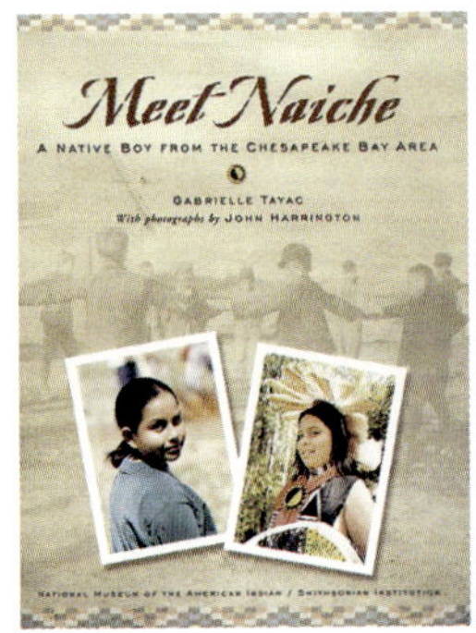

The books *Meet Lydia, Meet Mindy,* and *Meet Naiche* published by the Smithsonian's National Museum of the American Indian.

The first book took me not too far from home, to Maryland. The book was titled *Meet Naiche* and was about a young boy named Naiche and his participation in the ceremony of the Awakening of Mother Earth. We arrived at his home and met his parents. Both were eager to be a part of the project, and we met Naiche next. He was a young boy, along about in sixth grade. He showed us his regalia and talked about his culture. (Regalia is the proper name for Native American attire. Calling it an *outfit,* a *costume,* or some other word isn't right.) Following on the success of the first book, we next traveled to Arizona to work on the second book in the series, *Meet Mindy*. This book proved to be much more of a challenge, but it also had far more opportunities to make great photographs. Mindy is a member of the Hopi tribe and lives in a traditional suburban home in a tract of houses outside of Phoenix.

The first real day of shooting, we drove several hours to Fifth Mesa, a plateau of land that rises out of the Arizona desert. We arrived and met other members of Mindy's family—grandparents, cousins, and the like. Mindy was to go through a coming-of-age ceremony, much like a Bat Mitzvah, yet tribal in nature.

We worked very hard to ingratiate ourselves to the family. Amy, the editor, shifted into fixer mode and made sure we could photograph the ceremony that both Mindy and a number of other girls were to go through. Mindy's parents made inquiries, but I knew I was going to have a challenge—I could feel it.

After a day focused on making a few images and getting to know people, we left and came back the next day for the ceremony—our reason for being there.

After making a number of images in Mindy's grandparents' home on the third day, it was time for the ceremony. The many tourists who had come to see the ceremony, video cameras and snap cameras in hand, were admonished not to take photos because of the solemnity of the ceremony. Although Native Americans feel it is important that the general public witness their ceremonies in many instances, as it is believed to be a teaching tool to have Westerners present, photographs and video often are seen as a step too far in this outreach and educational effort. I, on the other hand, had been given permission by tribal elders and by Mindy's parents to photograph Mindy. Apparently, though, that message didn't make it to some of the other tribal members, who assumed I was a tourist. Despite other tribal members who continued to photograph, I was told I had to stop.

Once again, my appearance was misconstrued by others as something other than it was. Yet this time, it was working in the opposite direction. Even as a Native American, my conservative appearance was being second-guessed. Drawing near to Mindy's mother, I continued shooting, knowing I was essentially safe while in her proximity. Long lenses from that vantage point gave me a good perspective in the end, and one of the best images I made from that same spot—of the entire ceremony with a very wide-angle lens—ended up as a double-page spread in the book.

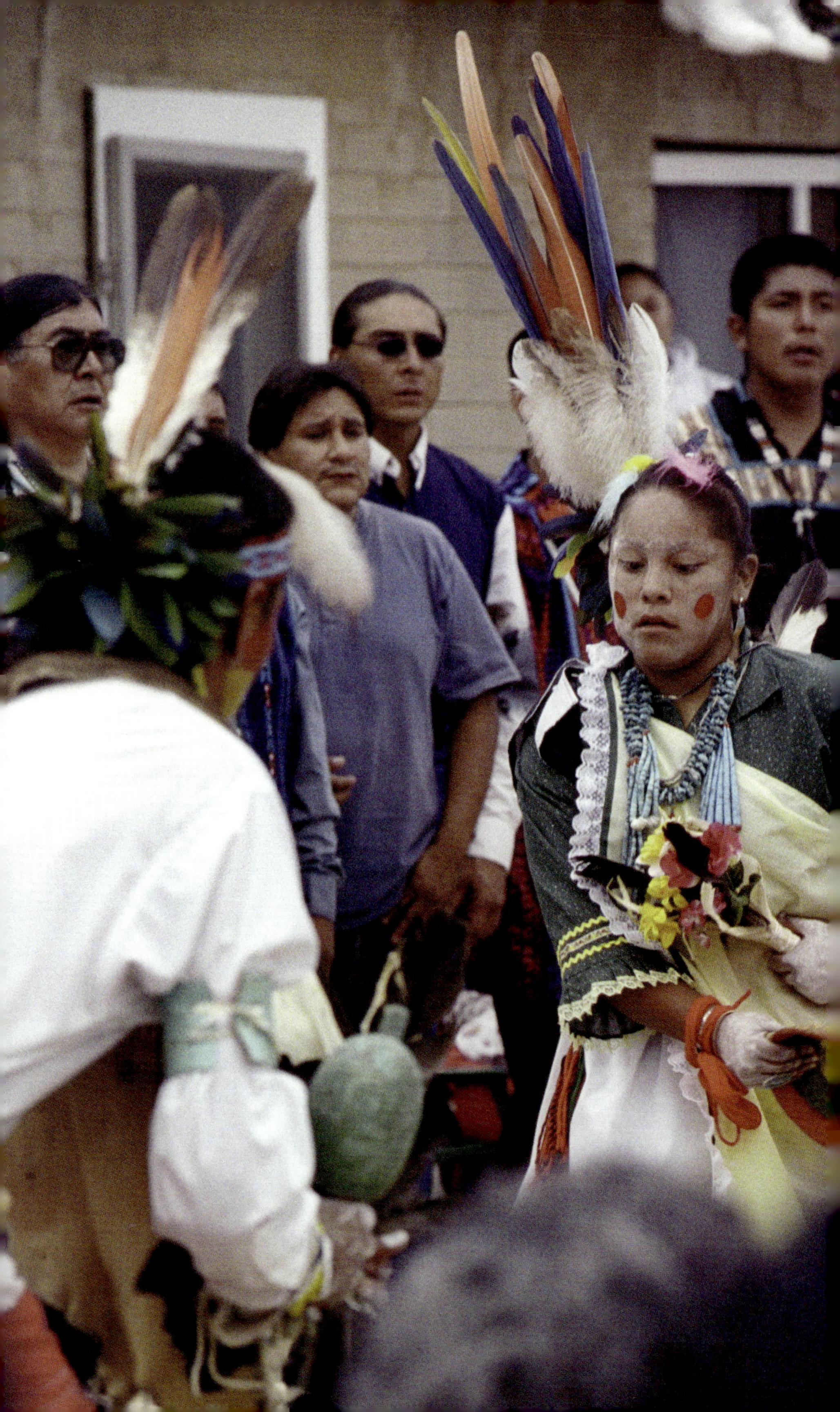

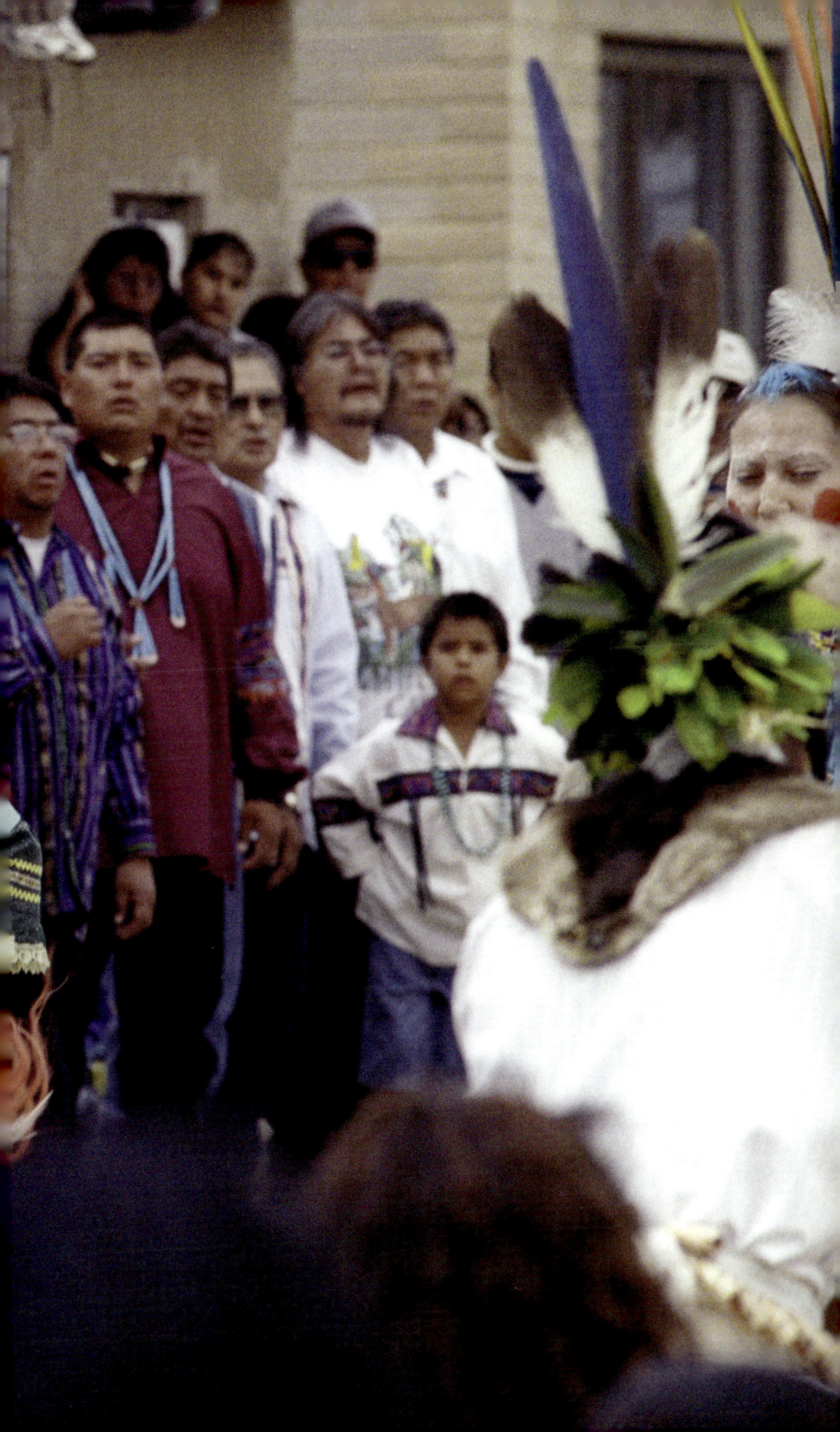

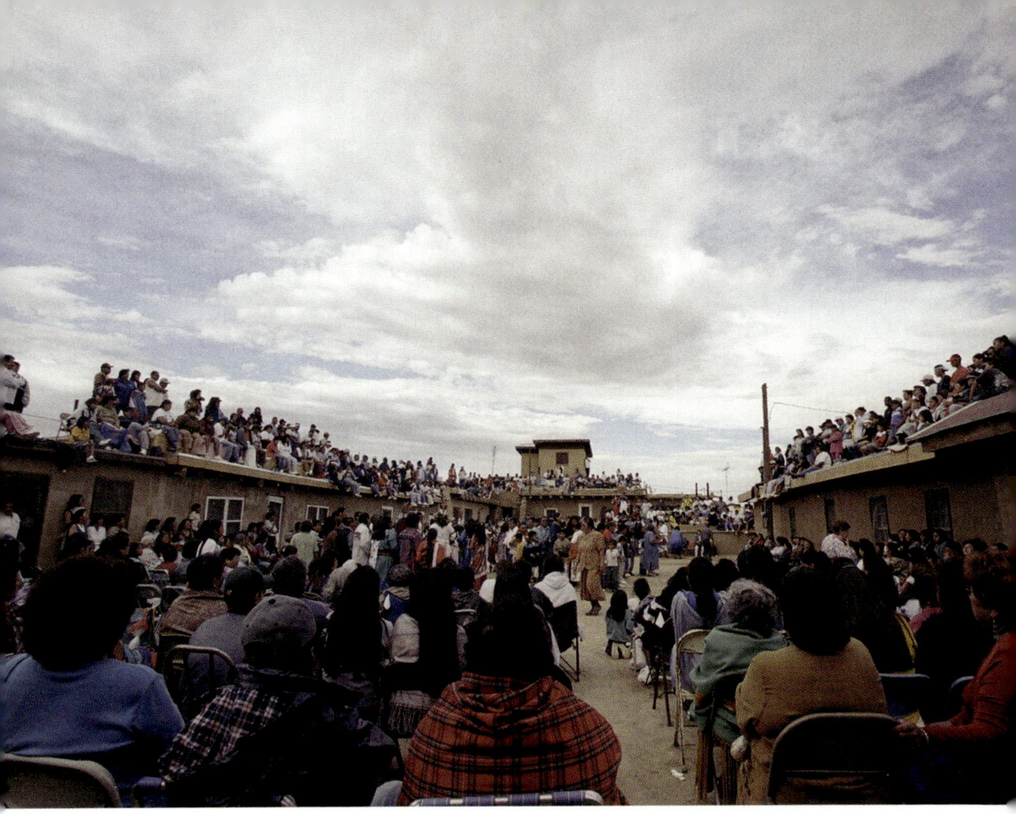

Following the ceremony, I had planned on a great portrait of Mindy at sunset on the edge of the mesa. I pulled about 300 feet of power cord from one of the few power sources on top of the plateau, all the way to the edge. One large softbox and a reflector lent themselves to just the right lighting mixed with the vanishing sun across the desert, and I had the shot I had envisioned from the beginning, of Mindy in her regalia just after the ceremony, having just become a woman in the eyes of her tribe.

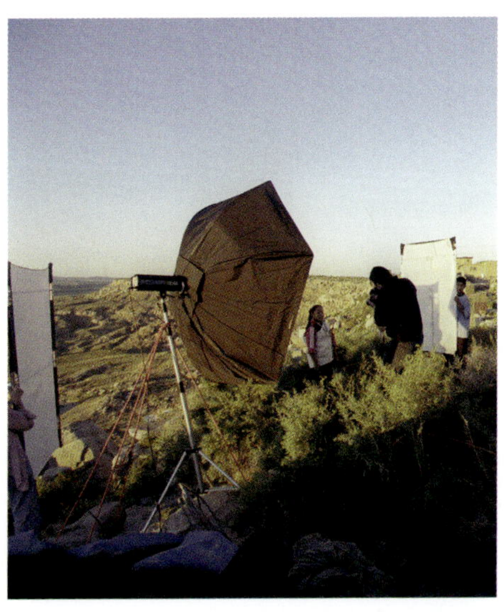

The setup for the portrait of Mindy at sunset on Fifth Mesa in Arizona, for the book *Meet Mindy*.

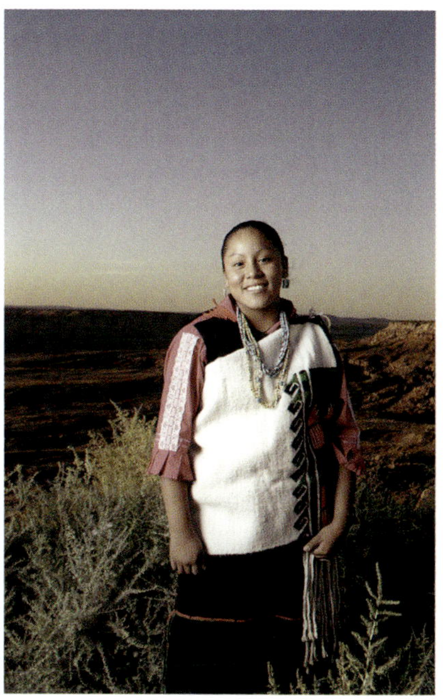

Mindy Secakuku, Hopi Indian Tribe teenager, photographed on Fifth Mesa at sunset.

With the second book edited and published, about a year later the opportunity came to work on the third book in the series—*Meet Lydia*. Lydia lived in Alaska, a bit of a trek outside of Juneau. For me, returning to Alaska was an interesting trip, as I had spent several years of my life living on the Yukon River in a small community of about 65 people called Stevens Village, about 30 miles south of the Arctic Circle and about 90 miles north of Fairbanks, accessible only by a small plane or a boat in the summer. This period of time in my life was filled with many harsh realities. There was the life-or-death reality of the cold temperatures—in fact, had I not been saved by two huskies from my sled team, I would not be here today. Then there was the isolation and subsistence-style living that called for me to work at fish camps during the summers catching fish for the winter. So, taking this assignment to Alaska was deeply personal, as well as an exciting professional opportunity.

When we arrived in Juneau, we trekked out to the small town where Lydia and her family lived. There wasn't a major ceremony like Naiche or Mindy had gone through, so this was more about Lydia's daily life in a small village on the shores near Juneau. We had to take a small plane to the airstrip near her town, which was alongside a marina that served many boats that not only fished for subsistence and commercial efforts, but also to take sport fishermen out on expeditions.

Our first outing took us plane-hopping to a grass airstrip, where we changed planes to one with oversized rubber wheels that were suitable for landing on gravel sandbars where there was no real airstrip.

Our pilot had already gone out once to our destination to clear the sandbar of driftwood—I have no idea how he landed the first time to do that—so we had a bit of a smoother landing than he likely did the first go 'round. As we were descending, the pilot warned us about where the black bears liked to hang out and told us that when the tide came in, we had to be gone. Otherwise, we were stuck, as his landing/takeoff strip would be underwater. We heeded this warning with great care.

I off-loaded my lighting equipment, looking to make a cover portrait of Lydia in this rural area, alongside an old log cabin that their family used to fish the area. A portable battery pack and large softbox, one stand, and an extra battery were my way of traveling very light. I had to be able to pack it on my back, as the site was about a mile from the sandbar on which we landed.

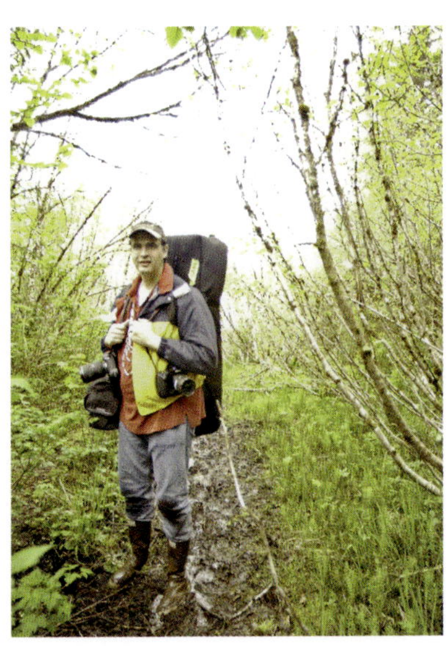

Packing cameras and lighting for a hike into the woods on the panhandle of Alaska for the book *Meet Lydia*.

Once there I set up, and even though it was overcast, I used the strobe and softbox to pop in just enough light so that Lydia was slightly brighter than the background and really jumped out of the image. We then left all of the equipment we didn't need and trekked into the woods to a waterfall that Lydia often would go to with her father. After what seemed like forever, and with the looming fear of the tide coming in, we made it to the waterfall with about 10 minutes to make images underneath a dense forest.

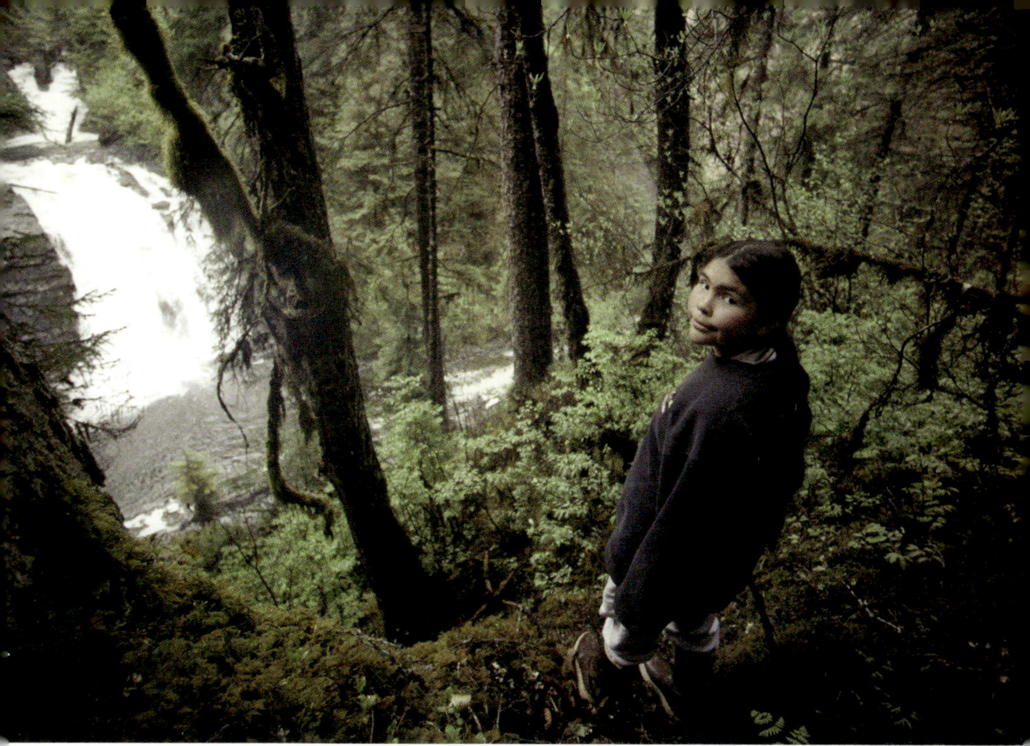

Yet the waterfall was in the light. Thankfully, with it being overcast, there wasn't too much differentiation between the light on the falls and an area alongside the path that had an opening above it that brought in just enough light that, by coupling it with a nominal strobe fill, I was able to make a few really great wide-angle images of Lydia with the falls in the distance.

We trekked back to the sandbar, and just as the tide was coming in, we lifted off and headed back to the waypoint airstrip, where we got onto a much larger plane (yet still a small one by anyone's standards) and headed back to her village.

Once back, I learned that Lydia and her grandfather would often go to a stream and fish, and so it was suggested that I go there to try to capture that, if possible.

When we arrived where they often fished, behind their smokehouse on the stream, the water was running quite cold, and there was no vantage point other than from the middle of the stream to capture the image of them fishing together. Seeing no other option, I recalled from my youth living on the Yukon that you could survive in waters below freezing (unfrozen because it was moving) if you were in there for just a brief period of time.

So, I slipped off my shoes and socks, much to the shock of those around me, and waded into the rushing water, which didn't seem very stream-like once I was actually fording it. I knew I had just a few minutes before my feet were numb and would not function well, and I had to balance that against my desire to not slip and get my clothing wet, which would be a problem later. I waded out, and the memories of being upside down in a kayak from my youth, as sub-freezing water drenched my clothing when I tipped over in the Yukon, came rushing back. I made about a dozen frames before I started to feel my feet and ankles numbing up—but not before I knew I had a workable frame.

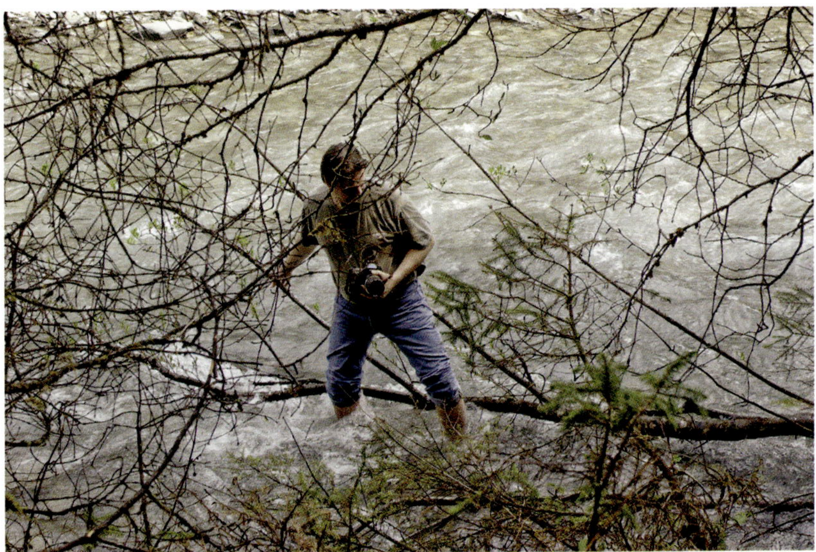

Determining that the water has taken effect on my feet and ankles as they numb up, I carefully return to the shore in an attempt to stay dry while working on assignment for the book *Meet Lydia*, published by the Smithsonian's National Museum of the American Indian.

With all of the images I wanted for the book finished, we headed back to the chartered boat and then settled in for a multi-hour trip back to Lydia's hometown. Once there, while people were off-loading the boat, Lydia and a friend of hers went to the receded waterfront, where mud, shells, and other freshwater creatures were exposed, and began playing on the beach in their waders.

I followed her down there and made a number of additional frames I had not intended, yet which I thought were apropos to the book.

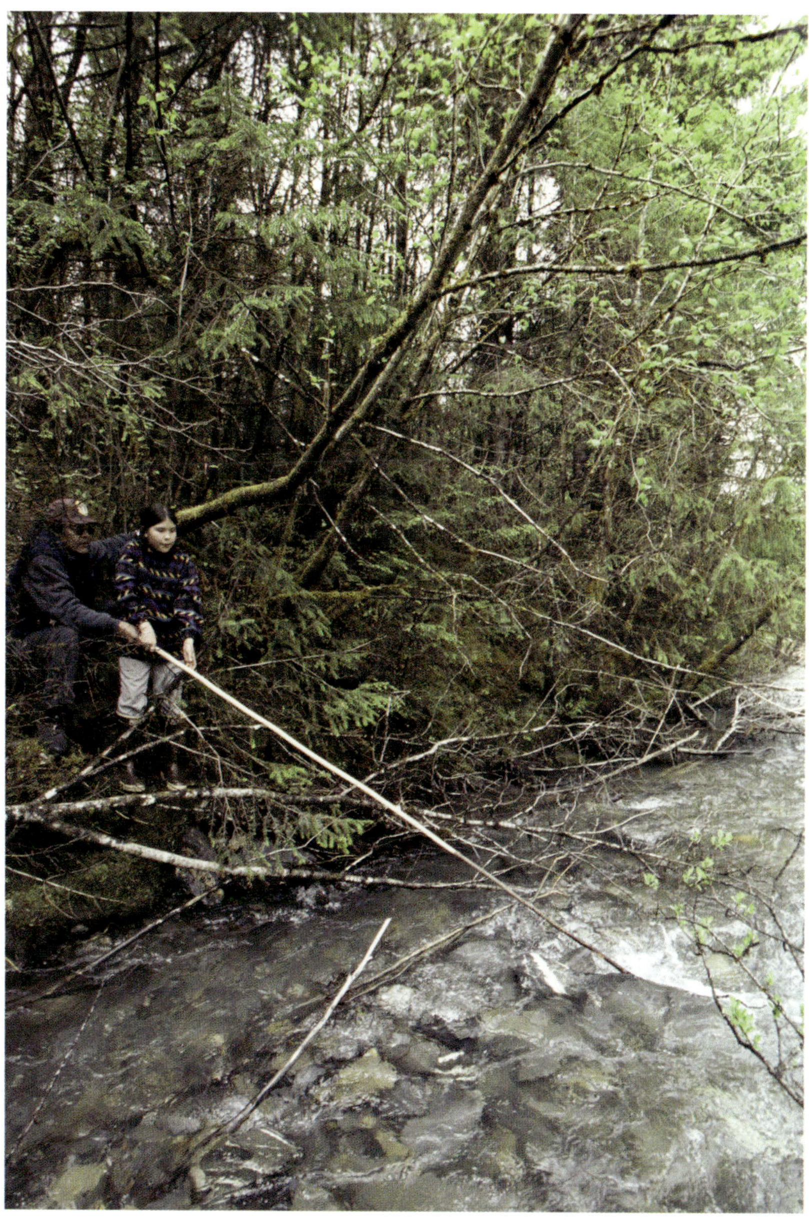

Lydia and her grandfather fishing, photographed while standing in the river for the book *Meet Lydia.*

When it came time to depart from Alaska, I told my editor that I had a side trip I wanted to make. It had been about 25 years since I had been in Stevens Village, so I decided to go back and see what the place looked like.

I caught a commercial flight from Juneau to Fairbanks and then overnighted with some friends I had made when I was living in the village. In the morning, I caught a small puddle-jumper for the 45-minute flight into the village. As we flew over the place where I had spent a few of the formative years of my life, it looked different. I suppose it should have, but I didn't want it to. The plane landed, and the old familiar feeling I'd had as a teenager as we ran to the airstrip to greet the plane and whomever was aboard was something I was on the receiving end of. This time, it was me who had arrived.

I recognized a number of the people who were kids when I was there and some of the elders, too. In this part of Alaska, the people are Indian, and along the coast it was Eskimo for the most part. I walked around, and the one-room schoolhouse I had gone to school in (and in which I lived in the other side of the building) had been torn down recently, with remnants of the building, wood, insulation, and the old diesel tank still about.

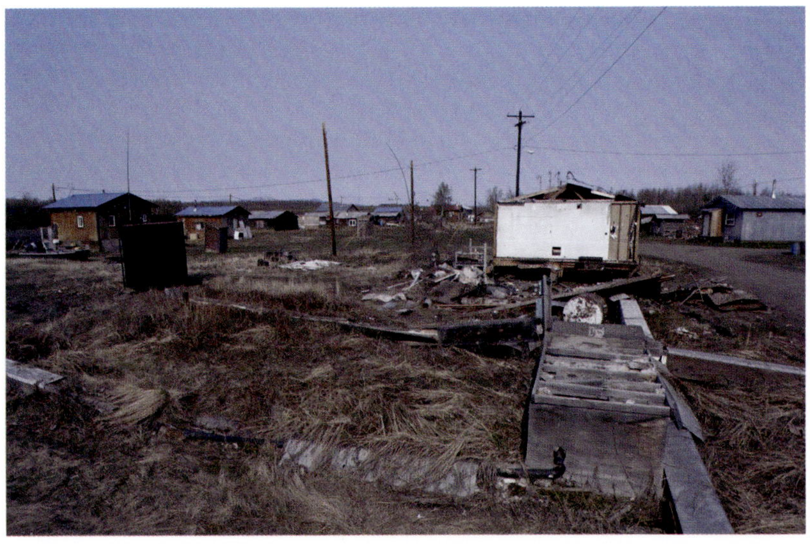

The school had been moved to the outskirts of town and was now a multi-room facility that looked as if it was a modern-day school from the lower 48.

As I meandered through the village, I looked for the house I was staying in for the night. I didn't take a lot of photographs there, although I did take some. This was more of a "this is your life" trek than anything else. A walk down memory lane, if you will.... The friends that I had overnighted with while in Fairbanks had made arrangements for me to stay overnight in the village. When I arrived at the cabin where I was going to stay, no one was there. I sat on the front porch for a while, watching the waters of the mighty Yukon River flow by, as I had some 25 years earlier, as I tended to my sled-dog team just up the way.

After a spell, I heard the familiar sound of an approaching plane and felt the rush of adrenaline that came from the excitement of the unknown winging its way into the village. I, along with everyone else, made the walk up the main gravel path to the airstrip to see who had come. This time, it was a second regularly scheduled flight that I had not been aware of. I watched as the few passengers deplaned and a few packages were handed off. Then and there, I decided that the old adage was right: You can go back, but you can't go home again. The village I remembered wasn't the same, nor, I guess, should it have been. I asked the pilot whether he had an empty seat back to Fairbanks, and he said he did, so I hopped that flight back to Fairbanks and back to my reality.

The third book was published, and it did quite well. The Smithsonian asked me a couple times to come and give a talk, once with Mindy. It was unusual for me to meet Mindy some five or so years later. This time, she was in high school and much older, it seemed. To me, Naiche, Mindy, and Lydia will always be those young children I photographed, and I will always have fond memories of my travels with them.

Next page: Lydia, wrapped in a traditional blanket made of squirrel fur.

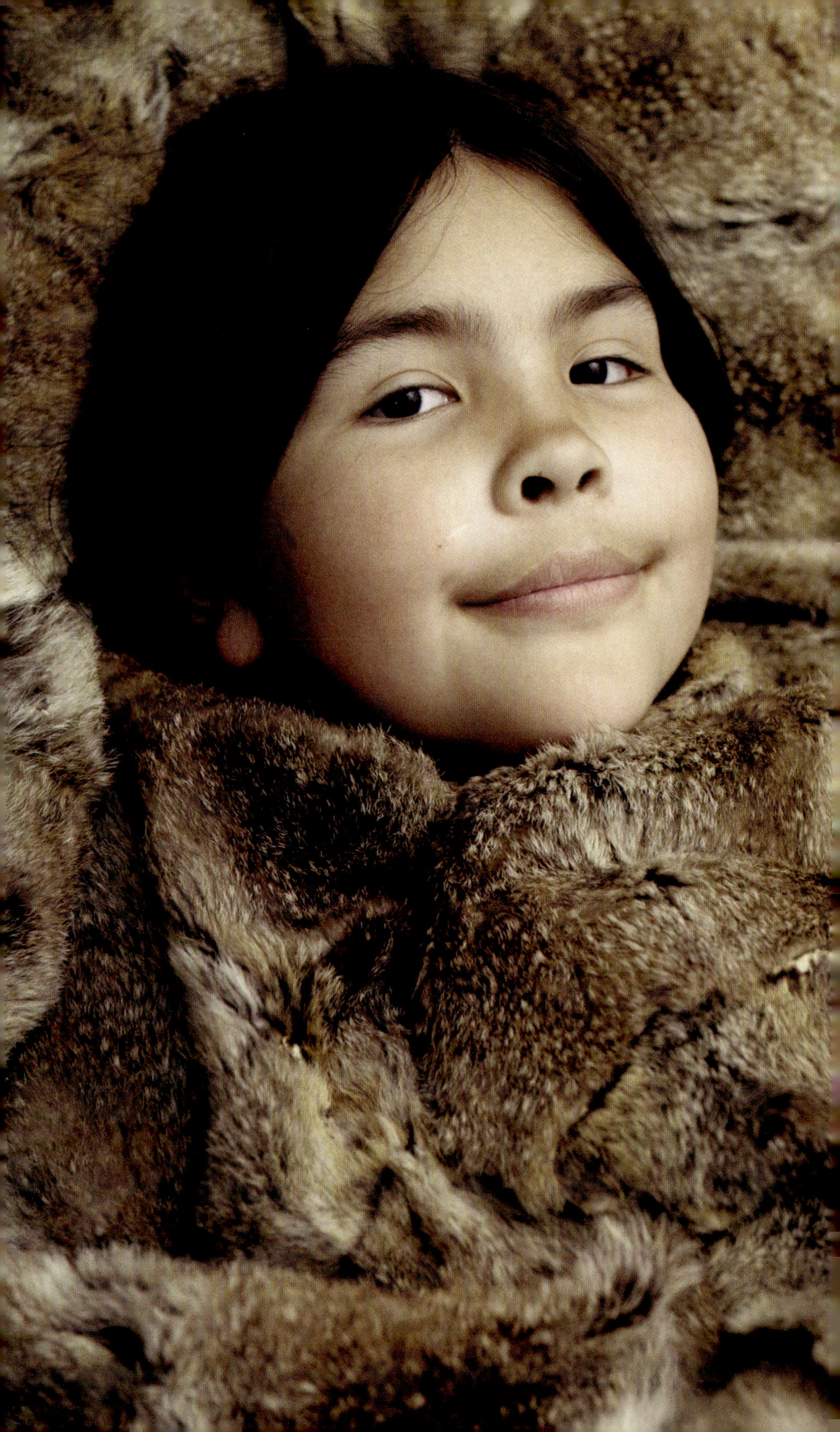

In the Studio with Sam Abell

I hold in high regard a select group of photographers. It would be easy to identify a number of them here; however, in all likelihood I would forget someone I hold dear in my heart—a true oversight, of course—and my friend would be miffed at me. So I won't do that, and instead I'll share a surreal moment with a legendary outdoor photographer, Sam Abell. I will also share that I asked Sam for permission to recount this story and the images, and Sam obliged my request. Sam is, in my humble estimation, a living legend. He has traveled the world for National Geographic and seen it all. The one thing he's never really done was work in a studio. You know, safe setup with lights and a seamless background. As Sam said, it wasn't a disdain for the environment, it's just that he had never done it.

Such was the scenario when Sam knocked on my door one spring night when we were both holed up in a hotel in Warwick, Rhode Island. Sam was there to give a keynote Friday night to the National Press Photographers Association's Northern Short Course, and I had lectured for two days to the attendees. One of the annual events I throw at the NSC has been a party Thursday and Friday nights, and this year I had decided to bring a "photo booth" setup to my party. It includes a 9-foot white seamless, a stationary camera, two umbrellas with flashes, a computer to preview the images, and two printers to print out as many 5×7 prints as we could do until the beer ran out.

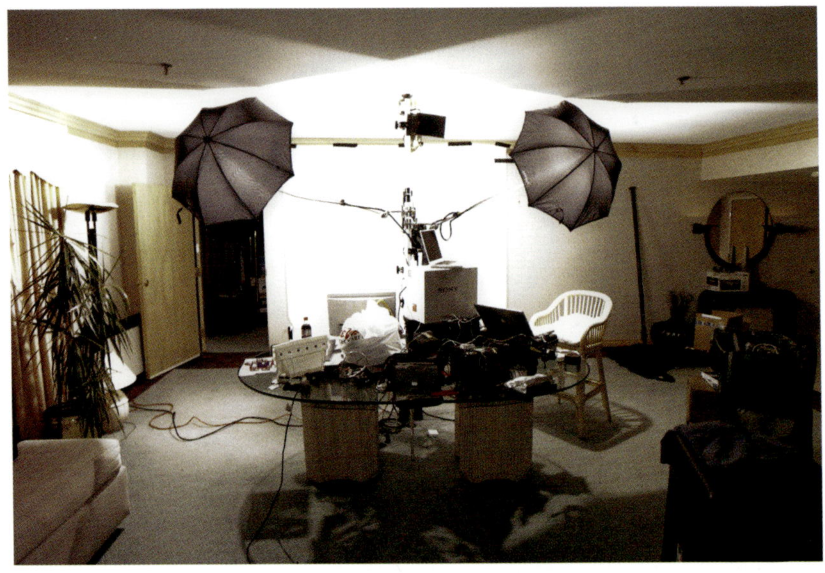

The ad hoc studio setup after the suite was rearranged and lighting fixtures were temporarily removed prior to the Suite Life Party during the 2007 Northern Short Course in Warwick, Rhode Island.

Sam stood in the doorway next to a friend of mine, Bonnie, saying he had heard I was throwing a party. I welcomed him in as humbly as I could, and Sam watched as the photo booth was in full swing. When you get a room full of 50 to 100 photographers with a white seamless and a printer, you get all manner of crazy ideas that make their way onto 5×7s. I encouraged Sam a few times, hoping to glimpse the master at work and out of his element.

After a brief period of observation, Sam decided to jump in. At first he stood in for a few photographs, and many people (including yours truly) quickly wanted their photo made with Sam. He was, of course, gracious to all who asked. As the prints began coming out of the printer, Sam decided he wanted to do something a bit more fun, so, with friend and colleague Jamie Rose, he suggested a play on the painting *American Gothic*, with a light stand filling in for the errant pitchfork.

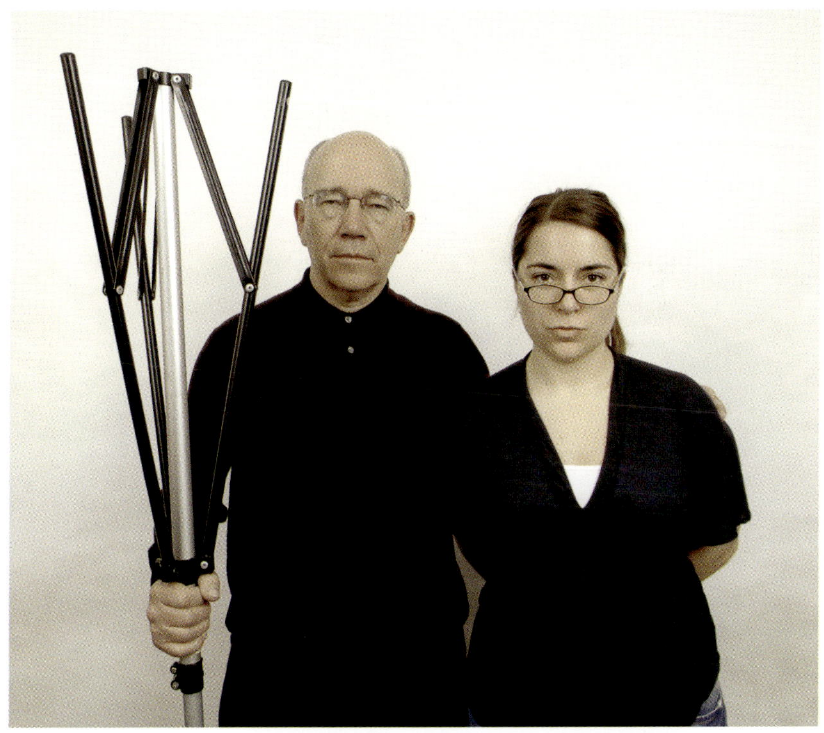

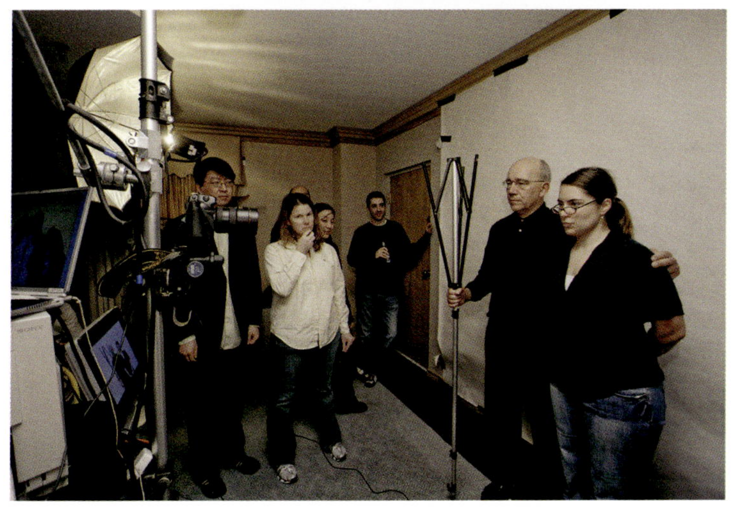

With this and the resulting print, Sam began to get into it, and he had this idea he called "the assaulto." Essentially, he would ask any long-haired person (man or woman) to stand with his or her back to the camera as Sam pretended to grab them from behind. the person would fling his or her head around in mock shock (and thus the benefit of long hair, for effect). After a few tries, Sam got a handle on it, and many people were game to be Sam's subject. Time and time again, Sam nailed it, with great looks on the faces of the subjects, and I stood in awe of his ability to quickly adapt to an environment he hadn't been in before.

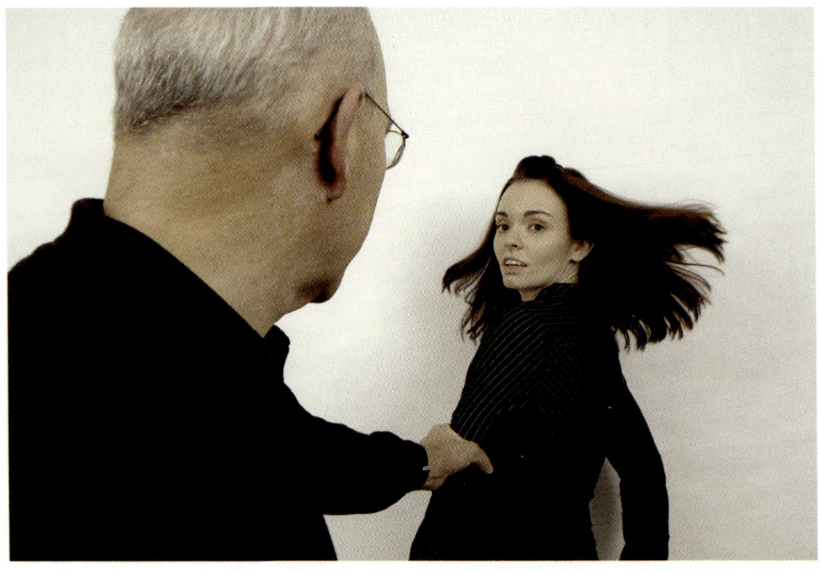

Sam Abell works on his "assaulto" idea in the ad hoc studio with Bonnie Biess.

Perhaps this story isn't of significant appreciation by the non-photographer reader; however, as the photographer-writer of this book, it was a surreal experience that, for me, was on the edge of reality.

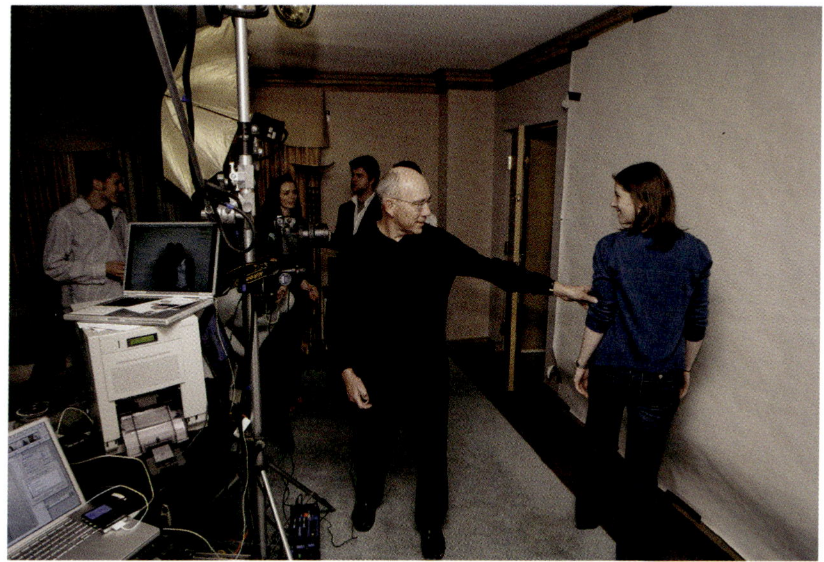

Sam Abell works on his "assaulto" idea in the ad hoc studio with Lauren Sandkuhler.

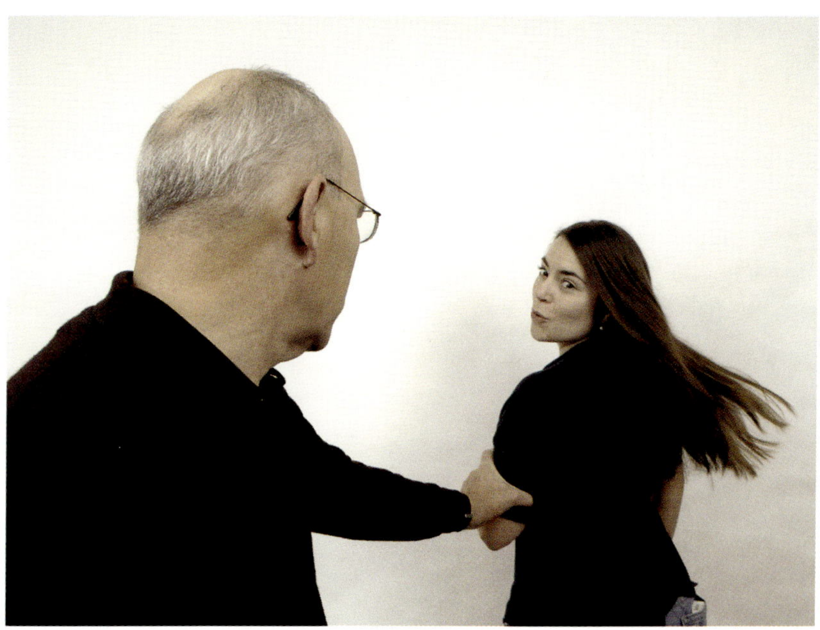

Sam Abell works on his "assaulto" idea in the ad hoc studio with Jamie Rose.

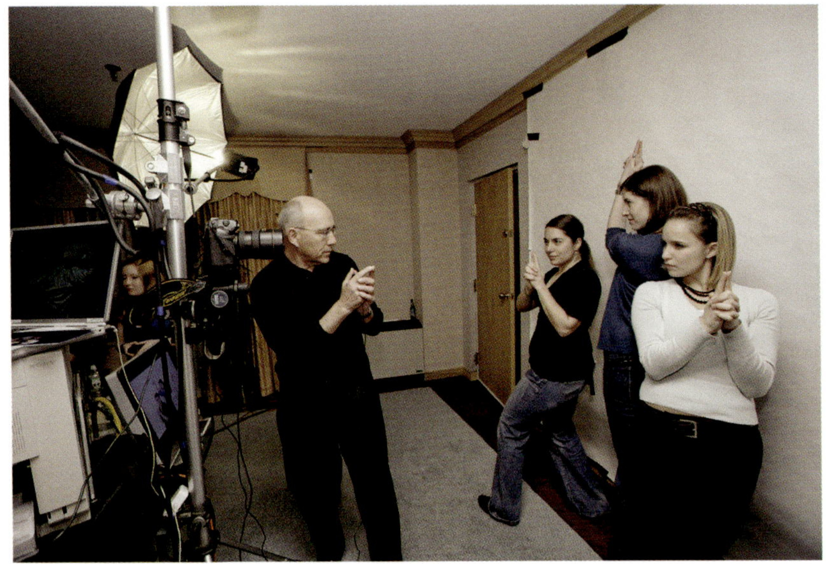

Sam Abell works on another idea, in homage to *Charlie's Angels*, in the ad hoc studio with Jamie Rose, Lauren Sandkuhler, and Katie Persons.

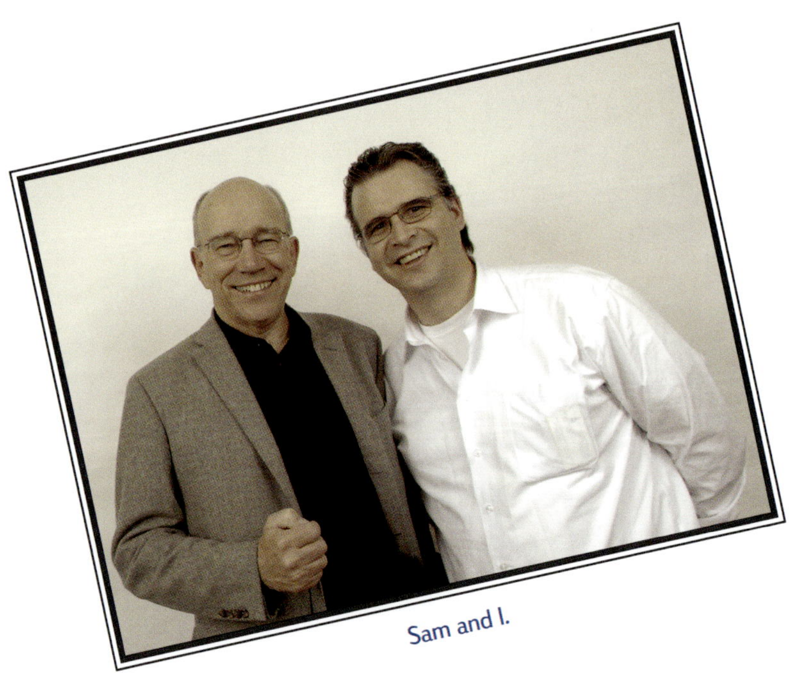

Sam and I.

Aretha Lets Loose

One thing I always strive to do is to ensure that the client holds whatever skills and talent I bring to bear with respect. Such was the case when I was called upon to photograph Aretha Franklin being honored by BET with their Walk of Fame Award.

During the preshow rehearsals, I encountered three or four photographers right in front of the stage, believing that they were going to be able to stay there during the show. Having done previous Walk of Fame events with Stevie Wonder and Patti LaBelle, I knew this was not going to be the case. I asked them who they were with, and each of them said, with a bit of bravado in their voice, that they were there for BET. Because I had been tasked with bringing in and leading the team of three photographers, which included a press-room photographer and a back-of-the-house long-lens photographer with me roaming the edges of the audience and backstage, this came as a surprise to me.

There was no need to debate the matter with any of them, but I did want to get to the bottom of it. So I went back to my contact and inquired about their status.

At this point I learned about—and was at the same time frustrated by the mindset of—these other photographers. My contact indicated to me that these photographers had contacted him and offered to shoot for free in exchange for a credential. Then he said, "I might get a few usable shots out of them, but I know everything I get from your team will be great."

Mind you, these weren't young college students or "newbies" with a camera; they were, in fact, photographers I had seen around town for years. Each of them had a press credential around his neck, as compared to the all-access pass needed to do this assignment justice. None of them came with the proper equipment, and when they were moved to the sides of the studio, all of them were under-lensed and were grumbling about how they were being treated.

You teach somebody how you want to be treated by how you present yourself, and they had presented themselves essentially as worthless as they offered their services and rights to their images for free. In the end, it didn't come as a surprise to me that they would do this, because much to my dismay, throughout the program these photographers acted more like audience members and fans than they did working professionals. They were hooting and hollering and applauding along with the audience, and anytime I've experienced that in a press area or by credentialed members of the press, I've taken great umbrage and shaken my head.

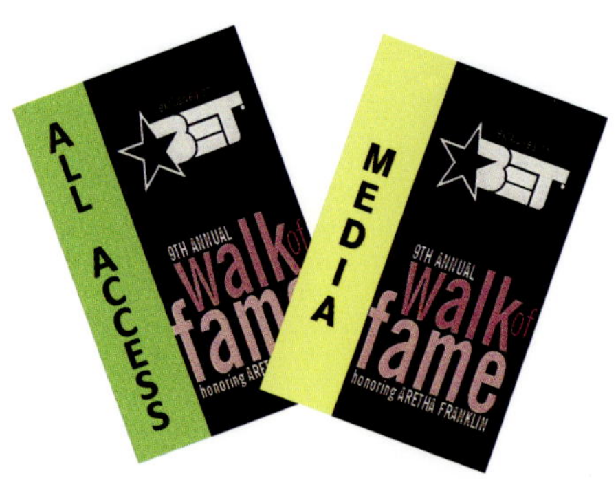

A word to the wise: A photographer's reputation can be tainted by inappropriate actions, especially when done in front of a crowd of potential A-list clients, so always be aware of your actions.

Having had the experience of doing this assignment previously, I was able to further refine my images this year. Clearly, we had done a good enough job to be asked back, but it is always our goal to deliver above and beyond what is expected and to always attempt to improve on what we've done previously. This assignment was no exception.

Having worked in the television studio and awards show environments before, certain things were a given: Dress in dark attire to minimize your being a visual distraction, and dress appropriately to the environment you're in. Also, with BET spending tens of thousands of dollars lighting everything perfectly, an on-camera strobe would not only take away from that lighting, but it would also be a huge no-no in a television studio environment. In addition, paying attention to the line of sight of onstage talent reading TelePrompTers and staying out of that line of sight makes you as invisible as possible to them. Knowing where the cameras are placed and which cameras are most likely to be used allows you to know the parameters within which you can move—and more importantly, when not to move.

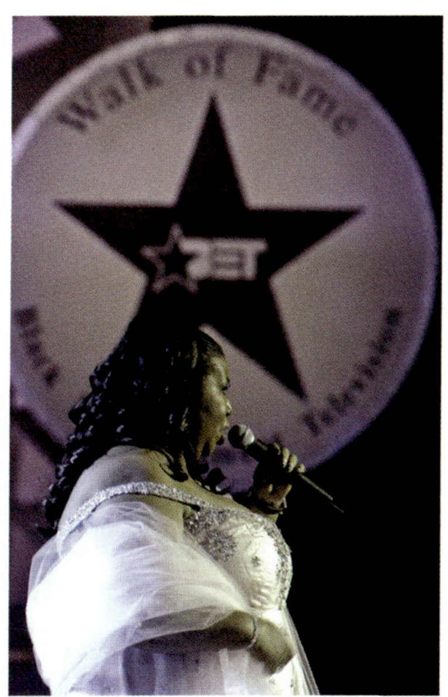

Aretha on stage with her wig on before she let loose.

In an ideal world, when you have a close relationship with the producers or director, you can get a headset that will allow you to know exactly which camera is being used and whether they are wide or tight, and thus what the probability is that you could be a visual distraction to a broadcast image. Further, when you're wearing a headset, it acts as just one more enhancement to your credential. However, such was not the case for this assignment.

As I contemplated which angles would be best for this assignment, I knew that one of the angles required me to be right in the front row, crouched in the aisle next to the last seat on the far right. The program consisted of a number of A-level artists performing the honoree's songs, the presentation of the award, and the artist herself performing a selection of her greatest hits. I obviously wanted to be down low, shooting up onto the stage to illustrate the greatness of the artist performing. Combined with the fact that I had to make my 6′ 7″ frame as small as possible, crouching at the front row was my best choice. I knew I wouldn't need anything longer than a 200mm lens and that I likely wouldn't need anything wider than a 20mm lens. Also, knowing that the long-lens work was covered by my photographer at the back of the house gave me comfort; this was part of the coverage plan that I conveyed to the client as important for the whole show.

As I moved about the studio, working very hard to minimize my obstruction of the views of the audience members, I knew that the point when I wanted to be down in front was right before Aretha went on stage. I needed to do this to get an unobstructed view of Aretha when she received her award, because I expected that the audience would give her a standing ovation. I also wanted to be there for her performance. I didn't know at the time how critically important this choice of position would become. I won't say that it was just luck, because I'm a firm believer in the adage, "Luck is what happens when preparation meets opportunity."

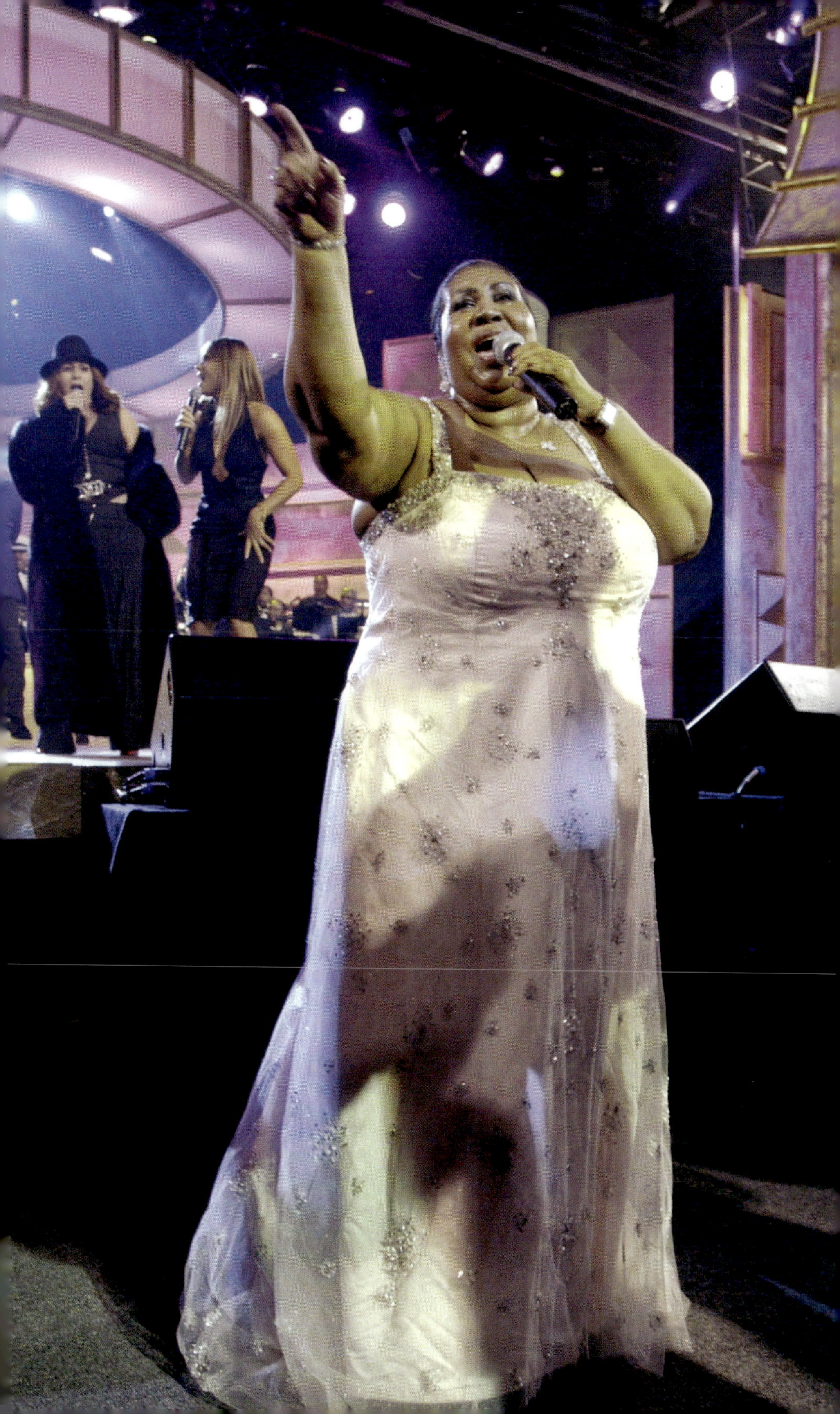

Atop the Golden Gate Bridge

It was 1988, and I was planning to head home from college for the summer. During my previous semester in college, one of my professors had introduced me to the photo editor at a magazine called *The World & I*. This was a small-circulation publication that was undeniably the largest monthly publication in the world, with 702 pages a month being printed. I had been hounding my professor for the entire school year to introduce me to the photo editor, and he finally did. I showed him my pitiful portfolio, and for some inexplicable reason, he suggested I come up with several story ideas—which I did, with great hopes of getting a story published. I proposed five ideas—one of which was about the painters of the Golden Gate Bridge.

With encouragement from the editor, I began writing letters. I contacted the Golden Gate Bridge Authority and told them of my plan. I intended to follow the daily lives of two of the painters, one an African-American woman and the other an Eastern European man. Both were well-respected painters and had been working on the bridge for some time. While researching for the story, I learned that the bridge is painted non-stop, with multiple crews working on it at all times. Bascially, that means when they get to the end, they return to paint the entire 4,200-foot bridge all over again!

I was excited to learn that my request to do the story had been approved, and we settled on a week of time I would spend with the both of them combined—a few days with each. As I worked on the piece, I spent time in their homes, getting ready for the day, going to the bank, and so on. I took copious notes and wrote what I thought would be an insightful piece on how both of these painters lived their lives and how they both contributed to the upkeep of an American icon.

Obviously, one of the things I would have to do is go with them as they worked, which meant—yes, wait for it—climbing up the Golden Gate Bridge. Well, not exactly climbing. I thought I would have to, but fortunately for me, there is a very small elevator that will take you up to the top inside one of the towers. From the bottom, the top looks so narrow, but it's actually quite a wide space.

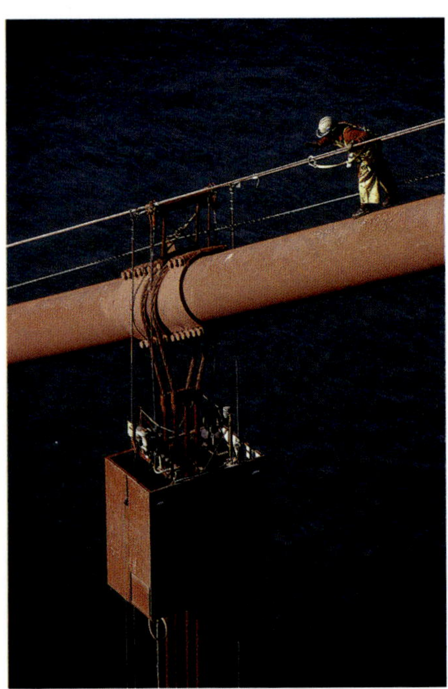

Looking down into one of the painters' booths from the ocean-side suspension cable.

We spent time discussing safety, and of course I had to wear a harness, lest I be flung by a gust of wind off into the ocean to my untimely death. Trust me when I tell you this: Looking over the edge of the bridge is a scary thing to do, and I'm not generally afraid of heights.

We went up the elevator in the tower closest to San Francisco, and when I looked toward Marin, the view was breathtaking. As you can see by the cover of this book, there was just the right number of clouds in the sky. I turned to focus on the painter I was following as she was climbing up and down the thick suspension cables that supported the bridge span.

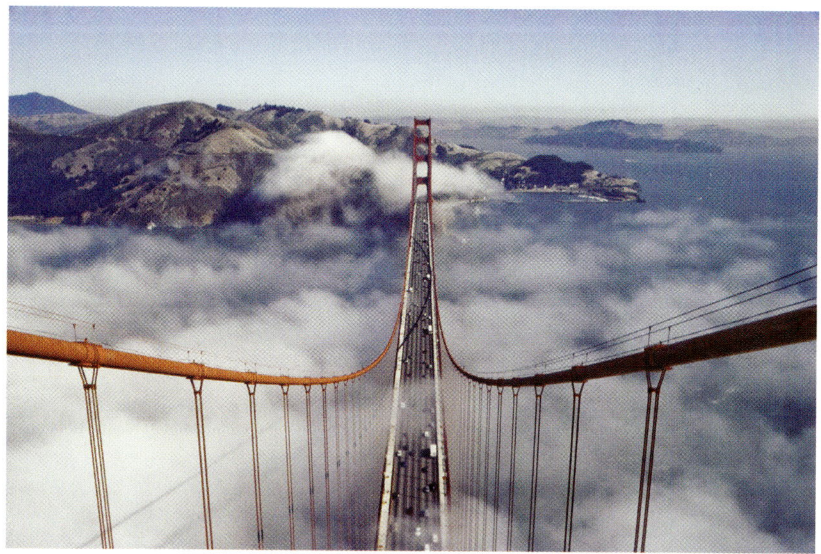

The view from the San Francisco tower looking toward Marin as the clouds begin to roll in.

A few moments later, when I turned back to look toward Marin again, the bridge was completely socked in with clouds, and we were so high up that we were above the clouds. I climbed into the crow's nest on the ocean side of the bridge so that I could shoot directly across at the painter enjoying a serene, peaceful moment in the crow's nest on the bay side of the bridge, with Alcatraz seeming to float in the clouds in the distance. She then went back out onto the cables on the bay side of the bridge, which, from my

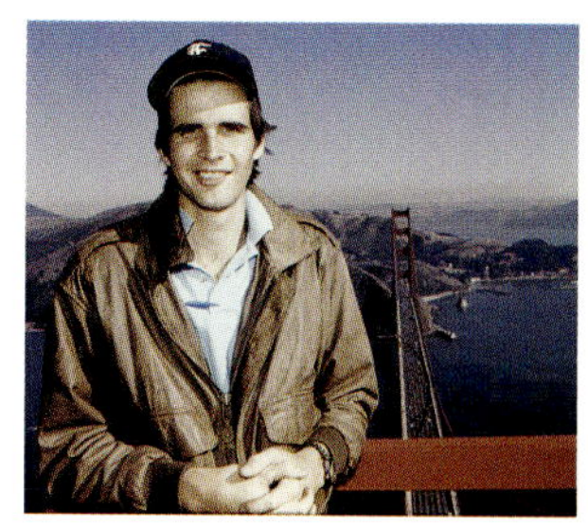

In the crow's nest atop the San Francisco tower.

vantage point at the top looking down, seemed to vanish into the quickly growing mass of fog that San Francisco is known for, enveloping the bridge. In short order, our photo opportunities at the top of the bridge vanished, and we took the elevator back down to focus on her work with a paintbrush at the street-level places where there was a dire need for a fresh coat of paint.

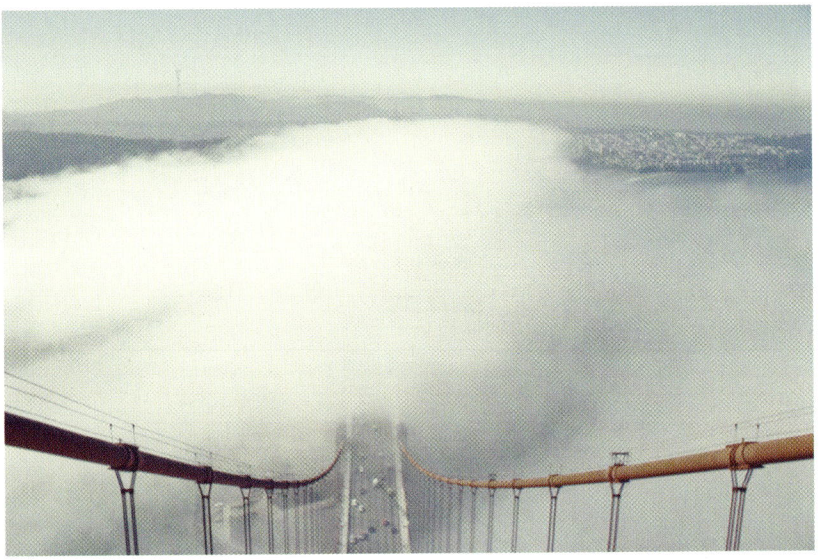

In just a short period of time, the fog rolled in, and the entire San Francisco tower was hidden by the fog, as seen from the Marin tower.

The following day I returned to the bridge and followed around the other painter. We spent most of our time on the sides and underneath the bridge, as that was his crew's location that day. Although I followed both of them home and on their errands around town, the best images I made were on that first day, and this self-assignment has always been one that I have held close to my heart as one of my favorites.

Opposite page: After the fog rolled in and the suspension cable faded into the mist, the painters remained hard at work, painting cabling.

Next spread: The bay-side crow's nest on the San Francisco tower is an excellent place to take a moment to reflect on life, as the island of Alcatraz sits off in the middle of the San Francisco Bay in the mist and fog.

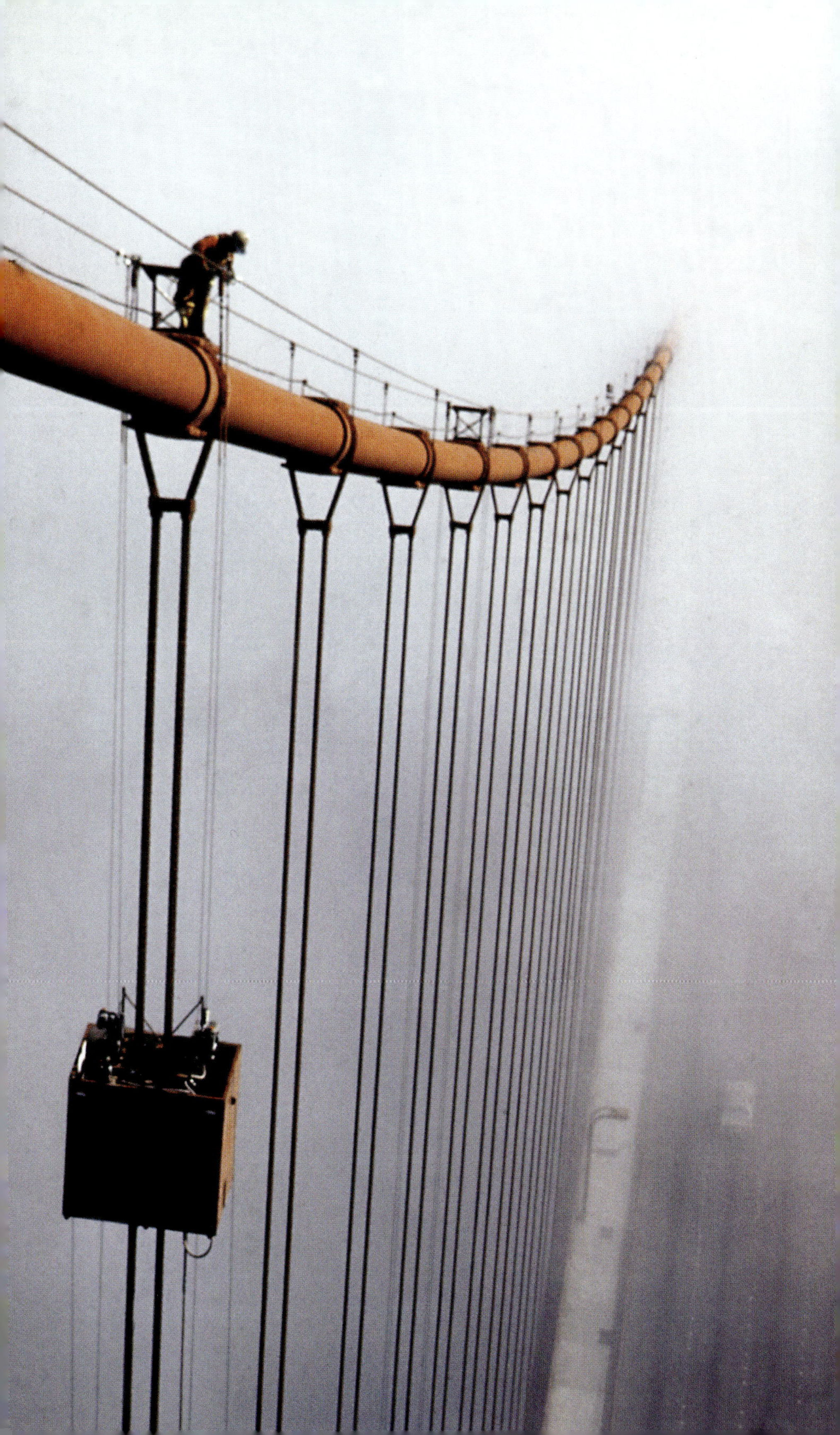

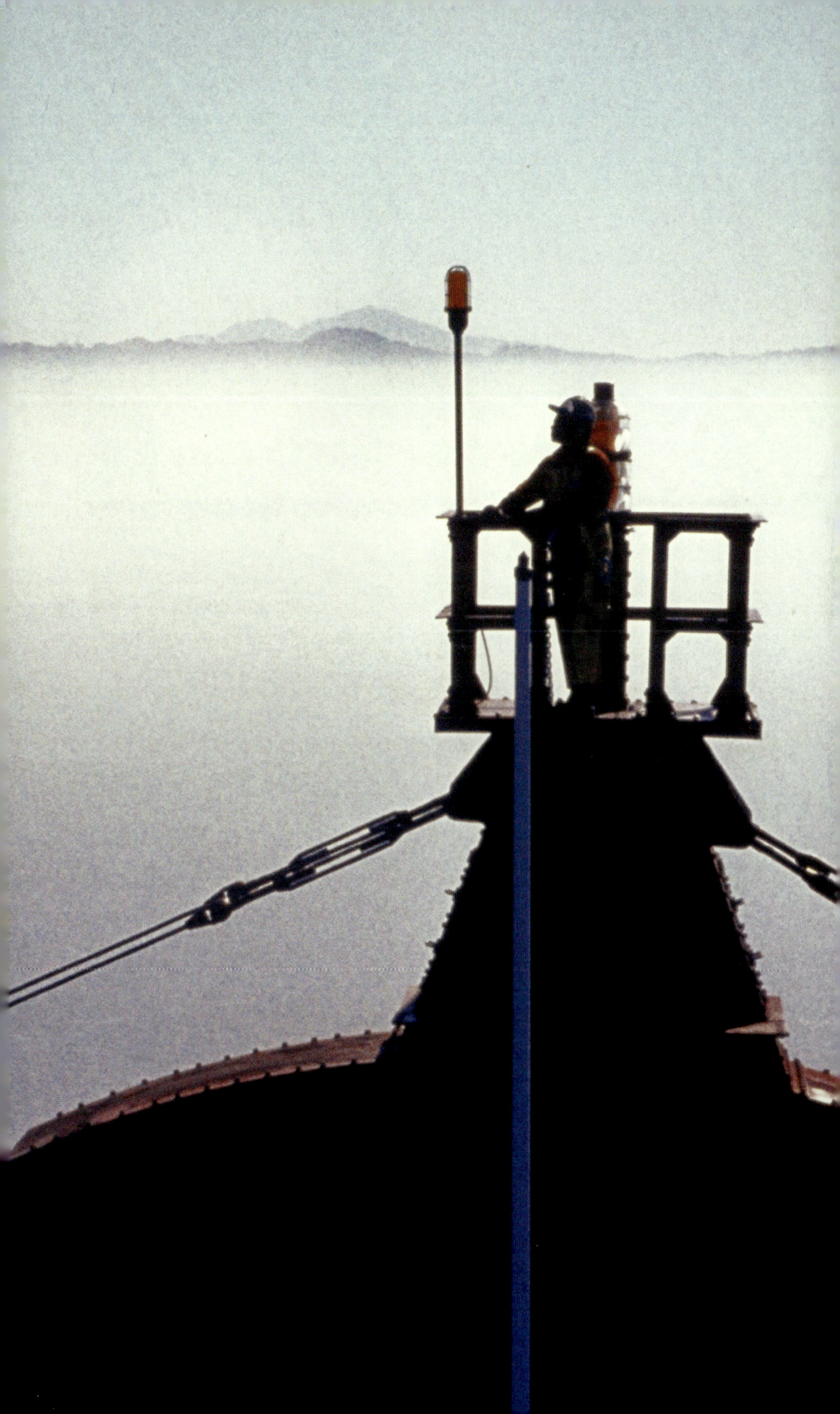

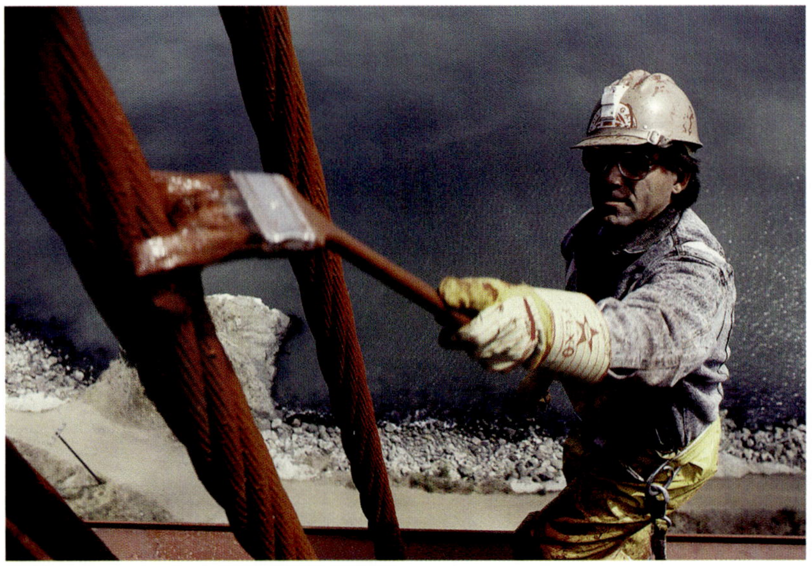

Leonid works on the lower side of the bridge, painting a cable.

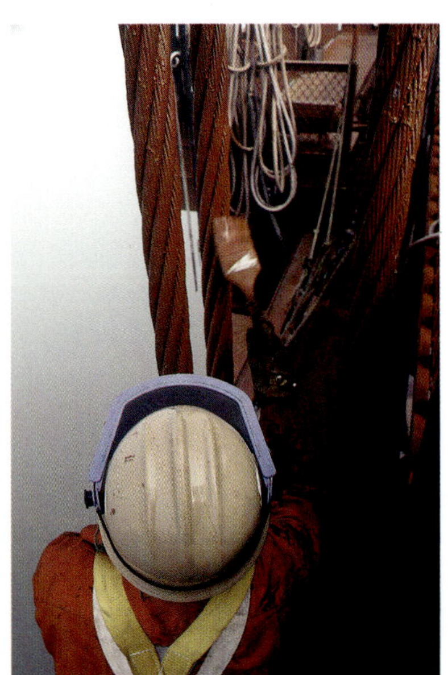

Another painter works on a cable.

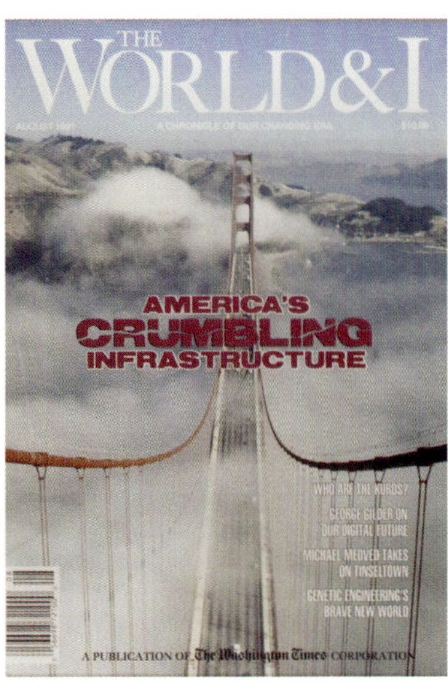

Several years after I shot the story, the magazine for which I was on staff licensed the image as stock for the cover.

John Lewis: Three Minutes or Less

On January 16, the phone rang. It was the art director for a publication group that was handling a regional publication. They wanted a portrait of a member of Congress—John Lewis. Lewis marched with Martin Luther King, Jr. in Selma, Alabama, and was a key (albeit young) figure in the infancy of the civil rights movement, so I was keen to photograph this very humble, yet awesome, man. The interview was scheduled for January 24, and the communications director also wanted the photography to take place that day.

I began a dialogue with the congressman's communications director about timing and logistics. She then proposed Thursday the 25th, and I agreed. Then she called back to say he would be out of town. No problem. How about the 24th? No, that wouldn't work, because it was the day after the State of the Union address, and he would be tired. No problem, how about the 26th? No, he would still be out of town. Then, she proposed 4:00 p.m. on the 24th, and I agreed and put it into my schedule.

About 30 minutes later, the phone rang, and it was the CD again. She indicated that the congressman was getting on a flight at 4:59 p.m., so the 4:00 slot wouldn't work after all. She proposed 10:00 a.m.—again, the morning after a long night on Capitol Hill. I agreed and shifted the schedule.

We then discussed location. I proposed the Cannon House Office Building terrace, right outside of the main door, but she had concerns about the cold. I suggested that it provides a great angle with nice dynamics, but I said I understood her concerns about the elements.

I then suggested the third-floor balcony of the Cannon House Office Building, and she liked that idea better. I called to try to schedule a window area to accomplish the photograph, as they are scheduled by the press gallery. I was told that CNN and Fox had both reserved the two window spaces for the entire morning, because they would be doing reactions to the speech the night before. And so I was, as they say, SOL.

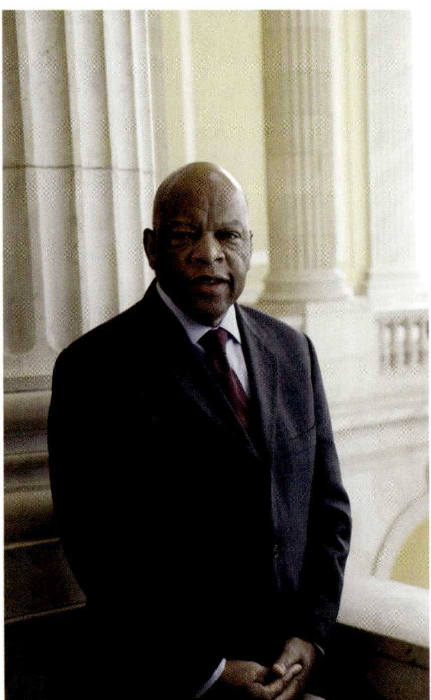

Portrait of Rep. John Lewis in the Canon House Office Building rotunda.

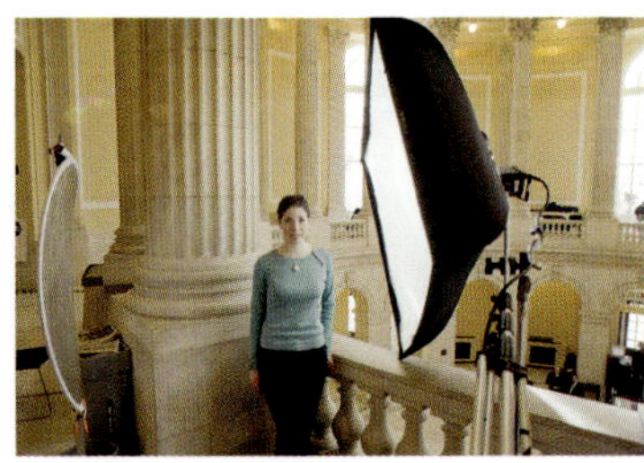

The lighting setup in the Canon House Office Building rotunda.

I then asked about the inside spaces between the columns, and I was told they're first come, first served. No problem—I'd take that, since there were alternative backup locations nearby if they ended up being full.

I called back, and the congressman's communications director then agreed that we could do the outside shot, weather permitting, and that the inside location would be our backup location.

We arrived at 9:15 a.m. to set up for what we believed would be a 10:00 a.m. shot. The communications director indicated that the congressman would be in between meetings, and that they would only have enough time for one location. When I indicated that we'd be finished with him in 5 or 10 minutes, maximum, she was nervous, suggesting that much time was not available. We set up both the inside and the outside locations so we'd be ready.

The inside location was lit with just one light, and the outside location also had a single light in a big softbox. I put a Full CTO gel into the softbox and set the camera to the tungsten setting so that all the ambient light from the sky would go blue. I very much like this look and feel, and it was the right first choice for what I was going for.

At 10:02, we learned that one of the House committees had scheduled a meeting for 10:00 a.m., and the earliest the congressman would be available was 11:00 a.m.

At 11:00 a.m., we learned that it would be at least another 30 minutes. At 11:45 a.m., the congressman arrived at the inside (secondary) location. I had chosen to wait for him inside, since at that moment I was in a secure area, having already been screened by security. My assistant, who helped set up, had been outside for two hours with the equipment, in a non-secure area. All the lighting had been tested and pre-set (of course), and I made the first image at 11:45:09.

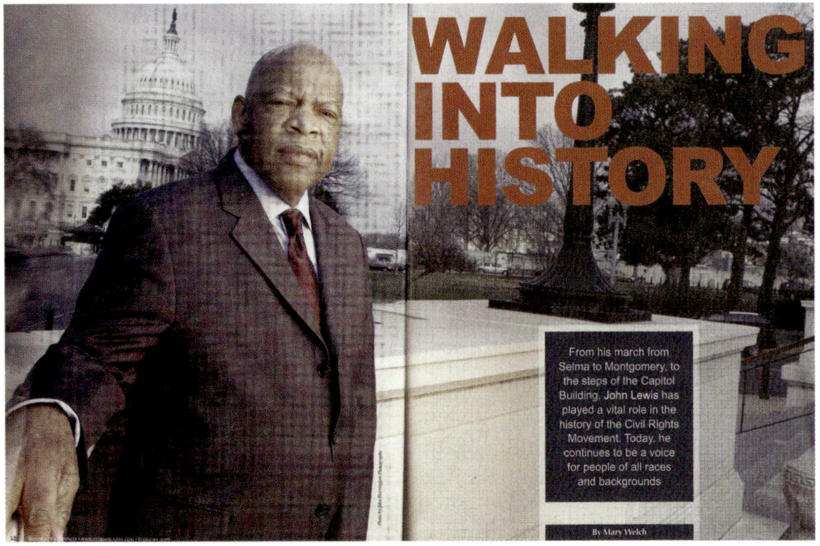

The opening spread of the magazine.

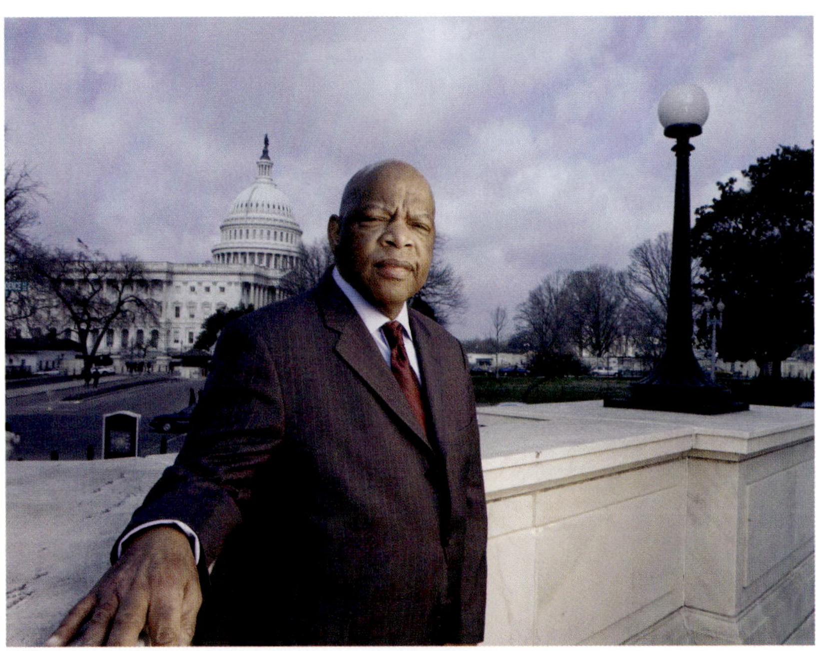

Portrait of Rep. John Lewis on the Canon House Office Building terrace.

Opposite page: Portrait of Rep. John Lewis on the Canon House Office Building terrace, shot for the cover.

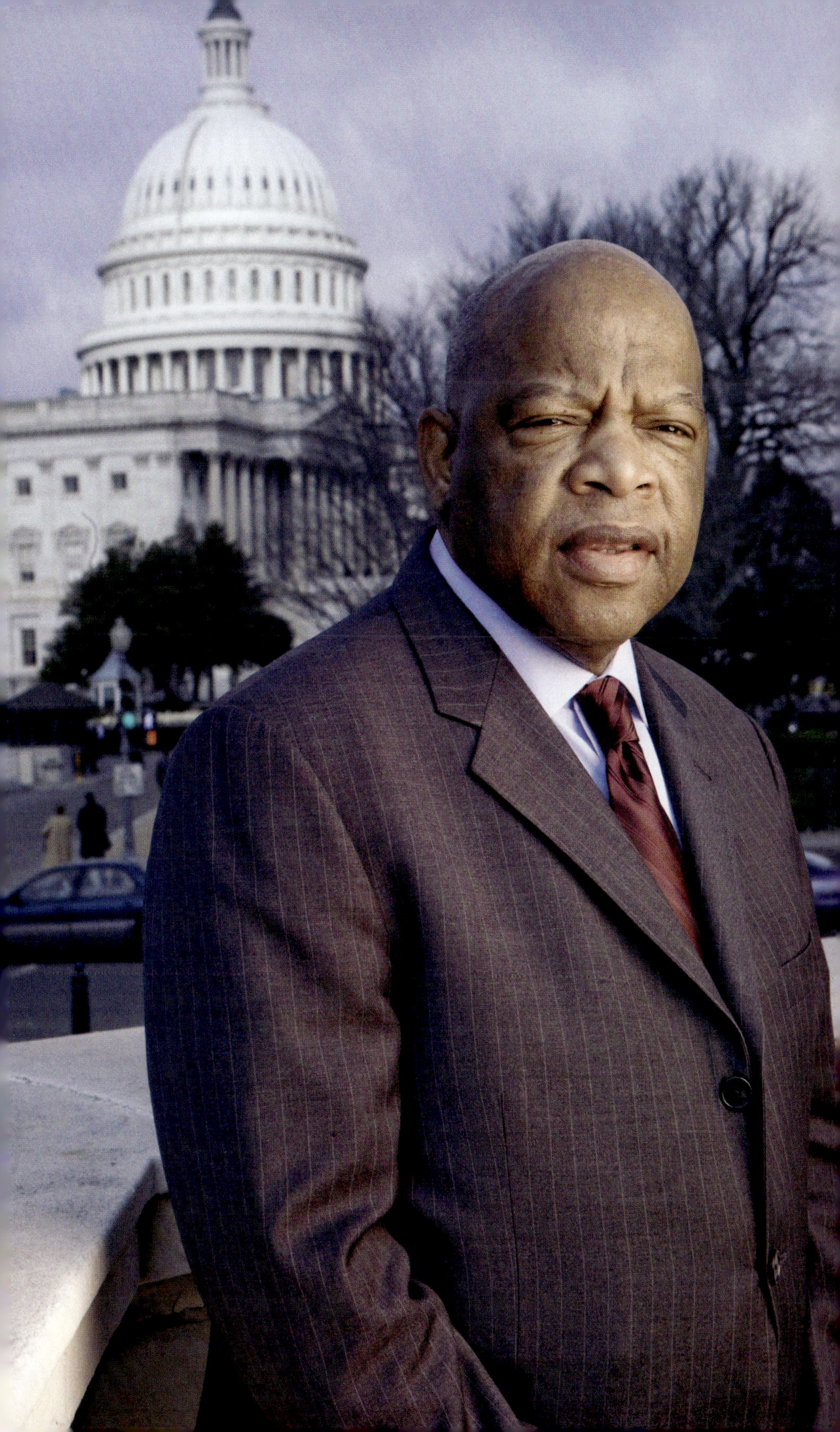

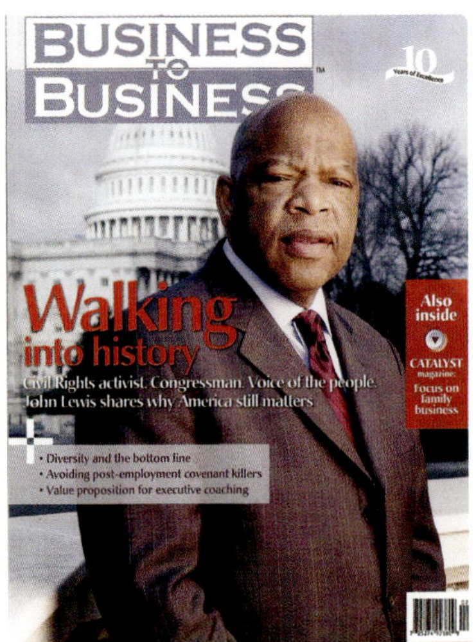

The shot used on the cover of *Business to Business* magazine

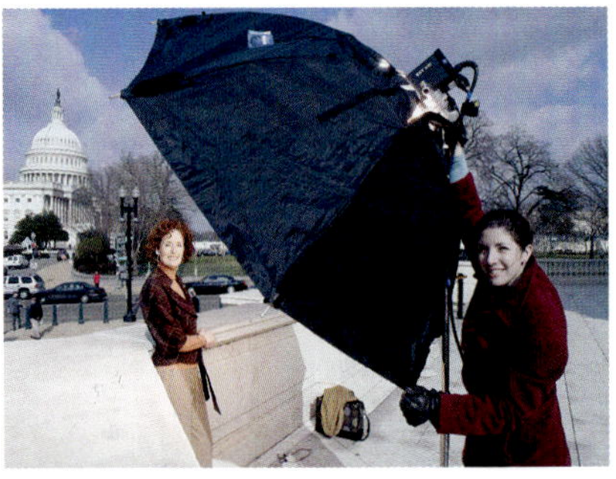

The lighting setup on the Canon House Office Building terrace.

After two dozen images, both vertical and horizontal, I said to the congressman, “We’ve got the second setup right outside the door, where my assistant is already waiting with the lights set up.” We walked downstairs and out the door, through security. Because we were leaving there was no delay; however, if we had started outside, I would’ve had to pass through the metal detectors, and my camera would’ve had to go through the X-ray machine. The congressman wouldn’t have had to wait if there was a line, whereas I would have. Tactically, it was best to go the other direction.

We got outside, and the light was different from how it was two hours earlier. It was sunnier, so I made a quick adjustment to the light power and made a test frame. Then I continued shooting outside. After about 30 seconds I asked the congressman how he was doing comfort-wise, because there were a few intermittent snowflakes falling. He said he was fine. After about another dozen frames, I stopped and said, “We’re done, sir. Thank you for your time.” And he was off to his next meeting, just three minutes after we started. Whew!

Pomp and Circumstance at the White House

It is said that history repeats itself, and thus, if you've been around long enough, you have an opportunity to witness it first hand. In May of 1991, Queen Elizabeth visited the White House on an official state visit and was received by President George H. W. Bush. In 2007, she came to the United States again, this time visiting with President George W. Bush. Both times she visited, she was received on the South Lawn of the White House, as are all heads of state.

In preparation for the queen's visit the first time, she held a reception for the U.S. press corps covering her visit, and I had the high honor of being invited. There were strict rules—this was an off-the-record reception, and there were absolutely no cameras allowed. At the ripe old age of 23, even I knew better than to disobey a monarch, and so I left my trusty cameras at home.

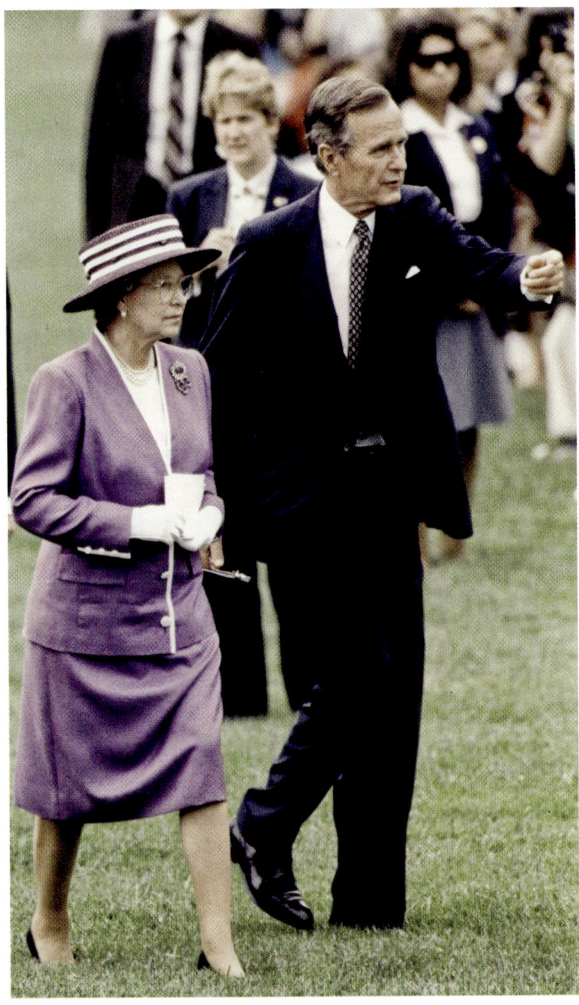

President George H.W. Bush and Queen Elizabeth II during her formal arrival ceremony on the South Lawn of the White House in 1991.

We queued up to enter the reception and were told that the queen would arrive shortly and that we should get into a receiving line. Admonitions were made not to touch the queen and to wait for her hand to be extended before extending your own, along with instructions not to be chatty and to move along. We were told that the queen would likely chat with reporters afterwards, and also that her husband, the Duke of Edinburgh, would be there as well.

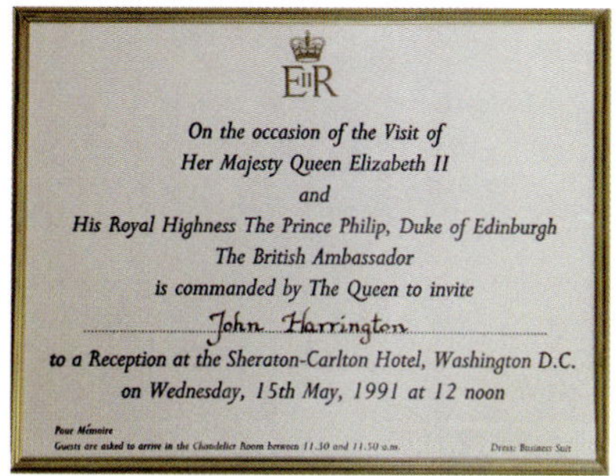
EIIR

On the occasion of the Visit of
Her Majesty Queen Elizabeth II
and
His Royal Highness The Prince Philip, Duke of Edinburgh
The British Ambassador
is commanded by The Queen to invite
John Harrington
to a Reception at the Sheraton-Carlton Hotel, Washington D.C.
on Wednesday, 15th May, 1991 at 12 noon

Pour Mémoire
Guests are asked to arrive in the Chandelier Room between 11.30 and 11.50 a.m.
Dress: Business Suit

The invitation I received from the British Ambassador on behalf of Queen Elizabeth for a press reception in 1991.

I got in line, and right behind me was the Gamma Liaison photographer. Unfortunately for me, he had ignored the admonition on cameras and had brought his in, thinking he could get a photograph of the queen. With him being about 10 years older than me, I didn't question him beyond saying, "Hey, they said we couldn't bring cameras in," to which he said something like, "It'll be fine." I should've known better.

I was nervous, as I think anyone would be when meeting the queen for the first time, and so I practiced my line: "Thank you for your hospitality, and I look forward to covering your visit." When I was about five or six people away from being received, the Gamma photographer asked me to take his photo. "Take my camera and just turn and shoot a frame of me after you are done. It's pre-focused and everything." I should've trusted my gut instinct to say no, but instead I said I would try, and so I shouldered his camera.

As it became my turn, I shook the queen's hand and delivered my remark, and she thanked me as graciously as you would expect a queen to do. Then I shook the duke's hand. At the end of the line, I turned to shoot a frame, and the duke turned and looked at me with a look of what can only be described as fear (although it wasn't) on his face. He then began a head-shaking admonition and verbalization of "No, no...." Two aides from the British Embassy came to me and started in on me, and my only response was "It's not my camera; it's his. He asked me to take the photo."

It was these facts that saved me from lasting embarrassment, although to this day I still cringe as I think of being duped by the Gamma photographer that day. I didn't see him for the rest of the reception, and I can't say whether or not he was ejected, but I did stay. I had no one to talk to—who'd want to talk to some young 23-year-old at something like this?—so I enjoyed the food. I still remember the rack of lamb that was one of the many passed hors d'oeuvres as being the finest I have ever tasted. I watched the queen as she made her way around the small, yet crowded room. She never did make it too close to me, which was just fine, but I had prepared two additional remarks just in case. The first was "Please don't send me to the Tower," and the second was, "You're looking especially regal this evening, your Majesty." (Actually, these were things I should have said—20 years later, I can't recall exactly what my two prepared remarks were.)

Coverage of her first visit went just fine—except for what was humorously referred to in diplomatic and journalistic circles as "the talking hat," because the president's podium was so tall that when the queen spoke, only her hat was visible above the microphone. It served to underscore the critical need to ensure that details such as speaker-versus-podium height are checked. This was somebody else's snafu and not mine, thank God.

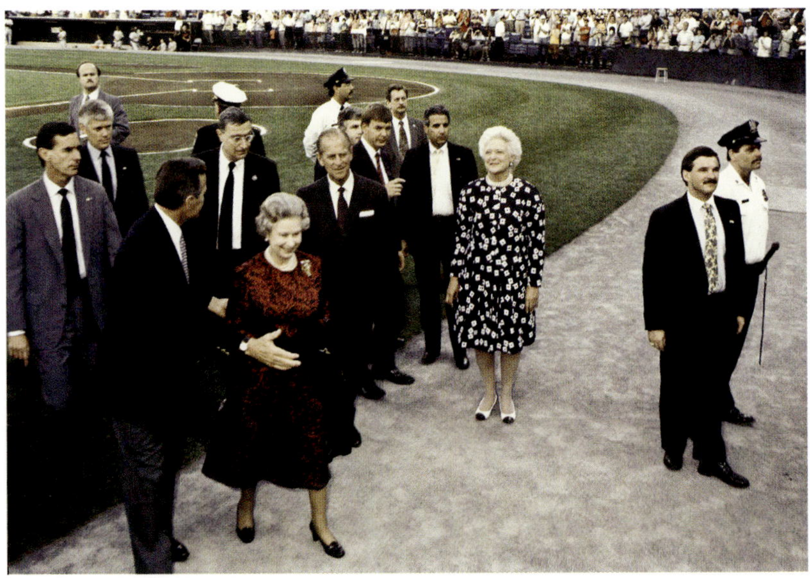

President George H.W. Bush and Queen Elizabeth II on the field at a Baltimore Orioles baseball game, at the conclusion of ceremonies honoring her attendance.

I covered the queen throughout her outings in the DC area, including a baseball game in Baltimore and a play at the Folger Shakespeare Library, where she sat onstage with the actors during the performance, as would have been done by the monarchy in Shakespeare's time. Afterwards, she greeted the actors and then was off to the Library of Congress to look at rare books and other items.

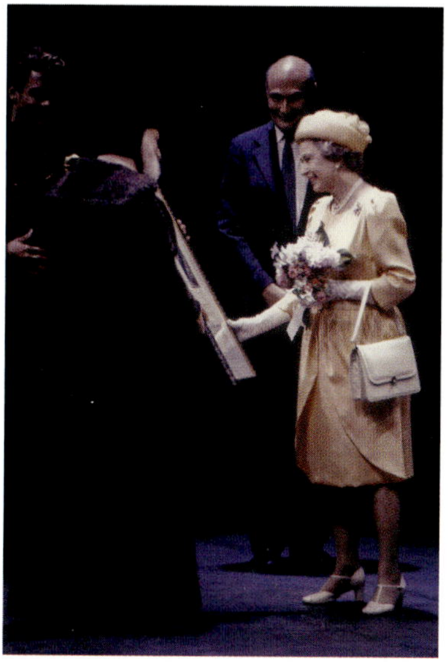

Queen Elizabeth II receives a gift after watching a play at the Folger Shakespeare Library.

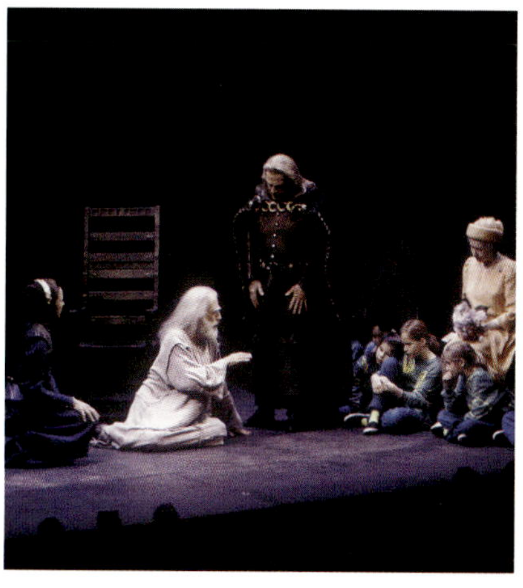

Queen Elizabeth II watches a performance of a play at the Folger Shakespeare Theater.

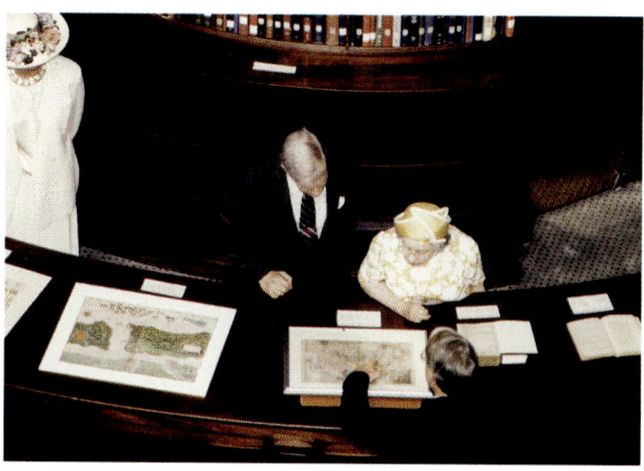

Queen Elizabeth II in the main reading room of the Library of Congress with James Billington.

Many years later, when she returned to visit George W. Bush, there were no podium errors. And this visit was more poignant, as I had matured and had more faith in my own decision-making abilities and was more confident in the protocols of the monarchy —what to do and what not to do. We were all ushered onto the South Lawn for the official arrival ceremony, and although the queen did not have a reception this time, and other assignments had me elsewhere during the other part of her visit, being there some 15+ years later was, in a way, a closing of the circle for me.

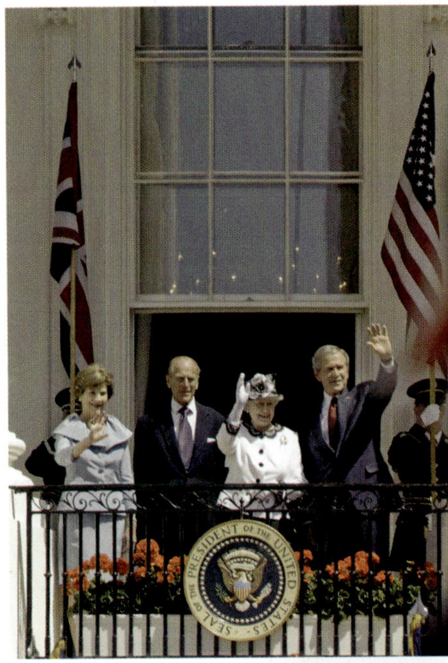

President and Mrs. Bush and Queen Elizabeth and HRH Prince Philip, Duke of Edinburgh, on the balcony of the South Portico following their official arrival ceremony for a state visit.

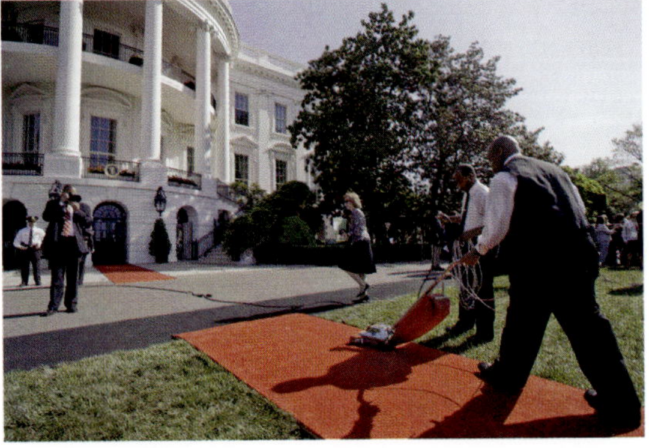

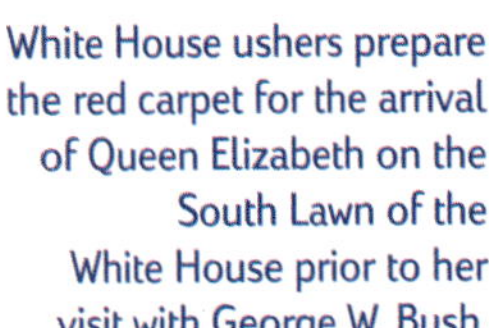

White House ushers prepare the red carpet for the arrival of Queen Elizabeth on the South Lawn of the White House prior to her visit with George W. Bush.

Air to Air over a Frigid Washington

From time to time unexpected assignments fall into your lap. The key during those opportunities is not only to be prepared for the unexpected, but also to stand your ground when it comes to a request for rights to the photographs that is not commensurate with the type of work being requested and/or the fees being paid. Such was the case with a defense contractor vying for a prestigious (and lucrative) government contract to provide helicopters to the military. These particular helicopters were to be a part of the fleet tasked with transporting the president, the rest of the executive branch, and top generals needing to travel in style, so it could not have been a more high-profile project.

I came to be involved in the project as much more of a public relations–type photography assignment. At the last minute, the client called because they had two helicopters that were of the make and model that would be used for the presidential fleet at a nearby regional airport in Virginia. When we sent over our contract, it included our standard public relations package of rights and standard duration. Our prospective client called following their review of the contract and expressed their concern about the scope of the rights package, telling us that they always "just get all rights," and could we change that?

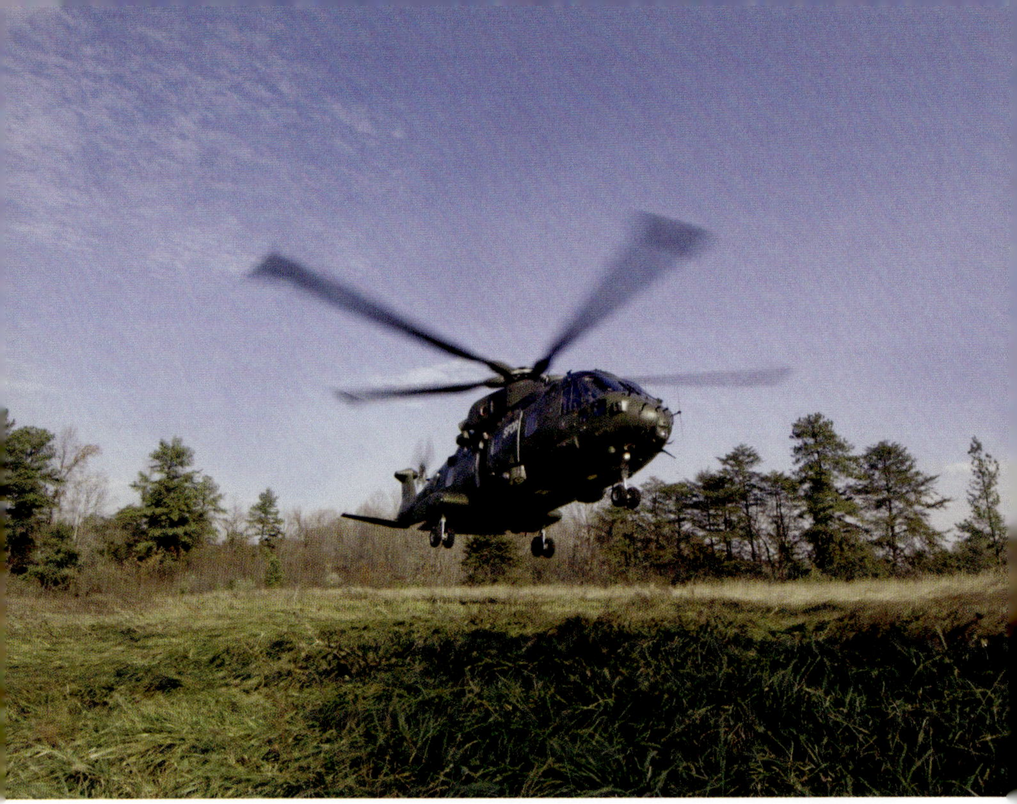

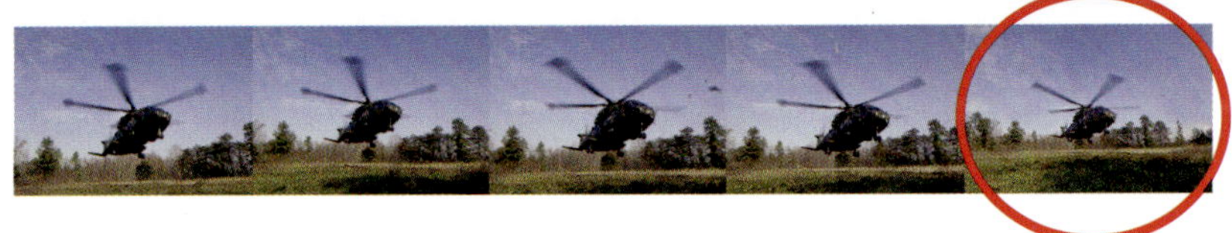

I politely responded that the fees outlined were commensurate with PR-type assignments, that conveying the broad scope of rights without an appropriate fee was not something we would do, and that from the description of the assignment, it didn't sound as if they needed anything beyond a PR package of rights. In the end, nothing could have been farther from the truth, but that was likely an unintentional result of some great photo opportunities and the preparation to take advantage of them, coupled with some favors conveyed to the pilots and crew of the helicopter in the form of a few photographs of them doing heroic acts and otherwise looking in full command and control of the situation. Throughout the course of the day, I not only shared the images with the client so they were assured that we were capturing the images they wanted, but I also showed select images to the pilots of their helicopter of what can only be termed as various heart-stopping maneuvers.

These various maneuvers were actually air-to-air photography that I had not anticipated doing but that I had been prepared for nonetheless. Once we arrived to do a few grip-and-grins and pictures of people looking into the aircraft, it was suggested that we go up to do some photography while the helicopters were flying. Having done helicopter work before, I knew that if I wanted to move around, I would have to be securely harnessed in. I approached the flight crew and identified the crewman in charge of the rear cabin. I indicated to him that I needed to get a harness and be briefed on safety measures within his domain. I did not ask for permission per se—I merely conveyed to him my need, which was ultimately a representation of the client's need. If I instead had begun the conversation with, "Do you think it would be okay if I roamed around the cabin?" I likely would have been told no, and my freedom of movement was critical to capturing the images I needed.

Next, I asked, "What would be the best way to view the other helicopter?" knowing that in previous cabin configurations, sliding open a door on the side or removing an outward-swinging door would give me an unobstructed view of the other helicopter, with the limitation that the other helicopter had to be on that side, and the sun had to be to my back. This ensured that I did not have to shoot through non-optical glass or, what is often the case, scratched clear plastic.

The crewman, interested in helping resolve my request, suggested that we could fly with the aft door open, allowing for a full view of the helicopter behind us. This was a remarkable turn of events, but the crew and pilot were still not 100-percent on board with what I had hoped to accomplish (yet).

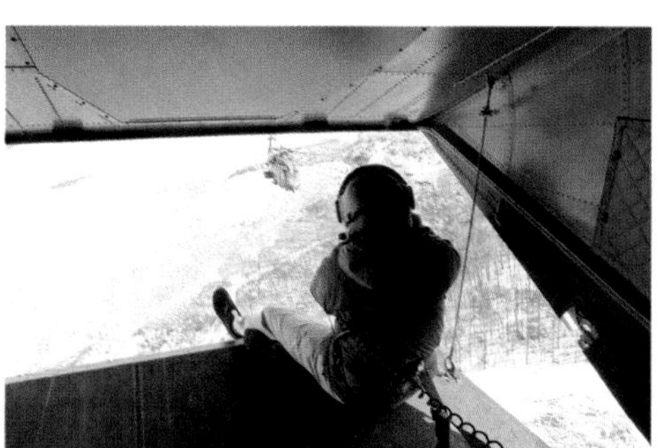

For those of you who have never flown in winter in Washington with the back of a helicopter open, here are a few things to keep in mind. When the ambient temperature is 25 degrees with a downdraft of 100 mph or so (which is necessary to keep the helicopter aloft), you can only imagine what the resulting wind chill feels like. To say I was frozen after just a few minutes would be an understatement. Despite knowing this, we still went up for a few sorties, and after each trip I would immediately load onto my laptop, review the images, and offer to the client (and more importantly the crew) a 30-second to one-minute review of the "best ofs" from the flight we had just completed.

The client was quite pleased with the results, and the crew, having had a few low-resolution images dropped onto their thumb drives, were increasingly on board with my objectives, which were not only to make great photos, but ultimately to deliver those best images to my client.

The next image we wanted to capture was of the helicopter touching down in a small landing zone (LZ), and the crew set about to find a suitable location. The plan was to take me to the LZ, drop me while the helicopter was "hot" (still running blades at a high speed), lift back off, circle back around, and land almost on top of me so that I could get a powerful wide-angle shot as the helicopter landed. We lifted off from the airport, flew for five or ten minutes, and they dropped me in the middle of a field—only they and God knew where I was.

As they lifted off, I protected my cameras from the flying debris that the rotor wash was buffeting around. As the helicopters vanished, it quickly became eerily silent because one of the features of this helicopter is how quiet it is. For a few moments, I wondered whether I might not get picked back up. I had been told that they would make a similar approach to the LZ as they had when they dropped me off, so I continued to look in that direction.

One of the most important things to think about when photographing helicopters is that you should not choose a shutter speed that freezes the blades completely, because the helicopter then looks as if it's falling from the sky. You also don't want to choose a shutter speed that's so slow that the blades all but disappear. Although every helicopter's blades spin at a different speed, a good starting point is 1/125 of a second, and that's where I set my shutter speed.

A few moments later, over the tree line came the helicopter, and I actually saw it before I could hear it. They came close, and I wanted to be closer, so I crouched down, camera pointing upward, and crawled forward, fighting against increasingly intense rotor wash that was now hurling debris straight at me. The blades of the helicopter were coming in at an angle and not straight down, because I felt that an angled landing would look more dynamic than a straight-up-and-down landing, and I had conveyed this desire to the pilot beforehand.

They were pleased with that type of approach, as it is not only more consistent with the approaches they use in theater, but also, as any helicopter pilot will tell you, their least favorite maneuver is a straight-up-and-down one with no front/back/left/right momentum.

The debris kept coming at me as they got closer and closer, and it felt like they were right on top of me, although I'm sure it was a safe distance. Once they touched down "hot" again, I climbed back aboard, and off we went. To this day, I still don't know whose field we landed in, but I do know that the pilots were 100-percent on board after I showed them the selects from this last sortie.

As the client continued their familiarization efforts with the members of the media, our next opportunity, which came along in short order, was an opportunity to fly from a small airport in Virginia to another small airport in Maryland, taking us up the Potomac River through what is referred to as the "Heli-Lane," right overtop of the Jefferson Memorial. The beauty of this route is that when properly positioned, you can capture the helicopter in the foreground and the White House in the background in one shot, and then quickly repositioning allows you to capture the helicopter and the U.S. Capitol in one shot.

Both ideas I proposed were presented as the main objectives for a picture that was to appear on the cover of *Rotor & Wing* magazine. I was able to rely on my previously established track record with the pilots and crew as we discussed the visual objectives for this outing, which served a dual purpose of also giving the writer for the magazine an opportunity to test-fly the helicopter. I was able to explain where the helicopters would need to be relative to one another, and I was connected into their communication system via headset and helmet to facilitate this tricky maneuver.

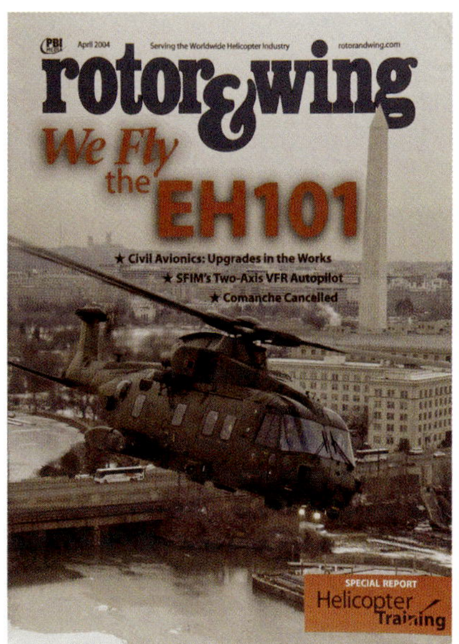

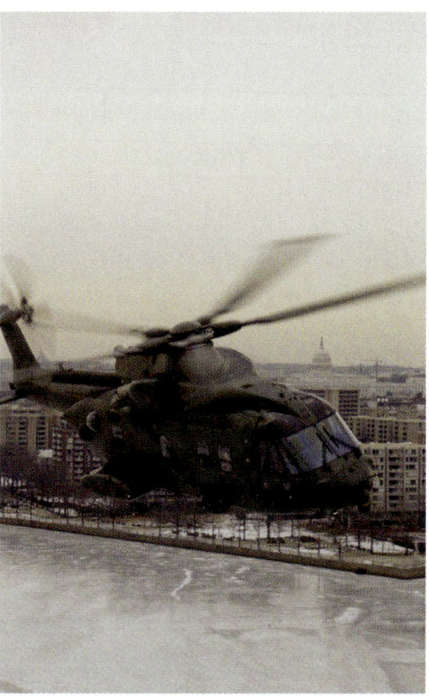

The cover of *Rotor & Wing* with the US-101 (referred to by them as the EH-101) from the shoot we did.

Opposite page: The US-101 with the Washington Monument and the White House in the background.

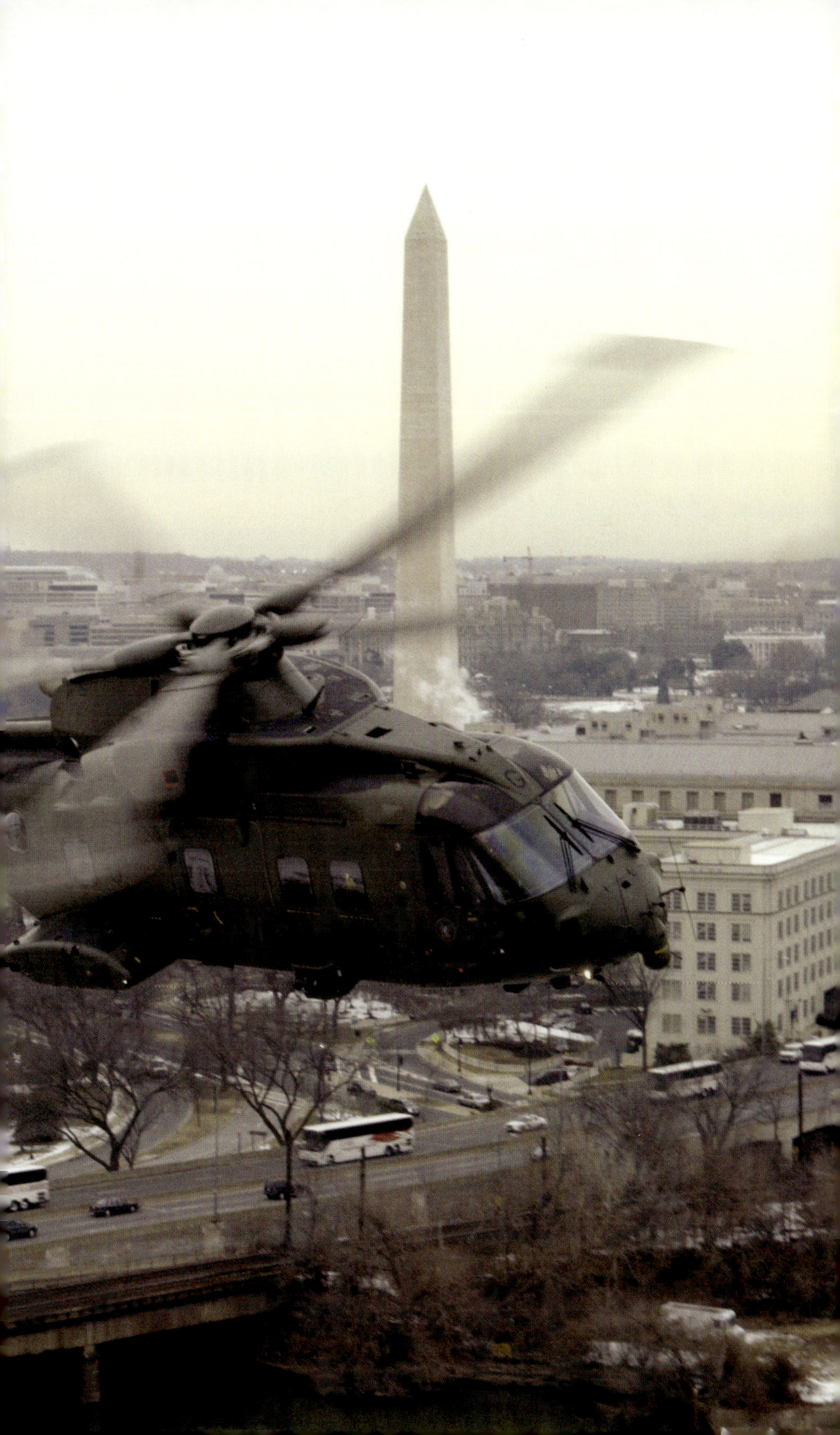

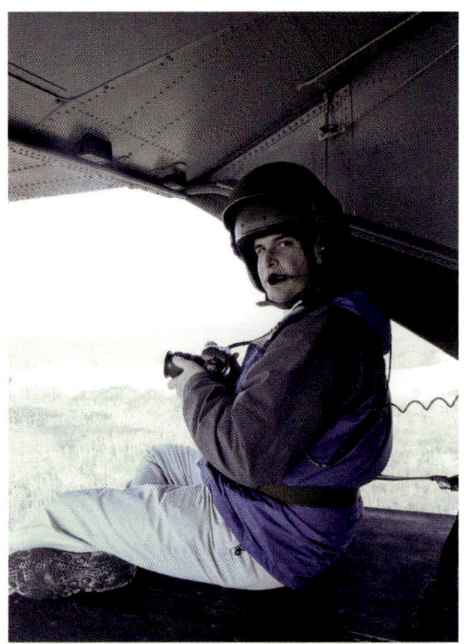

Tethered by a harness and with a helmet communications system, I was able to coordinate aircraft movements with the trailing helicopter.

Hanging out the back of this helicopter over the Potomac River, it was already cold because it was winter. Add to that the wind speed, and I knew I was in for a challenge. Fortunately, everyone was on the same page, and we were able to achieve the objective of capturing both images, as well as the cover of *Rotor & Wing*.

Flying over the Jefferson Memorial, with a frozen tidal basin below, the subject aircraft is juxtaposed with the U.S. Capitol after a position change from a few seconds earlier, where the White House was in the background. During some downtime standing next to the helicopter with my client afterward, I inquired about the hourly cost of these helicopters, as I am familiar with the costs of renting a variety of other much smaller helicopters. These birds were actually on loan back to the manufacturer by one of their European Union customers, and the deal was that the manufacturer would pay that customer for each hour flown. The client reported to me that each helicopter and crew was incurring charges at a rate of $25,000 an hour. My heart sank as I quickly did the math and realized that I had been responsible for about five hours' worth of flight time per helicopter. Fortunately for me, that was not a bill I would ever see, but we did fly in the future for at least another four hours.

In the end it was my good fortune that I had properly managed the rights to my images, because the client decided to use those images as the basis for an advertising campaign that ran repeatedly over a two-year period. The client was very pleased with all of the results and has returned for a number of additional rights-managed assignments since that first one when there was the suggestion that they would get all rights. The original contract allowed for the use of the images and unpaid media placements alongside editorial articles about the helicopter, as well as internal company use. These additional uses were paid advertising placements in public transportation locations, posters, tradeshow displays, and trade magazine ads, far and away greater than a standard PR need.

If you're not familiar with how to handle the rights to your images or with how I feel about all-rights demands, your best bet is to read my other book, *Best Business Practices for Photographers*, for insights into and solutions on this issue.

The US-101 over the Virginia countryside doing an evasive maneuver that caused more than one of the passenger-journalists to get sick.

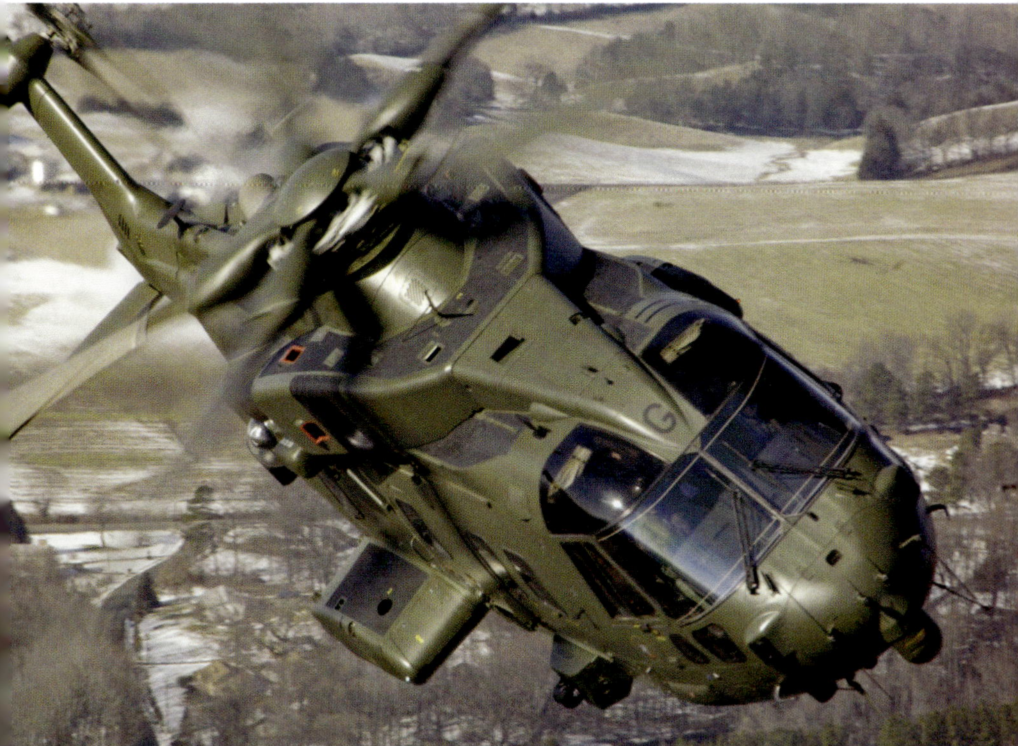

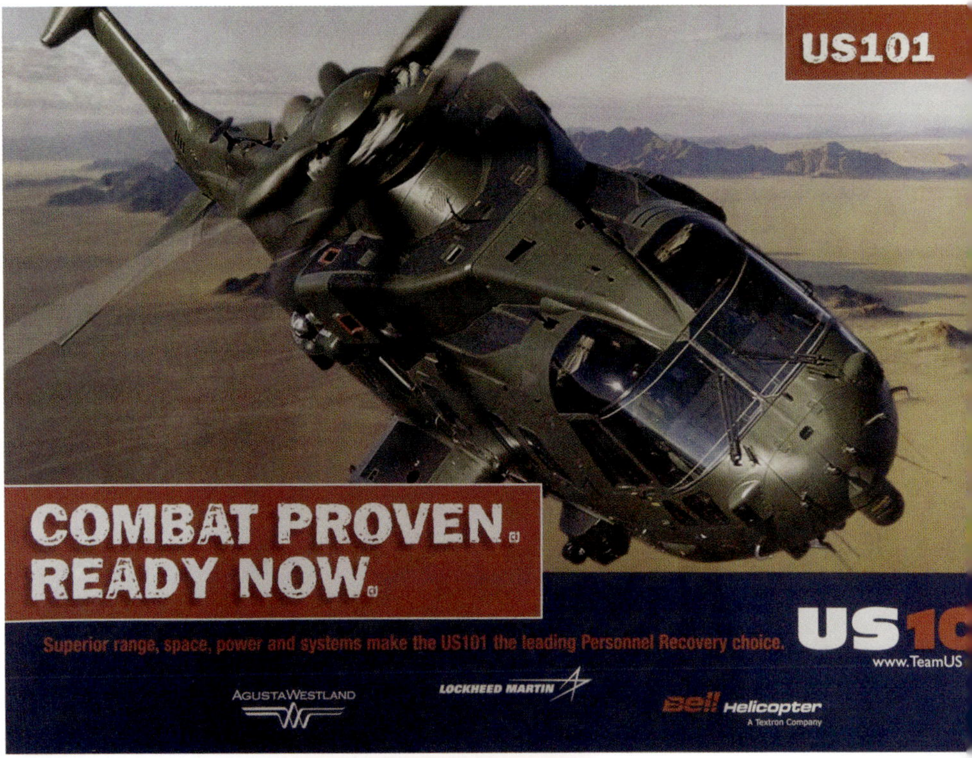

US101

COMBAT PROVEN.
READY NOW.

Superior range, space, power and systems make the US101 the leading Personnel Recovery choice.

US10

www.TeamUS

AGUSTAWESTLAND

LOCKHEED MARTIN

Bell Helicopter
A Textron Company

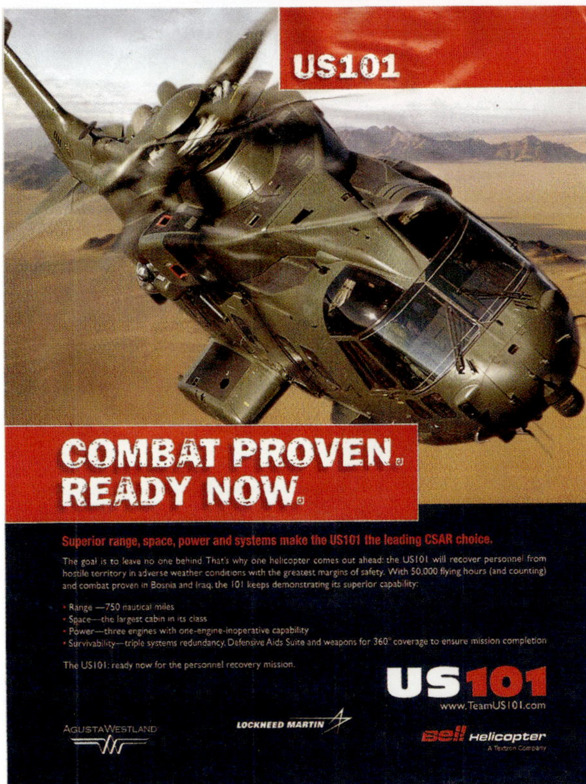

The client stripped out the Virginia countryside and inserted a desert scene in these two different ads.

Europe on a Shoestring

Traveling overseas, especially to locales where you don't speak the language, is always a challenge. My magazine had tasked me with a trip to Eastern Europe—Hungary, the Czech Republic, the now-unified East and West Germany in Berlin, Poland, and stops in between. The challenge, beyond language, was money. The magazine for which I was on staff did not have the budget, so I had to come up with a solution to save money. Plane hops and hotels soon seemed like a luxury, so I proposed a train trip from one city to the next. Not only would the train serve to get me from city to city, but I could also sleep on the train, saving hotel costs for a number of days.

I fleshed out an itinerary that had me flying into Budapest and taking the train to Warsaw, then to Berlin, then to Prague, then back to Budapest. I had built in two days for unexpected delays of the governmental and weather type, and I got the project approved.

I arrived in Budapest and started shooting immediately. I decided in each city I would come out of the train station and start talking to the taxi drivers. Whichever one understood me, I would book for the day as my driver.

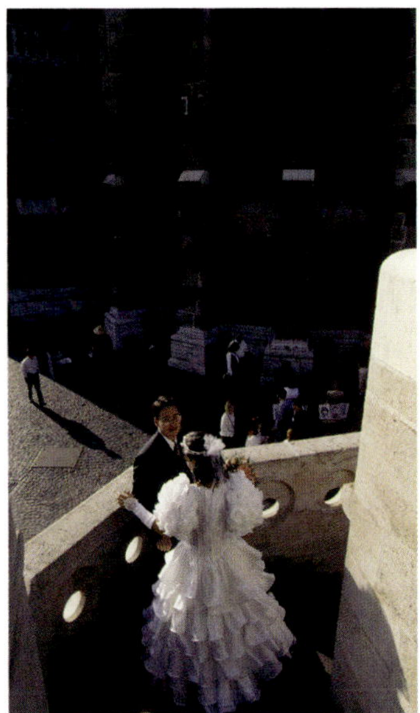

A couple just married at the Matthias Church on Castle Hill on the Buda side of Budapest, Hungary.

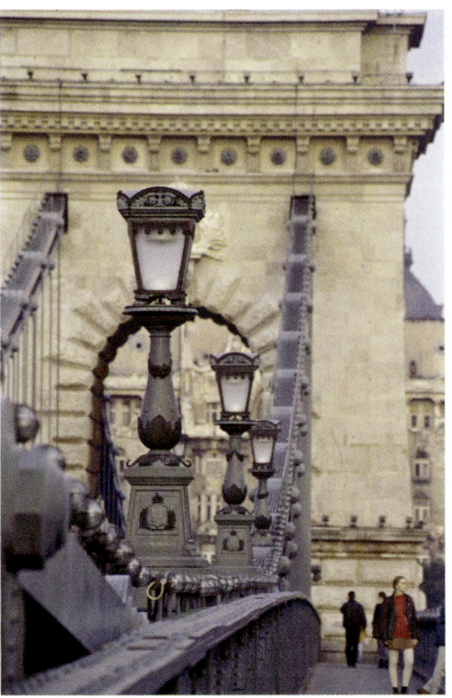

Detail of the famous Chain Bridge, with Buda Castle in a background, Budapest, Hungary.

On Day 1, I trekked about town with good weather, knocking out a large part of my shot list for Budapest. At the end of the day, my driver dropped me off at the train station, where I stumbled through my dialogue with the ticket agent as I tried to explain that I needed to get to Warsaw.

What I had missed was the fact that my rail journey would have me crossing several borders and at least one midway country I wasn't even stopping in. What I hadn't missed was that I expected the trip would be bumpy and noisy, so I got my doctor to prescribe what was, at the time, a new sleep drug—Ambien. When you mix the two—sleeping pills and border guards who, in the middle of the night, are opening your sleeping compartment and demanding to see your papers—you have a problem. The problem is compounded when they ask you questions and you don't understand them.

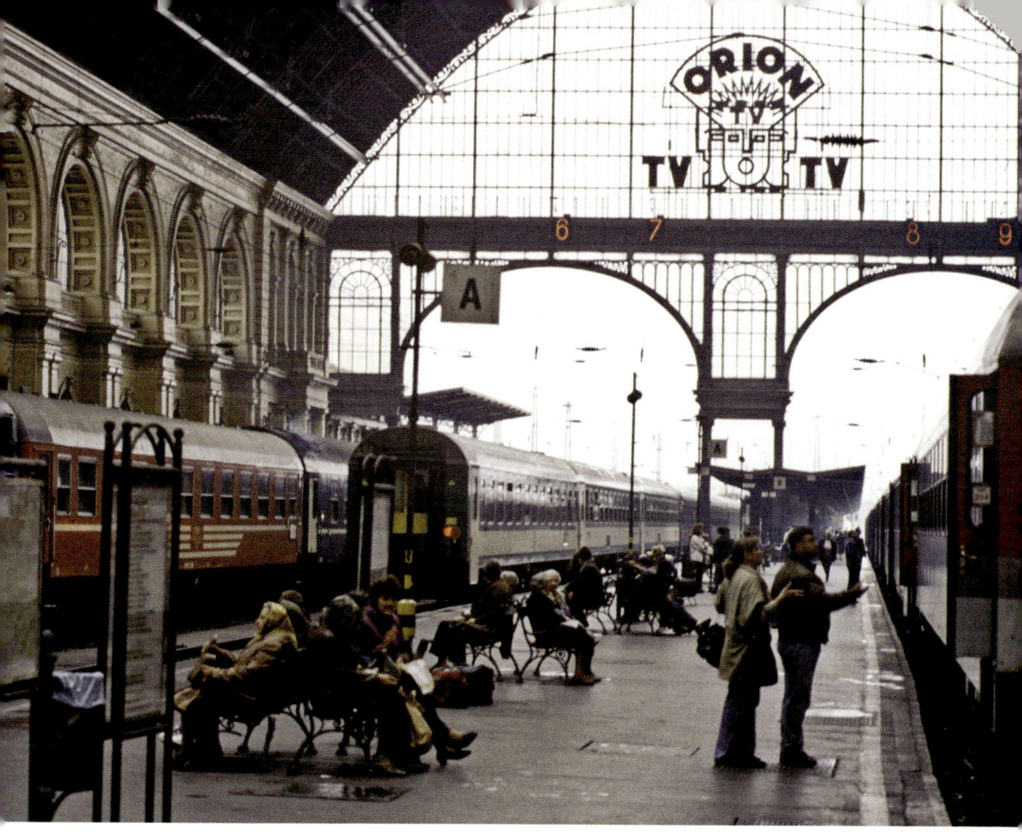

The Keleti train station in the eastern part of Pest. Taken in Budapest, Hungary.

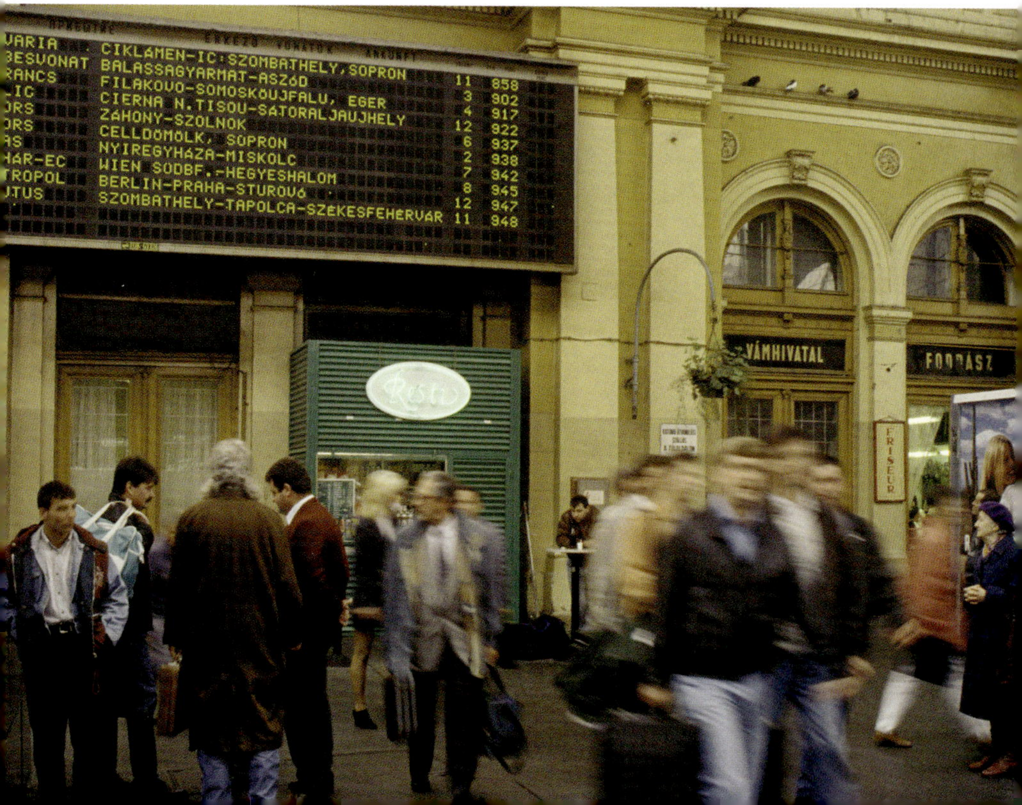

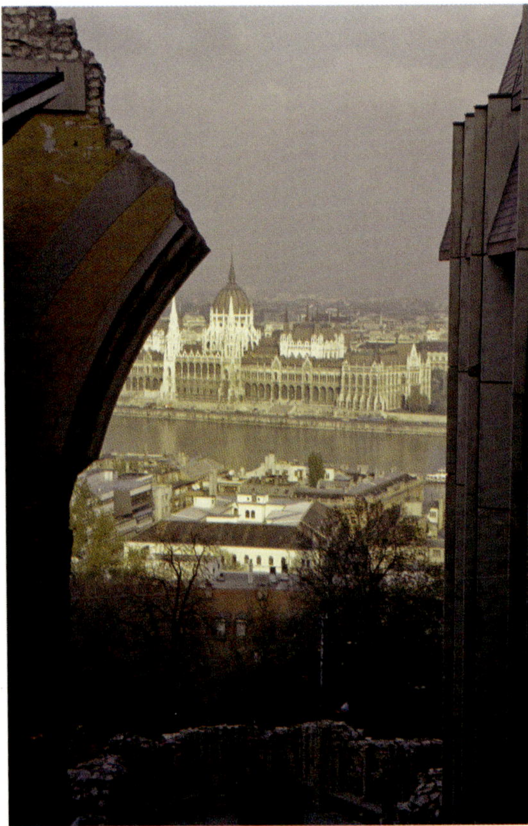

The Hungarian Parliament building, a huge neo-Gothic structure, was built between 1885 and 1902 on the banks of the Danube River on the Pest side of the city. Here it is seen through the structure of the Hilton Hotel. Taken in Budapest, Hungary.

As the sun rose on Warsaw, my train arrived, and I was able to make several images I could check off my list even before I left the train station. Before leaving, I stowed my extra clothes/gear/film in a locker and headed out. Once again, I found a great driver, finished my list, and made it back to the train station in time to catch the last train to Berlin. The only problem was, I was asking for a ticket using a language book, and the Polish language isn't the easiest to translate from English. I struggled, and after a while, as the ticket agent sat waiting for me to make myself understood, another ticket agent came over to help. It became apparent by watching their gestures and listening to the tone of their dialogue that she understood English and just wanted me to struggle through her language.

Finally, I got my ticket and found a spot to sit near the tracks. Unfortunately, as I was trying to type out captions from my day's excursions, it became apparent that where I was sitting wasn't the most hygienic spot. It seems that where I had decided to sit was where the city's homeless would relieve themselves. I didn't get this until some kind, English-speaking person took pity on me and enlightened me as to my whereabouts—needless to say, I promptly moved.

When the train arrived in Berlin, I was exhausted. I hadn't had more than an hour or two of sleep at a time, and I could barely see straight. I only had one day in Berlin and a long list of items to photograph. Once again, I dropped my extra clothes/gear/film, made a few morning images, and made my way to a restaurant near the Brandenburg Gate for lunch. I sat down, slipped the straps of my cameras and camera bags under the foot of my chair and around my leg, and placed my order.

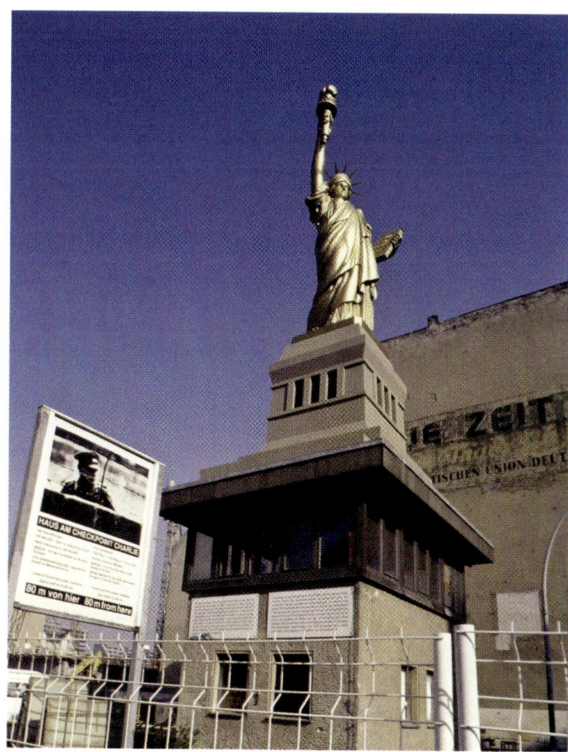

Formerly dividing the city of Berlin into east and west, the Berlin wall could be crossed here, at Checkpoint Charlie. The site will remain as a monument to the past.

Eventually, a tap on my shoulder awoke me, still seated upright, with drool on the front of my jacket, with my now-cold food on the table in front of me. I panicked and immediately looked down. Thankfully, my gear was still there, and nothing had been picked from my pockets. Next, I realized I had lost a considerable amount of time (but to this day I don't know how much), and I had a long list of images still to make, so I downed the meal as quickly as possible and headed out.

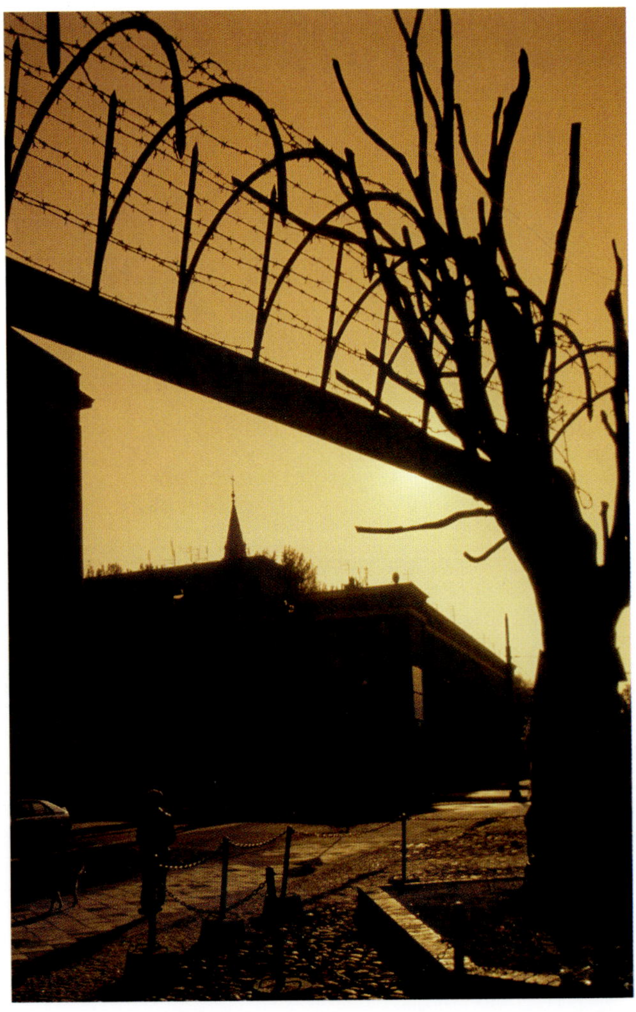

A former World War II prison structure named Powiak now sits as a reminder to the past, near the outskirts of the Jewish ghetto in Berlin, Germany.

Once again, the list got finished. I found a DHL office before heading to the train, and I shipped my shot film back to the office. I didn't want to worry about losing all of the shot film, and I also needed to offload it from my carrying pack. I headed off to the Berlin train station and found a much nicer ticket agent this time, who helped me with my ticket to Prague.

I boarded the train to Prague and once again fell asleep. It wasn't such a long ride, and I made it there by about midnight. I had a hotel in mind on the well-known Wenceslas Square. I thought it would be central to many of the places I had to photograph, so I cabbed it over there, exhausted after several days on the road and having not had a shower in as many days. I also needed to get online with my laptop and transmit an email with my update and my captions.

When I walked in around 1:00 a.m., I learned that the only phone in the hotel was in the lobby, and by no means could I open up the plug and banana-clip my telephone cord into the phone system to send an email, so I had to find another hotel. I left the hotel almost delirious, found a cab, and asked the driver to take me to my backup hotel. Apparently, the backup hotel I had chosen (in large part because of the price) was not in the best of neighborhoods. En route, I saw in the distance the Prague Hilton and dreamed of a day when I could afford to stay there.

I had been able to determine what the approximate cost of the taxi ride should be, but when we arrived at my hotel around 1:30 in the morning, the taxi driver wanted about four times what the ride should have cost. On a deserted street outside of this hotel we argued, and the driver threatened to call the police. I told him he should and gave him what I had thought would be a reasonable fare, and he sped off into the night. I then walked into the hotel and learned that there were no rooms at the inn—I was screwed.

After a moment of disbelief, standing there exhausted, I left the hotel lobby and began walking. I didn't quite know where I was headed, and I was definitely fearful for my life in the neighborhood I was in, but I didn't have a choice, as the hotel had told me that no taxis would come if they called, especially not at that hour.

In the distance, I spied the Prague Hilton again, rising above the glow of the city. I hastened my pace, now with a destination in sight. On my head was balanced my stuffed duffle bag of clothes and film—I must have looked like a homeless person, except with some really nice camera equipment. I walked into the hotel asked the front desk clerk whether they had any rooms. He said yes, and I said I'd take one.

"Don't you want to know how much they are?" he asked.

"No, I don't care. I need a room," I said as I plopped down my credit card. I had decided I would find a way to justify this expense to my boss.

With my room key in hand, I stumbled into my room. I pulled off my pants, which were almost able to stand in the corner of the room on their own, so disgustingly dirty they were. I called room service at 2:00 a.m., ordered four Diet Cokes, a cheeseburger, and apple pie, and turned on CNN. I ate and then fell asleep around 3:00 a.m., not waking until about 11. Exhausted but at the same time rejuvenated, I was behind, but fortunately I had two rain days I had not needed since the weather had held earlier in the trip, so I decided to spend one of them in Prague.

I stepped out of the hotel and quickly found an English-speaking taxi driver—much easier at this hour—and off we went. I hit all the items on my list and then came back to the hotel for a brief respite. I was able to connect into the phone system with my laptop and send off my captions, along with a tenuous explanation about how some conference was in town, and the only place I could stay was at the Hilton. My boss grumbled, but he understood (sort of).

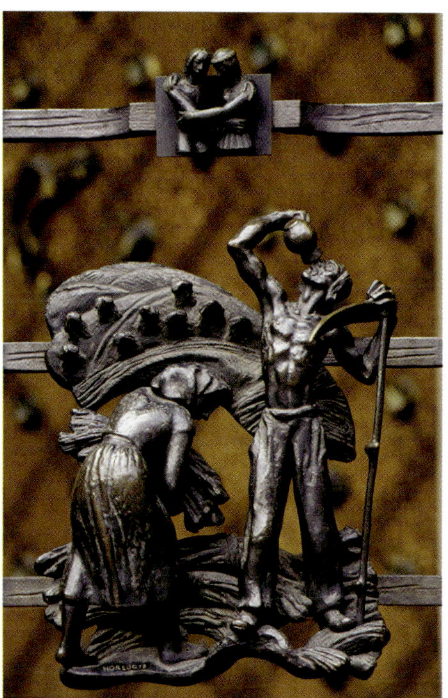

A relief on the golden portal of St. Vitus' Cathedral, within Prague Castle. The castle was begun in 1344 and completed in the 19th and 20th centuries. The cathedral houses the crown jewels and the tomb of "Good King" Wenceslas.

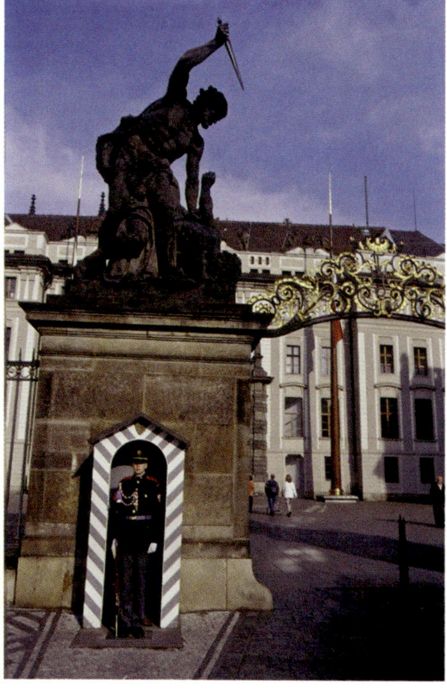

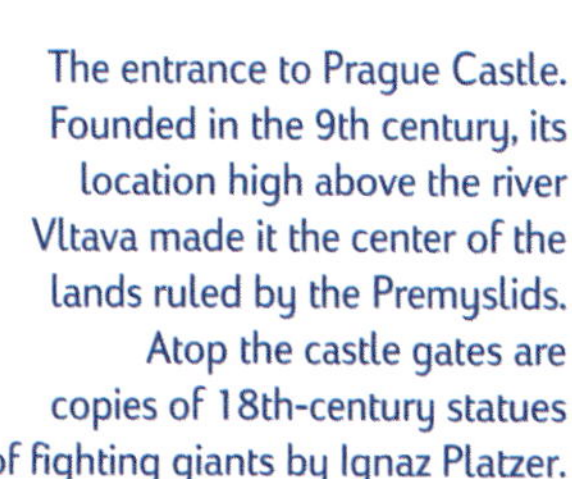

The entrance to Prague Castle. Founded in the 9th century, its location high above the river Vltava made it the center of the lands ruled by the Premyslids. Atop the castle gates are copies of 18th-century statues of fighting giants by Ignaz Platzer.

I spent the next day wandering off-list and made some fun images I was happy with. Finally, with two days of semi-rest, I caught my last train back to Budapest. There, I finished off my Budapest list, spent the extra weather day enjoying the city, and caught my scheduled flight home. It was a hellacious trip, but in the end, with all the trials and tribulations, a great one.

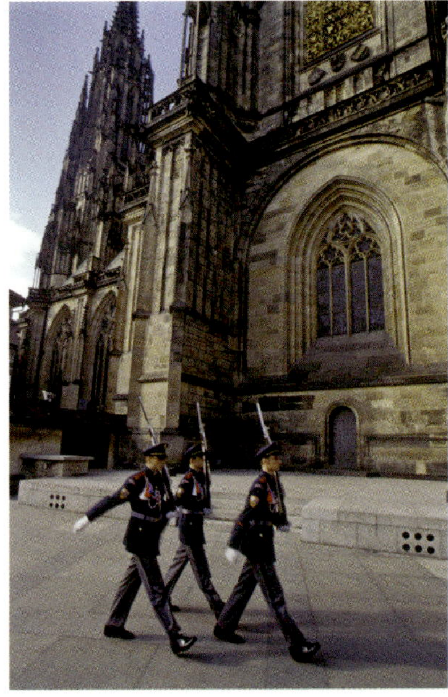

Soldiers march past St. Vitus' Cathedral inside Prague Castle.

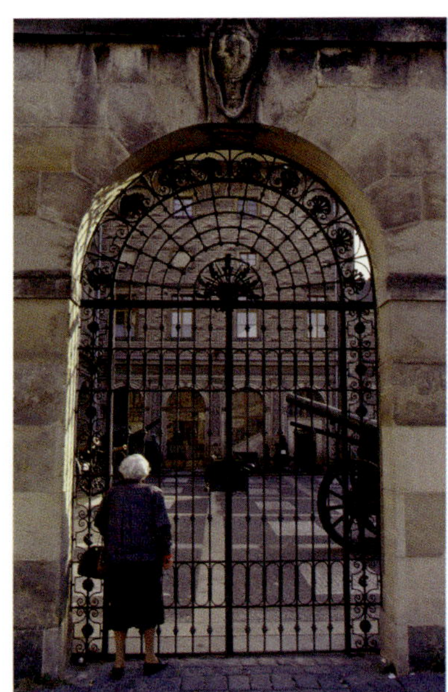

A woman looks into the courtyard of the Schwarzenberg Palace, near Prague Castle on Loretanska Street.

Live 8: Hallelujah! The Reverend Al Sharpton Delivers Destiny

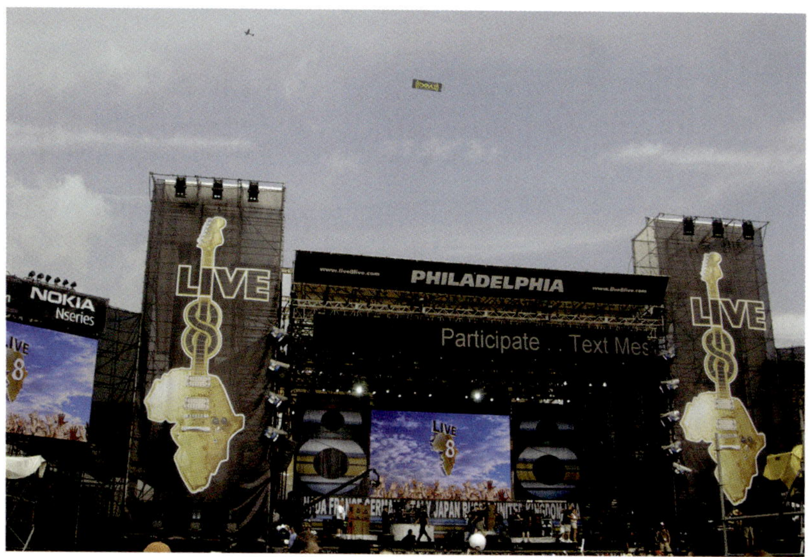

The front-of-house view of the Live 8 stage in Philadelphia.

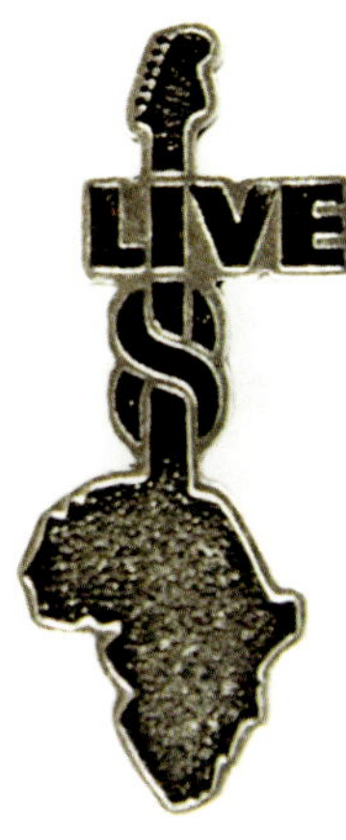

I had the opportunity to travel to Philadelphia to photograph the Live 8 concert. Eight concerts in eight countries simultaneously played around the world for a charitable purpose was a massive undertaking and was a follow-up to the Live Aid concerts from a decade or two earlier. I had hoped to be able to cover the front-of-house goings on, capturing all of the performers on stage and so on. Instead, I was quite surprised to find that this assignment took me backstage for almost the entire show.

My credentials included access to the front of house, but with every photographer crammed into the space in the front of the house, being backstage afforded me opportunities that don't always come along. Pictures backstage are often what you make of them. There are usually no publicists pre-grouping artists, telling you where to stand or the artists where to stand—it is truly a free-for-all (properly credentialed), and this carries with it not only the potential for awesome images of artists unguarded and being themselves, but also great responsibility to demonstrate restraint and respect for the artists. When you find yourself in these types of situations, discretion is always the better part of valor because if one or two artists decide that you're a nuisance, the event organizers will likely defer to the desires of the artists, and you will lose your credential.

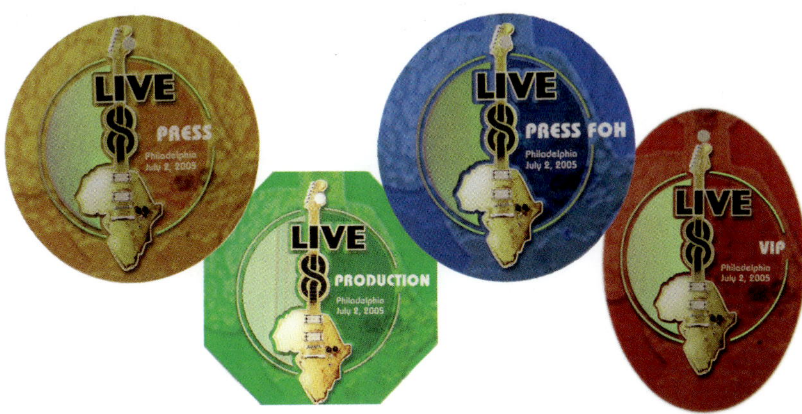

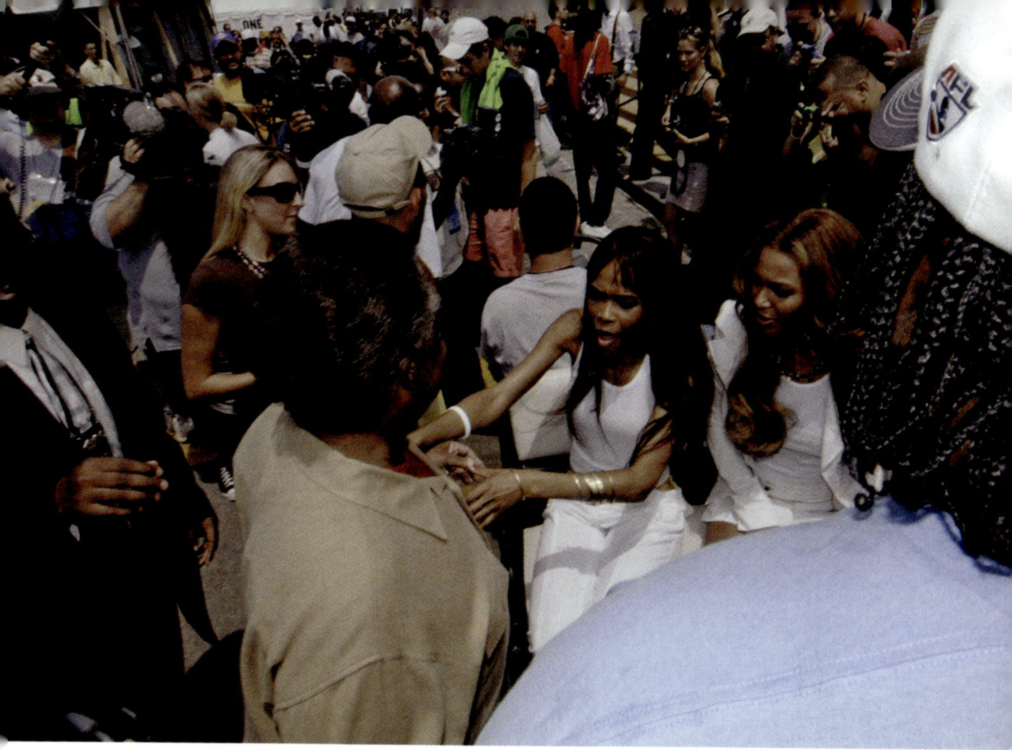

The fandemonium surrounding Rev. Al Sharpton and Destiny's Child backstage at Live 8.

At this event, artists like local boy Jon Bon Jovi and legends like Stevie Wonder were all over backstage. One photo I really wanted was of Destiny's Child, but they were notorious for controlling the images taken of them and avoiding having images taken for this reason. I saw them pause briefly, as they were passing by, to talk to Al Sharpton, and I knew that if I wanted to get Destiny's Child, then it had to be a photograph that included Al Sharpton.

Years ago, a close friend and colleague, Michael Spilotro, taught me a little tip: When you want to get a big celebrity's picture, sometimes you need to include with them a slightly lesser celebrity or one who loves being photographed. Michael had shared with me a story about how he had been able to get a photograph of the elusive Robert Duvall by asking the camera-friendly Pat Boone if he wouldn't mind posing with Duvall, and since Pat Boone said sure, Duvall, not wanting to offend Boone, acquiesced. I used the same approach with the camera-averse Destiny's Child and the camera-friendly Al Sharpton.

Bear in mind that even though the artists are milling about backstage, they still have a full entourage of private security and are trying to avoid the many credentialed VIP guests who are really just fans with connections. The key, in this situation, is to engage the talent quickly and politely, before they signal their minders.

As Reverend Sharpton was chatting with Destiny's Child, I waited for a brief lull in their conversation and said to Sharpton, "Reverend, can I trouble you for a photograph with these lovely ladies?" Sharpton, of course, responded, "It would be my pleasure." I turned my camera toward them, and Destiny's Child wore a huge smile in a picture that I would have never gotten had I not asked for the photo to take place via the good Reverend.

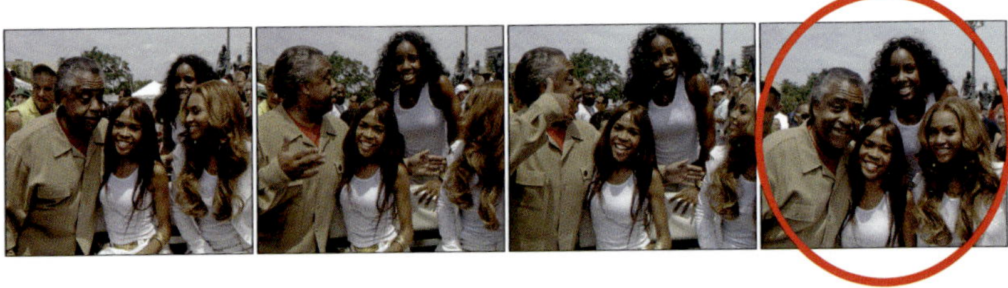

In the end, although these photos may not be "studio perfect," they are great, unguarded moments that my client wanted of these artists having a good time at the Live 8 concert. Although we used the good-natured Al Sharpton for the picture we really wanted, he enjoyed the moment just as much as Destiny's Child, which afforded me the opportunity to get the three of them smiling beautifully for the camera.

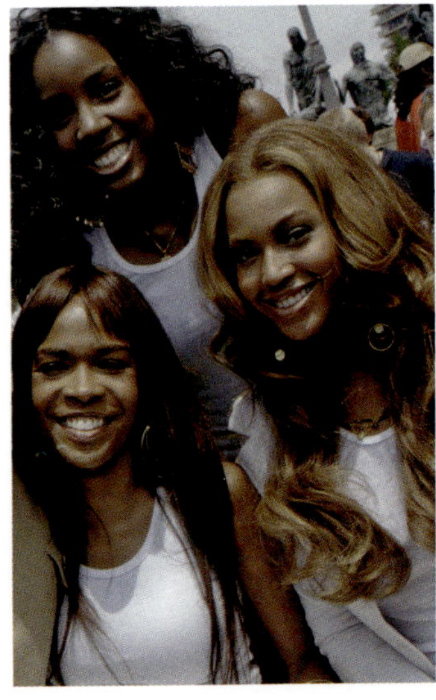

The final crop of Destiny's Child, as I had originally wanted.

Fireworks at Iwo Jima

Every year, Washington, DC throws an awesome party on the Mall among the monuments, and a 20-minute fireworks extravaganza caps it off, celebrating the nation's independence on July 4th. One of my first published photographs was of the fireworks, shot from the top of the Lincoln Memorial, and each year I contemplate where I want to photograph them from next. I've had a number of ideas over the years, but one that continued to vex me was the Iwo Jima Memorial.

The Iwo Jima Memorial, a roughly 60-foot sculpture made from the historic photograph of the raising of the American flag on Iwo Jima, is a memorial to the U.S. Marines and sits on a site overlooking the Potomac River, with DC and the Mall in the background. For me, the memorial was the perfect foreground subject for the photograph I wanted to make, because the idea of the fireworks behind the soldiers brings to mind the warfare that was taking place around the raising of the flag.

I had photographed the memorial a number of times before and found that it had some horrendous industrial lighting on it. Not to mention it's a pea-green statue with a black marble base, so there really was no "normal" color to see.

The challenge was, how do I color-correct for the statue? I knew that color-correcting for the statue would throw off the sky and skew all the colors of the fireworks, but I was okay with that, since who's to say what colors the bursts were anyway?

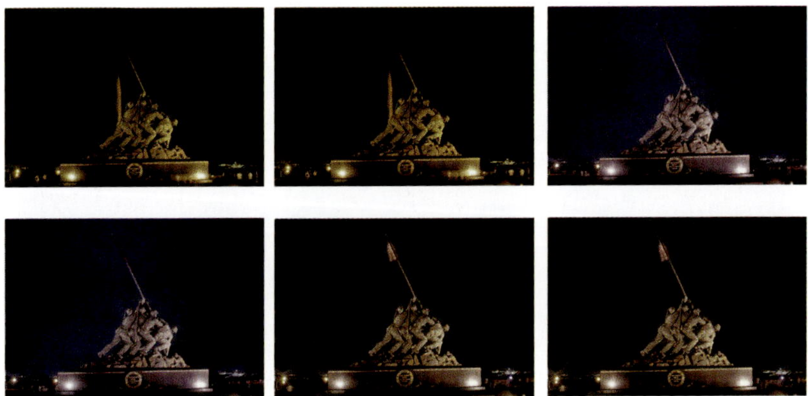

Above: A series of test images taken to check for the right filter pack and exposure settings before the 4th of July. Opposite page: One of the resulting finished images of fireworks going off behind the Iwo Jima Memorial in Rosslyn, Virginia.

Knowing that the fireworks would start at 9:00 p.m., earlier in the week I went over to do a trial run. I set up in exactly the spot I wanted, and I placed a series of Kodak Wratten gels over the lens, adding in magenta, blue, and greens in a methodical order. I also bracketed my exposures for each one so that I could find not only the correct filter pack, but also the best exposure. I did this also knowing that at about 100 ISO, fireworks look their best around f/8. Further, I knew that I wanted the exposure to be about 15 seconds or so. Since I was shooting this on slide film, I knew this testing was critical, as slide film has very little latitude to get it wrong. I went to the lab, processed the film, and studied the results.

With an exposure of 15 seconds, I could use a black card in front of the camera to manually "open and close" the lens, allowing for just the bursts I wanted to be exposed. I knew that this would allow me the most control over the final result.

Satisfied with the filter pack, I arrived on July 4th and set up five cameras—three 35mm bodies and two Hasselblad cameras. Each had its own timer and was on a separate tripod, and each had its own release. Knowing that an exposure would last about 15 seconds or so, that would be four frames a minute, or 80 frames total for the 20-minute show. This meant that for the 35mm

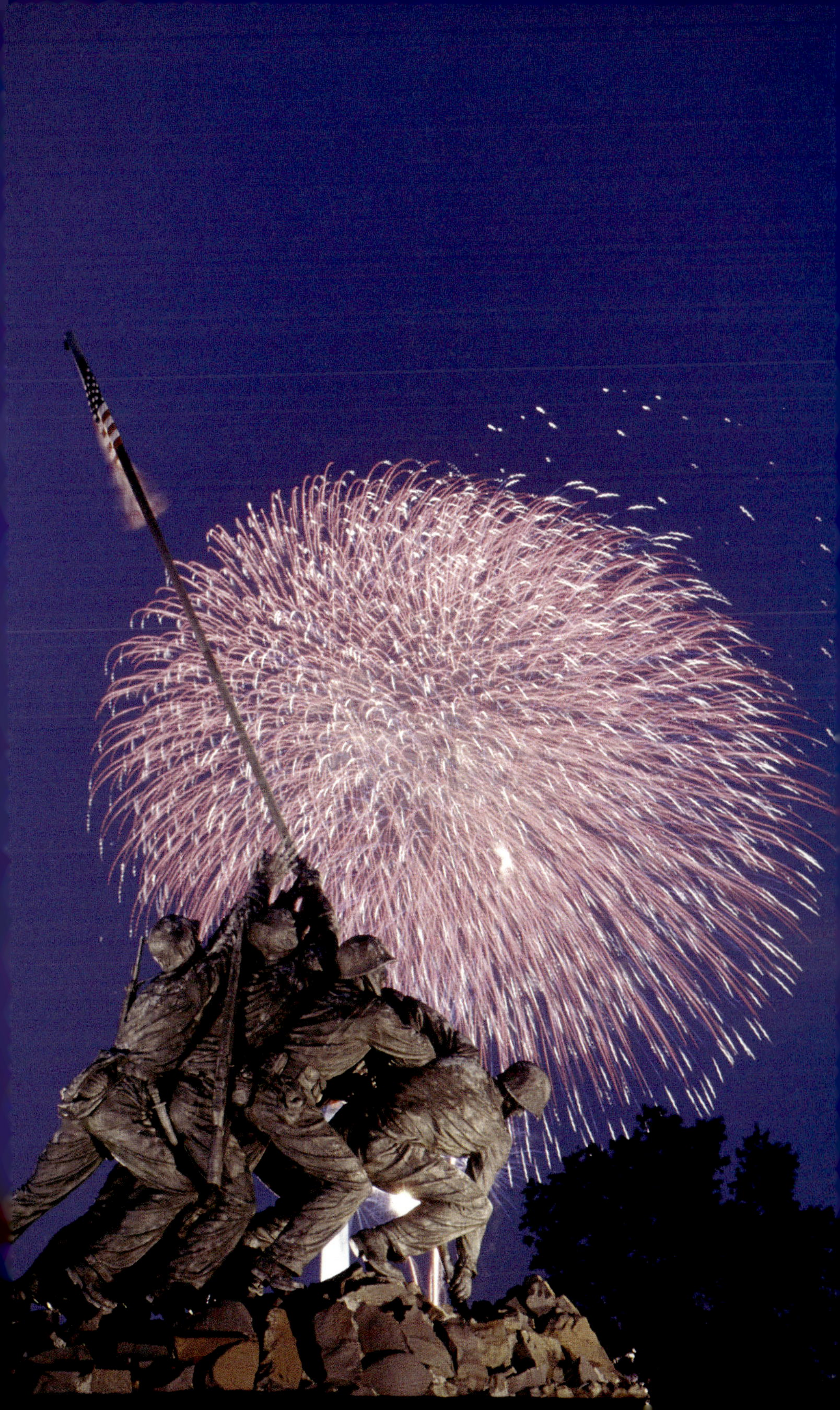

bodies, I would likely get two rolls each, and I loaded the Hasselblad with 220 film and pre-loaded additional backs. Time was of the essence, and every manner of delay had to be reduced to its bare minimum.

As with any event, you arrive early and stake out your spot, and this one was no different. What worried me—since I was there easily eight hours beforehand because I expected picnickers to be there, too—was that people would come in and set up right in front of me, ruining my foreground, so I roped off a sizable area in front of the cameras to preserve my foreground. Throughout the day, more than one person tried to enter the space I had set up, and I would politely explain that this was my space, and they would wander off to some other location. (This was an assignment that required me to have a permit from the National Park Service, which I did.) About an hour beforehand, a colleague from the local paper turned up for her assignment, and we chatted. She hadn't photographed fireworks before and didn't know much about how to do it properly. I gave her a few tips, she set up her camera next to mine, and we waited.

At the appointed hour, the controlled explosions in the distance meant that we were a few seconds from the first blooms, and sure enough, things started out amazingly. One important note about fireworks is to not only get your first images just right, but also to pray for winds that are perpendicular to your position—or, in a perfect world, blowing in the direction from you to the fireworks—because that way all the clouds of smoke don't stick around or blow in your direction, obscuring your remaining view of the show. On occasion, I've seen the wind so still that the smoke just lingers, and it really becomes a horrible photograph, as gray smoke is illuminated by the blooms bursting above it.

This time, the smoke did not obscure the fireworks, and several of the bursts were huge. All of my testing and planning resulted in a number of images that were very worthwhile, and one became an inspirational poster series that more than compensated me for all of the effort.

The Captain's Jersey Retirement

Next to Wayne Gretzky, one of the greatest hockey players of all time (or so I'm told) is Mark Messier. Messier played in Madison Square Garden for the New York Rangers, and when he retired, the Rangers decided to retire his number at a ceremony before the game on January 12, 2006. Messier had brought great regard to his team, and the fans loved him. The outside of the stadium was adorned with full-length, building-sized murals of him in full hockey attire. Inside, red carpet was laid out on the ice for the ceremonies.

My initial objective was to get down on the ice, but then I decided I could make a far better image from a skybox. I made a few images from ice level of the standard check-presentation ceremonies, but then I hustled upstairs to a skybox because, fortunately, I had access to one. I made my way up to get in position.

I wanted to show the actual raising of his number, and I believed that "the Captain," as he was known to his teammates, would be "i-magged" (short for *image magnification*) onto the center-ice Jumbotron, so all the fans could watch as he watched the number rise to the rafters.

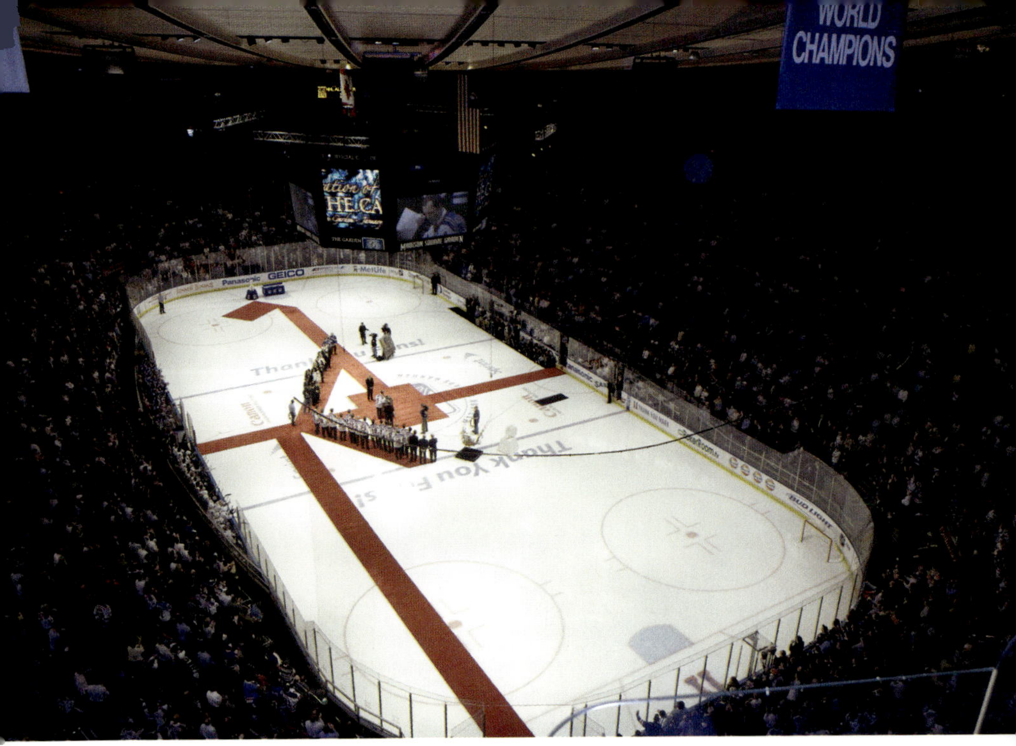

The on-ice red-carpet activities surrounding the retirement of "The Captain's" jersey.

As the number went up, the camera on the Captain's face stayed static so all the fans in the audience could see Messier, holding his son in his arms, watch it go up. I watched as it rose slowly—I knew that at just the right moment, it would look as if he was looking at the number from the Jumbotron. The camera angles worked in just the right way for this optical illusion so that anyone shooting from the ice could not juxtapose the Captain with the jersey and the act of it rising up to the rafters.

Sometimes, it pays to think about how you can make images from a different angle than anyone else. Just because the pack chooses one location, that doesn't automatically mean that you should be there, too. If your experience and forward-thinking approach gives you an opportunity to make a different image, it becomes easier to differentiate the type of photography you can offer. It's often said without risk there is no reward, and in this instance, the reward was well worth it.

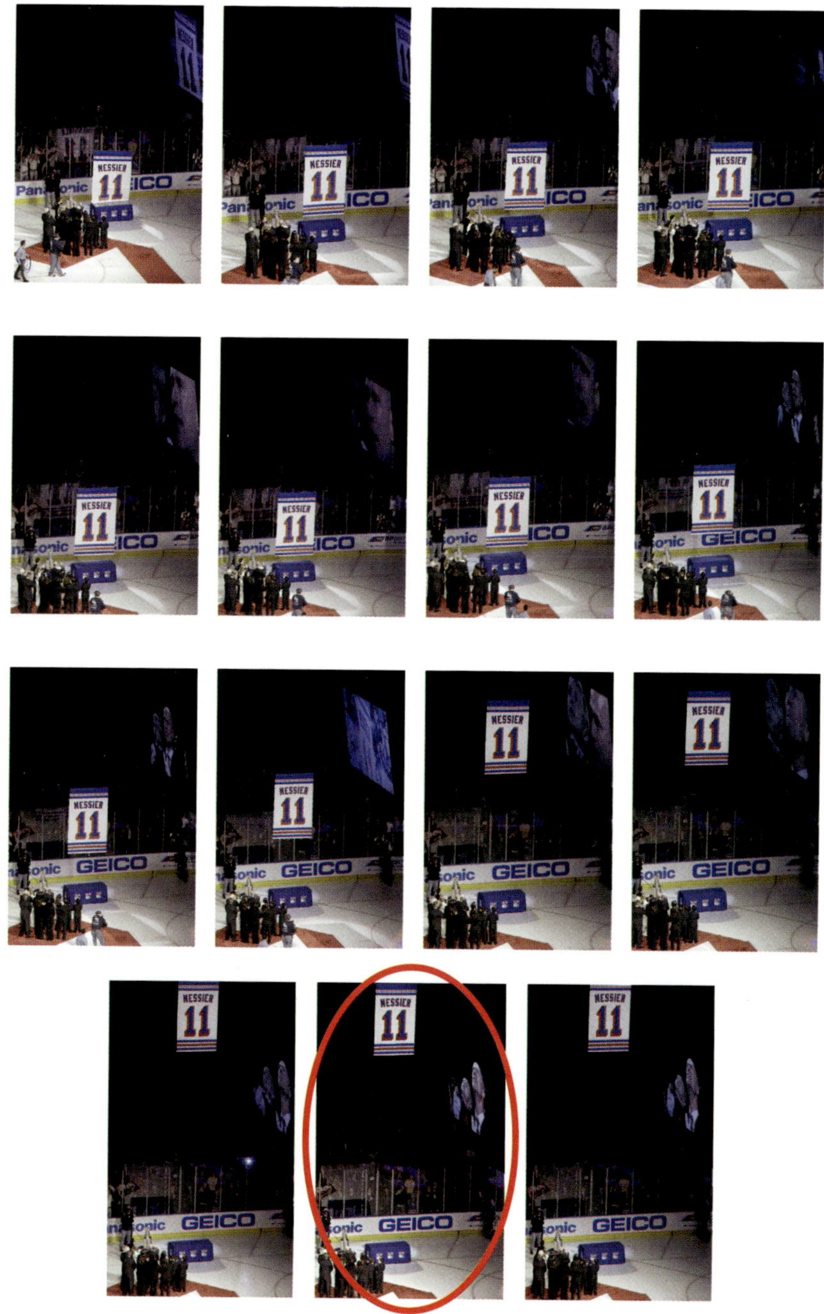

Mark Messier and his son, seen on the Jumbotron, look up as his number is raised to the rafters.

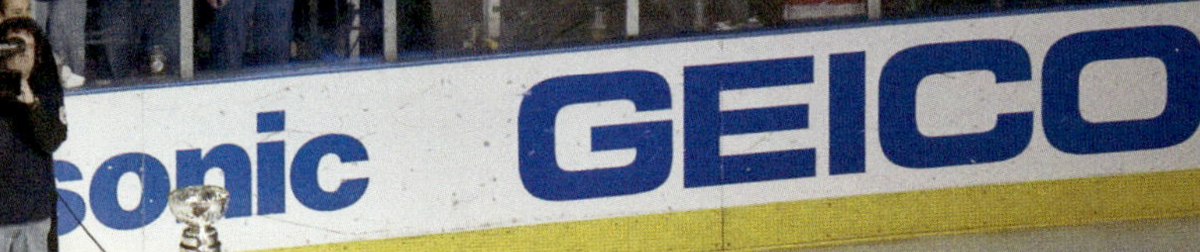
MESSIER
11
asonic
GEICO
MSG
RANGERS

Danica Patrick and the 20×40 Softbox

All NASCAR and Indy car drivers wish that all they had to do was focus on driving, yet the reality is that the ability to fire up the engine and race around a track costs millions of dollars a year. That's why every one of those cars that you see racing around the track has countless sponsorship stickers on it, as do the drivers' fire-retardant racing suits. If you were a sponsor, in an ideal world you would not want your corporate branding to be crowded by every other brand that is also a sponsor. Such was the case with my client, XM Satellite Radio, who was a primary sponsor for Indy racing superstar Danica Patrick.

Danica had come to XM with cars and her trailer as a part of her contractually obligated days of personal appearances to a sponsor at this level. It was coordinated with the cars and other support vehicles traveling through the area to a nearby scheduled race. The day XM chose would be known as an employee appreciation day, where XM's headquarters parking lot would be taken over by opportunities for employees to put on and take off tires with the air tools the pit crews use, play videogames, and enjoy a lunch comparable to that which they would get at a racetrack—without all the high prices, as the food and ice cream that was provided on this day was free.

The star attraction was Danica Patrick, who signed autographs and posed with fans who seemed to go beyond the employees who were in the building—no doubt a few race fans who were friends with employees just happened to be visiting XM that day. The line stretched a good distance, and I shot representative photos demonstrating how long the line was and how much of a hit Danica was, along with a select few showing her chatting and engaging with the fans and employees. Because I was close with a few of those employees, I would hop in at the right moment and make a frame or two of them posed with her, rather than having them rely on a point-and-shoot that just didn't have enough flash fill on a hot summer day to beat the sun.

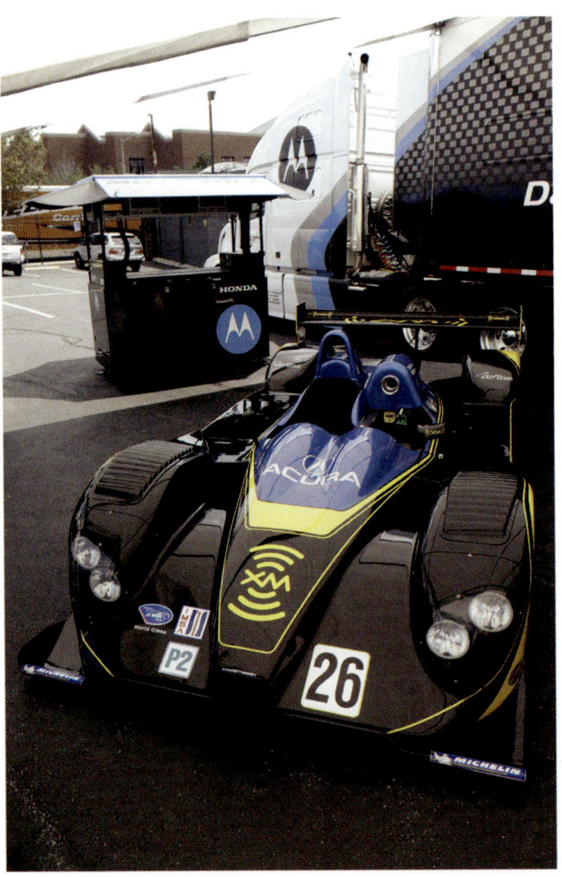

Underneath the tent, which provided soft light all around, including on nearby cars.

Danica and her cars were underneath a translucent white tent, and I started looking around at the opportunity that this presented. If I got up high enough, not only could I rotate my on-camera strobe and point it at the white above me, but the rest of the car would be illuminated by a huge softbox that would have otherwise cost me a fortune to set up and staff in an outdoor environment. The beauty of popping in the strobe was that I could overpower the sunlight cut back by the translucent tent and illuminating the car but still have what amounted to soft, flattering light that would be slightly brighter thanks to the strobe pop into the white tent surface.

I knew I would have about 10 seconds to make this happen as she wrapped up signing photos for the fans and made her way back to her VIP holding room before departing. So I grabbed the chair, got up high, and got a quick test shot to see what my best settings were and check the framing. With about 10 minutes to go and the line dwindling, I made a statement to Danica and did not pose a query. Asking permission might yield a "no" response, and the opportunity would be lost. Instead, making the casual statement, "Hey, we'd like to get a shot of you next to the car on your way out," gave me a far better chance of getting the shot.

I also didn't want to wait to present this request as she was getting up, because by then she would be surrounded with handlers who might squelch that opportunity. As the last fan got his signature, she got up to go with her handlers by her side, and I said to her, "Hey, Danica—that quick shot I mentioned," and she said, "Oh yeah, right. Where do you want me to stand?" I had my ten seconds ticking down.

I pulled my chair into position as I asked her to sit on the front right tire of her car and cross her arms. She crossed her arms right below the XM branding that stood alone and would be so coveted because of the uncluttered presence of that logo relative to all of the other portraits that she would otherwise do when wearing branding. After about four frames I knew that I had the shot, and she, of course, looked fabulous: the obvious focus of the picture but in the context of what she does—driving an Indy racing car.

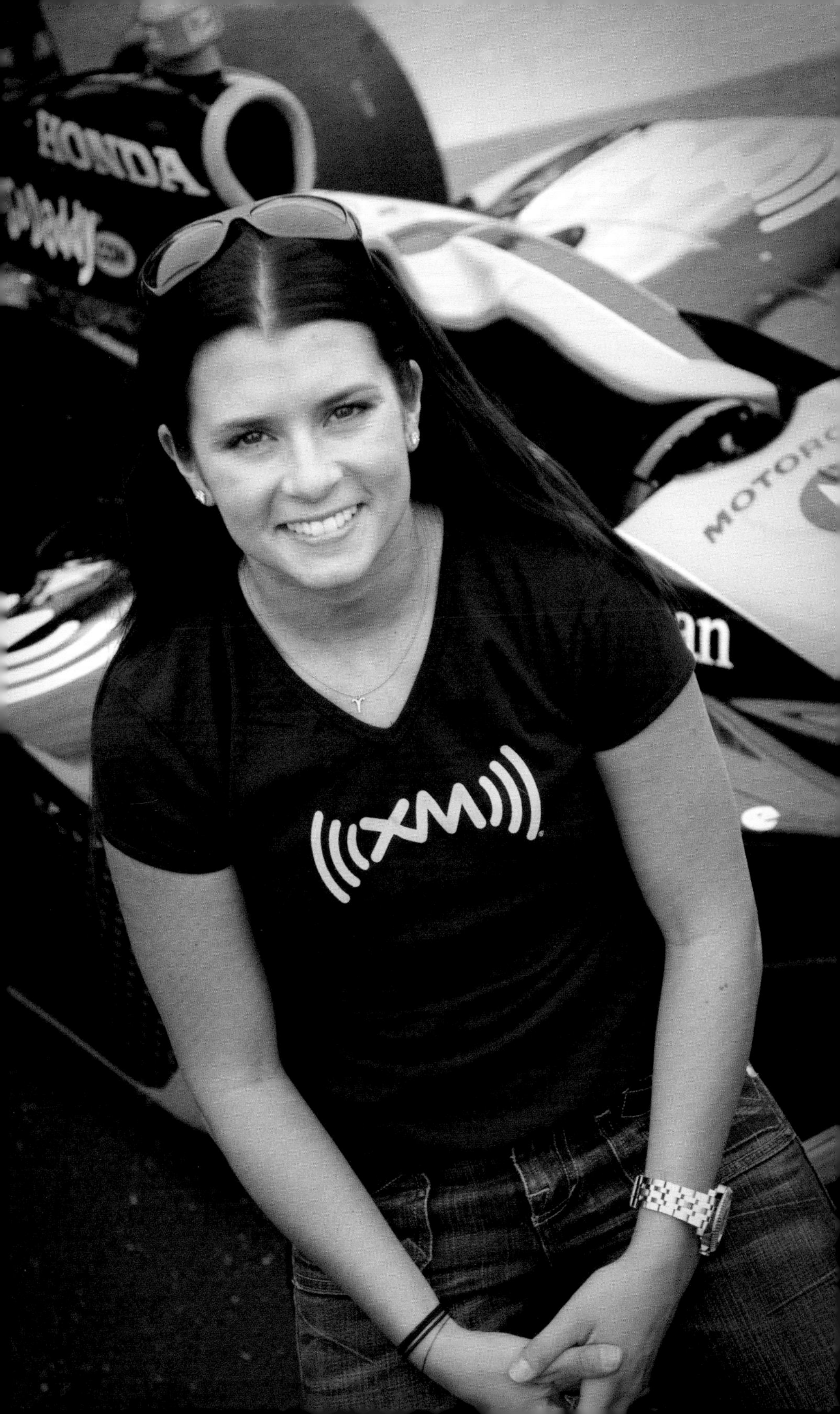
HONDA
XM

Clarence Thomas and Anita Hill: Head to Head

Few news events in the modern era caused such a stir as that of the confirmation hearings of Clarence Thomas to be a Supreme Court justice. The only other media circuses I can think of that rival it were the trials of OJ Simpson and Bill Clinton. As it happens, I had a front-row seat for the Clarence Thomas fiasco as it played out before the eyes of the nation.

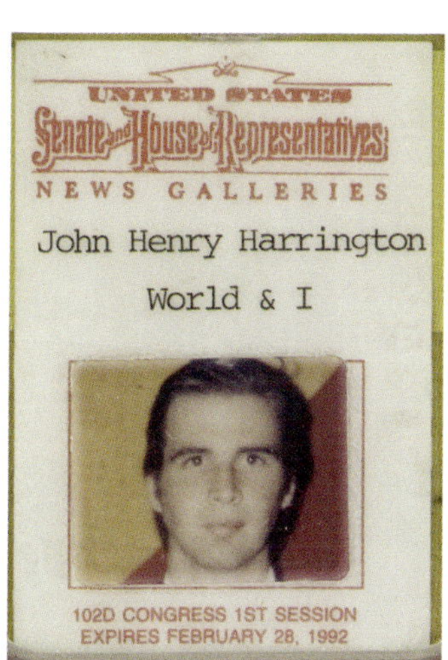

The hearings started out relatively normally on September 10, 1991. President George H.W. Bush had wanted to nominate Thomas when Justice Brennan stepped down in 1990; however, the discussions at the time suggested that this could be misperceived as a race-based appointment, so instead, David Souter was nominated.

On July 1, 1991, Thomas was nominated as Thurgood Marshall had just announced his retirement, and some experts suggested that Thomas was the only plausible black candidate for a conservative vote on the court.

Day in, and day out, the senators challenged Thomas, who they were all but certain was a conservative. The democrats were in control of the Senate at that time, so with a majority they could continue to beat on and pillory Thomas in the hopes of tripping him up and finding something that they could nail him on to deny him the nomination as the next Supreme Court justice.

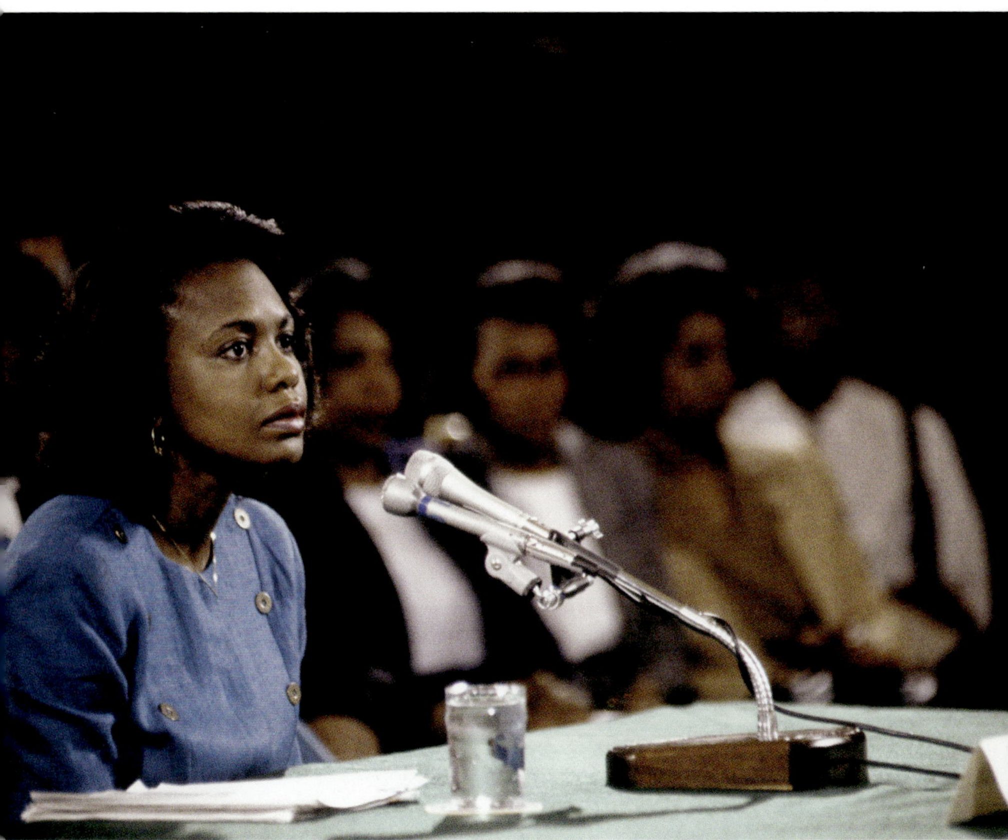

Anita Hill testifies at the Clarence Thomas hearings.

Near the end of the hearings, a confidential interview with a former co-worker of Thomas's, Anita Hill, done by the FBI, was leaked, and journalistic pandemonium ensued as Hill was brought in to testify. I had already made several images of Thomas from one side, and I envisioned photographing Hill from the other, so that the spread in the magazine could place them "head to head," facing left and facing right. I sat, crouched, for hours and days on end, making the images of each of them from the left and from the right. How many rolls of film exactly did we need of these two?!

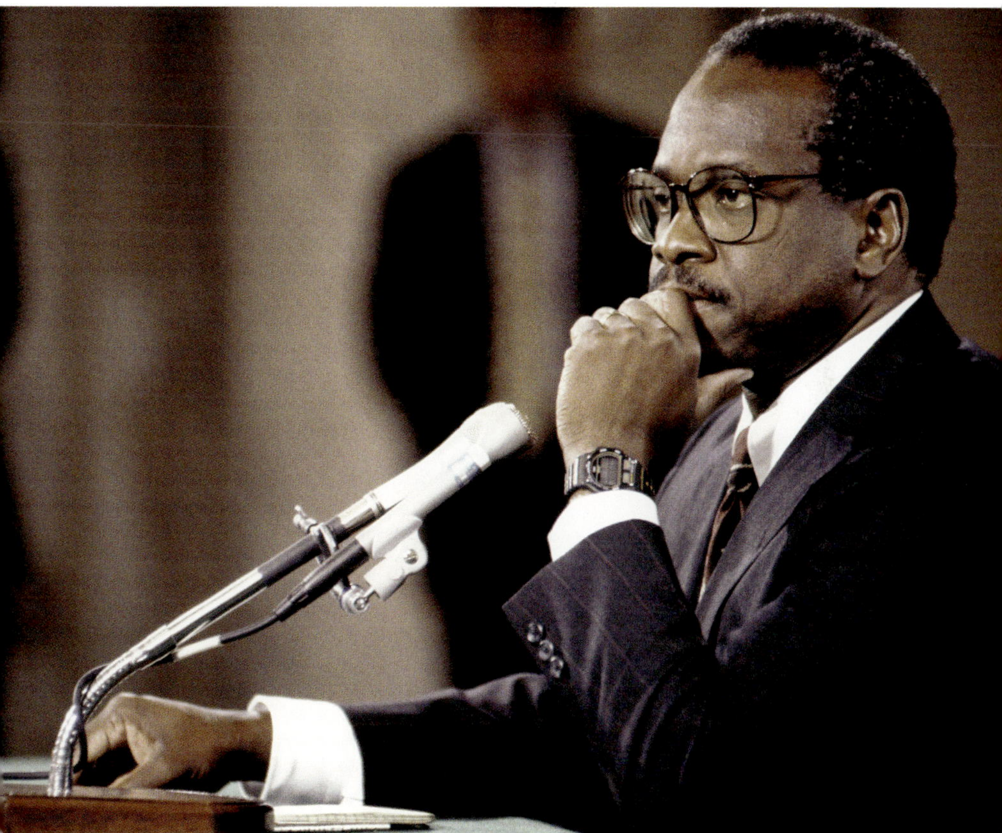

Clarence Thomas listens to a senator during his confirmation hearings.

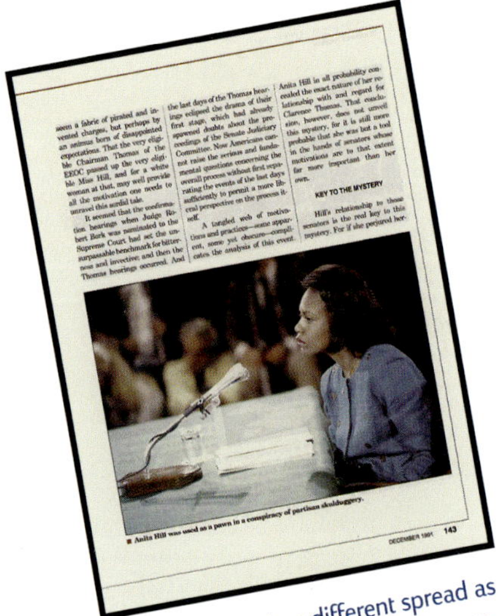

seem a fabric of pirated and invented charges, but perhaps by an animus born of disappointed expectations. That the very eligible Chairman Thomas of the EEOC passed up the very eligible Miss Hill, and for a white woman at that, may well provide all the motivation one needs to unravel this sordid tale.

It seemed that the confirmation hearings when Judge Robert Bork was nominated to the Supreme Court had set the unsurpassable benchmark for bitterness and invective; and then the Thomas hearings occurred. And the last days of the Thomas hearings eclipsed the drama of their first stage, which had already spawned doubts about the proceedings of the Senate Judiciary Committee. Now Americans cannot raise the serious and fundamental questions concerning the overall process without first separating the events of the last days sufficiently to permit a more liberal perspective on the process itself.

A tangled web of motivations and practices—some apparent, some yet obscure—complicates the analysis of this event. Anita Hill in all probability concealed the exact nature of her relationship with and regard for Clarence Thomas. That conclusion, however, does not unveil this mystery, for it is still more probable that she was but a tool in the hands of senators whose motivations are to that extent far more important than her own.

KEY TO THE MYSTERY

Hill's relationship to those senators is the real key to this mystery. For if she perjured her-

■ Anita Hill was used as a pawn in a conspiracy of partisan skulduggery.

DECEMBER 1991 143

Anita Hill shown in a different spread as a part of the coverage of the Clarence Thomas hearings—not "head-to-head" with him as I had hoped.

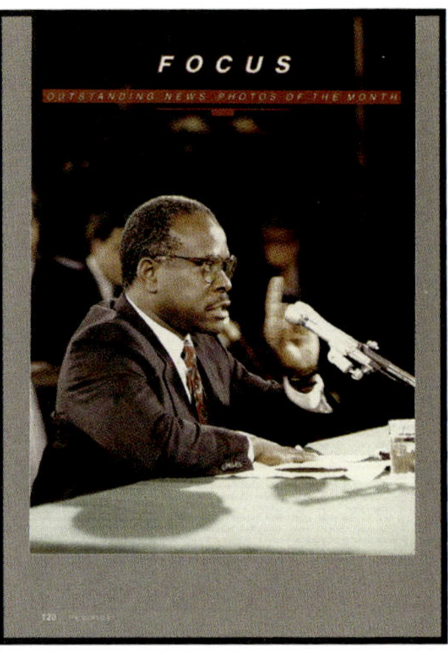

The opening page of the "Focus" section with Clarence Thomas running full page during his confirmation hearings.

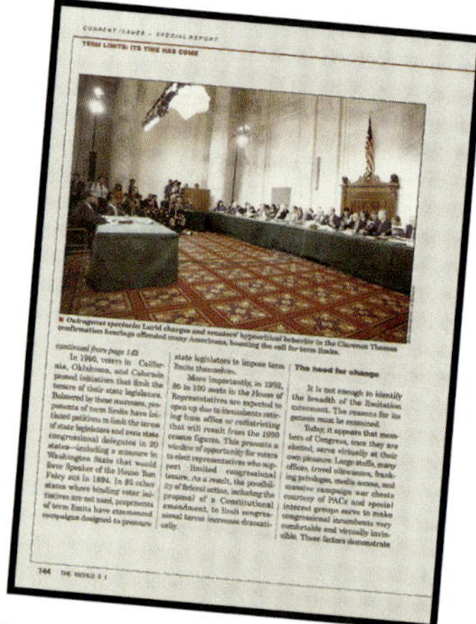

CURRENT ISSUES – SPECIAL REPORT

TERM LIMITS: ITS TIME HAS COME

■ Outrageous spectacle: Lurid charges and senators' hypocritical behavior in the Clarence Thomas confirmation hearings offended many Americans, boosting the call for term limits.

continued from page 143

In 1990, voters in California, Oklahoma, and Colorado passed initiatives that limit the tenure of their state legislators. Bolstered by these successes, proponents of term limits have initiated petitions to limit the terms of state legislators and even state congressional delegates in 20 states—including a measure in Washington State that would force Speaker of the House Tom Foley out in 1994. In 25 other states where binding voter initiatives are not used, proponents of term limits have commenced campaigns designed to pressure state legislators to impose term limits themselves.

More importantly, in 1992, 80 to 100 seats in the House of Representatives are expected to open up due to incumbents retiring from office or redistricting that will result from the 1990 census figures. This presents a window of opportunity for voters to elect representatives who support limited congressional tenure. As a result, the possibility of federal action, including the proposal of a Constitutional amendment, to limit congressional terms increases dramatically.

The need for change

It is not enough to identify the breadth of the limitation movement. The reasons for its genesis must be examined.

Today, it appears that members of Congress, once they are elected, serve virtually at their own pleasure. Large staffs, many offices, travel allowances, franking privileges, media access, and massive campaign war chests courtesy of PACs and special interest groups serve to make congressional incumbents very comfortable and virtually invincible. These factors demonstrate

144 THE WORLD & I

One of the other images showing the nominee before the full Senate Judiciary Committee as it appeared in the magazine.

In the end, although the magazine I worked for—*The World & I*—did publish the images, they didn't follow my design idea of placing them on facing pages, as I have done on the preceding pages. Somewhere in the universe, a design wrong is being righted.

Plant—The Pure Professional

Few rock-and-roll stars are as renowned as Robert Plant. Plant has filled stadiums in cities around the world. Yet, on the day I photographed him, there were about 40 of us in a small recording studio in Washington, DC, at the headquarters of XM Satellite Radio.

It was March of 2005, and Plant had been working with his newly formed band, the Strange Sensation, and promoting his album *Mighty ReArranger*. He was scheduled to come to XM and do an "Artist Confidential" event for an hour or so. These events typically included an interview portion as well as the artist performing several of his or her songs.

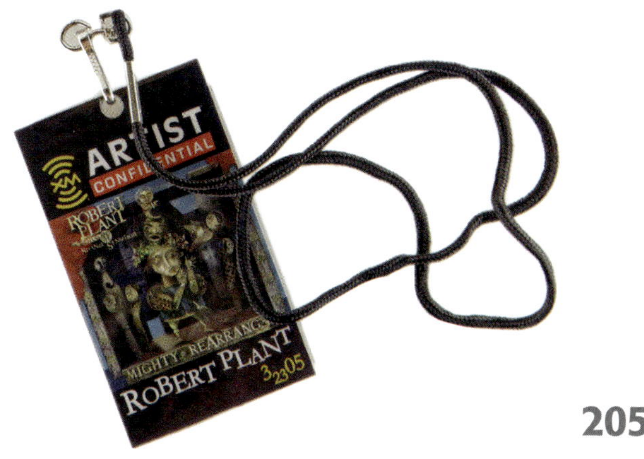

The purpose of the audience is to give the artist an intimate crowd to play to, as well as a few questions from those who are ultimately the artist's most avid fans. No doubt almost everyone was there because of Plant's legendary status with Led Zeppelin, yet Plant wanted to talk very little about those days, as he was focused on his new endeavors. The radio host did a remarkable job of coaxing from Plant just the insights that the audience wanted and dovetailing them very well with insights about Plant's current projects.

All the while it was my responsibility to silently (or as silently as possible) capture the magic in the studio on camera to promote the event when it aired and to have in the can for possible future use. This included images of Plant speaking, images of the interviewer speaking to Plant, shots of Plant performing, as well as a few "trade" shots with the interviewer and other XM execs posing with the artist.

The room was laid out slightly differently than normal because of the size of the band Plant brought in. In addition to the challenges of being as quiet as possible, I also had to be aware of where the three-plus remotely operated video cameras were and which direction they were pointing, so as not to be in those shots.

To capture Plant head-on and to be able to juxtapose him with the XM logo in the background, there was only one place I could be, and that was about 7 feet in front of Plant standing, and leaning up against a column. The problem with this position was that throughout the entire performance, rather than being hidden or less obvious (as is always my goal), I had to be front and center in his line of sight. This made me very uncomfortable, but it was the only choice.

Opposite page: Robert Plant looks directly into my camera's lens (one of many times) during his performance in the Hugh Panaro Performance Theatre at XM Satellite Radio, promoting the album *The Mighty ReArranger.*

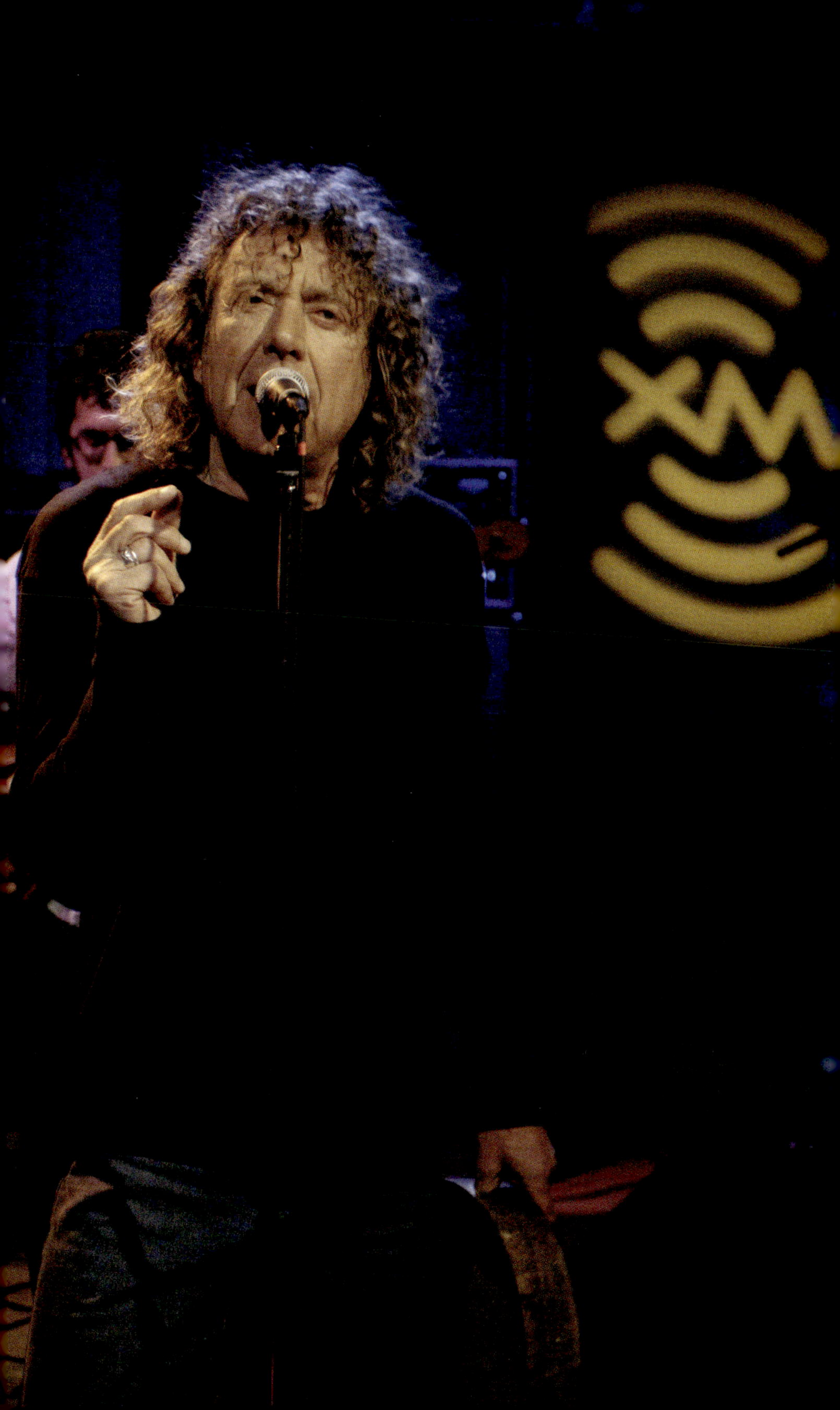
XM

Fortunately, when Plant was being interviewed, he wasn't looking my direction; but for much of his performance, when his eyes were open, he was usually looking right at me. Rather than shrink from this opportunity that I'd never had before, I decided to take advantage of it. Plant, being the consummate professional, seemed unfazed by my being in his line of sight, and rather than being distracted by my presence, I felt a symbiotic connection being made between us as he was giving me the best he could as well.

Since my camera was silent, using a Jacobson Blimp, I wasn't making any distracting audible noise. If you're unfamiliar with a Jacobson Blimp, it is the best solution for working on movie sets, on sound stages, and in recording studios, and many directors and sound engineers won't let you into their space without one. By placing your camera in a custom-made soundproof housing (specific to each make and model of camera), the sound-dampening foam inside the hard-shell plastic case eliminates any noise from inside that the camera makes, from about one foot away. The case also includes a series of interchangeable tubes for each lens you have on your camera, depending upon how long or short the lens is. Lastly, there is a custom-made triggering wire that comes through the foam and hard-shell so you can trigger the camera's shutter and make pictures.

Plant performed an amazing set of music, and even though they weren't the tunes from Led Zeppelin that were so familiar to me, he still had a remarkable voice to share. I couldn't believe that I was experiencing what stadiums full of people had paid top dollar to hear—and I was doing it in an aurally perfect studio with an intimate group of people. It truly was a surreal experience, which was compounded following my review of the images where Plant is staring directly into my lens.

The key to working successfully in an incredibly intimate setting and close quarters is to have the best tools at your disposal so that your creative efforts are not thwarted by the needs of the many other elements of the project that are either equally—or in some cases more—important than you.

Vanity Press Corps

When a client calls for a photographer, one of the questions I often ask pertains to the scope of the event. Is it a 30-minute press conference or a reception? But the questions continue: Is it a simple reception or one with a lengthy receiving line? Is there a meet-and-greet beforehand? All of these questions help me determine the scope of the project and what tools and talent we need to bring to bear with this assignment.

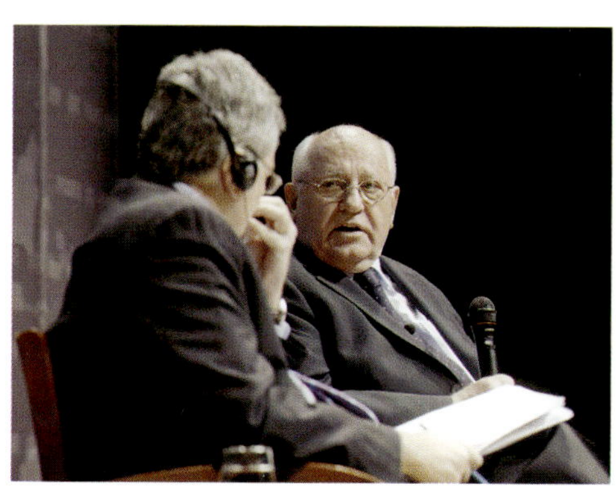

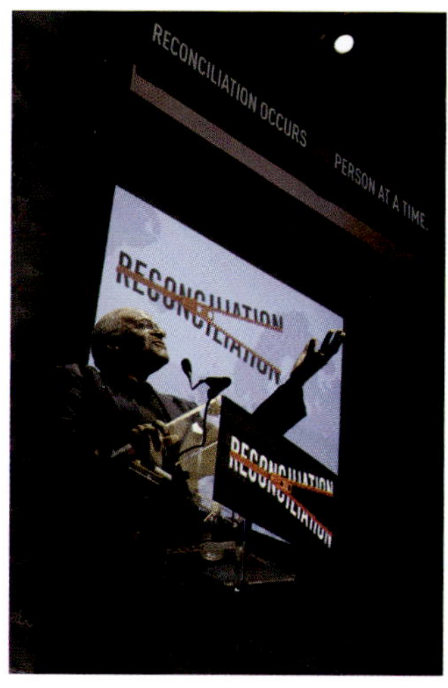

Such was the case when we were called upon to do a multi-day conference that brought the likes of Desmond Tutu and Mikhail Gorbachev to Washington to discuss human rights issues and how to begin the healing process around the world. At first, the client asked for 12 photographers for three full days. A simple math equation will help you to quickly understand that this was potentially about $50,000 for the job.

Although I completely trusted my client, I thought back to a lesson I learned from an employer I had in college, Tony. I was a limousine driver then, and he shared with me a story about a couple who were getting married and needed somewhere around 50 limousines. Although I can't recall the exact number, suffice it to say that with multi-day drivers and cars, the bill was astronomical. Tony was a smart guy, and even though every other limousine company wanted to be the prime contractor for this job, Tony won it, and he had to bring in extra cars from as far away as New York City. Tony had one requirement: For a job this big, he wanted it prepaid. At first the client balked, but Tony said he wouldn't take the job any other way.

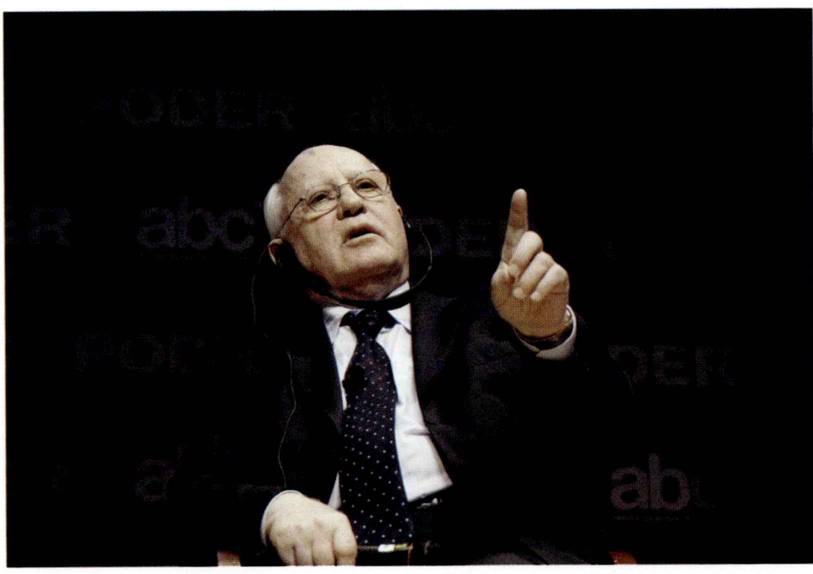

Mikhail Gorbachev makes a point during the program.

The sad fact was that in the end, the hotel, florist, band, and every other vendor besides Tony got stood up for payment. The florist reportedly went out of business, as this well-to-do South American family skipped town and left behind all the unpaid bills. I wasn't about to let this happen to me—not when it was potentially 11 of my friends who would be upset with me if they didn't get paid for work they had performed.

I conveyed to my client that because they were U.S. based and because I had a working relationship with them, I would need 50 percent to secure and confirm all of our photographers, and the remaining 50 percent would be due on the final day of shooting. Ultimately, my client's client would be responsible for making sure this happened, and it did.

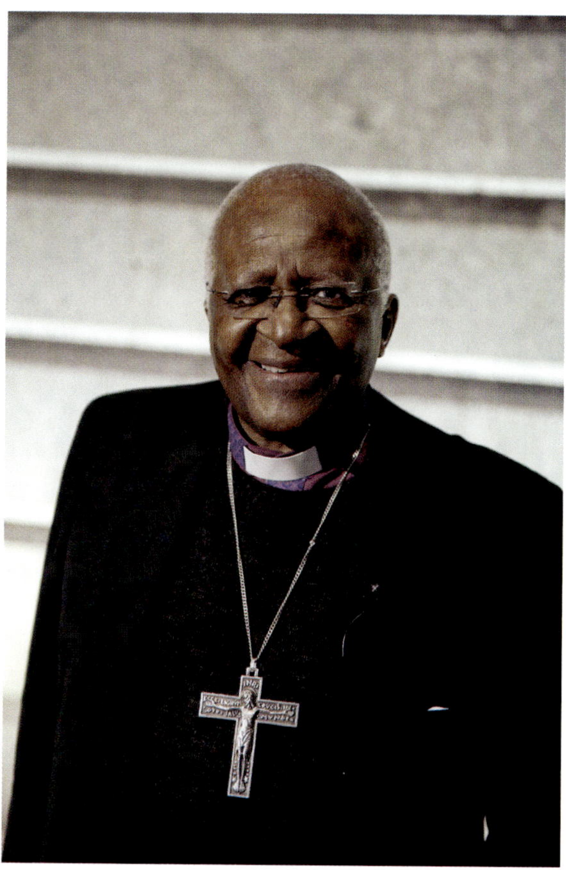

Desmond Tutu, prior to participating in the program.

The client seemed relieved to know that we would handle all the photographers ourselves, rather than them having to manage each of the photographers' positions and ensure that there would be little to no duplication. As we went back and forth during the initial conversations, it became clear that part of why they wanted so many photographers was to essentially buy themselves a press corps—a press presence—that would make the event seem more important than it might be. After reviewing their budget, they settled on six of us, from 8:00 a.m. to 6:00 p.m. each day, and we also had to bring in a post-production person, as the client wanted same-day delivery of a number of images. The post-production person had to be dedicated to taking in everyone's cards and making sure that happened.

The challenge with these types of multi-photographer events is that if everyone were left to his or her own devices, the images would be duplicated. It's natural for a professional photographer to ascertain not only the best angles, but also the best moments when photographing an event such as this. Take, for example, a wedding. If you were a wedding client and booked two photographers, in all likelihood you'd have both of them at the end of the aisle as you were coming up the aisle after your ceremony.

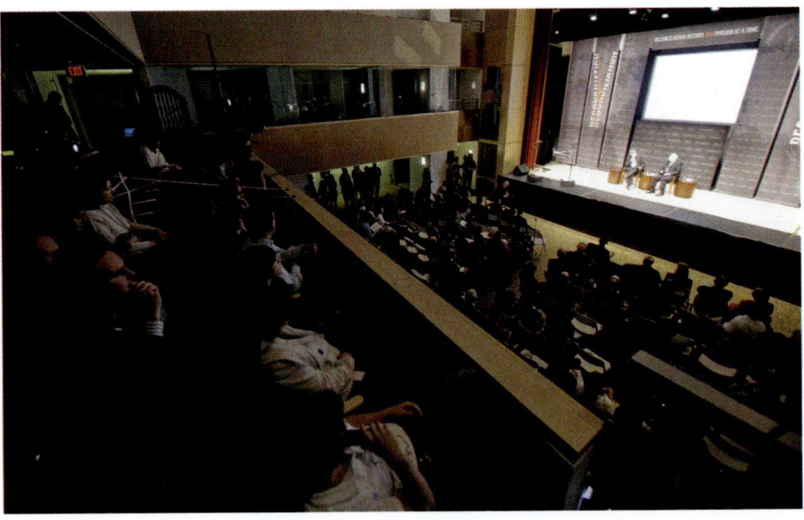

The view from the balcony during the program.

Instead, having one capture the image from the top and one from the back would give you better coverage. The same holds true when there are a half-dozen talented photographers looking to make the best images possible. Directing each photographer to cover from a particular position ensures full coverage of the event.

For this project, I assigned one photographer to the back of the room, shooting everything with a long lens; one on the left side of the room; and one on the right. There was a balcony area, so we covered things from both balcony sides, and we had a rover who could capture audience reactions to the speakers. All in all, we could have done this project with just two or three photographers working very hard; but in the end, everyone was appreciative of the work, and for a change none of us had to work hard, hustling around the room—we could just focus on one part of the event, from one angle. After a while, this did challenge us to do something different and make images that challenged us. Further, the client got the ambiance of "press" everywhere, so the audience felt as if it was an important news event.

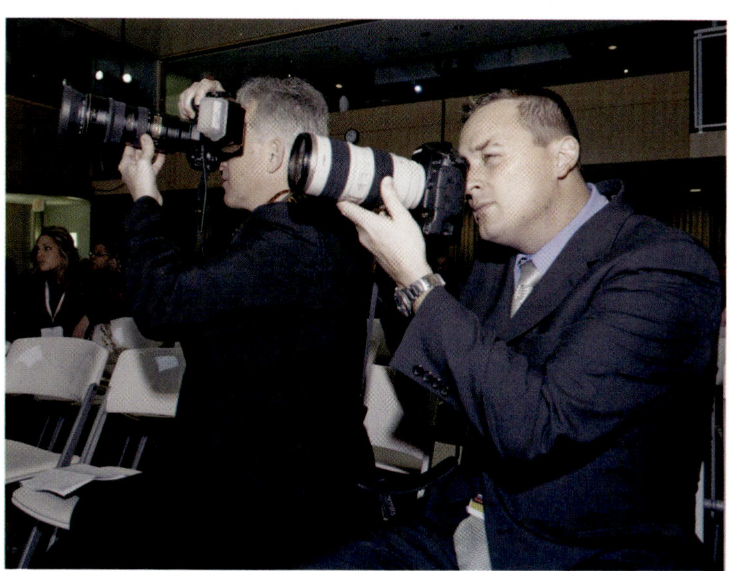

Good friends and colleagues Nick Cretter (left) and William Foster (right) work the angles as a part of the photo team covering the event.

Several of the key speakers were exciting to see. Photographing Desmond Tutu was especially interesting, as was photographing Mikhail Gorbachev. Because he was one of my first professional photography assignments just under 20 years prior, when he was the Soviet Premier, seeing him on stage at this event and making an image of him backstage with actor Val Kilmer was a unique experience, to be certain. In the end, the client was very happy with the results, and fortunately, everyone got paid—not just me.

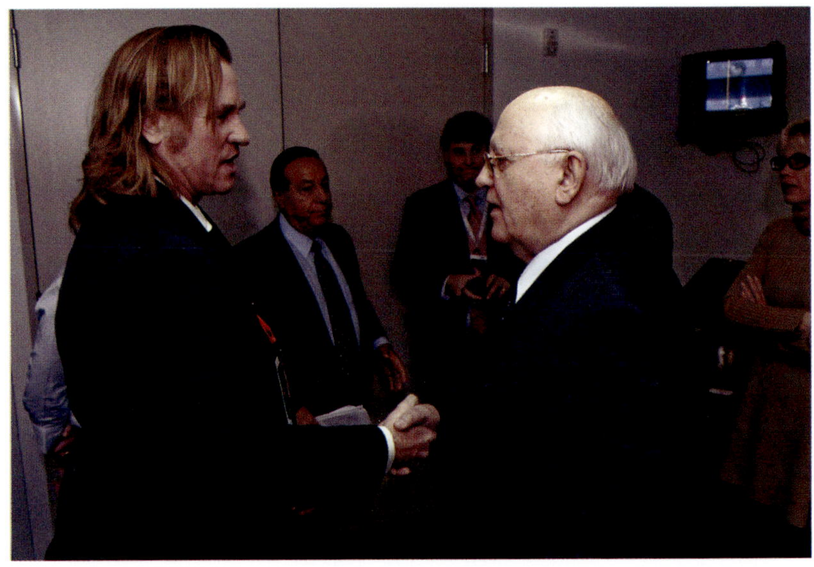

Actor Val Kilmer meets with Mikhail Gorbachev in the green room backstage.

September 11, 2001

I think almost everyone remembers where they were on September 11th, 2001, and this is my story.

I was scheduled to be at a client's office at 8:00 a.m. in Maryland, just outside of Washington, DC, doing portraits for several hours. I had an assistant with me, and we began setting up at 8:00 in the client's conference room. We were ready for our first portrait at about 8:30. We finished that subject and were waiting for the second of three to come into the room when someone came in and turned on the overhead projector to CNN, which was broadcasting the news that at 8:46 a.m., American Airlines Flight 11 had "crashed" into the north tower of the World Trade Center. I remember being dumbstruck by this and, along with everyone else, thinking about it as a tragic accident. The second subject came in, and we were able to accomplish that portrait. Just after that, with cameras trained on the towers, United Airlines Flight 175 crashed into the South Tower at 9:03 a.m.

Our third subject was a no-show, for obvious reasons, and my assistant and I watched the news as it was unfolding before our eyes on the huge conference-room screen. We were packed up by about 9:20 and out the door. We were in our car listening to the radio on the 495 Beltway surrounding the city, headed back to the office, when we heard the news that at 9:37 a.m., American Airlines Flight 77 was flown into the Pentagon. I turned to my assistant and said, "We're going back to the office, dumping this lighting equipment, getting extra provisions and gear, and then heading to the Pentagon." She said, in a very quiet voice, "Okay."

About 10 minutes later my cell phone rang, and it was *People* magazine: "Are you available for an assignment right now?"

"Of course, what do you need me to do?" I replied. The editor told me he had heard of fires on the Mall, and he wanted me to go check things out. "How about the Pentagon?" I said. "No, I don't think so" came the response. I decided not to listen to him.

We arrived at the office at about 10:00 a.m. and literally threw all the equipment cases out of the Jeep 4x4. We loaded in long lenses, all the batteries I had, and some provisions. I also grabbed a change of clothes, because, as crazy as it sounds, I did have other contractually obligated assignments that day/evening, and I wanted to be prepared.

We headed toward the Pentagon, and traffic was backed up on the freeway cutting across the city toward the Potomac River, where the Pentagon was located. I saw the smoke in the distance as I turned north onto Route 110, just east of the Pentagon. At 10:36 a.m., according to the metadata in the first image I shot, I saw a local fire department ambulance from the Cabin John Park Volunteer Fire Department, and then I passed by some firemen taking refuge under a tree at 11:11 a.m.

Opposite page: The view into the point of impact at the Pentagon as fire trucks worked to put out the fire.

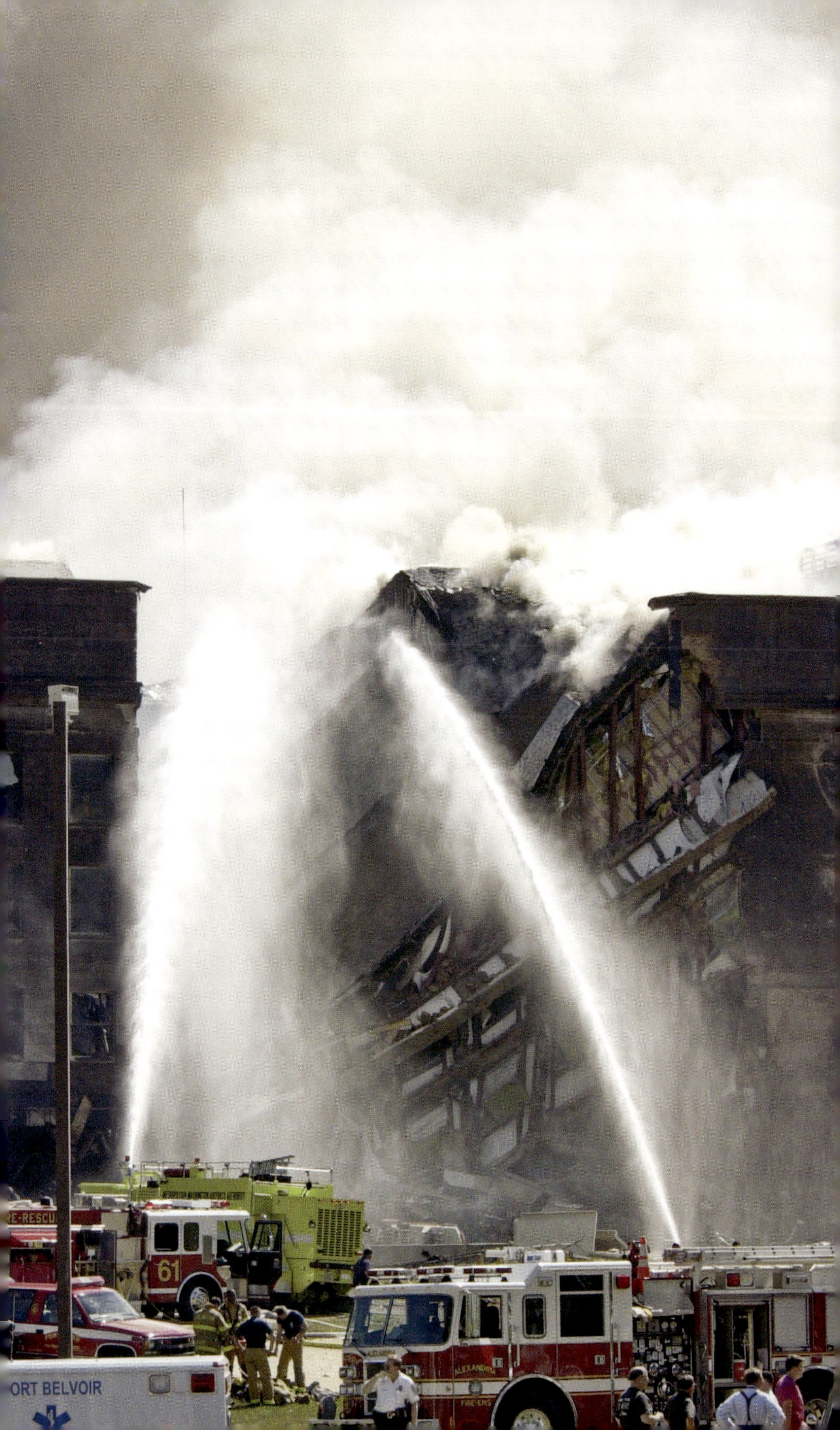
RE-RESCU
61
ORT BELVOIR

Traffic by now was chaos, and we abandoned my Jeep on the side of the road. I posted my press placard in the windshield and hoped the Jeep would be there when I returned. Attempting to walk toward the Pentagon, I was stopped by security, and I made a few frames from that perspective. In the distance, I noticed a vantage point that would give me a remarkable view of the crash site, elevated just enough to give a clear view. It required some serious walking to get there.

Trekking north into Arlington National Cemetery, which is immediately across from the Pentagon at the crash site, I entered the grounds and began walking south, toward the maintenance entrance at the southeastern side of the cemetery. Thirty minutes further on, I made my way up behind a tree line, up to the elevated position I had seen. I came through the tree line and found one other photographer there. We were fairly obscured and behind a fence, high enough up that we could see right into the crash site. Every other news outlet was relegated to a point about a half-mile away, at the Citgo gas station on South Joyce Street. Although this entire trek took the better part of an hour, it was well worth the effort.

I began making images, not knowing how long it would be before the other photographer and I were kicked out. Technically, no one legally had the right to throw us off what was public property—especially not when we were in a fenced-in area and not interfering in any way with the emergency efforts, and given that we were both properly credentialed by the U.S. government as *bona fide* members of the news media.

As the flames billowed from the wreckage in the building, firemen diligently worked to put out fires through broken windows. Priests were walking among the rescue workers, giving last rites, as first responders below my vantage point moved fresh stretchers to the site.

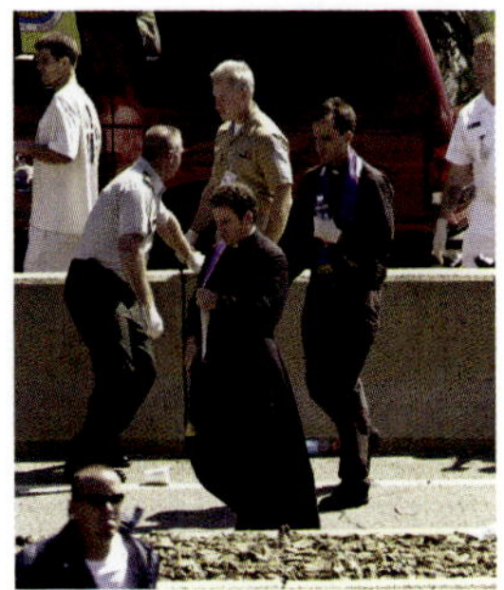

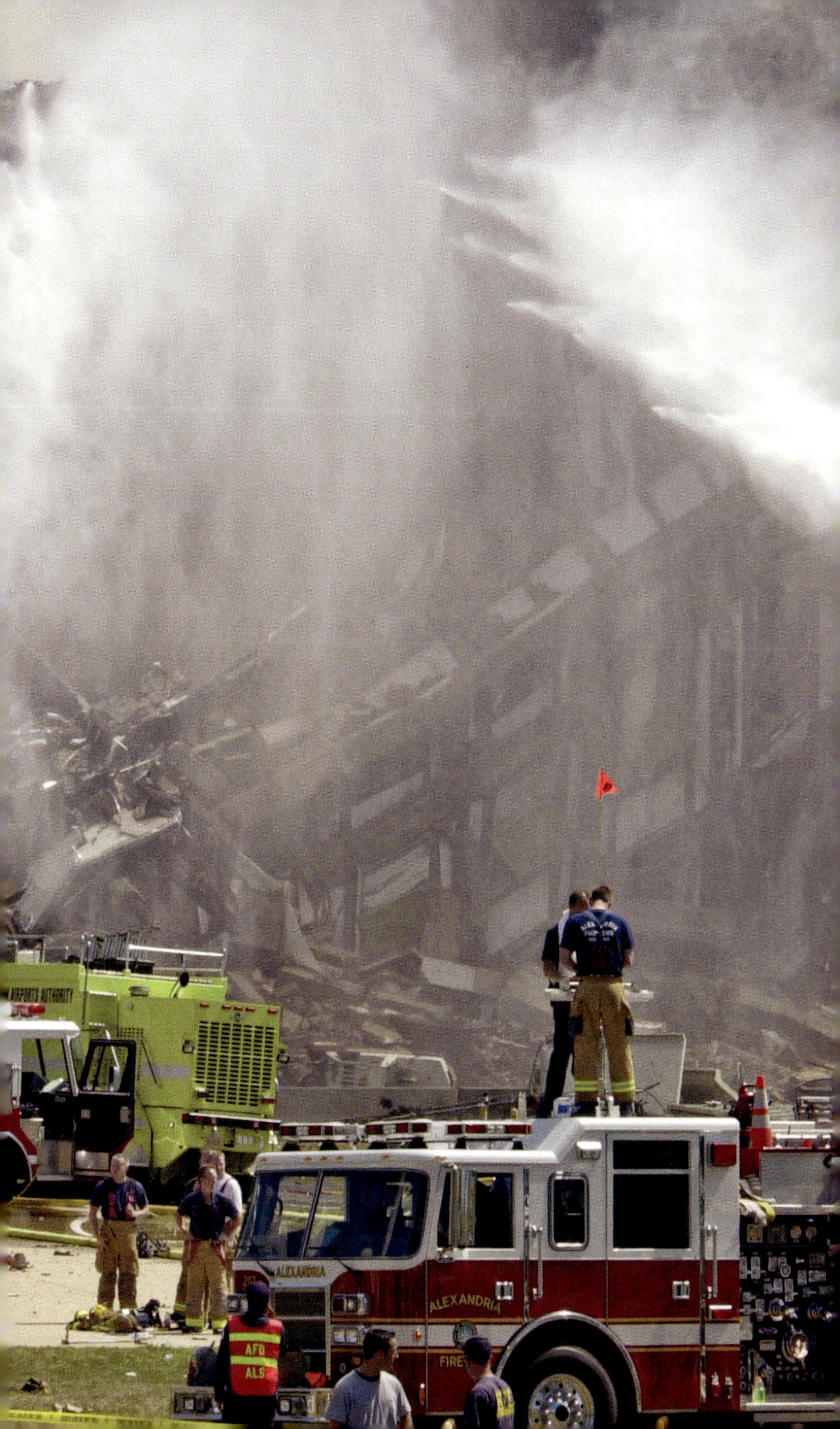
AIRPORTS AUTHORITY
ALEXANDRIA
ALEXANDRIA
AFD
ALS
FIRE

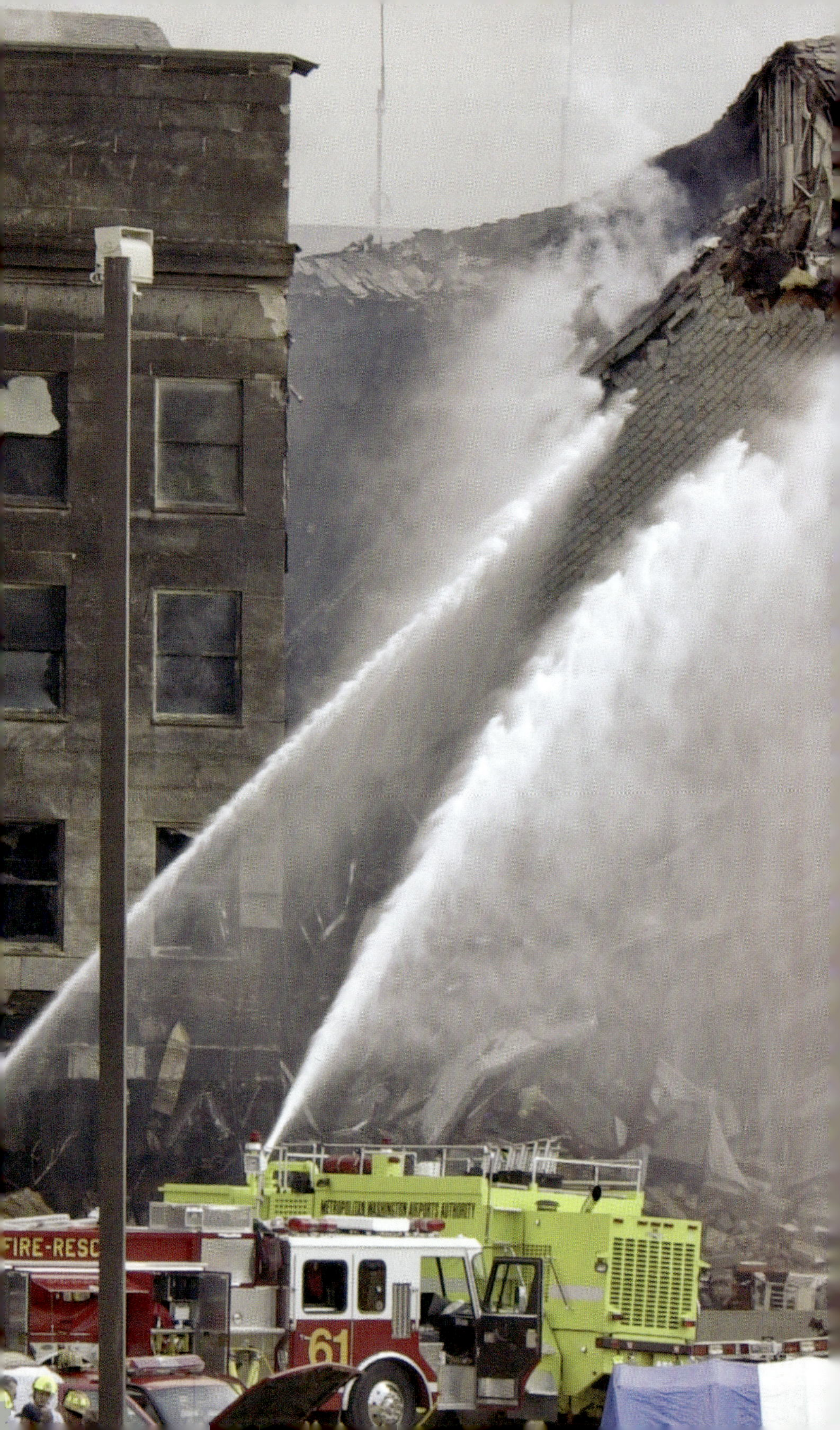
FIRE-RESC
61

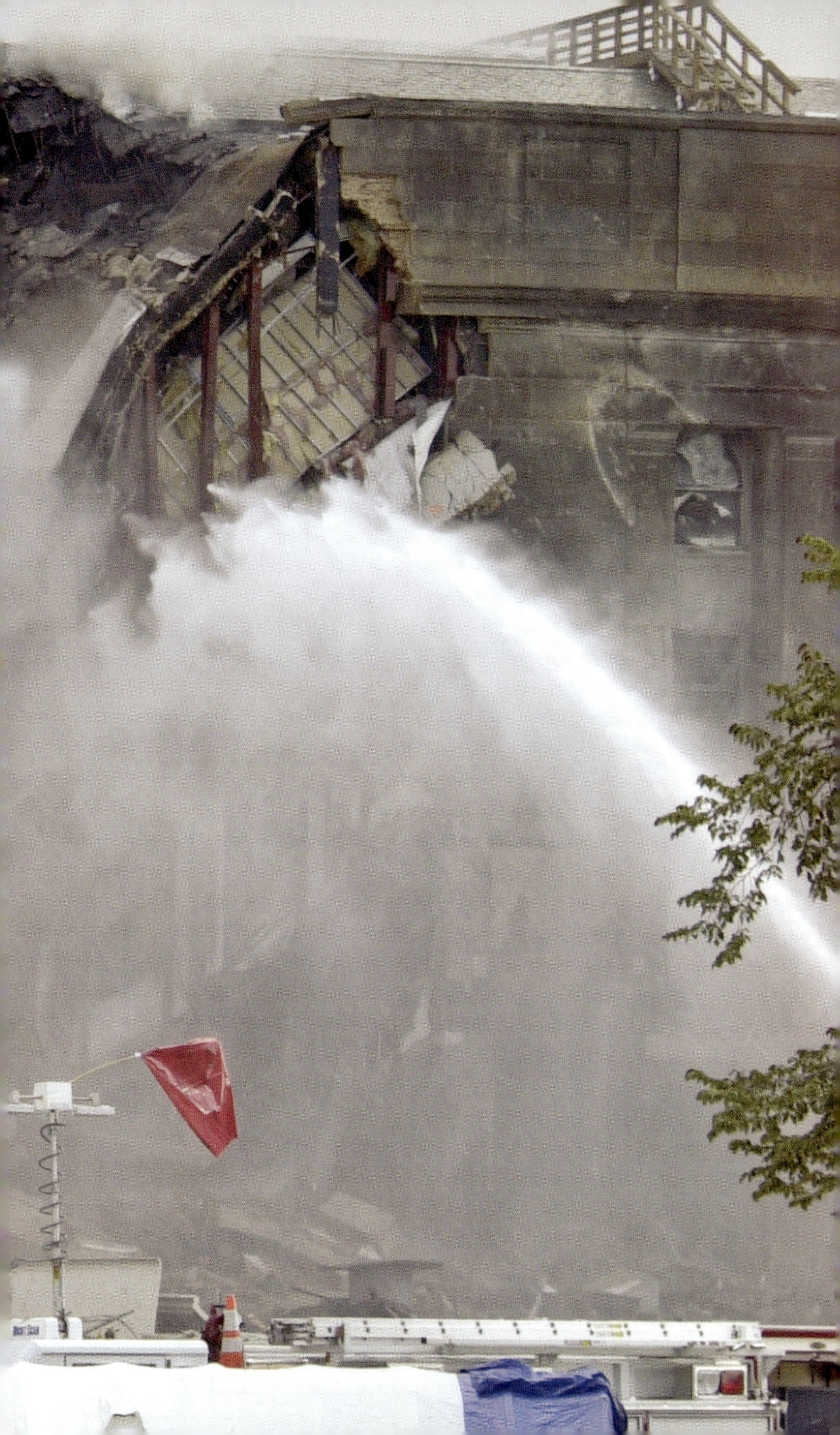

At about 1:45 p.m. I saw two firemen headed toward a burned-out section of the building, where the flames had been extinguished, one with an American flag on his shoulder. The one carrying the flag went to a steel post protruding from the ground and raised the American flag. Then he raised his fist high in the air, and I felt a chill run through my body.

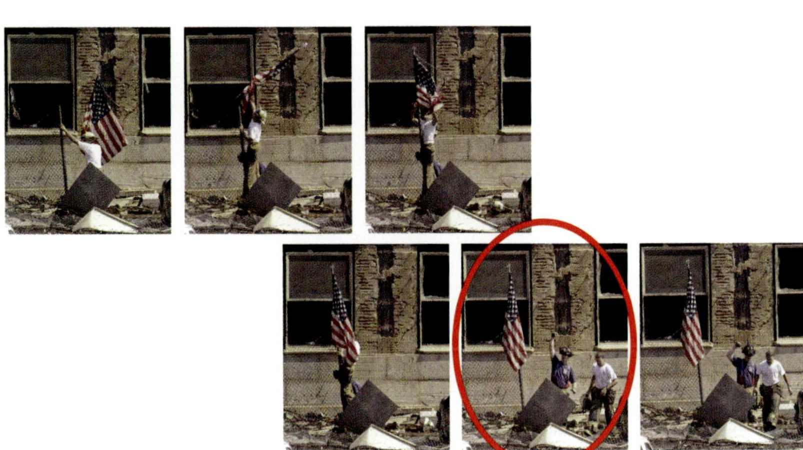

Shortly thereafter, FBI agents came through the area flashing their badges and ordered us out. We both protested loudly, identifying ourselves and arguing, but today was not a day to be aggravating federal agents, so the better part of valor was to depart the area. With that, I walked down to the Citgo station, and many of my colleagues were already there, bemoaning the poor nature of the viewing angle. "Where were you?" came the questions. "Oh, over there on the rise, looking right into the crash site," was my casual answer, yet I knew that it was the best vantage point anyone could've ever asked for when covering an incident like this. Being willing to go the extra mile (literally) for the angle was the difference between nothing and everything. I made a few images of a press conference, but the hour was late, and I had somewhere else I was contractually obligated to be.

Over the course of an hour, I made my way back to my car. On my way, *Business Week* called me to ask whether I was available that evening and beyond. Because I had other commitments, I had

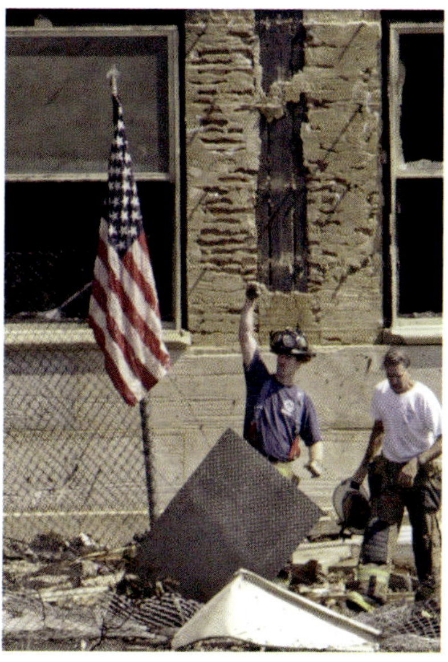

A local firefighter posts the American flag and pumps his fist into the air.

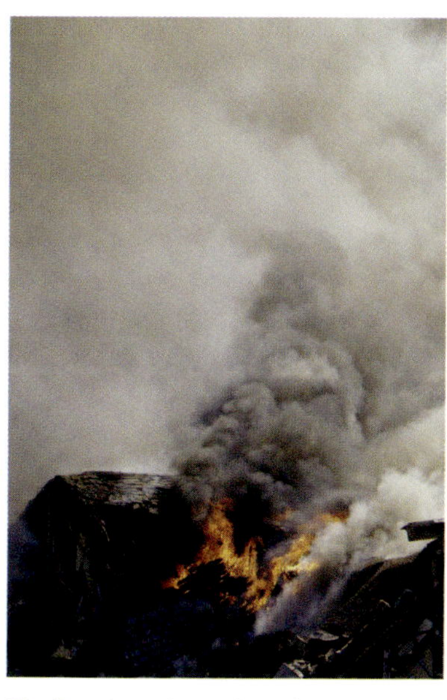

The flames on the rooftop of the Pentagon at the point of impact.

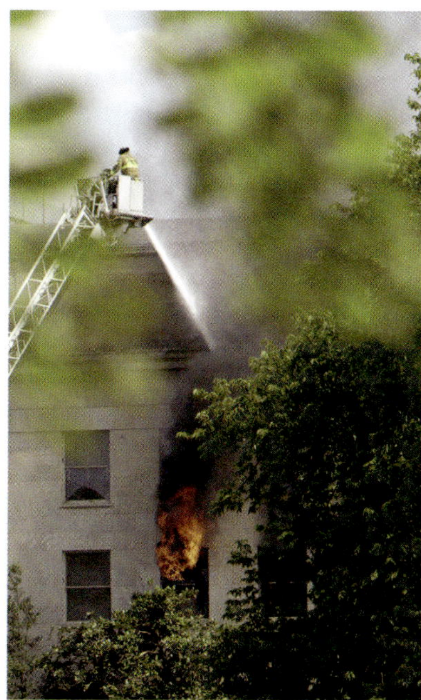

A firefighter putting out a fire through a broken window near the point of impact.

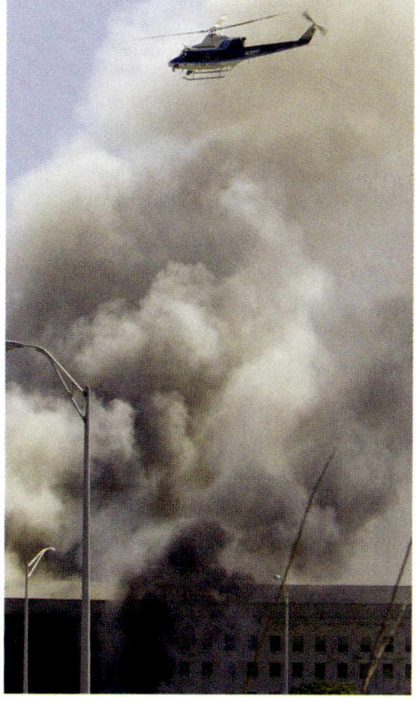

A U.S. Park Police helicopter surveys the scene amid the smoke coming from the point of impact.

to decline, though I had just wrapped up my *People* magazine commitment for the time being. I got to my car and made my way to the nearby Ritz-Carlton Hotel. I changed into my suit and presented myself at the appointed hour of 5:30 p.m. to my client, who was scheduled to have a reception there. The client, as was to be expected, had cancelled their event, so I was free to go. I called back *Business Week*, but of course they had already found someone else for their multi-day needs.

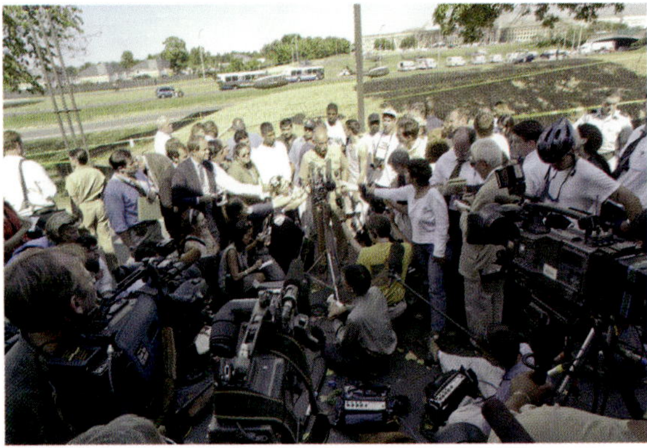

The press conference I encountered just before calling it a day.

Over the course of the next few days, I divided my time between the local hospitals and the Pentagon, on assignment for *People* and a nursing magazine. The nursing magazine had assigned me to do a portrait inside the Pentagon of a nurse, Eileen Murphy. When I walked into her examination room, I immediately recognized her—I had seen her outside at work on the 11th. I commented briefly on this, but she didn't want to discuss her work out there, nor see the images I had made of her on the 11th. So, we proceeded with the portrait, and that was that.

To date, these images have not been published. *People* magazine, a New York–headquartered publication, focused on their hometown and opted for a few DC images from the wire services. So, the select few images you see here from the many that I have are being published for the first time, in this book. From the raising of the flag, to the fighting of the fires, to the people who made a difference that day, I commend you.

Seal Wins Approval from Ambassadors to Bullfighters

When I got the assignment to travel throughout Mexico, I didn't know what to expect. I knew that I would be completely self-contained, and I had a limited amount of money to hire fixers to make my life easier. I also had next to zero comprehension of the Spanish language. However, this had not thwarted my travels to Cuba or elsewhere in the world where I had an equally poor comprehension of the language. I had just finished watching the movie *Salvador* with James Woods, and I recalled a scene where Woods, who played a photojournalist, had found himself stuck in El Salvador on the 4th of July and attended a 4th of July party at the U.S. embassy there. Thinking I would do the same thing, since I was stuck in Mexico City in the days leading up to and on the 4th of July, I called the embassy. To the very pleasant woman who answered the phone, I introduced myself as a photojournalist on assignment in Mexico City. I indicated that I was stuck in town and wondered whether the embassy was planning anything for the 4th of July. At that time I had no clue of what I was in for.

The woman said that they were, but she didn't say anything more. I mentioned that I was used to celebrating it on the Mall, covering the fireworks displays in Washington, and I was feeling a bit homesick for it. Was there a possibility of my coming to the party? Now, I'm not generally somebody who invites myself to parties, but I was under the misguided impression that it would be as informal a party as I had seen in the movie, which was fine because all I had were jeans and a variety of casual shirts.

I hopped in my rental car and made my way over to the ambassador's residence. As I parked my car and got out, I realized that I was in way over my head. This apparently was the hot ticket for the entire social scene in Mexico City that day—people were dressed to the nines in suits and beautiful dresses despite the summer heat. Instead of turning tail, I wanted to speak to the woman who had so graciously allowed me to come and express my appreciation—but acknowledge that in jeans and a polo shirt, I was clearly underdressed. Then I would make my way back to my hotel.

When I presented myself to the person with "the list," she looked me up and down as if surely I couldn't be on the list, but her attitude when she asked whether she could help me suggested that she might feign a cursory perusal of her list before sending me on my way back to where I came from. Instead, I asked to speak to the person with whom I had spoken on the phone, and I waited outside for the few minutes that it took for her to come out. When she did I greeted her, expressed my appreciation, and told her that I knew I was underdressed and I appreciated her last-minute courtesy of extending my invitation, but I didn't feel like coming in given my attire. To her credit, she was most gracious when she said, "No, no, please come in. We're happy to have you." I asked whether she was sure, and she reiterated her desire again, so I joined the line of people waiting to be received by the ambassador and his wife just inside the door. I could tell by the look on the list checker's face that she was not pleased with this turn of events, but clearly this decision had been made above her pay grade, and she had nothing more to say.

As I arrived and shook the hands of the ambassador and then his wife, followed by other senior embassy staff, I did have one ace up my sleeve. The one shirt that I brought that I thought might get me out of a jam was a dark-blue polo emblazoned with a variation of the Presidential seal that said "Clinton/Gore 1992." The seal was positioned prominently on the left side of my chest so it was visible and eye-catching to anyone giving me a cursory preview. When I shook hands with the ambassador, I expressed to him my apologies for being under-attired and said that I appreciated his graciousness in celebrating the 4th of July here in Mexico. After he thanked me, he immediately focused on the shirt, which I had gotten during the 1992 Clinton-Gore campaign, and asked whether I was from Washington. I indicated that I worked in Washington as a photojournalist and that I was here in Mexico City on assignment. He said simply, "Enjoy your stay in Mexico and let us know if there's anything we can do while you're here. Happy 4th of July, and enjoy the party." And with that he moved on to the next guest, as if I had been standing there in a three-piece suit the entire time.

Crooner Ben Vereen had been flown in to sing patriotic songs a capella at the poolside, and many stations with American food dotted the backyard, from ice cream bars by Dove to hot dogs, hamburgers, and, yes, apple pie. When I left the party, I began thinking about my assignment for the next day, covering a bullfight in Mexico City.

It was on my list of things to photograph, and I had been fortunate enough to find that one was taking place during my time in the city. I decided to hire a fixer to help me make the pictures I wanted happen, which included a portrait I wanted to do of a bullfighter. I wore my emblazoned polo for a second day, thinking it might help gain me access to the tunnel where the bullfighters waited before going into the arena. My fixer started gesticulating and pointing at the seal on my polo shirt. Although the ambassador did not happen to help me directly, my interaction with him the day before spurred me on and filled me with self-confidence as I knowingly smiled back at him and nodded.

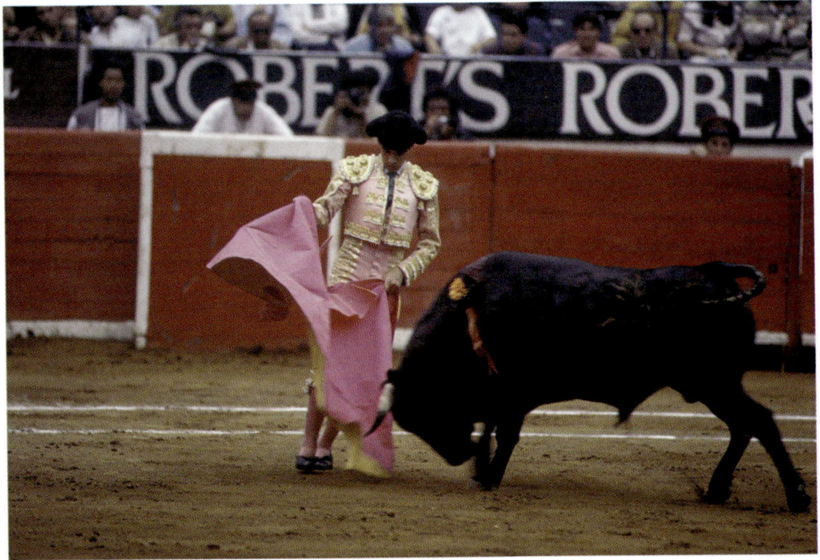

Battling with the bull.

The security guard let us pass, and my fixer, now believing he was escorting somebody important, and I found ourselves in the tunnel.

A young bullfighter from Spain was waiting in the wings a few moments before it was his time in the arena, and my fixer translated for me as I inquired of the bullfighter whether I might photograph him; the bullfighter said that it would be fine if I did. The stucco wall made for a beautiful and otherwise nondescript background, and the ambient light at this late hour in the day meant that a beautiful, soft light was coming in from the sky above the arena and getting darker farther in the tunnel. I positioned myself with the sky and the arena to my back, and the bullfighter simply struck a proud pose. After a few frames I asked my fixer whether the bullfighter would sign my release. He translated it, and the bullfighter signed the release.

Opposite page: Jose Tomas of Madrid, one of the world's most famous and dramatic bullfighters, at the young age of 18, before going out to meet the day's bulls in March, 1994.

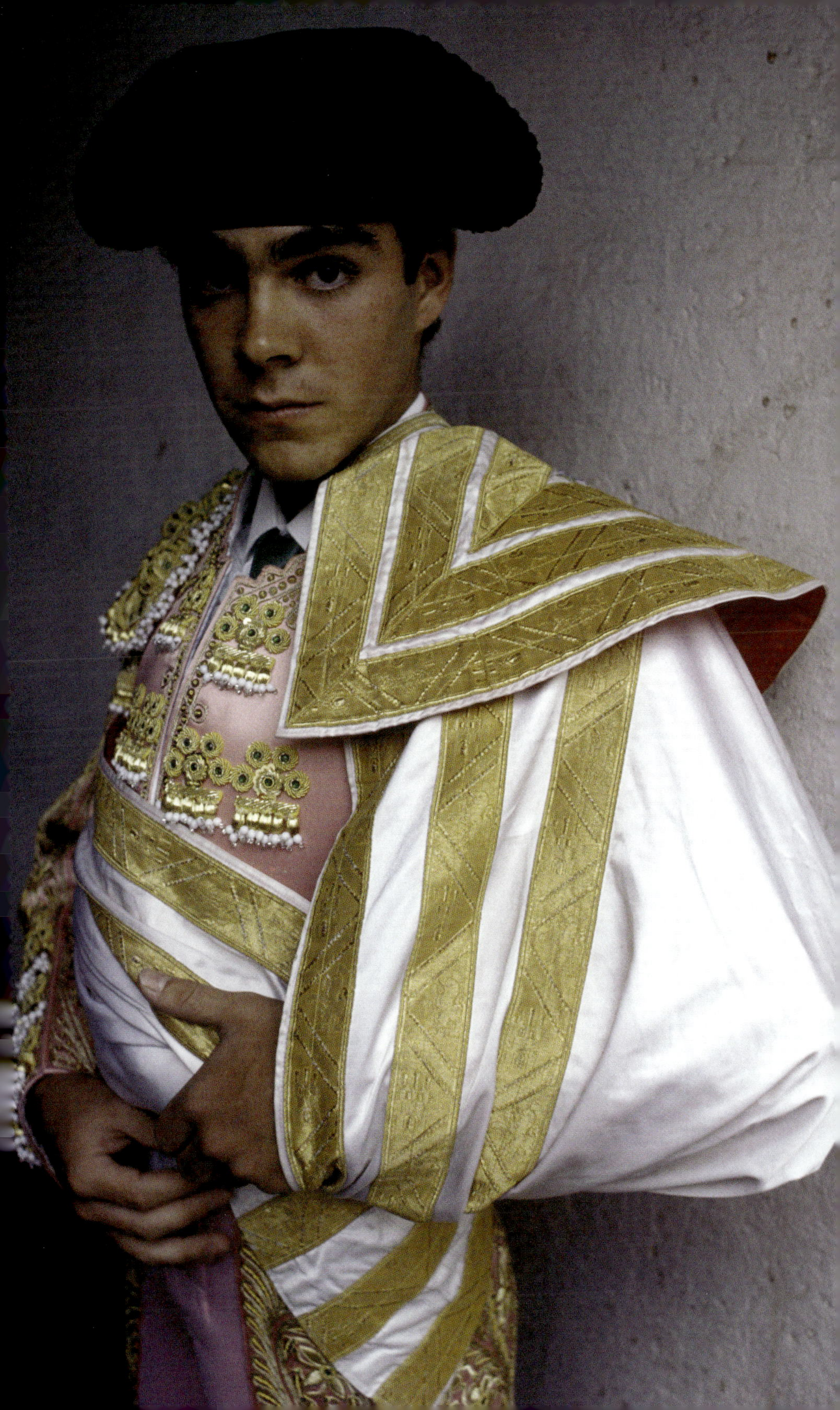

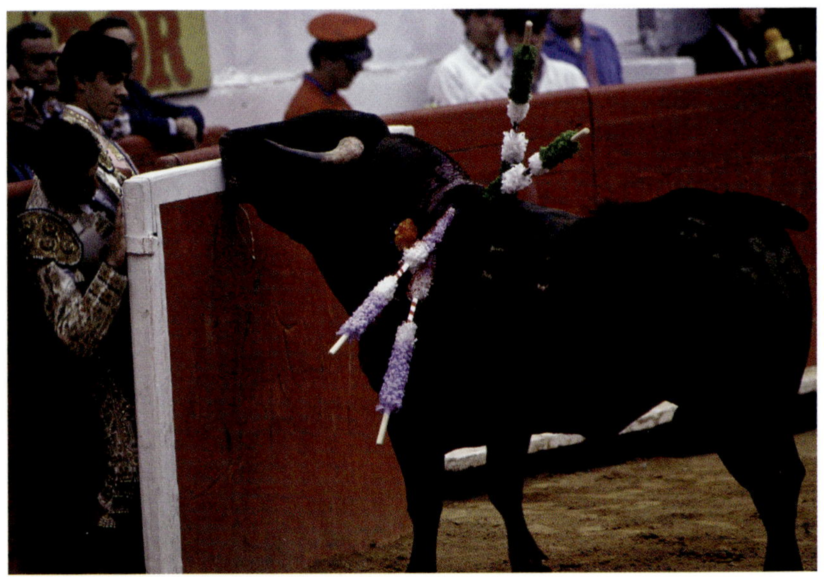

A wounded bull attempts to get at two bullfighters behind a shield.

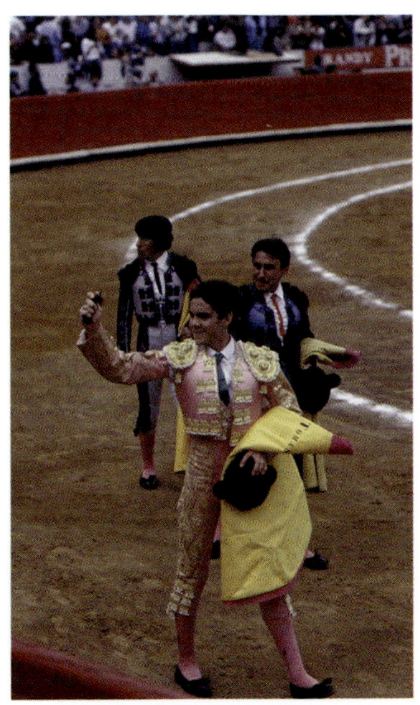

At the end of a bullfight, showcasing the tail of the bull.

He then went out into the arena and was successful in his bout with the bull. He paraded proudly around the arena after a close call had him scurrying behind a protective panel on the edge of the arena. I shot all the while, capturing those things, but knowing that my best picture was the portrait before his fight.

On leaving the arena, I had to chuckle at the authority my polo shirt from the gift shop at the Clinton inauguration had imbued in others.

Nelson Mandela: Dignity with Disability

I had always heard Nelson Mandela's name spoken in almost hushed tones, with reverence about his fight for justice and his principles for equality among his people.

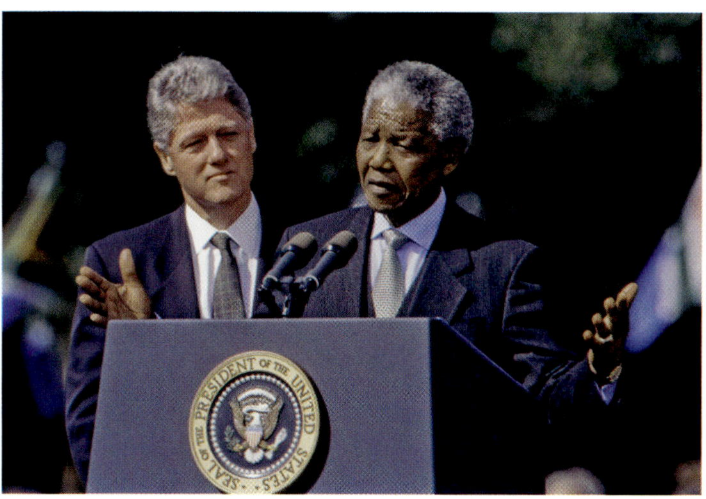

Nelson Mandela, the president of South Africa, during his arrival ceremony on the South Lawn of the White House during a state visit with President Clinton.

My first opportunity to photograph Mandela was when he visited the White House with then-President Clinton. A ceremony on the South Lawn, with all the pageantry that the White House could seemingly muster, was set out. It was a sunny day with a slight breeze blowing on a cool October morning in 1994.

Mandela had come to promote South Africa and to seek additional help from the United States in his fight for equality, now as a free man and a leader of his country. The ceremony on the South Lawn was moving, with Mandela captivating the crowd.

During the course of his remarks, I was able to move around a bit. First, I was able to make several great images of him head on —waiting for just the right moment as President Clinton, behind him and to camera left, looked on. Much the same as Ronald Reagan, President Clinton was always aware of his on-camera presence, so you could always count on him to do just the right thing (at least visually!) at the right time.

After I captured several images from the head-on position, I was able to move to a position at an angle and capture an image that was less about the White House and more about Mandela and South Africa. I juxtaposed his country's flag, flying in a gentle breeze in the background, with Mandela at the podium.

Several years later, I found myself up close and personal with President Mandela, but this time without all the pomp and circumstance. Mandela made his fifth—and what is believed to have been his last, given his health—trip to the U.S. He came and visited with President Bush and promoted his agenda of fighting AIDS (after his son had died from the disease earlier that year), as well as educating students of modest means.

My encounter with him occurred on the tarmac of Dulles Airport, as he was about to depart U.S. soil. Several people instrumental in the trip had called on me to do some meet-and-greet images as Mandela left on a private jet. He could barely walk, and it was determined that he couldn't make it comfortably up the dozen or so stairs to enter the jet.

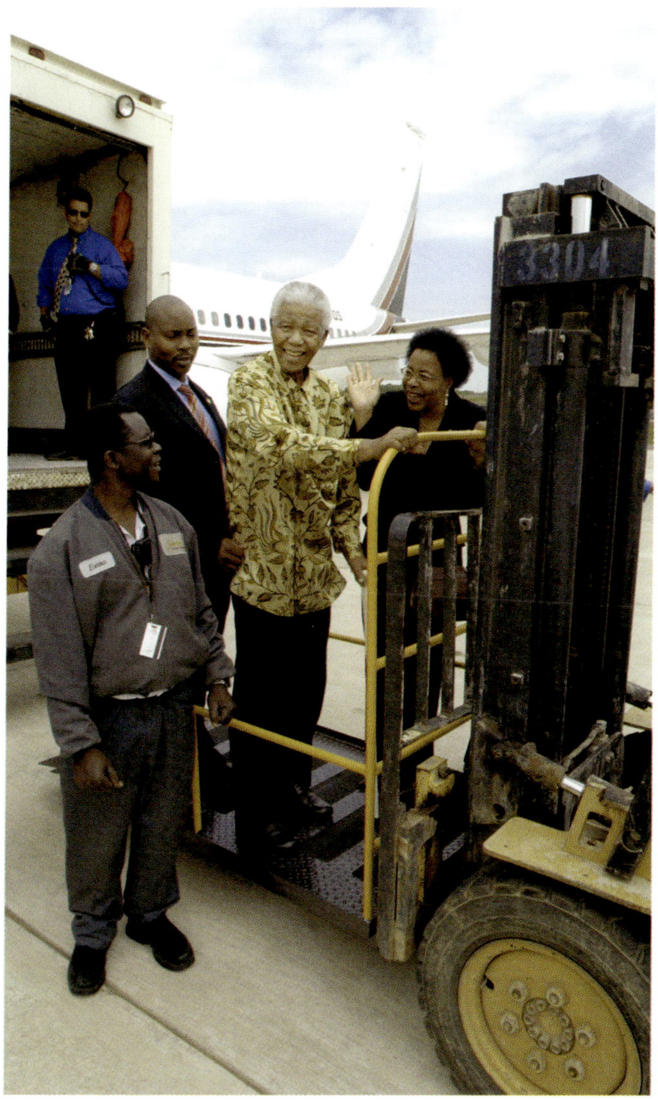

An ailing Mandela is raised to a catering truck via forklift to board a private jet at Dulles Airport in Virginia.

After the meet-and-greet concluded, I made several images as a forklift raised Mandela into a catering container, which raised him the last few feet, and he walked into the jet via the galley service entrance. I did so with the belief that I was capturing history, as Mandela left the U.S. for the last time.

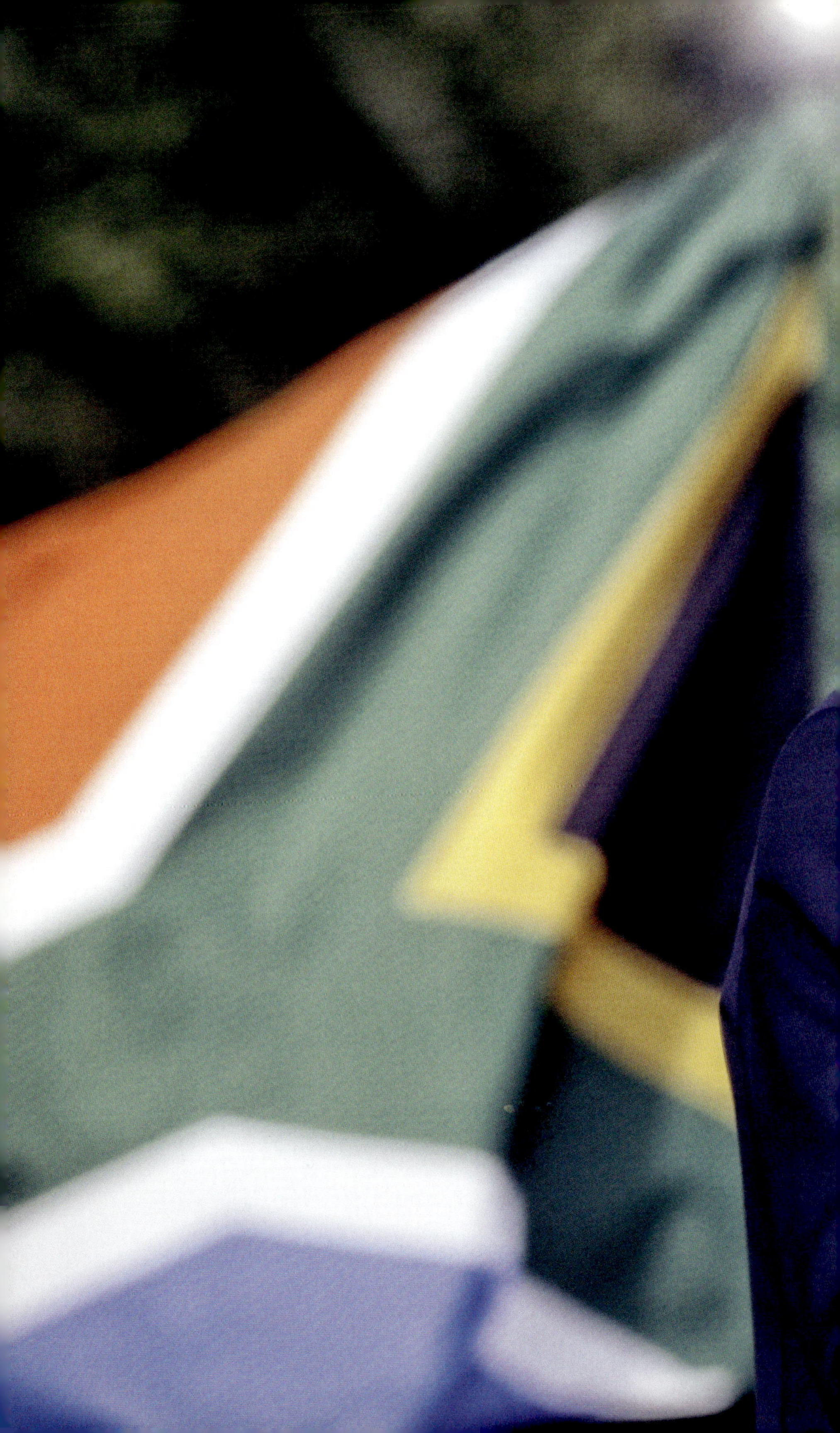

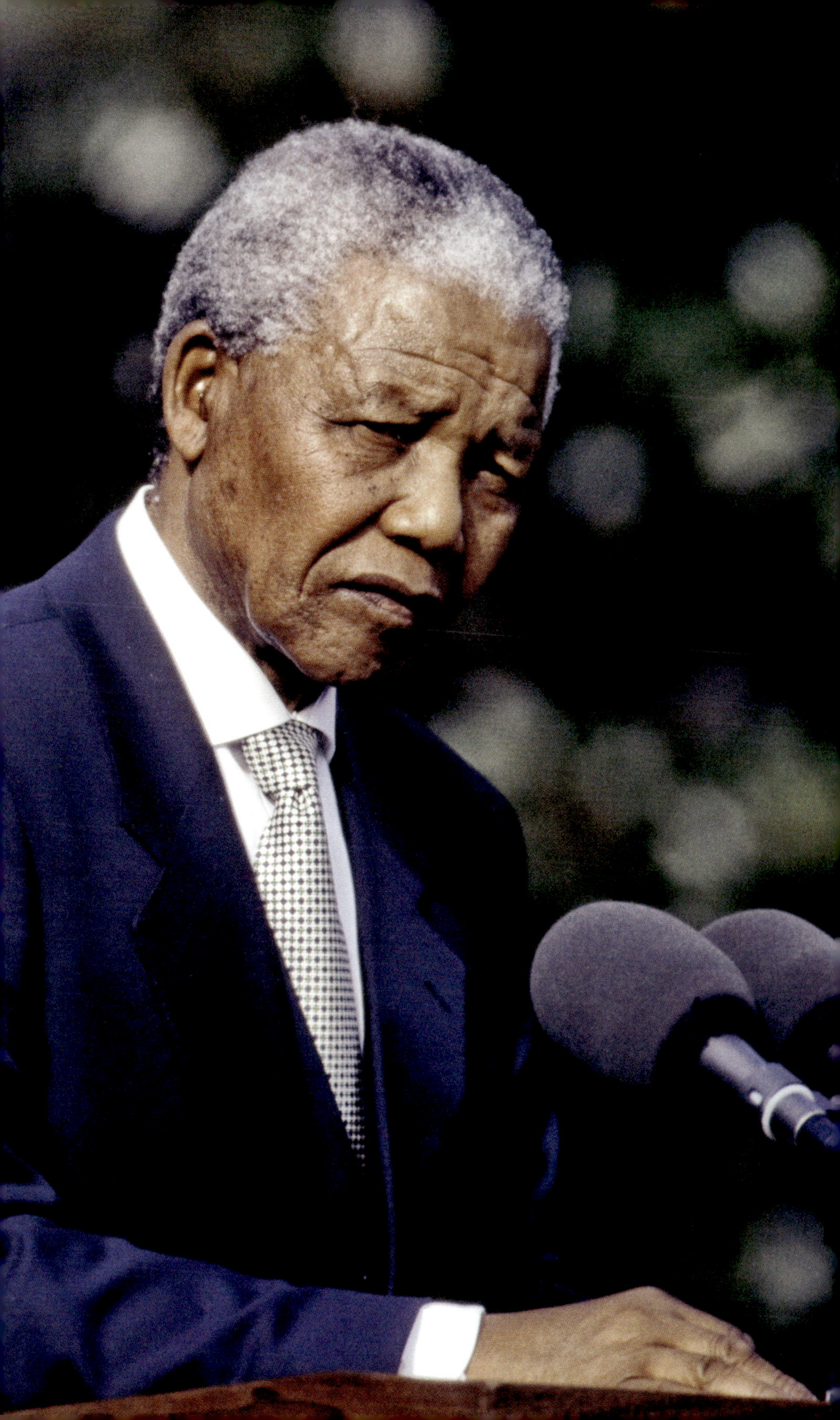

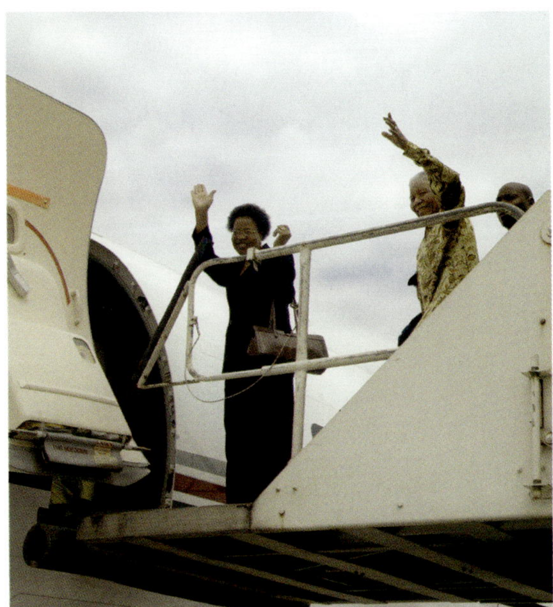

Nelson Mandela departing Dulles Airport in Virginia as he boards a private jet.

Mandela, the former president of South Africa, boards the jet.

I find so compelling the images of Mandela as a statesman at the White House, contrasted with him being hoisted on a forklift into a catering truck for access to his ride home. I found myself humbled by being present as this great man left the U.S. for the last time, sadly in such an undignified manner.

Keeping Cool in New Orleans

Following the devastation of Hurricane Katrina, large swaths of New Orleans were wiped from the cityscape. Arguably the epicenter of the jazz and blues musical movement is New Orleans, and the roots of that musical genre come from the real life and living conditions that the players experience. So, when Katrina wiped away people's living quarters, even as dilapidated as they were, they were their homes—and now they were no more.

A movement started to rebuild homes in the lower Ninth Ward, specifically for artists and musicians, and I was called upon to photograph one of the volunteers involved in the project, along with one of the beneficiaries of the homebuilding. The promotional campaign was to be sizable, so we had an art director, a stylist/makeup person, and representatives from the organization I was working for, as well as the organization that provided the hammer-toting volunteers.

On my side of the fence, I had a digital technician and an assistant. We scouted the location the day before and found a really beautiful row of houses, colorful and finished. The one challenge we faced was that I wanted the two subjects to be on the doorstep of the house and to use the stairs of the front porch and the railing for them to be standing upon, to give context and finishing to the foreground of the image. The challenge, of course, was that in order to get the steps where we wanted them, we had to build them in the middle of the front yard. Fortunately, our volunteer offered to bring the tools necessary to assemble the scraps of stair pieces in the area the next day. It was overcast on the scout day, and we prayed for blue skies.

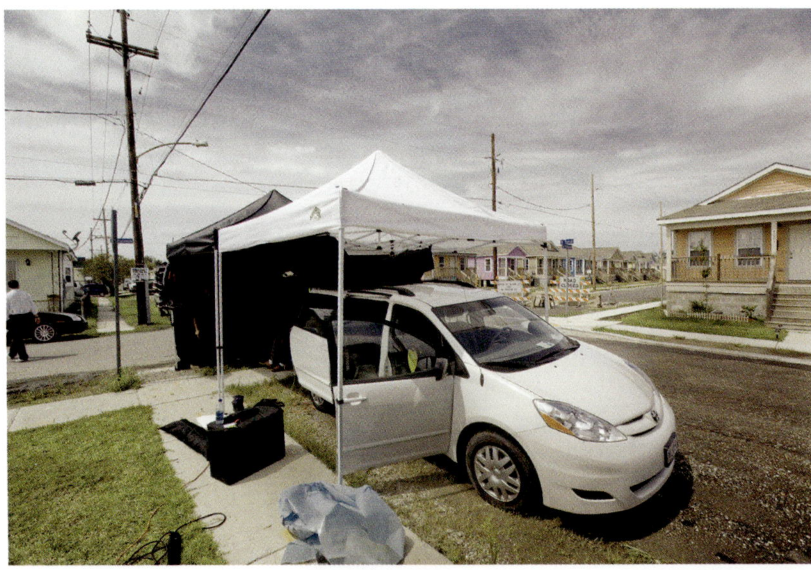

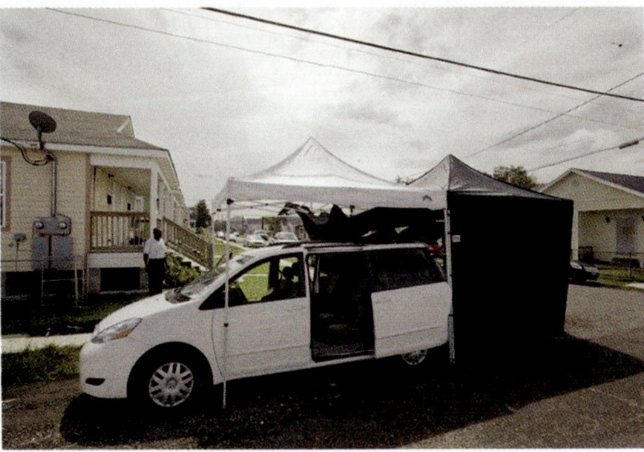

The setup of the production vehicle and tenting.

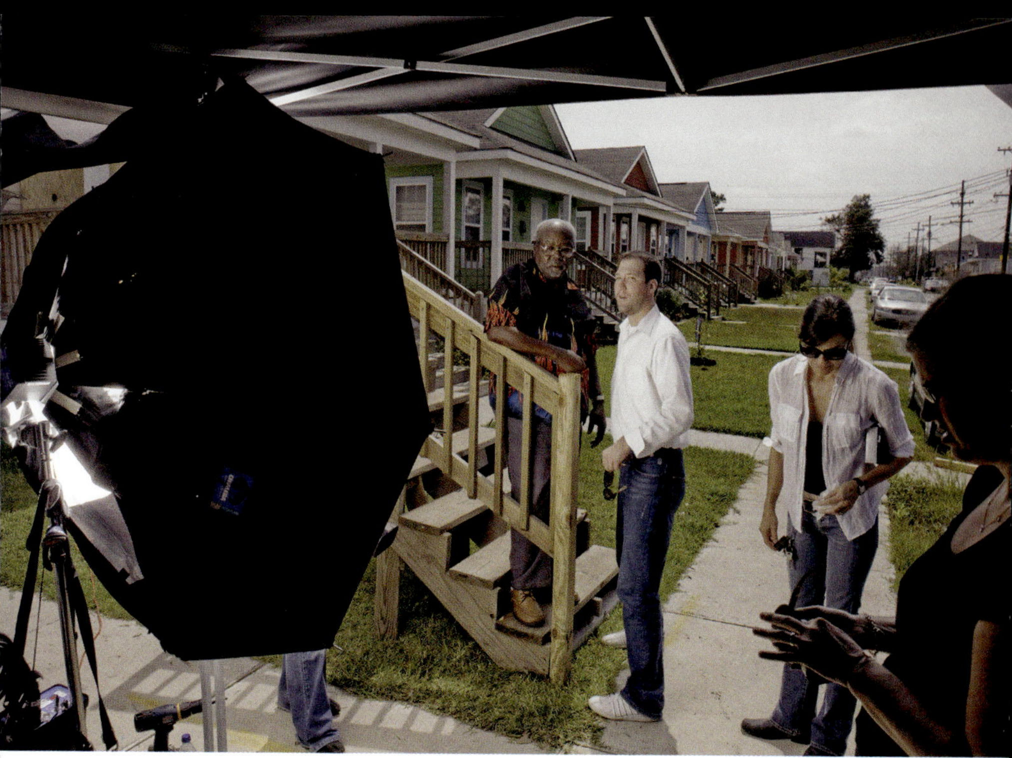

The setup as seen from inside the tent.

The gods must have been smiling upon us, because we awoke to crisp blue skies with the occasional cloud sailing through. We arrived on location and started setting up tenting. The hot sun would quickly beat down on us, and we needed the computer to be protected not just from the heat, but also from the glare of the sun that would affect the art director's view of the screen. Fortunately, one of the houses had power, and we pulled a hundred feet of power cord to the vehicle and started booting up the computers and setting up the lights.

One of our subjects was nowhere to be found. Our friendly volunteer was busy building us a new set of stairs that would put them in just the right position to juxtapose them against a rainbow of row houses. The entire environment surrounding these homes, however, was surreal. Even a block away the devastation of Katrina was still evident, but these multicolored sentinels of New Orleans artists stood out quite prominently.

The subject turned up in a Hoveround wheelchair, and we knew this could be a problem. We hadn't planned for him to be in a wheelchair, as we needed him standing alongside the volunteer.

Further, he didn't have the wardrobe of a jazz and blues musician. Because of this, the seemingly unnecessary stylist/makeup artist became worth every penny, as we sent her off to the artist's home to find some suitable wardrobe options, which she did.

About 30 minutes later, she returned with a great shirt that had flames on it. It didn't quite fit, but it looked great! Fortunately, the musician was able to stand, and his use of the Hoveround chair was more for convenience than a critical need, so he was able to stand on the steps without a problem. We shot a few test images, but something was missing. He didn't look "cool" enough. I turned and looked at the art director, and the solution became clear immediately—I took the sunglasses off the art director's head, slipped them onto our musician, and the final touch of cool was added. A few images later, and we were a wrap, with the art director and other stakeholders very pleased with the results.

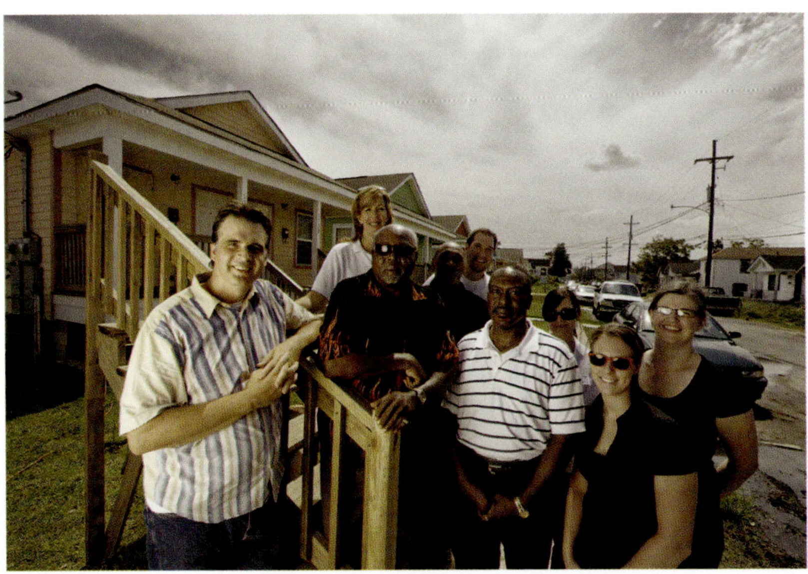

The crew, including the client, assistants, talent, makeup, and me, around the "front steps" built on the front lawn.

Opposite page: The finished image.

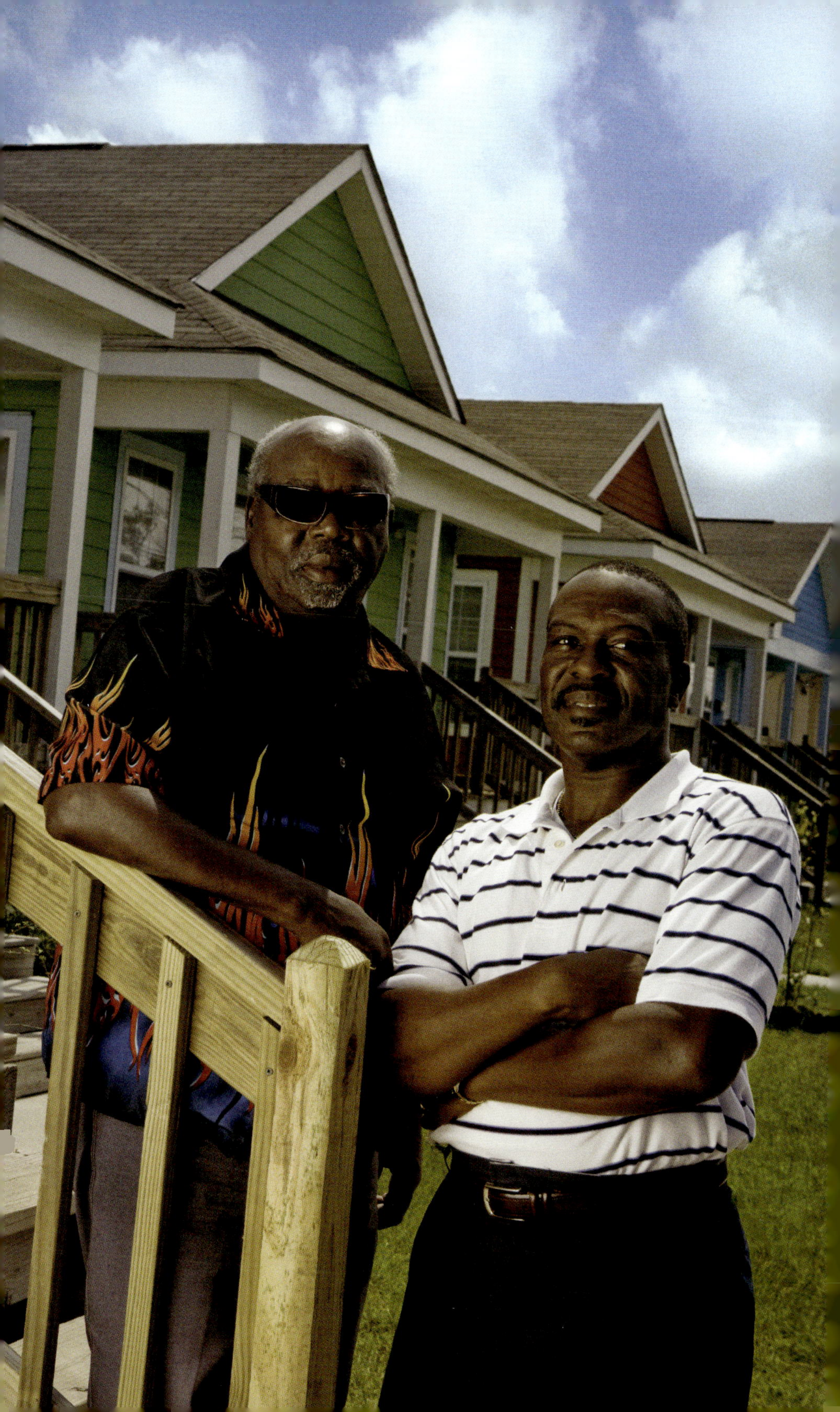

The 9/11 *United We Stand* Concert

In the days following the tragedy of September 11, 2001, people everywhere were united not only to avenge the attacks, but also to support America. The musical community was no different. Led by the genius of Michael Jackson, artists came together to perform during a star-studded show at RFK Stadium, just over a month later, on October 20, 2001.

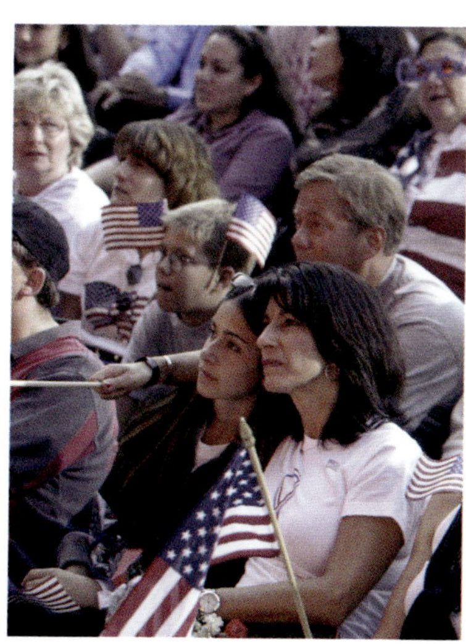

Washington, DC: fans at the *United We Stand* concert at RFK Stadium.

I was tasked with working both the backstage press areas, where MTV, VH1, and every other network was doing interviews with the artists, as well as all the on-stage activities.

It was remarkable to see the likes of Beyonce (with Destiny's Child), Puff Daddy (as he was known then), Huey Lewis and the News, Bette Midler, the Backstreet Boys, MC Hammer, Mariah Carey, James Brown, and about a dozen others come together for this show.

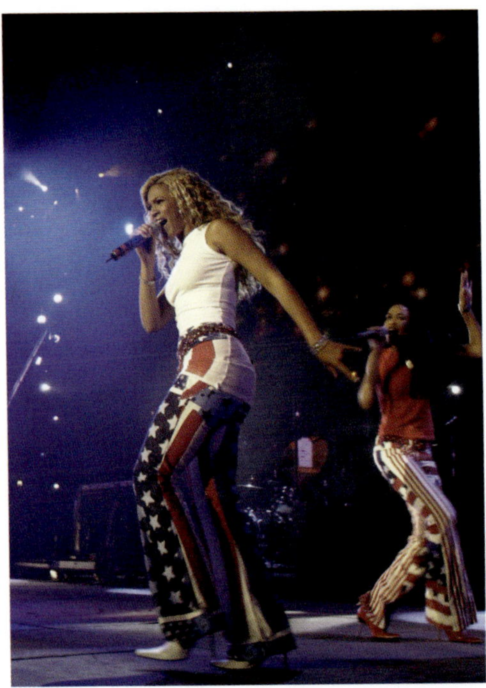

Beyonce, with Destiny's Child, performs at the *United We Stand* concert.

The show kicked off at about 1 p.m with the Backstreet Boys, and the artists performing in the middle of the day did not have the benefit of the theatrical lighting that the later acts did, yet their performances shone as each belted out their greatest hits. This show wasn't about money; it was about giving back to the country. The artists were really pumped and primed to be there, as this wasn't just another concert for them. Many of them adorned themselves with American flags and other patriotic symbols to show their support for their country and the victims of the 9/11 attacks.

Huey Lewis and the News, a personal favorite of mine, came on stage following the Backstreet Boys, and James Brown followed Huey with several soul-stirring renditions of his hits. Following Brown came Usher, Carole King, Al Green, and John Mellencamp. Puff Daddy came on dressed in military fatigues.

I actually saw him earlier in the evening, when I was doing my reconnaissance backstage—as I usually do at concerts because I find that this is when you may stumble across something interesting that could portend things to come later in the show. I knew when I saw Puff Daddy backstage in an interview room that he was up to something with those fatigues, so I made sure I was out in front for him.

Just as he came on stage, he grabbed the American flag and began waving it wildly, and I was prepared and primed as the "United We Stand" graphic came on the screen behind him. I had positioned myself so that he would be statuesque and in military might because of the fatigues, and the American flag was the icing on the cake that pulled together this 9/11 concert for me.

When *NSYNC came on, there were issues regarding the network's right to broadcast them—apparently because of some contractual obligation to another network—so although the cameras went unmanned, we were able to continue shooting without having to work around the Steadicam operator and other fixed cameras we would generally work around.

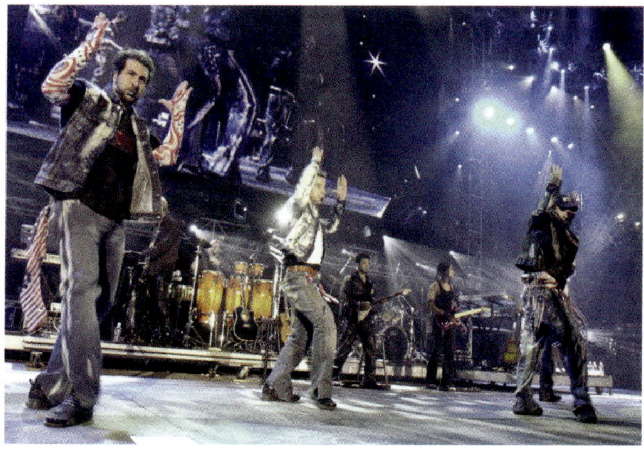

*NSYNC performs at the *United We Stand* concert.

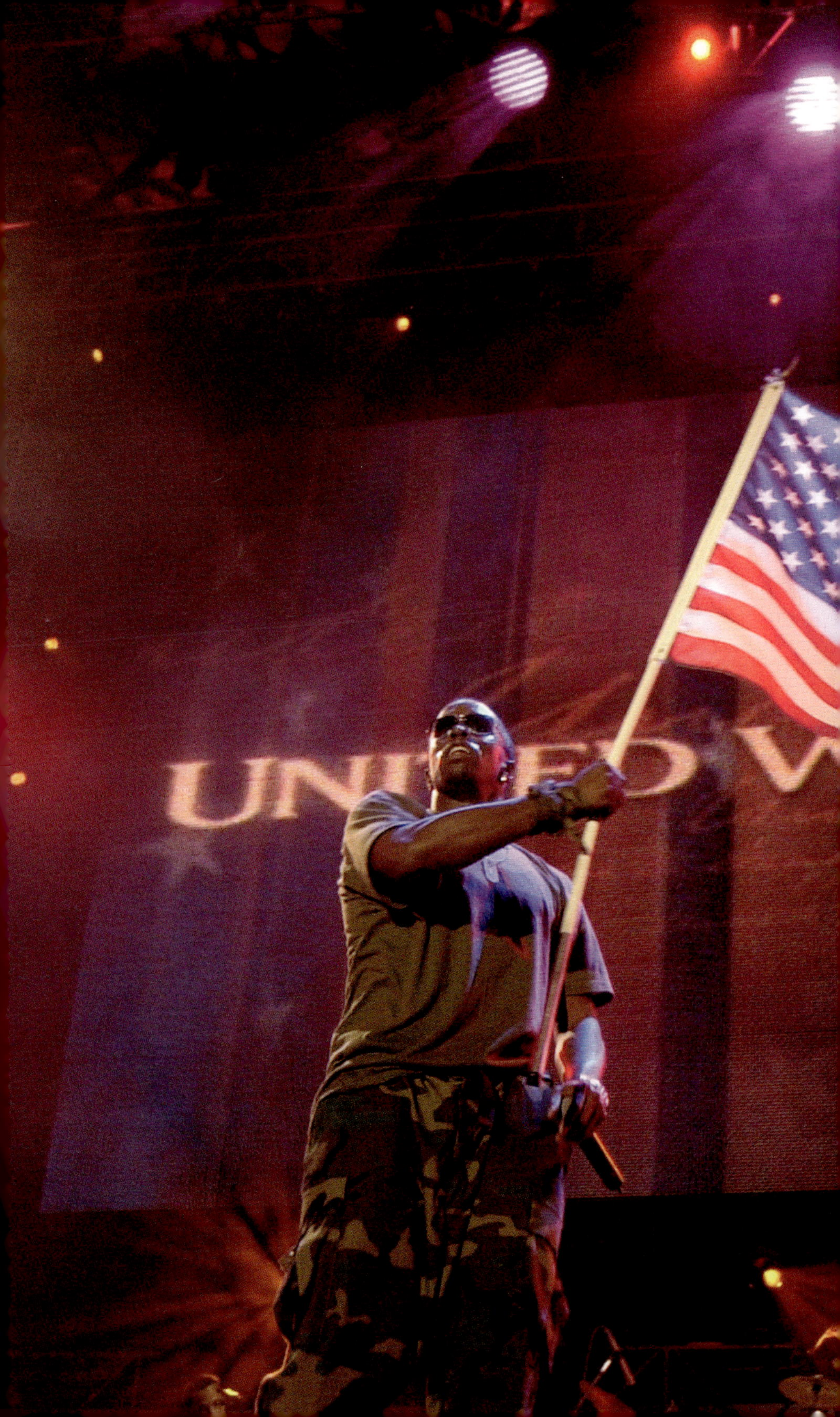

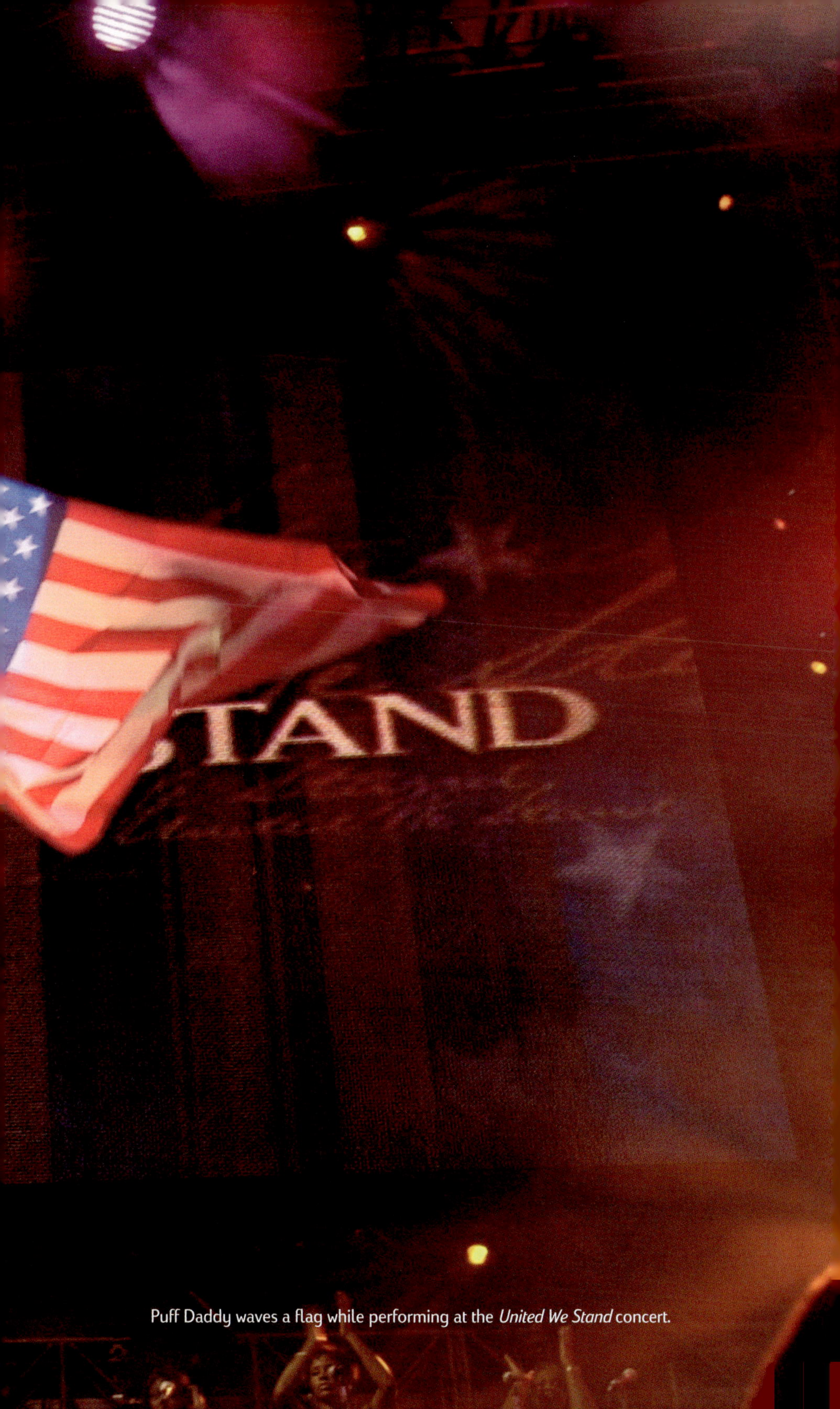

Puff Daddy waves a flag while performing at the *United We Stand* concert.

Train came on next as the cameras were re-manned, and Pink followed shortly thereafter. Aerosmith came on, and I made some images of Steven Tyler that to this day are showcased on my website. Ricky Martin wowed the ladies, as you might expect, and the Goo Goo Dolls pleased the crowd as well. Beyonce, on next, wore an American flag–styled skintight pair of pants—in the way only Beyonce could—alongside her band mates, bringing back together Destiny's Child for the night. Mariah Carey followed, and Rod Stewart, the consummate performer, delivered his hits as well, with Michael Jackson closing the show.

The show, which all took place on one stage, had little time for set changes, and you just knew that the lighting directors and each of the sound technicians that artists at this level require were really working their tails off in the tent at the center of the stadium floor, which was the nerve center of the show.

As a part of the official team of photographers, I was able to work not only in the photo pit and backstage, but also in the area near the tent at the center of the stadium, which is where all the sound technicians and lighting/special effects technicians run the show.

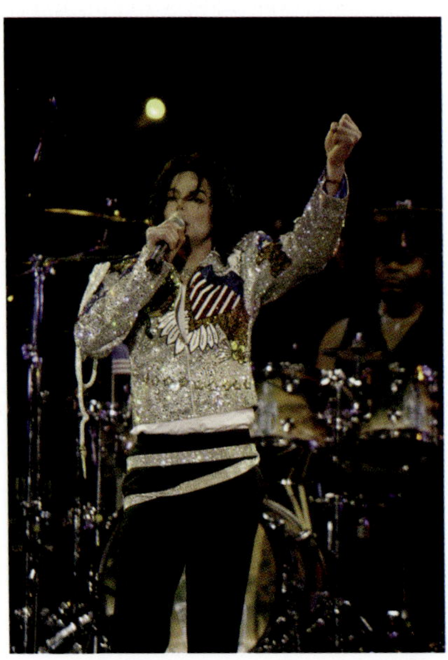

Michael Jackson performs at the *United We Stand* concert.

Opposite page: Steven Tyler of Aerosmith performs at the *United We Stand* concert.

Next spread: Confetti drops at the finale.

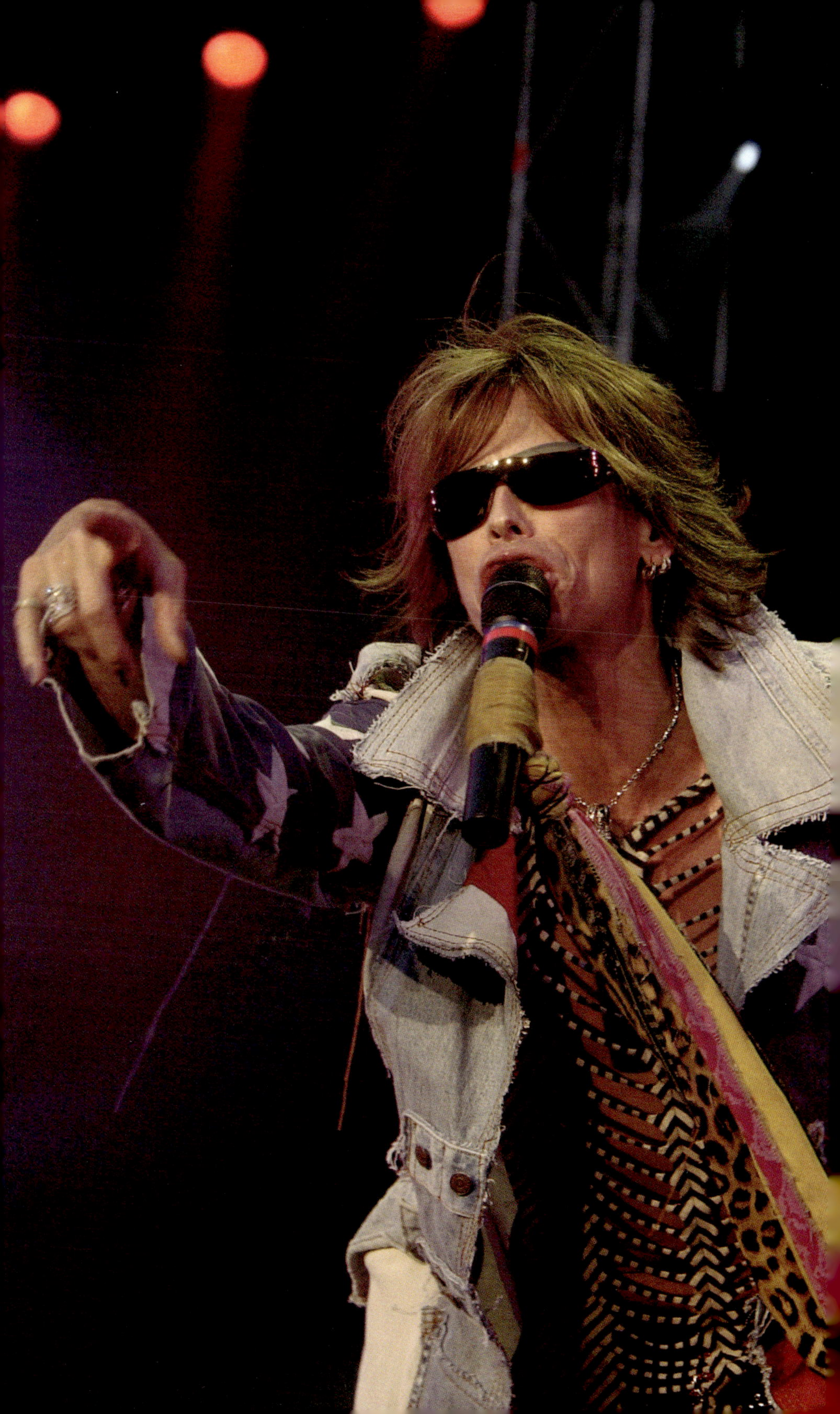

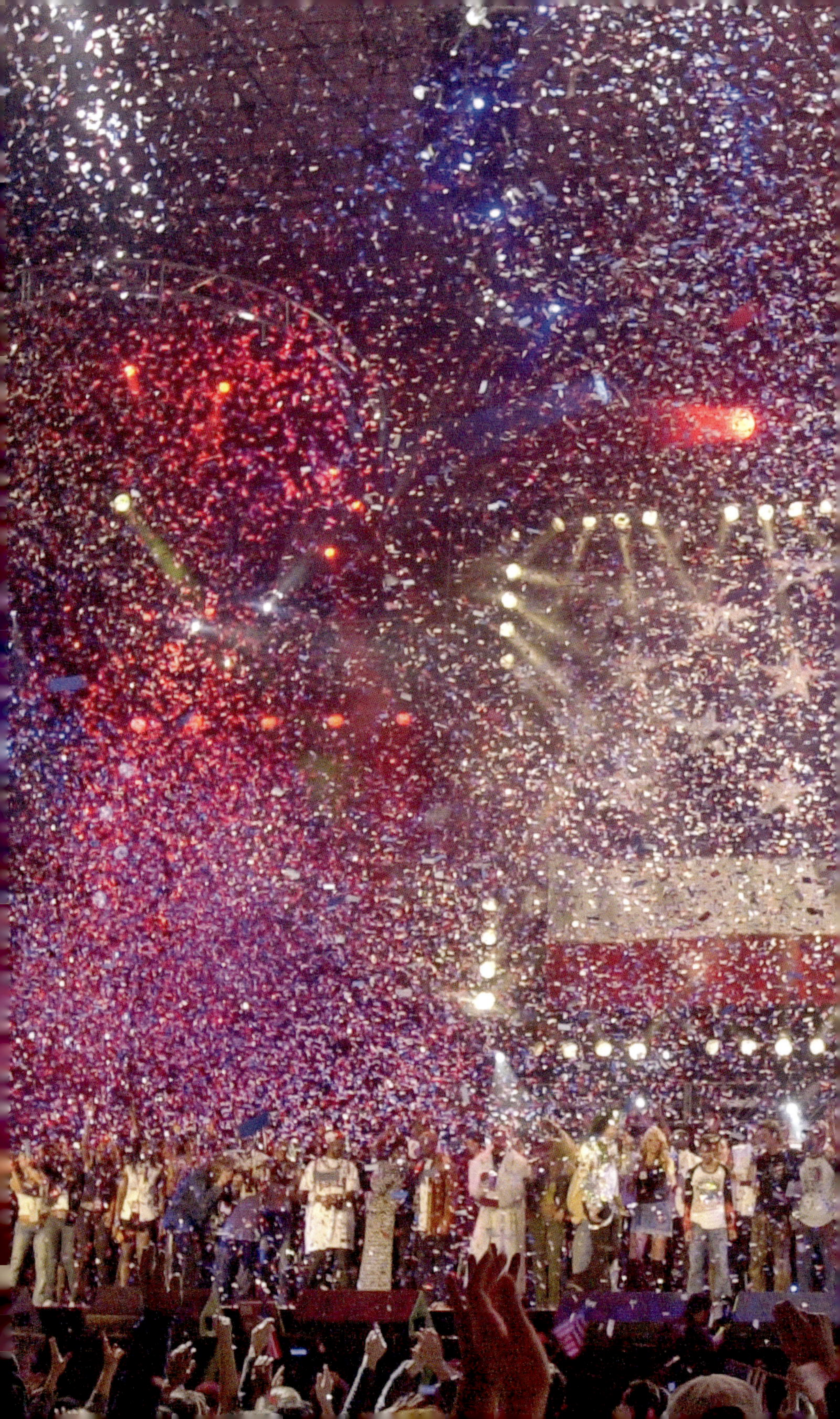

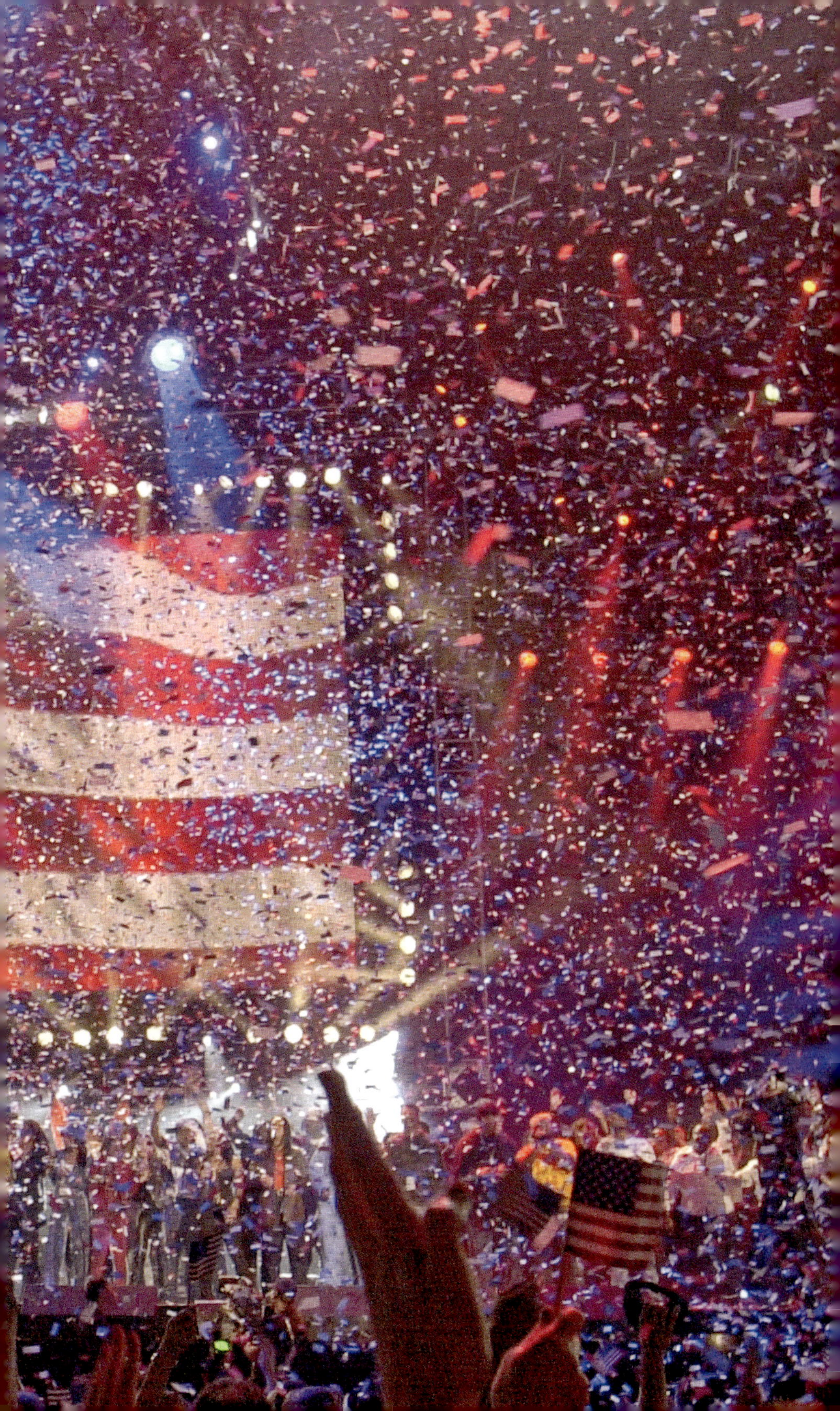

As a part of my reconnaissance earlier in the day, I had availed myself of the official run-of-show—which, in layman's terms, is the producer's list of how the show will play out, including cues for special effects. So, knowing how the finale would look, I knew that the tent was the best place to get the overall image I had envisioned. It was at this location that, during the finale where all the artists came on stage, I made a really great image of the confetti falling down and creating this colorful curtain that shimmered in the late-night ambiance.

You always need to be prepared for the unexpected at major events involving high-profile talent like this—especially when it's for a beloved cause. That means that you need to step out of your comfort zone and politely, with a sense of self-confidence, put yourself where you need to be to find out the most information you can to ultimately produce the best possible images from the event.

Ten Seconds with the President

I've had the privilege of photographing presidents going back to the first George Bush, and if you count President Reagan's visit to the White House and ceremonies at George Washington University Hospital, where he honored those who saved his life, Reagan too. Almost every time it was a news event, although from time to time I was the exclusive photographer traveling with a foreign dignitary for a private meeting with whichever president was in office. Once, when on assignment for National Geographic Television, I had behind-the-scenes access to the White House for a state dinner. Yet, I had never had the opportunity to have studio lighting and the undivided attention of the president before.

When I have photographed each president, the opportunities have ranged from a 20-second stint in the Oval Office with a collection of my colleagues, to 20 or so minutes during a ceremony in the Rose Garden, or even 45 minutes to an hour during a primetime press conference. In this case, the valuable time I had was boiled down to about 10 seconds.

The initial assignment—grip and grins with the president—wasn't all that. In the end, however, it's not what something is, it's what you make of it. It was my assignment to, in a private room, photograph the president in a receiving line with about two-dozen VIP guests who had sponsored an event that the president was attending.

The entire time in the room was about 10 minutes or so, and because of the VIP nature of the guests, we brought in lights, both for recycle time and for a flattering quality of light. Beforehand, we tested the lights—two umbrellas, left and right, with the left light about half a stop brighter than the right.

At the appointed time the president came in, and the guests were queued up and waiting for the president to arrive, so I determined that my opportunity to photograph the president alone would likely come at the end. With precision, the White House staff shuffled each guest pairing in, each had a moment to chat with the president and first lady, and then the foursome would pose for the camera. For each guest we would make two frames, just in case one of the four people in the image had his or her eyes closed. In fact, in one pairing the president had his eyes closed in the first image, and in the second image one of the guests had his eyes closed, so we had to "swap heads" in that image so that the VIP guest could have his picture suitable for framing.

Typically, as the president wraps up a meet-and-greet, there is a brief moment or two while security mobilizes to advance the president, staff gets into position, and the president bids farewell to the organizers. When all of the pairings were done, just such a moment occurred, and there were no guests surrounding the president; it was just me and him. I lifted the camera and said, "Mr. President, look this way for a moment," and I made two frames of him—eyes to camera, all by himself. The strobes fired as desired, and the background was nondescript enough that I liked it. And with that, he was whisked away to his next engagement.

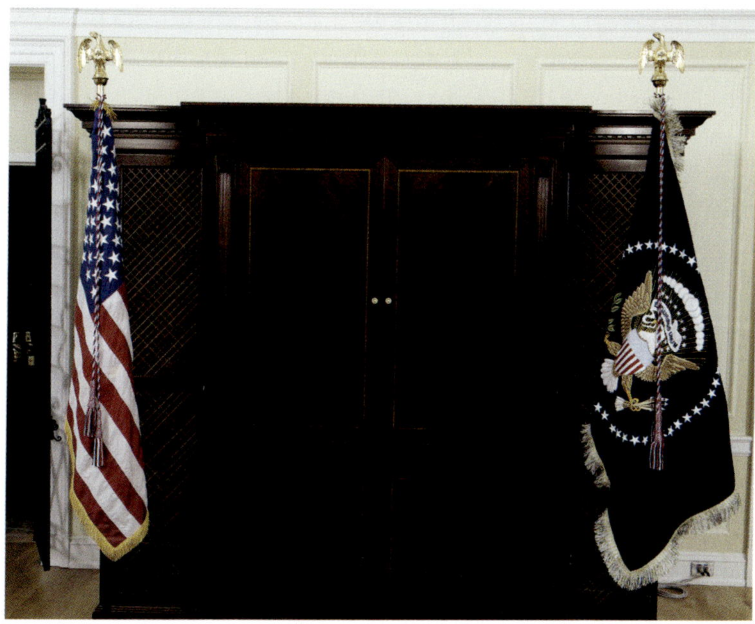

The American and presidential flags alongside a wooden cabinet in the Library of Congress, awaiting the arrival of the president for the grip-and-grins.

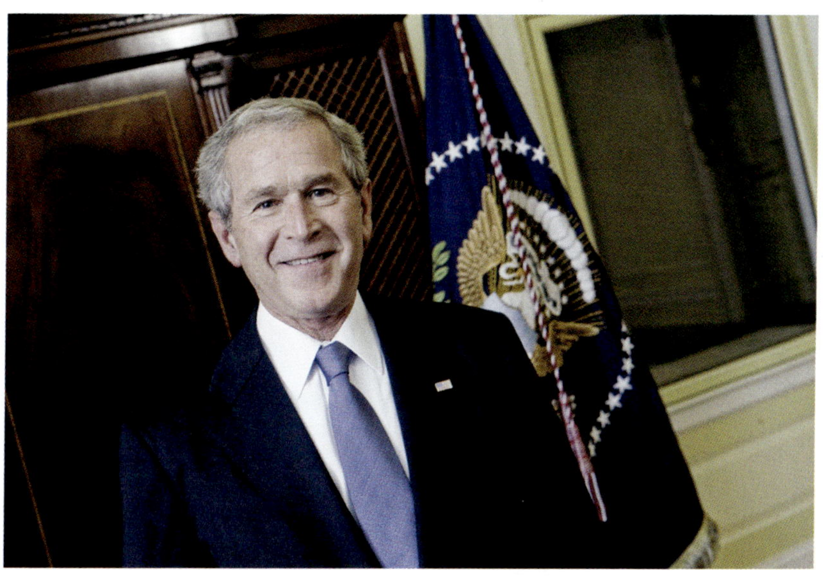

The color image of the president I was pleased with.

When I reviewed the two frames, I was quite pleased, and either would have served quite well. All too often, clients will call with an assignment request and say that the shoot will only take about five minutes, suggesting that it should cost less because of the mistaken notion that we bill by time. In point of fact, when you only have a few seconds to make a photo, and you're able to accomplish the creation of a good image in that amount of time, you should be able to command a premium because of that ability. Almost anyone can make a great portrait if they have hours—the test is, can you make one in 10 seconds?

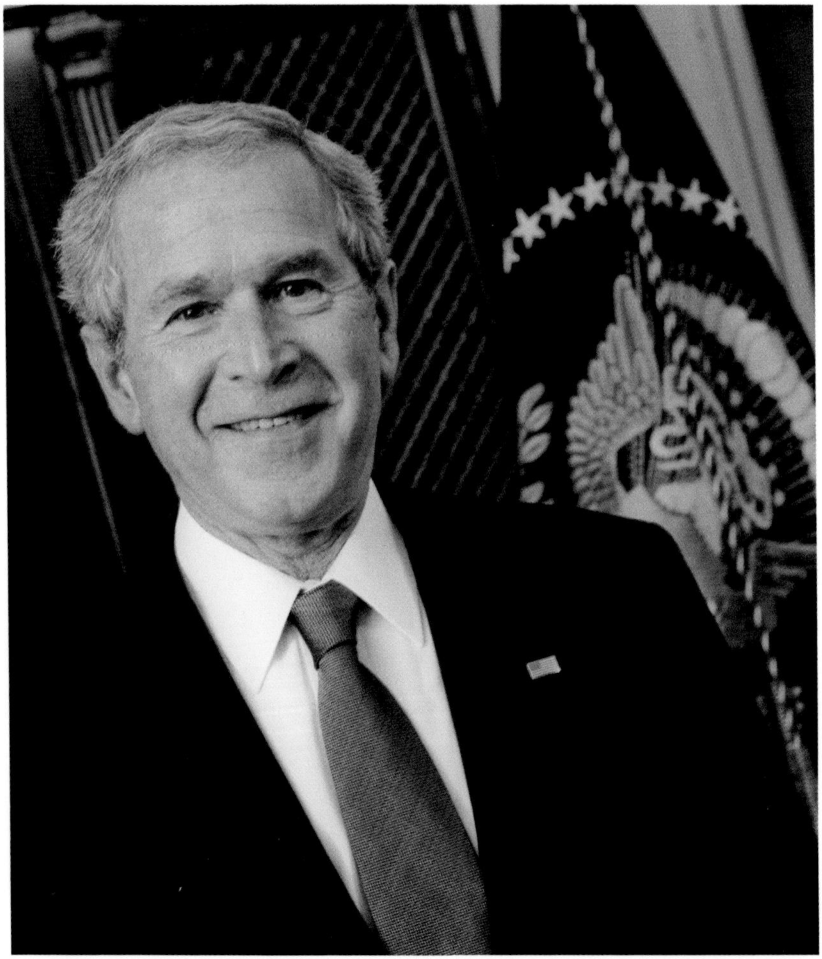

The final black-and-white cropped version of the president.

Kristin Davis: Dogs and the City

It is often said that as an actor, you should never work with dogs or kids. As a photographer, however, this can be a great opportunity for unscripted moments. But when the actress is Kristin Davis, and you only have about 10 minutes to make a big shot happen, on-the-fly, unscripted moments are not what you want.

In this case the client was a dog-food company, and Davis was brought in to promote charitable activities on the part of the dog-food company, which helped dogs that were neglected, homeless, or otherwise in need. To showcase the event, the dog-food company wanted an image of Davis in Washington with pets. I suggested the Capitol as the de facto "DC scene setter" and the steps next to the Grant Memorial as a way to showcase Davis and several rescued dogs.

I discussed the logistics and timing of the shoot, which preceded her speaking at a press conference at the National Press Club. It was critical that Davis be able to immediately review and approve the images from the shoot, and we set up a digital workstation for her to review the images. Also, because we were doing the shoot so rapidly, I recommended we do it with as little production as possible—no big lights, flash-fill on camera, and so on—and the client agreed.

When Davis turned up on set, she was as pleasant as the last time I had photographed her, pre–*Sex and the City*. Working under tight time constraints is difficult enough, but when you add animals to the equation, it's even harder. With that in mind, I did many walkthroughs with the dogs and handlers before Davis arrived, so I would have the exact angle and speed at which I wanted the dogs to walk nailed, and so the dogs would be familiar with what they would be doing. When Davis arrived I gave her a 30-second walkthrough, and with the dog handlers for each of the rescued dogs just out of the camera's frame on the right, Davis did just four takes. We reviewed them each time.

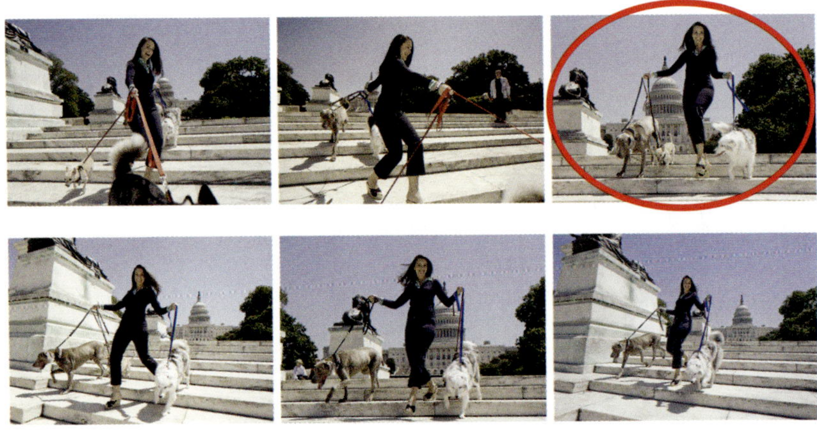

In the end, we decided she had nailed it best on the first take—her long, slender legs gracefully stepping down off the steps, with the dogs looking good, too. Ten minutes later, Davis was off to the National Press Club (and a wardrobe change) for the press conference, and we were distributing the image to the press to promote the rescue-dog program that the dog-food company was supporting.

The key to the success of this project was taking the time to do the setup before the talent arrived. This way, the dogs were able to learn quickly what was expected of them, and we only had to wrangle the talent!

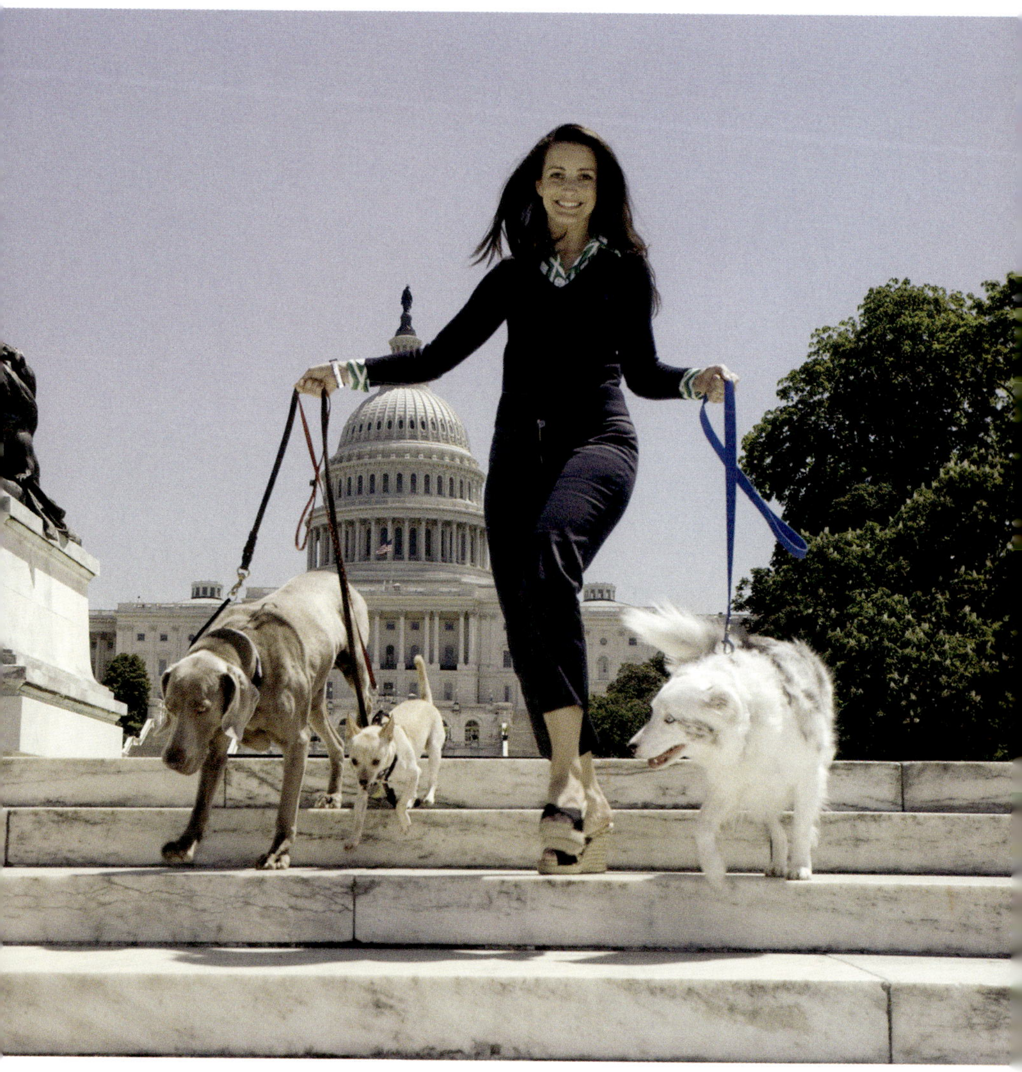

A Presidential Debate and an Exercise in Diplomacy

Once in a blue moon, you get a blessed phone call. I had heard that Senator Obama was going to be among the panelists during a PBS-sponsored presidential debate at Howard University. I couldn't believe my lucky stars when the phone rang, and it was a longtime client of mine telling me that he was the lead in handling the PR for the event. Would I mind managing a team of photographers, but also providing logistical counsel for the event?

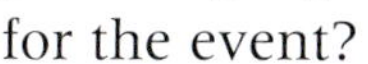

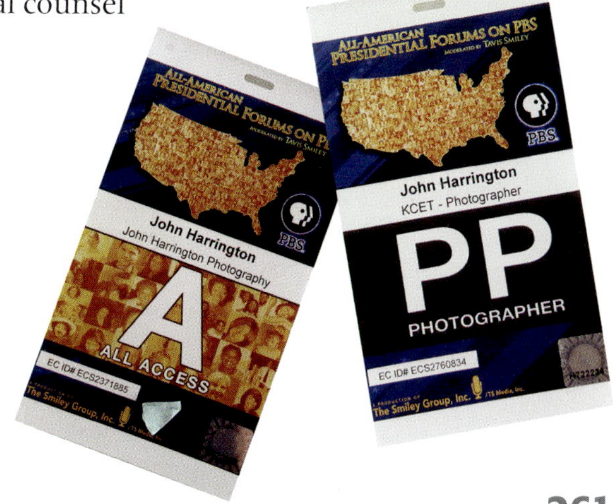

I have worn many different hats as a photographer, but this particular event was important because it allowed me to position my fellow photographers and be an advocate for their craft in what would normally be a very controlled environment.

The two obvious frontrunners would be there—Hillary Rodham Clinton and Barack Obama—so everyone was keyed up for a big event. I came on site a few days beforehand to meet with the PR team in the morning, followed by the representatives from the wire services and newspapers.

Right off the bat, I could see problems arising, as certain high-profile newspapers were not being given access to the event, and choices needed to be made as to who would get access. I found myself in the uncomfortable position of being on the other side of the fence from my fellow photographers and being the one who had to advise on these hard decisions. I had to make the case for the variety of positions that the news media would need, as the production crew were understandably sensitive to having photographers in the line of sight of the candidates at this historic presidential debate.

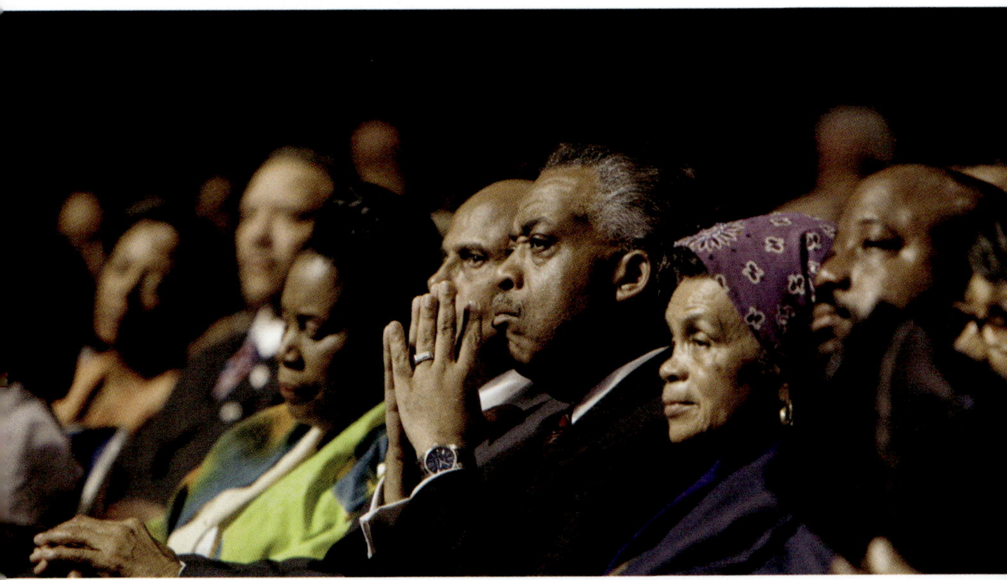

Al Sharpton, front and center during the debate.

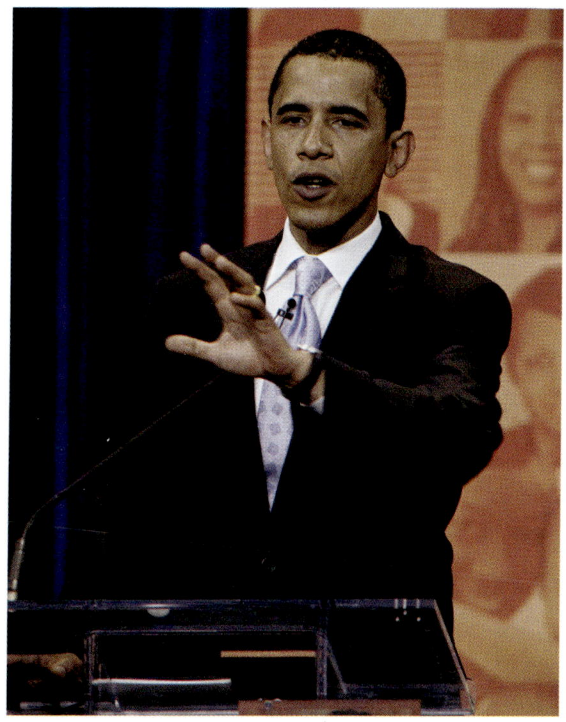

Barack Obama makes a point during the debate.

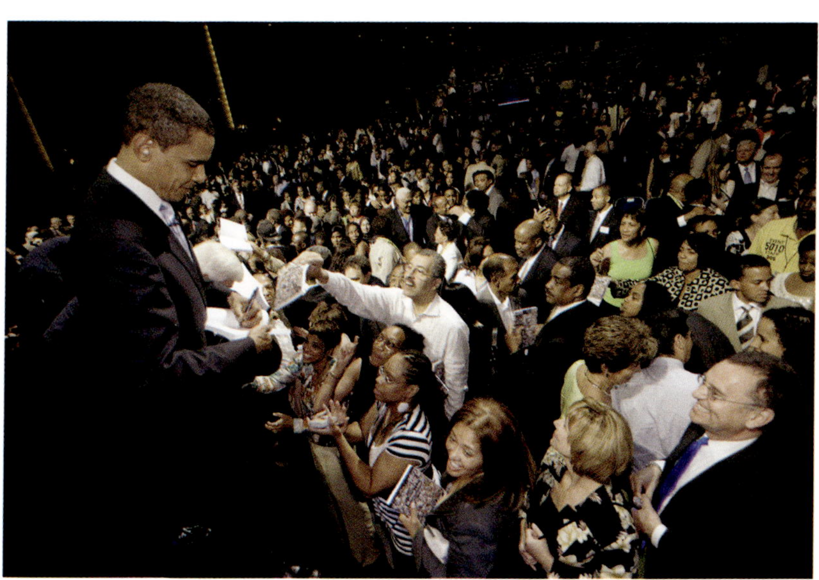

Following the debates, Barack Obama signs autographs for fans.

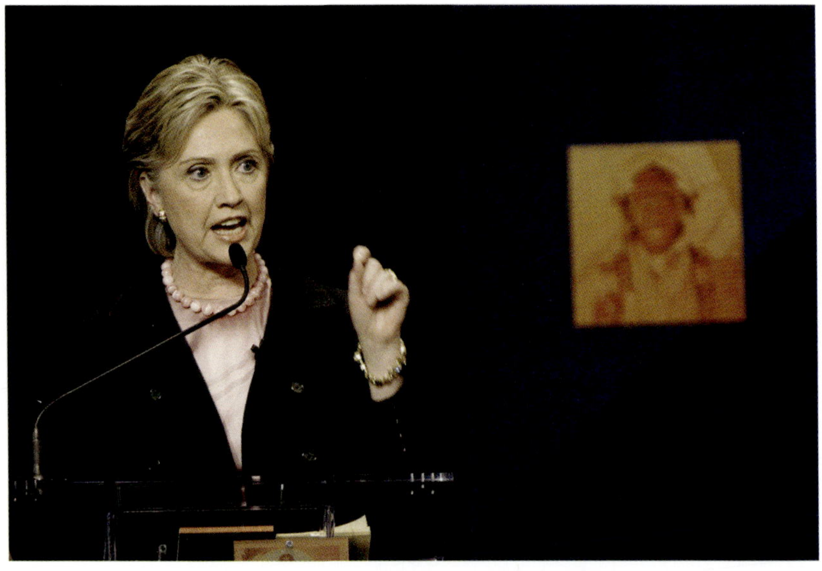

Hillary Clinton makes a point during the debate.

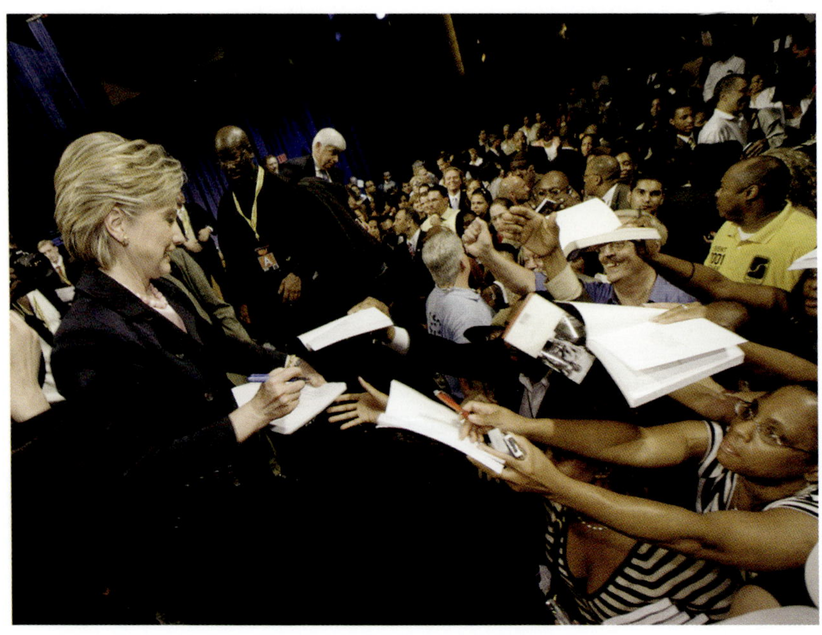

Following the debates, Hillary Clinton signs autographs for fans.

On the day of the event, we arrived to set up our equipment well before the press were allowed in. From multiple tripods and long lenses to the digital workstations we needed to get the images out as soon as possible, it was a logistical challenge and very tedious. As the PBS crew was setting up camera positions, and the various campaigns were checking out staging and lighting, we tested our equipment and the Internet connection we would need to feed out images to the news media who did not get a spot inside the theater where the debate was happening.

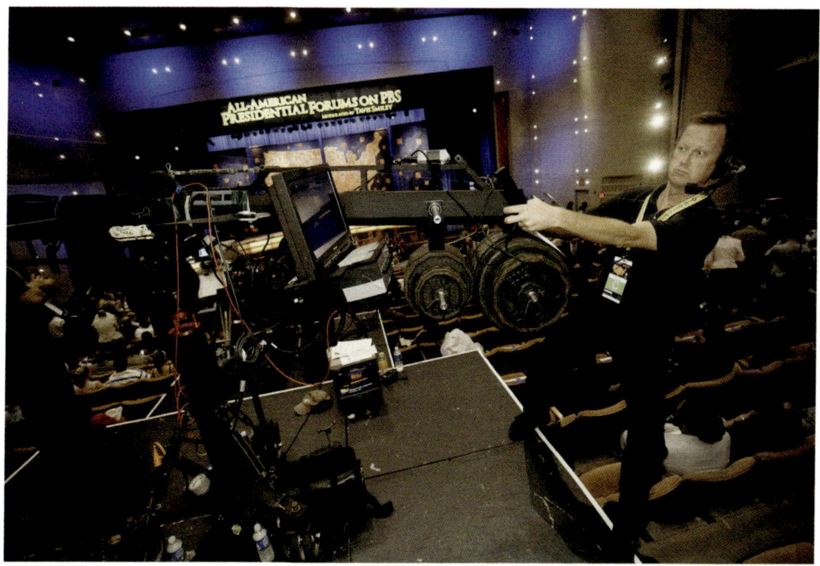

The PBS crew at work during rehearsals.

When the candidates came on stage, it was clear who the frontrunners were, despite the admonition to the audience not to show any audible favoritism toward one candidate or another. I had arranged with the PBS team that there needed to be a "down in front" shot, and they agreed, provided we could accomplish it during the first 20 to 30 seconds as the candidates greeted the crowd. They insisted that the photographers needed to follow the "that's a wrap" instructions and head back to their positions immediately thereafter—and, fortunately, they did.

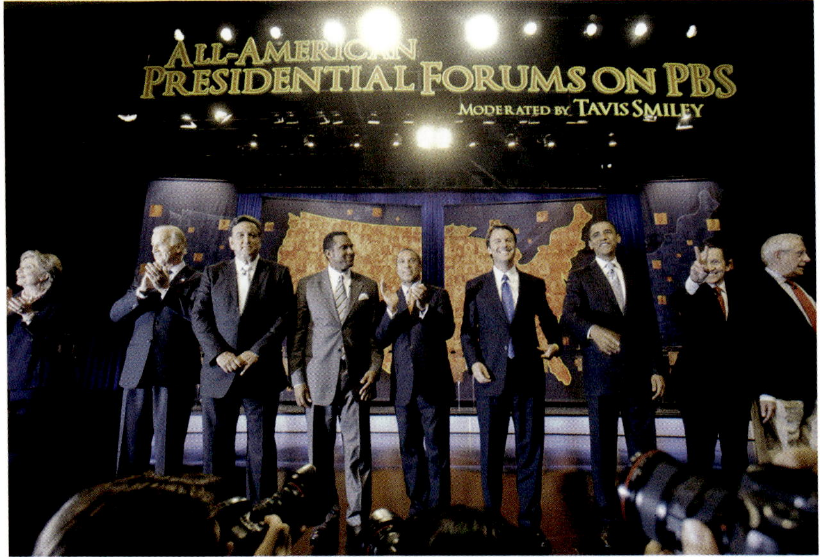

The group photo of Democratic candidates just before the debate began.

During the debate, I was able to work all around the theater—not restricted by a locked-down position—and get images from the various stage-left and stage-right positions. I also was able to get some shots of the notable audience members—Al Sharpton among them. Also on the shot list were images of the crew at work, so we went into the production truck to get a few of those images.

Afterwards, the candidates stayed on stage to greet the audience, and I wanted to make several images of them interacting. Fortunately, both Obama and Clinton had books out, and many of the audience members had brought the books to be signed, so there were a number of great images I could make of both Obama and Clinton interacting with the audience. Throughout the evening, we fed out upwards of 50 images of the debate, being careful to ensure that each candidate had an equal number of images sent, as well as images of the event's scene-setters.

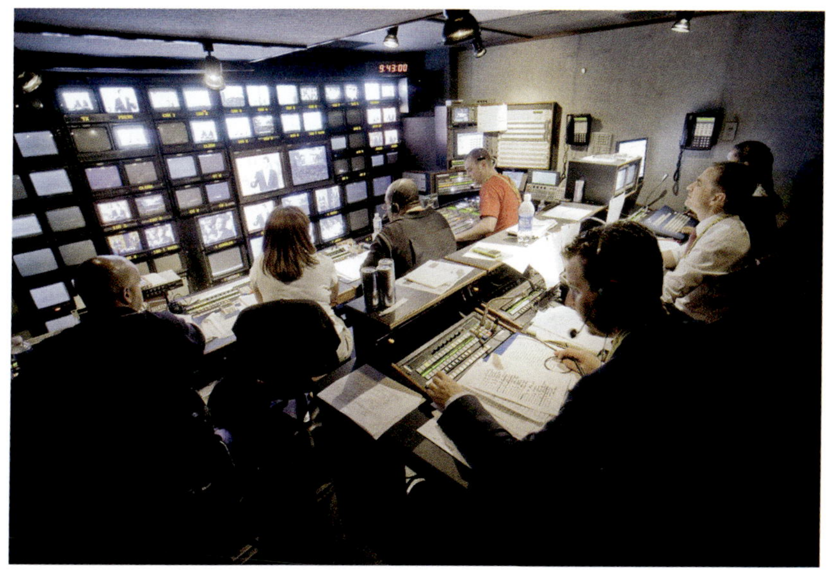

The nerve center of the debate, where the show is produced.

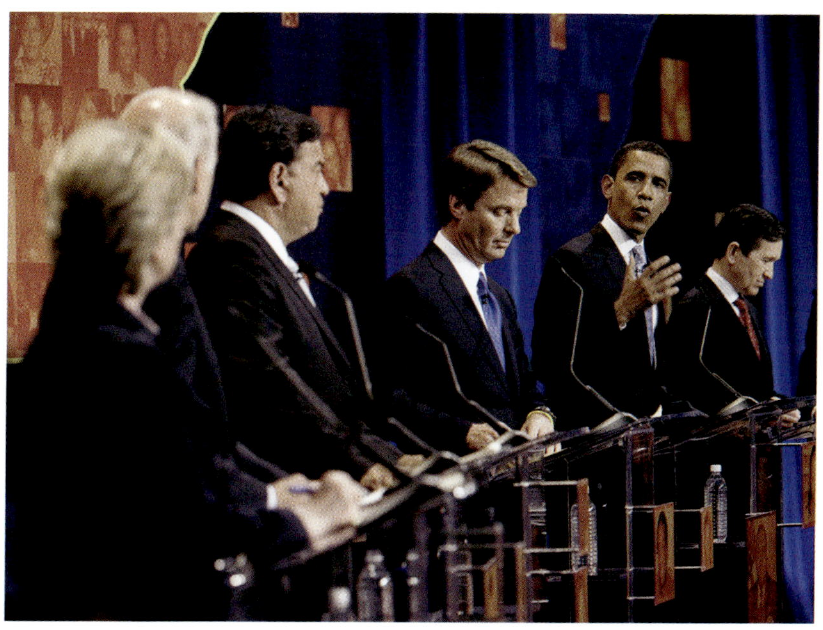

From the wings of the stage, Barack Obama is seen making a point in Hillary Clinton's direction.

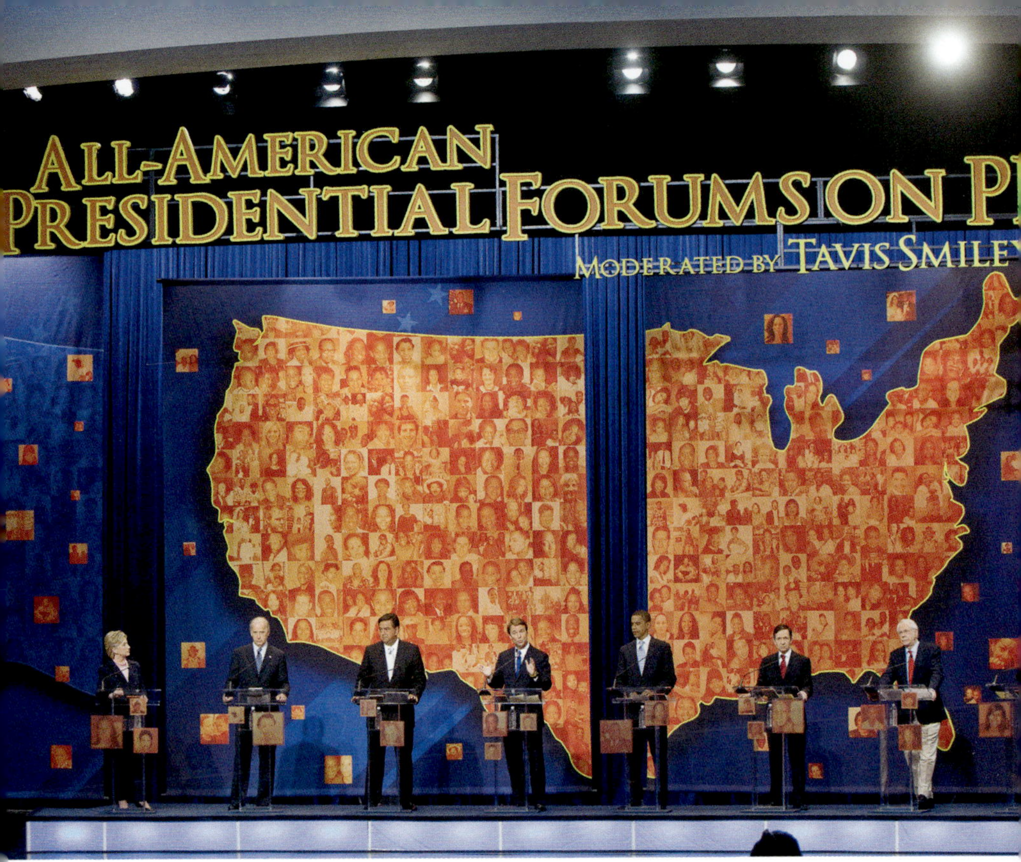

The PBS Democratic Presidential Debate from the balcony.

When you take into consideration that the location for this debate was at Howard University, a historically black college, and then-Senator Obama was vying for the presidency, you will understand the extreme pressure I felt at trying to ensure that publications such as *Ebony* and *Jet* received equal treatment, even if at the expense of moving another publication to a less favorable position to shoot. Diplomacy is an art form that many people strive to perfect. This experience taught me to respect great statesmen and the fine lines they dance along. At the end of the day, I think the event was a huge success, and the advocacy I fought for all the photographers present I believed to be without prejudice.

Stevie Wonder: Portrait Composite

There are just some legends that you are humbled by and honored to be able to photograph once, let alone several times. For me, one such legend is Stevie Wonder. I had photographed him twice just prior to this project, once for the BET Walk of Fame and once at Live 8. However, this time was supposed to be different, and in many respects it was.

Steve Wonder was being honored by the Library of Congress with its Gershwin Award, and that included him playing a few of his songs and receiving the award. One objective was to get a good portrait of Stevie that could be used in materials that the Library was sending out. (The Library was my client for this project.) I had brought in lights, but I didn't have a 100-percent commitment that we would be able to make the portrait, so I had a backup plan! Plan B...

In the librarian's ceremonial office, in the Jefferson Building of the Library of Congress, is an amazingly ornate arch above the tall windows in that room, and that was the background I wanted.

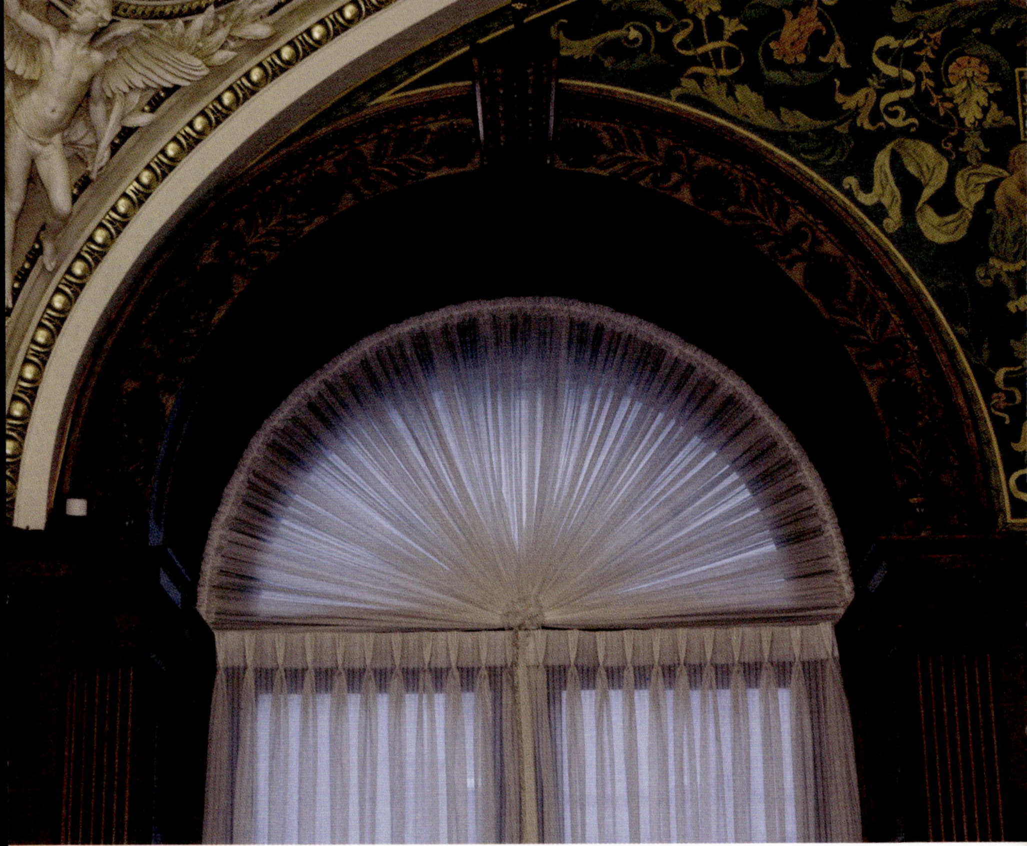

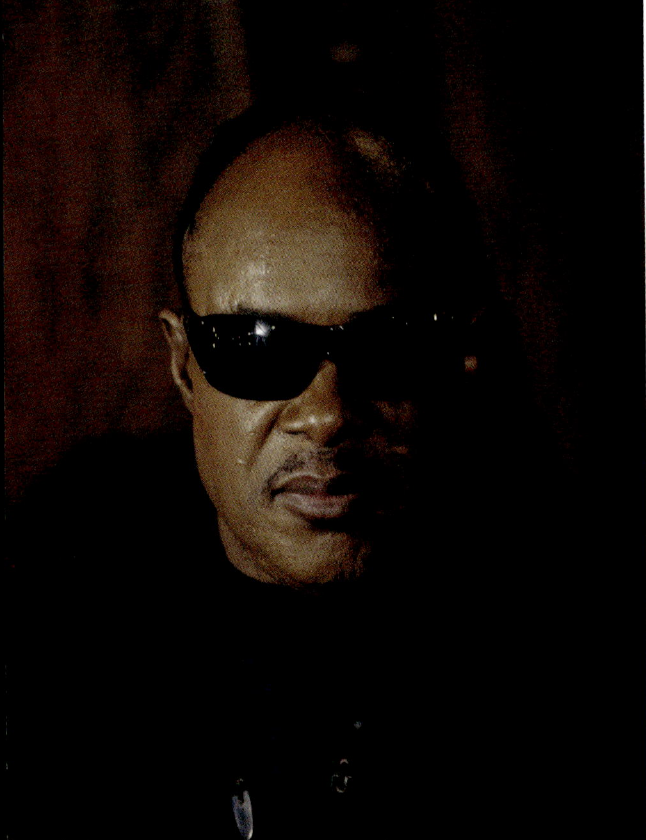

Opposite page: The finished image of Stevie "in" the librarian's ceremonial office. Above and left: The components of the image—Stevie during the press conference and the ceremonial office image.

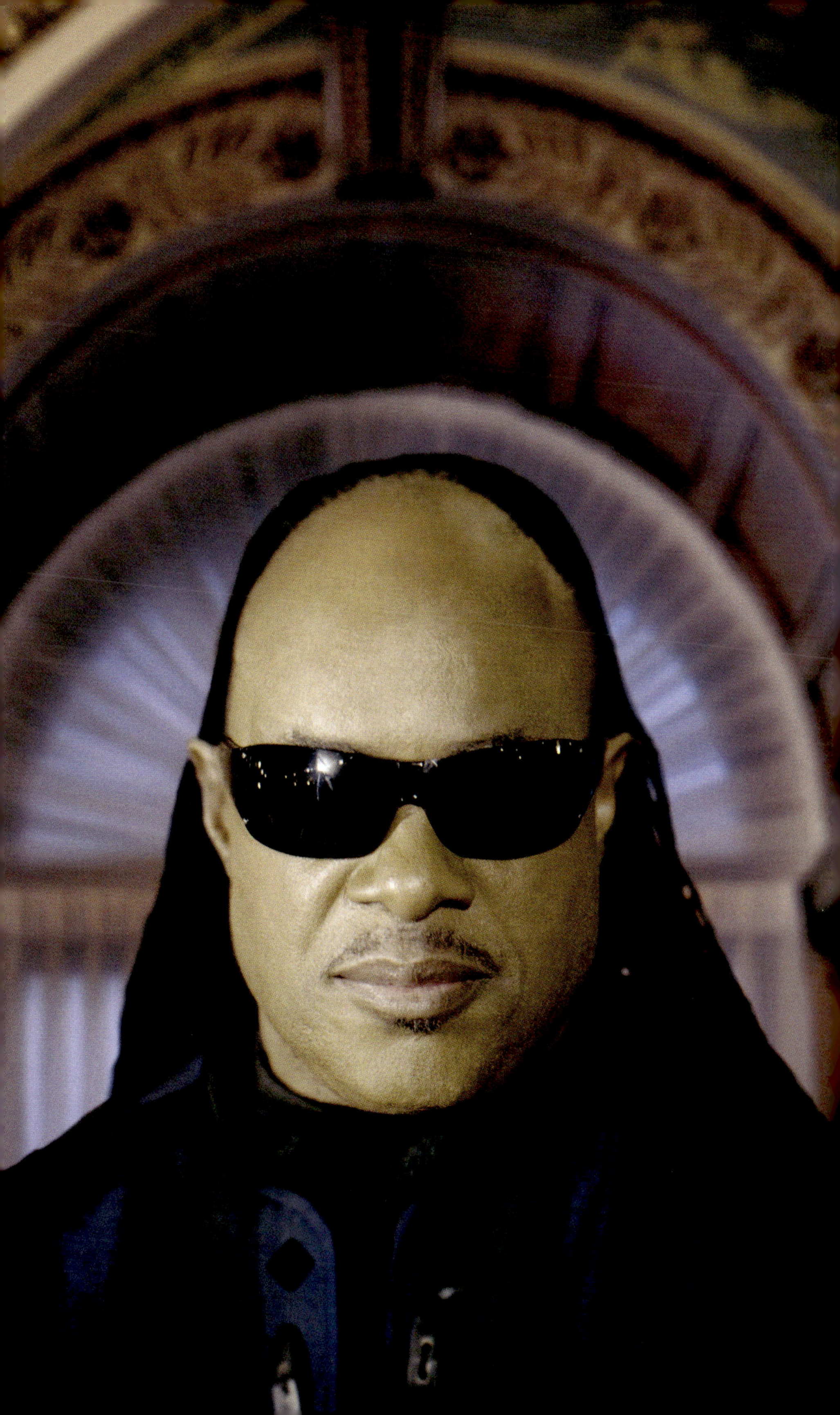

And while Wonder did come into the room and spent a great deal of time in there just before his press conference, no opportunity presented itself to make the image that I had envisioned, due to the commotion around him. From the entourage to the hangers-on, the moment just didn't materialize.

We next moved to the press conference, where I had an assistant holding a dead-center spot so I would be facing Wonder directly head-on at the podium. So begins Plan B.... Typically for me, this is a really big no-no, as I always want some dynamic angle where the speaker looks more active. As Wonder spoke, I shot a number of images. I was concentrating on a straight-on, shoulders-squared, head-straight-toward-me image, where, for a change, the speaker wasn't speaking.

Fortunately, the room was lit for television cameras, so I didn't have to rely on my strobes, and instead I could shoot available light. I selected a lens length that would give me not only the framing that I wanted, but also the right compression for a portrait. For a change, it helped that my subject was wearing dark glasses. Not only did I not have to worry about whether he was looking at me or into the camera, but more importantly, this is a look that is very familiar to people who have seen Stevie Wonder.

As Wonder left the press conference, I knew I had a number of candidates for my idea. While he was preparing for the performance, I slipped back into the librarian's ceremonial office, selected a similar lens length, and made several different frames of the archway I had originally wanted to do the portrait in front of, also with the camera at a similar angle.

I then moved on to the performance, where Wonder performed a number of his most amazing hits and talked throughout each break. It truly was a humbling sight to see and hear him. The last time I heard him perform, I was out to the front of the house for the Live 8 concert—one of my rare forays there from the backstage area I was in. This time, however, the crowd was just a few hundred in an intimate amphitheater in the Library of Congress.

I returned to the studio and began a conversation with my post-production team. We discussed in detail what I was looking for, and each step of the way I would tweak and fine-tune the composite image so it looked just right. Because I was not representing this image as a news/editorial image to anyone, and it was, in fact, a portrait of Wonder at the Library of Congress, I felt that doing a composite was within the bounds of ethics. (That is why, for example, the image does not appear in the editorial section of my website, but rather in the portraits section.)

I had not shared with the client that I was doing this, and I knew they were disappointed that they hadn't gotten the portrait they wanted. So, when I delivered the final images to them, I made a print and included the composite image on the CD as well. When I showed the print to my client contact, he was blown away and excited; I knew he wanted very badly to have a portrait and thought it wouldn't be happening. In this case, having a plan and then a backup plan not only gave me a great portrait (albeit in a composite, which I rarely do), but it also made the client happy with the results. Sometimes you have to be able to see beyond the restrictions you are faced with in order to deliver.

Arlington Cemetery: Grieving Mothers

Photographing in cemeteries—any cemetery—is not my idea of fun. As most people do, I hold them in great reverence. I'm always careful not to step on the areas where a casket might be underfoot. The reverence grows exponentially when the cemetery holds the fallen soldiers of America's wars, with the most revered, Arlington Cemetery, being the ultimate final resting place of the country's fallen. Although I had been a tour guide in DC during my college days, the only other times I had really photographed events in Arlington were for ceremonies for the Kennedys and the laying of wreaths by heads of state.

The call came in on a Friday from a client in need of a last-minute portrait in the cemetery. The last-minute need was on Sunday, just two days away. Last-minute portraits are something I have become a specialist in, not by design but by happenstance. Clients often seem to forget they need a photographer for a project, and that's when my phone rings. As such, I have a system in place to do portraits even within a few hours of a phone call. This one, however, had some sizable hoops I needed to jump through.

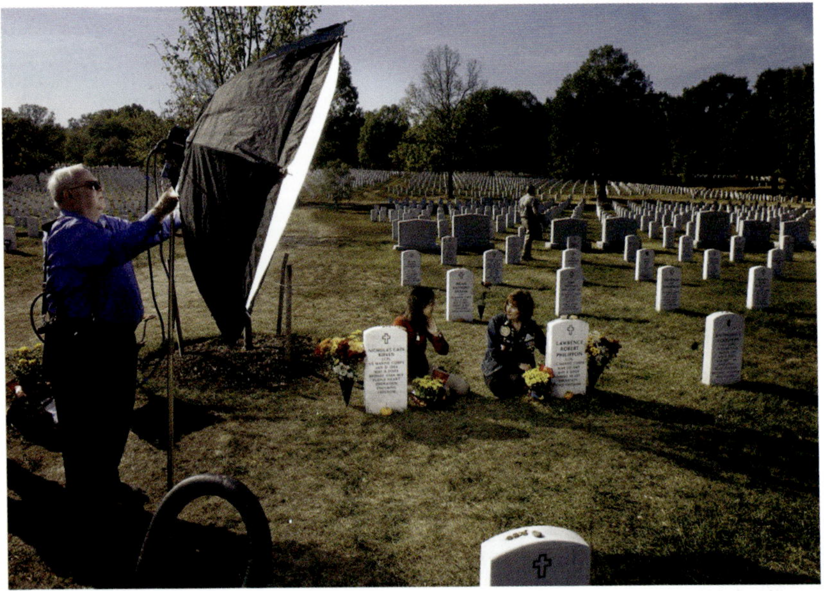

The setup for the images was just one light on a stand. The black arch in the foreground is the top of a step ladder I used to get up slightly higher for one series of images.

One of the biggest was getting permission to shoot in the cemetery. This shoot was to be a commercial portrait of the grieving mothers of two fallen soldiers. I advised the client that I didn't have sufficient time to get the permission and that they would need to handle that hurdle. Within a few hours, an email came in from the client clearing me into Arlington—much to my surprise.

I contacted the mothers, and we arranged to meet graveside. I was given the coordinates to where their sons were buried. I believed that the sons would be somewhere mid-row, and I was struggling mentally with how I would set up a light and do this portrait amidst the other headstones. I thought long and hard about how to do this, as I was en route to the cemetery. I had packed a very light kit, a portable battery-powered strobe, and one softbox. I arrived and entered the cemetery with my assistant. We immediately located the two mothers and introduced ourselves.

Much to my relief, their sons' headstones were the last two in a row. I surveyed the scene and wondered what the best perspective would be. How do you photograph two women who've lost their sons, ostensibly with their sons? Hugging the headstones? Leaning on them? Sitting on them? Standing next to them? Holding hands between them? How do you show the vastness of the cemetery while still having the focus be on the mothers?

I decided that I would start with a slightly higher angle, getting the mothers in the lower foreground and allowing the expanse of the cemetery to play out in the background. The sun was fairly high in the sky, but I caught a break because it was behind them and would provide a bit of a rim light around their heads. I could use my one light and softbox to fill in their faces from camera left.

I had a two-step stepstool and climbed up one step for just the right angle. I made several solemn images, and my usual comment of "Smile!" to a subject before me almost passed my lips before I realized what I was about to say. This was not the case

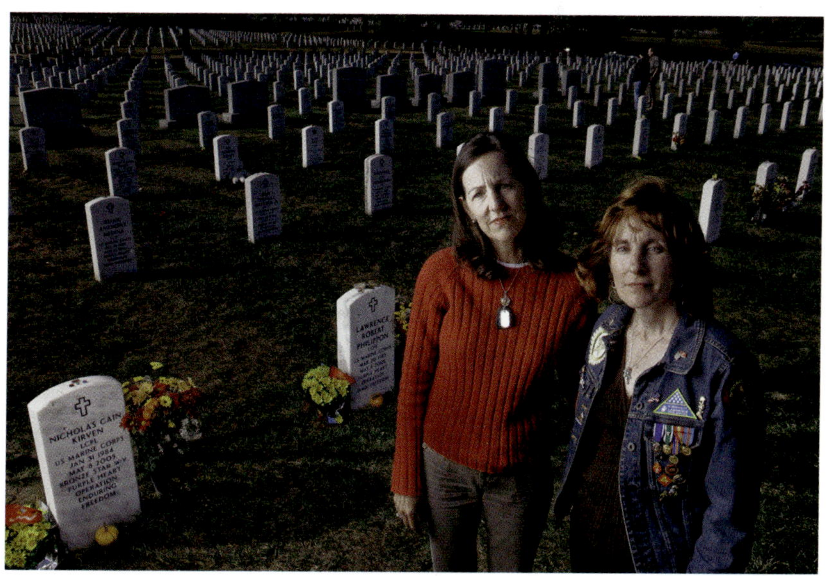

The first image that I really liked of the two mothers, photographed in Section 60 at Arlington National Cemetery.

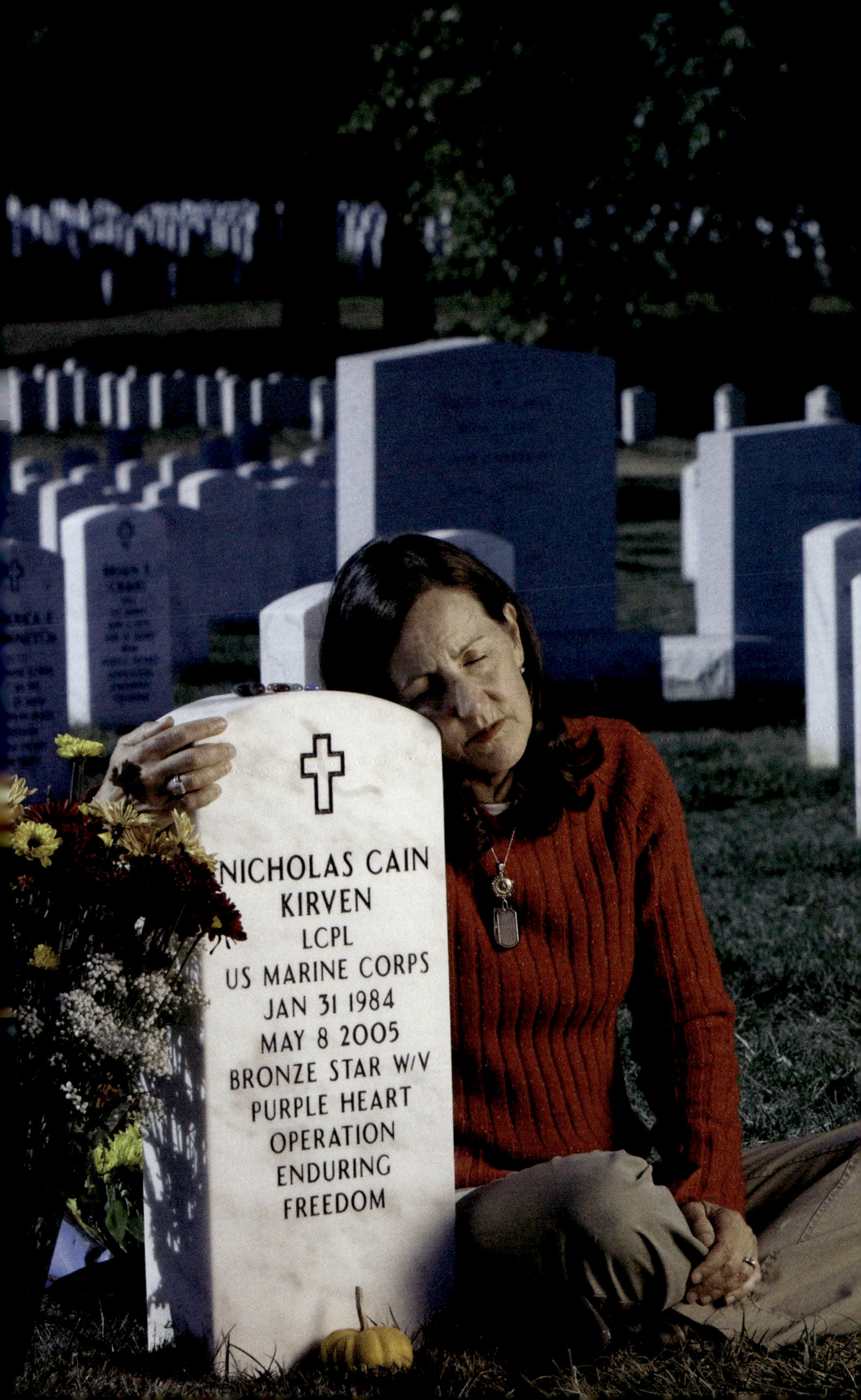
NICHOLAS CAIN
KIRVEN
LCPL
US MARINE CORPS
JAN 31 1984
MAY 8 2005
BRONZE STAR W/V
PURPLE HEART
OPERATION
ENDURING
FREEDOM

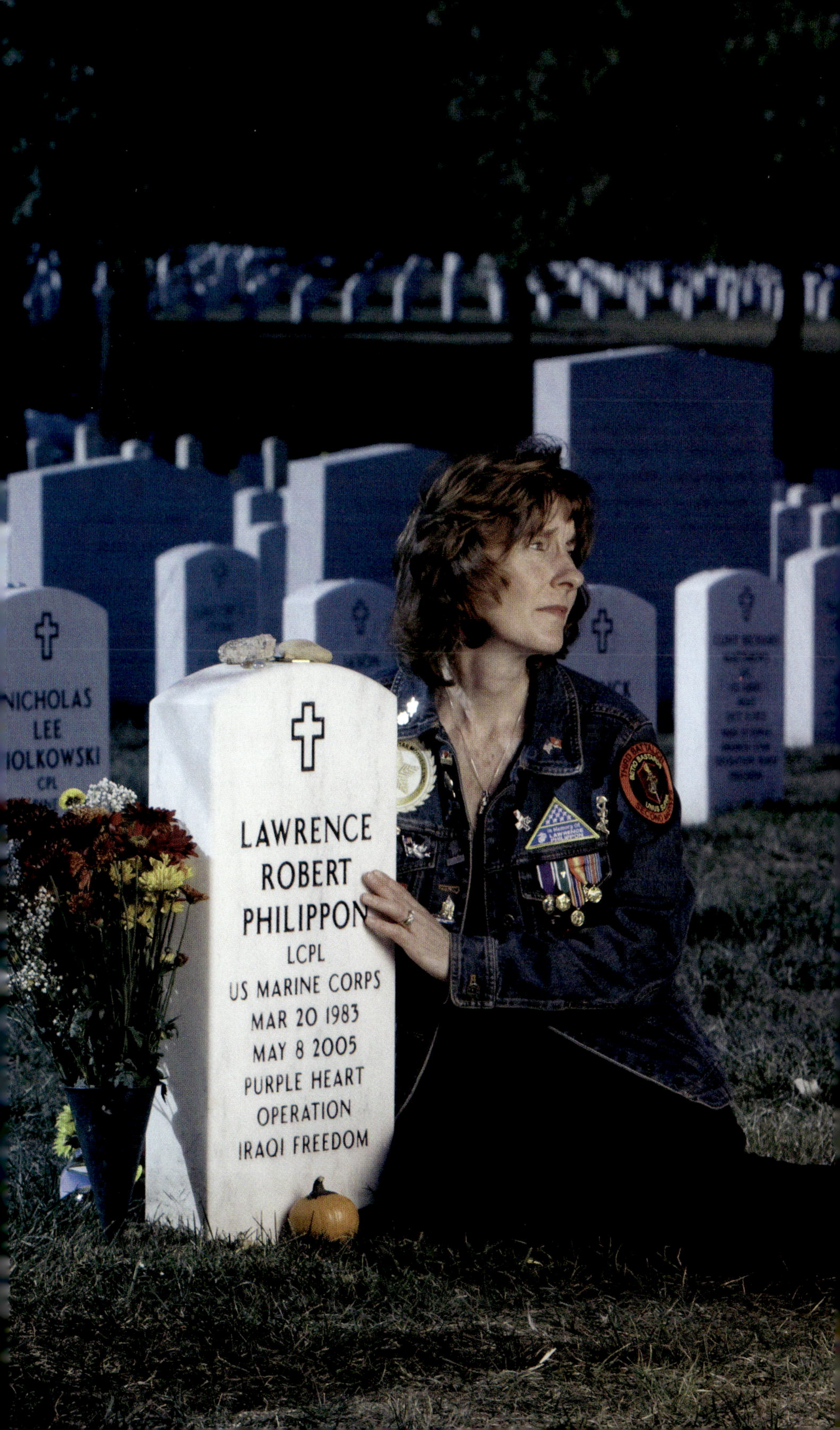
NICHOLAS
LEE
CPL
LAWRENCE
ROBERT
PHILIPPON
LCPL
US MARINE CORPS
MAR 20 1983
MAY 8 2005
PURPLE HEART
OPERATION
IRAQI FREEDOM

some 20 years earlier, when I was covering the Loma Prieta earthquake in 1989. I made the mistake of asking a California Highway Patrol officer, standing before the collapsed Cypress overpass in Oakland, California, to "smile" while making his portrait. (I immediately realized just how inappropriate the request was and apologized.)

After several different images, I decided I had enough variety on this perspective, so I reset my position and that of the mothers to be between the headstones, as their sons were buried side by side. I slid into the row for a straight-on angle, legs crossed, with my back almost up against the row that was next to theirs, yet not encroaching on the area above where their sons' caskets would be.

After just a few frames, I decided I didn't like the straight-on position, and I was uncomfortable being where I was anyway, so I shifted back to the place where my stepstool was. Still sitting cross-legged, I repositioned the light. Each of the mothers was on the right of her son's headstone, looking at me, looking at each other, and in several other varieties of poses.

By this time in the shoot, the mothers were paying attention to the cadence of the strobe pack's recycle tone—a short beep indicating the pack was recharged and ready to flash again. It was about a three-second recycle time, and they could tell I was about to shoot because I was doing so right after the pack had recycled.

As I was making these images, I felt that I didn't have a "moment," which I really wanted—something where the mothers were just being themselves, even though I was there with a camera. So, I paused a moment, lowering the camera, which was pre-focused, and said to them, "I need to adjust something; give me a moment." And for just a split second, the mothers were themselves, caught off guard in an unscripted moment, as I raised the camera and squeezed off one frame of them, showing their sorrow, pain, and loss. One frame of two mothers who had both lost their sons in a war overseas on the same day—Mother's Day.

Index

T

X-Y